MODERNIZATION AND THE CRISIS OF DEVELOPMENT IN AFRICA

Interdisciplinary Research Series in Ethnic, Gender and Class Relations

Series Editor: Biko Agozino, Cheyney University of Pennsylvania, USA

This series brings together research from a range of disciplines including criminology, cultural studies and applied social studies, focusing on experiences of ethnic, gender and class relations. In particular, the series examines the treatment of marginalized groups within the social systems for criminal justice, education, health, employment and welfare.

Forthcoming in this series

Democratic Policing in Transitional and Developing Countries
Edited by
Nathan Pino and Michael D. Wiatrowski
ISBN 0 7546 4719 6

Modernization and the Crisis of Development in Africa

The Nigerian Experience

JEREMIAH I. DIBUA
Morgan State University, USA

Routledge
Taylor & Francis Group
LONDON AND NEW YORK

First published 2006 by Ashgate Publishing

Reissued 2018 by Routledge
2 Park Square, Milton Park, Abingdon, Oxon OX14 4RN
605 Third Avenue, New York, NY 10017

First issued in paperback 2021

Routledge is an imprint of the Taylor & Francis Group, an informa business

A Library of Congress record exists under LC control number: 2006000106

ISBN 13: 978-0-815-39055-8 (hbk)
ISBN 13: 978-1-351-15292-1 (ebk)
ISBN 13: 978-1-138-35653-5 (pbk)

DOI: 10.4324/9781351152921

Contents

To the loving memories of my father, Peter Dibua and my sister, Blessing Dibua; and to my mother, Madam Okaima Agnes Dibua for her selflessness and nobility of heart

List of Tables

Acknowledgements

Although the writing of this book started in earnest in 2003, the ideas expressed here have greatly benefited from years of interactions with numerous colleagues, friends and students. I cannot name all of them here. I am, however, greatly indebted to them. I particularly wish to thank my colleagues in the College of Arts and Social Sciences of the former Bendel State University (now Ambrose Alli University), Ekpoma, Nigeria, where I started my university teaching career. The frank, often "brutal" and yet lively, debates we had in the weekly faculty seminar series and along the hallways greatly helped to shape my ideas. In this regard, I am particularly grateful to Bright Ekuerhare, A. C. Unomah, J. B. Webster, Onaiwu Ogbomo, Peter Egbon, Bona Chizea, Polycarp Ikuenobe, Biko Agozino and the following colleagues who are now deceased, Austen Adeoye, Frank Mowah and Ben Efoghe. At the University of Benin, Benin City, Nigeria, I benefited greatly from my discussions with colleagues in the History Department as well as those in the social sciences. I acknowledge the encouragement and support of A. D. Nzemeke, a retired Professor of History, University of Benin. I also wish to acknowledge the support and encouragement of Burney J. Hollis, Dean of the College of Liberal Arts, Morgan State University, Annette Palmer, Chair of History Department, Morgan State University, and my colleagues in the History Department, especially Rosalyn Terborg-Penn and Glenn Phillips. I thank Bana Okpu, Imounu Ikhimioya, Joseph Osagie, Owen Kalinga, Sylvia Jacobs, Tunde Adeleke and Willie Lamouse-Smith who contributed in various ways to the successful completion of this work.

I am grateful to Musa Abutudu for the very beneficial discussions we have had over the years and for his incisive comments on some of the chapters of this book. The initial draft of chapter 6 was written during an NEH Summer Seminar fellowship at the University of Illinois, Urbana-Champaign. I am grateful to the Directors of the Seminar, Don Crummey and Cynthia Radding, and fellow participants for their comments. I am also grateful to Abubakar Momoh, the subsequently named reviewer of the manuscript, for his insightful comments. I acknowledge the assistance of my graduate assistants, Frederick Kumolalo and Dana 'Yaa' Hammond in helping to locate source materials; I also acknowledge the excellent job Yaa did in the preparation of the final version of the manuscript.

I want to thank Caroline Wintersgill and Mary Savigar of Ashgate Publishing for offering me the opportunity to write this book and for their patience and encouragement during the period of writing. I am grateful to my mother, my brothers, Emman, Victor and Isaiah, and my sister, Angela, for their constant support and encouragement. Words cannot express the depth of my gratitude to my wife and children, Genevieve, Ohiremen, Ihinosen and Ohiole for their encouragement, companionship and for making the home a very warm and lively place in spite of the sacrifices they made during the writing of this book.

List of Abbreviations

ABN	Association for Better Nigeria
ABU	Ahmadu Bello University
AD	Alliance for Democracy
ADPs	Agricultural Development Projects
AFEM	Autonomous Foreign Exchange Market
AFRC	Armed Forces Ruling Council
AG	Action Group
APP	All People's Party
ASC	Agro Service Centers
ASUU	Academic Staff Union of Universities
AWU	Abeokuta Women's Union
BLC	Better Life Committees
BLP	Better Life Program
BP	British Petroleum
Bpd	barrels per day
BWAC	Berlin West African Conference
CA	Constituent Assembly
CBN	Central Bank of Nigeria
CD	Campaign for Democracy
CDA	Colonial Development Act
CDC	Constitution Drafting Committee
CDWA	Colonial Development and Welfare Act
CDWF	Colonial Development and Welfare Fund
CKD	Completely Knocked Down
CNC	Congress for National Consensus
CRC	Constitution Review Committee
DFRRI	Directorate of Food, Roads and Rural Infrastructure
DP	Dynamic Party
DPN	Democratic Party of Nigeria
ECA	Economic Commission for Africa
FAO	Food and Agricultural Organization
FEAP	Family Economic Advancement Program
FEDECO	Federal Electoral Commission
FEM	Foreign Exchange Market
FSP	Family Support Program
FSTF	Family Support Trust Fund

GBM	Green Belt Movement
GDM	Grassroots Democratic Movement
GDP	Gross Domestic Product
GNP	Gross National Product
GNPP	Great Nigeria People's Party
GR	Green Revolution
IBRD	International Bank for Reconstruction and Development
IFIs	International Financial Institutions
ILO	International Labor Organization
IMF	International Monetary Fund
INEC	Independent National Electoral Commission
ING	Interim National Government
ISI	Import Substitution Industrialization
JAMB	Joint Admission and Matriculation Board
KPP	Kano People's Party
LMWA	Lagos Market Women Association
MAMSER	Mass Mobilization for Social Justice and Economic Recovery
MAN	Manufacturers Association of Nigeria
MDF	Mid-West Democratic Party
NAC	National African Company
NADECO	National Democratic Coalition
NAFPP	National Accelerated Food Production Program
NANS	National Association of Nigerian Students
NASENI	National Agency for Science and Engineering Infrastructure
NBCI	National Bank for Commerce and Industry
NCC	National Constitutional Conference
NCCC	National Constitutional Conference Commission
NCEI	National Committee on Engineering Infrastucture
NCNC	National Council of Nigerian Citizens
NCPN	National Center Party of Nigeria
NCW	National Commission for Women
NCWS	National Council of Women Societies
NDC	Niger Delta Congress
NDE	National Directorate of Employment
NEC	National Electoral Commission
NECON	National Electoral Commission
NEPA	National Electric Power Authority
NEPB	Nigerian Enterprises Promotion Board
NEPU	Northern Elements Progressive Union
NES	Nigerian Economic Society
NICs	Newly Industrializing Countries
NITEL	Nigerian Telecommunications Limited
NLC	National Labor Congress

NNA	Nigerian National Alliance
NNDP	Nigerian National Democratic Party
NNOC	Nigerian National Oil Company
NNPC	Nigerian National Petroleum Corporation
NOIP	National Office of Industrial Property
NPA	Nigerian Ports Authority
NPC	Northern People's Congress
NPN	National Party of Nigeria
NPP	Nigerian People's Party
NPRC	National Political Reform Conference
NRC	National Republican Convention
NSTDA	National Science and Technology Development Agency
NSTF	National Science and Technology Fund
NUC	National Universities Commission
NUF	Northern Unity Forum
NUNS	National Union of Nigerian Students
NUS	Nigerian Union of Students
OAU	Organization of African Unity
OFN	Operation Feed the Nation
OIC	Organization of Islamic Conference
OPEC	Organization of Petroleum Exporting Countries
PAN	Peugeot Automobile of Nigeria
PDP	People's Democratic Party
PLO	Presidential Liaison Officers
PPA	Progressive Peoples Alliance
PPP	People's Progressive Party
PRONACO	Pro-National Conference
PRP	People's Redemption Party
R and D	Research and Development
RBDAs	River Basin Development Authorities
RNC	Royal Niger Company
SAPs	Structural Adjustment Programs
SDP	Social Democratic Party
SFEM	Second-Tier Foreign Exchange Market
SPP	Social Progressive Party
SSRC/CCP	Social Science Research Council Committee on Comparative Politics
TC	Transitional Council
TNCs	Trans-National Corporations
TVA	Tennessee Valley Authority
UAC	United Africa Company
UMBC	United Middle Belt Congress
UNCP	United Nigeria Congress Party

UNCTAD	United Nations Conference on Trade and Development
UNDP	United Nations Development Program
UNEP	United Nations Environment Program
UNIDO	United Nations Industrial Development Organization
UPE	Universal Primary Education
UPGA	United Progressive Grand Alliance
UPN	Unity Party of Nigeria
UPP	United People's Party
USA (US)	United States of America
USAID	United States Agency for International Development
VAG	Volkswagen AG of Germany
VWON	Volkswagen of Nigeria
WACCB	West African Cocoa Control Board
WAFF	West African Frontier Force
WAI	War Against Indiscipline
WAPCB	West African Produce Control Board
WID	Women in Development
WIN	Women in Nigeria
ZCP	Zamfara Commoners' Party

Chapter 1

Introduction: "Experts," Africanists and Africa's Development Crisis

Discussions on what can be termed the "African Dilemma" have largely focused on the issue of development. The post World War II period, which witnessed the beginning of the process of political decolonization in Africa, coincided with the rise of modernization and its ideological cousin, developmentalism. Developmentalism experienced a great deal of intellectual ferment in the 1950s. Expectedly, development economics occupied a preeminent position in the developmentalist discourse. There was also a significant preoccupation with political development variously defined as political system, national integration, increasing secularization, increasing space for political participation, among others. However, a common concern of the political and economic developmentalists was how to "modernize" the respective "traditional," "primitive," "barbaric" and "backward" African societies through transplanting into them the "civilized" and "modern" features of Western societies. Walt Rostow's "stages of growth" theory became the "gospel" on which the "catechism" of modernization and economic developmentalism was based.[1] On the other hand, modernization and political developmentalist discourse was anchored on the structural-functionalist approach developed in the 1950s, by political scientists associated with the Social Science Research Council Committee on Comparative Politics (SSRC/CCP).[2] While stating that the political functions performed in each society regardless of its level of development are the same, these scholars emphasized differentiation in social structures and the erosion of traditional social institutions as crucial indices of political development.[3] Essentially, the developmentalist perspective adopted the Weberian binary division of societies into polar opposites: traditional and modern.

The preoccupation with developmentalism became of even more abiding interest with the attainment of political independence by majority of African countries in the 1960s. Development economists, preoccupied with how to effect a rapid transformation of the economies of African countries from their "traditional" state to a "modern" state, placed great faith on development planning. Scholars interested in political development were more interested in the issue of nation-building, a process that was expected to result in the replacement of the "traditional" structures of African societies with transplanted "modern" structures.[4]

Development economists adopted a state-centrist approach, which eschewed politics and regarded a developmental and authoritarian state as the primary agency for promoting economic transformation through the instrumentality of development planning. This was in contrast with political development scholars who adopted a more society-centrist approach and saw the state as an arena of political struggles for the authoritative distribution of scarce resources, rather than as the primary agency for national development. However, the shared belief of development economists and political development scholars on modernization and the linear conception of development made them to link authoritarian state or authoritarian political organization to rapid economic development.[5] Indeed, the 1960s and 1970s witnessed the proliferation of modernist, state-centrist and developmentalist works on Africa.

In any case, the pervading interest on developmentalism, created the opportunity for sending many Western "experts" to African countries by Western governments, international financial institutions, and Western-based aid agencies, to help in bringing about the rapid "modernization" of "traditional" and "backward" African societies. As noted by John Toye, the modernization paradigm fostered a situation in which Western "experts" occupied "an extremely prominent and powerful position as guides and advisers," in African and other non-Western countries.[6] Development economists were the greatest beneficiaries from this enterprise as they were widely sought after to help in formulating development strategies. Based on often-cursory visits to Africa and without collecting sufficient data, these "experts" drew up elaborate development plans and programs, even if as some of them conceded, this amounted to "planning without facts."[7] Underlying these plans and programs were prescriptions on how to promote development by replicating the "stages of growth" of the European countries. In spite of the fact that the prescriptions of the "experts" were not normally based on extensive empirical evidence and failed to take into account the socio-economic realities of the respective African countries, modernist scholars did not blame the shortcomings of the prescriptions for the failure of the development programs. Rather, the argument usually made is that the recommendations of the "experts" were sound but the programs failed because of internal irrationalities such as poor implementation, corruption, neo-patrimonialism, etc.

Nevertheless, the African economic crisis, which became acute from the 1980s, led to the neoliberal revolution anchored on the neoclassical economism championed by the World Bank and the International Monetary Fund (IMF), and the public choice school largely championed by North American-based Africanists. This new orthodoxy blamed excessive state intervention and the resultant anti-market policies, as well as the neo-patrimonial nature and rent-seeking proclivity of policy makers for the crisis. The new orthodoxy therefore advocated state-retrenching policies that would lead to the ascendancy of market forces and the enthronement of liberal democracy and good governance as the solution to Africa's economic crisis. These policies were embodied in the World Bank sponsored

Structural Adjustment Programs (SAPs) and the linkage of these programs to democratization.

Like the developmentalist era, the new neoliberal orthodoxy created opportunities for a new generation of "experts," this time, mainly monetary economists to be sent to African countries to assist in drawing up structural adjustment programs. Furthermore, like their development economists' precursors, the new "experts" occupied very influential positions in the policy-making bodies, and financial agencies and institutions of African countries. In fact, they occupied strategic positions in the central banks and the ministries of finance of these countries, as clearly exemplified by the case of Ghana – the so-called star pupil of structural adjustment in Africa. In addition, domestic "experts" who had been affiliated with the IFIs were appointed into strategic government positions in African countries. In Nigeria for instance, Idika Kalu Idika, a former World Bank official who was appointed as the country's minister of finance, presided over the introduction of the structural adjustment program in 1986. Furthermore, Olusegun Obasanjo's second term in office as Nigeria's president, which began in 2003, saw the appointment of Ngozi Okonjo-Iweala, a former World Bank vice president as the country's minister of finance and Charles Soludo, who had been associated with the World Bank as the governor of the central bank.[8] However, the implementations of the neoliberal policies worsened, rather than improve the economic crisis of the respective African countries. Reminiscent of the modernization scholars of the 1960s and 1970s, the neo-modernization advocates of the neoliberal orthodoxy exonerated the "experts" while blaming internal factors, such as poor implementation, neo-patrimonialism and corruption for the failure of the reform programs. They argued that the neoliberal policies, which were fundamentally, sound, rational and sought to restore rationality to African economies, failed because of the irrational and neo-patrimonial nature of the African state systems and societies. This exoneration of the "experts" is clearly faulty because their prescriptions were not based on concrete analysis of the African reality; rather, they sought to subordinate the African reality to preconceived theories, models and paradigms.

James Ferguson has noted that most "experts" who formulate development policies in Africa, often demonstrate a startling ignorance of the realities of the locale that their policies are intended to help. Indeed, development "experts" and institutions generate their own forms of discourse, and this discourse simultaneously constructs the locality as a particular kind of knowledge while creating a structure of knowledge around the object of development. Development policies are therefore organized on the basis of this inadequately conceptualized structure of knowledge.[9]

Indeed, the discussions of Africa's development trajectory and the economic crisis have revolved around two broad themes: the state and individual/collective values. These themes, which are squarely situated within the modernization paradigm, have been largely based on the Weberian perspective. However, of great significance is the fact that Western-based Africanists have disproportionately dominated the discourse. According to Kwesi Yankah, this dominance is manifested in "the complete alienation of scholarly authority to the Western academy, which dictates the paradigms and metalanguage in which . . . (African) reality should be ordered, as well as controls the strategic outlets of knowledge dissemination."[10] Nevertheless, the commitment of Western Africanists to Weberian themes and their modernist perspective resulted in a situation in which it was deemed that the African reality could only be more relevantly analyzed by finding a comparable stage in early modern European history. This Eurocentric and universalist approach not only privileged the European experience over the African experience, but resulted in a situation in which the African reality was lifted out of context.[11] Central to this approach was the production of various paradigms and fancy appellations that perhaps, inadvertently promoted what amounted to the "pathologization" of the African experience.[12] In the process, the specificity of the African situation was missed.

What accounts for the dominant position of Western-based Africanists in the analysis of Africa's development trajectory, and the African experience in general? In answering this question, Tiyambe Zeleza stated that the dominance is a reflection of "the historical and contemporary relations of domination and dependency between Africa and the West," and that "the production of knowledge is related to the structures of power." Zeleza further argued that "the way in which the field of African studies has historically been imprisoned by languages, epistemologies and discourses that are externalist, often means that . . . Africa becomes no more than an empirical lab to test pretentiously universalistic models, theories and paradigms," developed by Western Africanists.[13] This externalist orientation and the claim to universalistic perspective is particularly applicable to the field of political science where Western based scholars, especially North American Africanists, have been very prolific in periodically churning out adjectival phrases and models that purportedly explain the African reality.

Nevertheless, the epistemological dominance of Western Africanist discourse is equally prevalent in the branches of African studies in which African based scholars, at least in the 1960s and 1970s, played a leading role. A significant example is the field of African history, which was largely developed by African based historians in response to the denigration of the African past by colonialist and imperialist historians. While the resultant African historiography greatly helped to disprove the myths and lies propagated about the African past and, therefore, helped to rehabilitate the African past, the scholars could not escape from the Western epistemological traditions under which they were trained. This gave rise to an African historiography that was based on Western empiricist and universalistic tradition and therefore uncritically accepted the modernization paradigm.[14] This for instance, accounted for the attempts at seeking "modernizers" in the African past.

In essence, the modernization paradigm in trying to seek meaning and relevance in the African experience, only to the extent that it approximates or mirrors a specific stage in European history, promoted the distortion of the African experience. It tended to foster a racist and imperialist perspective that completely denigrated the African culture and practices and, so, created a situation in which these indigenous factors were portrayed as irrelevant, and indeed hindrances, to Africa's development. The liberal/neoliberal political economy of markets and liberal democracy fostered by the modernist scholars and "experts" is therefore out of tune with the realities of the African situation. This paradigm helped to entrench the peripheral location of African countries in the international capitalist system. The consequences of this peripheral location have been extremely detrimental to Africa's development.[15] The liberal/neoliberal political economy perspective thus helped to aggravate the development crisis rather than promote development.

Scholars operating from what can be termed the radical political economy perspective have vigorously challenged the prescriptions of the modernist liberal/neoliberal political economy advocates. Apart from subjecting the modernization paradigm to serious criticism, they put the main blame for Africa's development crisis on the peripheral location of African countries in the global capitalist system. As noted by Adebayo Olukoshi, "the insights that emanate from the perspectives of the radical political economy school appear to be far closer to reality in much of Africa than the positions conveyed by the neo-liberal 'political economy'/public choice theorists."[16] However, while the radical political economy school clearly interrogated the issues of dependency, authoritarianism and the role of the state, much attention was not paid to significant issues like gender and culture that are crucial for a more balanced and elaborate analysis of the crisis of development in Africa.

This book, then, aims at interrogating the central role modernization played in Africa's development trajectory, and the paradigm's contribution to the crisis of development and the entrenchment of the peripheral role of African countries in the global capitalist system. The book demonstrates that contrary to the popularly held belief, the influence of modernization did not end with the decline of development economics in the late 1970s. It states that the neoliberal political economy as manifested in the structural adjustment programs, good governance and liberal democracy projects from the 1980s, were firmly situated within the modernization paradigm. The book combines elaborate theoretical and empirical analyses in drawing attention to the dialectical and contradictory relationships between modernization, and the indigenous African realities and culture. Using Nigeria as a case study, the book points out that by advocating the replication of Western institutions and experiences as the credible path to development, modernization discountenanced the crucial roles of culture and the indigenous realities for the development process. This shortcoming adversely affected the development project. The book conducts a far-reaching theoretical and empirical analysis of how this process occurred in different aspects of the Nigerian economy and society.

Furthermore, this book adopts the radical political economy approach in demonstrating the centrality of the adverse effects of the modernization paradigm for understanding the nature and dynamics of Nigeria's development crisis. In essence, it adopts a multifaceted and transdisciplinary method rooted in the radical political economy approach. The approach incorporates issues of state, class, gender and culture into an analysis of Nigeria's development crisis that emphasizes the centrality of the acute limitations of the modernization paradigm. At this point, it is necessary to dwell a bit more on the Weberian/modernist and state-centrist explanations of the African development crisis because they constitute the core of the modernization paradigm, and the fact that the subsequent chapters are devoted to critically analyzing these issues.

Weberian/Modernist Explanations of Africa's Development Crisis

Talcott Parsons, the interpreter and translator of Max Weber's works into the English language, helped to popularize Weber's theory of rationality/ideal type societies (Western societies) and irrationality/non-ideal type societies (non-Western societies) to the English audience. In line with Weber's binary categorization of societies, the modernization paradigm stated that non-Western societies could only attain modernity if they acquire the instrumental rationality of Western societies. The Western based, particularly North American Africanists, adopted this Weberian binary division of societies, in this case, the existence of two realms: the private realm (communal and ethno-regional sectors) and the public realm (governmental sector), in their analyses of Africa's development crisis. The kernel of their argument is that while moral principles were applied to the private realm, the public realm was considered as immoral and therefore subjected to the irrational practices of exploitation and corruption. As a result, the desire to satisfy the material interest and wellbeing of the individual and his/her communal group, made him/her to corruptly appropriate government resources for individual and group interests. Yet the corrupt appropriation of government resources was not looked upon as corruption or frowned at so long as the individual used part of the resources to satisfy the material needs of his/her extended family and communal group: on the contrary, such an individual was hailed as a hero.[17] Thus, while moral values applied to the private realm, what Goran Hyden characterized as the irrational economy of moral affection,[18] the public realm was regarded as amoral. The essence of this Weberian argument is that the amoral values associated with the public realm gave rise to corruption, patrimonialism/neo-patrimonialism, clientelism, and in short, the exploitation of public office for the satisfaction of private and communal ends.[19]

Perhaps Richard Joseph's prebendal theory more clearly illustrates the essence and limitations of this Weberian and modernist perspective. Joseph's theory of prebendalism is highlighted here not because it is fundamentally superior to the other theories, but because of Joseph's claim that it combines elements of the other theories, and transcends their limitations through adjustment and refinements thereby providing a more relevant framework for analyzing the Nigerian/African society.[20] Joseph did acknowledge that there are similarities between prebendalism and clientelism, and that in significant respects, both are mutually reinforcing. Nevertheless, he stated that while clientelism "defines the nature of individual and group relationships within the wider socio-political sphere, ... prebendalism is primarily a function of the competition for, and appropriation of, the offices of the state." In other words, clientelism points in the direction of relationships of power and attachment while prebendalism points towards the material resources needed to cultivate or maintain such relationships and consequences of such pressures on the nature of the state.[21] But what exactly is prebendalism? According to Joseph, a prebendal system is not only "one in which the offices of state are allocated and then exploited as benefices by the office holders," but also "one where such a practice is legitimated by a set of political norms according to which the appropriation of such offices is not just an act of individual greed or ambition but concurrently the satisfaction of the short-term objectives of a subset of the general population."[22] Nonetheless, in spite of Joseph's insistence, his construct did not fundamentally deviate from patrimonialism/neo-patrimonialism, Peter Ekeh's the two publics or Kenneth Post and Michael Vickers' systems of reward, for instance.

More fundamental is the fact that the prebendal construct is based on the paradigm of modernity's perspective, which presumes that the modern African situation can only be significantly or relevantly analyzed in so far as it approximates a particular stage in the history of Europe. Hence, the postcolonial Nigerian situation is analyzed from the perspective of the prebendal system that existed in feudal Europe where a prebend was an office of state, which an individual procured either through examinations or as a reward for loyal service to a lord or ruler. The irrelevance of feudal Europe's experience to the postcolonial African situation is apparent. But as is the practice with the modernization paradigm's penchant for subordinating the African reality to theory in the quest for finding similar stages in European history, Joseph justified the application of prebendalism to postcolonial Nigerian politics by stating:

> The peculiar political and economic conditions of the post-colonial world have contributed to the entrenchment of a form of state organization, and of attitudes regarding the uses of state offices, which are pre-modern. Instead of the constitutional and legal systems, as well as the stated impersonal norms, determining the form of this state organization, such legal-rational features largely serve to camouflage extensive prebendal practices.

The preoccupation with seeing the African situation as mirroring a particular stage in the European historical experience led to his description of "extensive corruption" in Nigeria as equating Weber's characterization of prebends in feudal Europe, as "the economic assurance of ... office."[23]

Some critics of the prebendal construct did not really quarrel with the Weberian and modernist themes underlying it, rather, they raised issues with some of the observations regarding the Nigerian society. Tom Forrest criticized prebendalism and patrimonialism for focusing too much on the personalization of the state, the use of state regulation and control for unproductive accumulation and the characterization of political competition as focused entirely on access to state resources. He further noted that they failed to give adequate attention to the social and political space that is autonomous of the state and that they neglected forms of political conflict that are not focused on the struggle for material benefits and access to state power.[24] However, Forrest accepted the modernization paradigm that underlined the prebendal perspective. Eghosa Osaghae has argued that as dependent, rather than independent variables, prebendalism and other Weberian themes that focus on internal factors, cannot adequately explain the reasons for the failure of democracy, and indeed, the problem of underdevelopment in Nigeria. He stated that a more complete explanation must include external factors and dimensions that helped to perpetuate Nigeria's peripheral location in the international capitalist system.[25] Osaghae's observation about the failure to take into account external factors is valid to the extent that it pertains to Nigeria's dependent position in the international capitalist system. But in a rather contradictory way, he accepted the Weberian and modernist perspectives as crucial tools for analyzing the nature and failure of democracy in Nigeria while accepting the successful transplanting of Western-style liberal democracy into the country, as a valid goal. On this basis, Osaghae was preoccupied with recommending ways of making this brand of "ideal type" "rational" democracy work successfully in Nigeria.

Nevertheless, in spite of the limitations of prebendalism as a tool for analyzing the development experience in Nigeria and other African countries, some modernist scholars have adopted it as a valid analytical tool.[26] But as already noted, prebendalism and similar Weberian influenced modernist perspectives cannot adequately capture the African reality in so far as their major preoccupation are with showing how the African situation mirrors a particular stage in pre-modern or early modern European history. This kind of analysis results in a situation in which African issues are not analyzed in, and for, themselves. In other words, such an analysis is not African centered. In addition, the claim to comparative and universalistic perspective which privileges the European experience over concrete African realities, usually lead to the subordination of the African reality to theory. In the process, the specificity of the African situation is lost.

Moreover, many of the issues, which these Africanists purport to explain in their grand theories, are equally present in contemporary Western European societies, and some of them are, in fact, entrenched aspects of the capitalist system and the developmentalist paradigm. For instance, much of the allegation of irrationality and corruption that the Africanist scholars make with respect to Nigeria and other African countries centers on the privatization of public offices. This privatization of public offices of course exists to a very high degree in African countries. But the phenomenon also exists, albeit to a lesser degree, in Western capitalist countries as epitomized for instance, by the case of pork-barrel projects in the United States (this issue is discussed in greater details in chapter 4). The higher degree of this incidence in African countries can be partly attributed to the peripheral nature of their capitalist system. In addition, there is a sense in which it can be said that the privatization of public offices is fostered by the very logic of the developmentalist paradigm. Nevertheless, while rather derogatory terms are used to explain the presence of these phenomena in Africa, many of which are, as already pointed out, products of the inherited capitalist system and the developmentalist paradigm, their existence in the Western societies are either overlooked or less derogatorily analyzed. How do we account for this difference in approach? The answer lies mainly in the structure and control over the production of knowledge about Africa. In any case, I do not believe that the African situation can be concretely analyzed by looking at how they mirror the European historical experience because the circumstances, historical, socio-cultural, material and political realities of the respective societies are different. This approach also contains some features that can be portrayed as fostering Western racial superiority and imperialism, and in a sense, serves as an apologist for European imperialism in Africa and the resultant adverse effects of neo-colonial dependence and exploitation, on Africa's development. Moreover, the preoccupation with grand models and fancy appellations often couched in abstruse language, perhaps wittingly or unwittingly, made the Africanist modernist inquiry to become more of "an agenda for esoteric discourse within the Western academy," rather than concrete analysis of the specificity of the African situation.[27] In essence, because of their acute shortcomings, prebendalism and similar Weberian/modernist constructs cannot adequately explain concrete African realities. They are therefore not of much analytical value in terms of explaining the African development experience.

Postcolonial State, State-Centrism and Africa's Development

The postcolonial African state is a product of colonialism. Since the colonial state was imposed by force and was primarily concerned with maximizing the extraction of wealth from the colonies, coercive means were deployed to ensure the attainment of its exploitative goals. The colonial state was therefore primarily a law and order state. As a result, it exercised absolute and arbitrary power.

According to Claude Ake, since for its subjects, the colonial state was, at any rate, "an arbitrary power, it could not engender any legitimacy even though it made rules and laws profusely and propagated values." As a result, "in struggling to advance their interests, the colonial subjects did not worry about conforming to legality or legitimacy norms," rather, the primary concern was with capturing power.[28] In addition, in order to satisfy its exploitative goals, the colonial state assumed an extremely statist character. It intervened in, and controlled all aspects of the economy, introduced new relations of production, and was the primary instrument for surplus accumulation.

Although attainment of political independence brought about some structural changes and Africans became the managers of their respective states, the postcolonial state retained most features of the colonial state. It remained authoritarian and was primarily preoccupied with maintaining law and order. Various instruments of coercion were used to ensure compliance on the part of the citizens. The postcolonial state remained the primary instrument for production, surplus accumulation and capitalist development. This character of the state was fostered by the developmental state paradigm of development economists, which justified paternalistic and authoritarian tendencies on the part of the state in the name of producing national consensus for the development project. This promoted a form of statist or state-centrist development process. Given the neocolonial and peripheral nature of the state, the developmentalist state paradigm fostered a form of state capitalism under which the postcolonial African state became a primary instrument for accumulation for both the fledgling domestic capitalists and foreign capitalists. As noted by William Graf, "the peripheral (African) capitalist state exists mainly to guarantee the conditions for the reproduction and expansion of capitalist property relations and mode(s) of production." However, since the state "lacks the socio-economic 'base' to sustain and develop a relatively autochthonous capitalism . . . (it) intervenes in the economy, in collaboration with the external elements of this economic 'base', to create the preconditions for, and to promote, private accumulation."[29]

Another significant feature of the postcolonial state in Africa is its very limited form of autonomy in the sense that its apparatuses are not well developed and the fact that it enjoys limited autonomy from the social classes that are themselves involved in intense struggle to capture it. This lack of autonomy had severe consequences for the political economy of African countries. As stated by Ake:

> In the absence of autonomizing mechanisms in the post-colonial state, the resources of physical coercion become the tools of particular groups, especially the hegemonic factions of the ruling class, and the affinity between the coercive institutions and these hegemonic fractions has inevitably become particularly visible. Also, the only effective check on the use of the coercive resources becomes merely the prudence of enlightened self-interest of those who control them. So we have essentially relations of raw power in

> which right tends to be coextensive with power and security depends on the control of power. The struggle for power, then, is everything and is pursued by every means.[30]

The above limitations of the postcolonial state, which were accentuated by the kind of developmentalism promoted by development economists and other modernist proponents, resulted in political instability and economic crisis, among others. By the 1980s, the severity of the crisis led to the neoliberal revolution, which blamed state-centrist policies for the economic crisis and advocated the minimization of the role of the state as the way out of the crisis. It was argued that this state retrenchment policy would put Africa back on the path to economic recovery and development. By advocating minimal state, the ascendancy of market forces, good governance, democratization, and through the increased attention paid to civil society, neoliberals argued that emphasis shifted from state-centrist policies to society-centrist policies. On this basis, they stated that the modernization paradigm, which had fostered state-centrism, had become irrelevant and obsolete because of its failure to engender development. However, contrary to the claim of the neoliberals, their policies were squarely situated within the modernization paradigm. Like the earlier modernization policies, the essence of the neoliberal policies was the promotion of Westernization in Africa through the replication of Western institutions, and the use of authoritarian state power to achieve this objective.

Furthermore, contrary to the claim of state minimization, the neoliberal orthodoxy was state-centrist in many significant respects. In fact, their analysis of the economic crisis, which was hinged on the twin themes of the failure or success of the state, and the preoccupation with the issue of state versus markets, actually puts the state in the center of the neoliberal analysis. More significant is the fact that given the unpopularity and massive resistance to the neoliberal economic and social policies, the neoliberals relied on, and actually advocated a strong and authoritarian state that could forcefully push through the reforms. Ben Fine and Colin Stoneman have pointed out that the neoliberal "appeal to market forces is also, in reality, an ideological proxy for state intervention on behalf of capital." They also opined that "privatisation is better seen not as the withdrawal of the state in favour of the market, but as a particular form of (state) intervention which . . . inevitably favours some capitalists and disadvantages others."[31] Even the issue of instituting liberal democracy inevitably entailed state intervention because of the neoliberal linkage of economic liberalism with liberal democracy. The countries implementing structural adjustment programs were therefore expected to ensure that the adjustment policies formed part of the democratization process, and were in fact, entrenched under a future democratic dispensation. This therefore resulted in authoritarian and state controlled democratization processes in many African countries.

Moreover, the area of civil society, which was portrayed as the core of the society-centrist policy of the neoliberal orthodoxy, was not immune to state intervention. In line with the dictates of the modernization paradigm, the neoliberal reforms encouraged the massive use of state power to construct civil society that mirrors the Western image.[32] It thus follows that the neoliberal policies were largely statist and that the distinction between state-centrism and society-centrism is at best tenuous. According to Yusuf Bangura and Peter Gibbon:

> One major problem with the neo-liberal perspective, however, is its limited view of the way structures of incentives operate in concrete African societies. It posits two contrasting models of resource allocation with different structures of opportunities – one based on state interventions leading to price distortions and economic rents for a privileged few; and a second based on free competitive markets which allocate resources optimally. Quite apart from the obvious fact that some of the elements of the statist model never get completely eliminated even in economies with fully developed markets, the rigid distinction between state and non-state, public and private, rent-seeking and market-oriented is misplaced in the African context.[33]

Crawford Young has argued that the postcolonial state in Africa ended by 1990 and that it is therefore not valid to talk about the postcolonial state and postcoloniality in general, after 1990.[34] Young's argument is best captured in his own words:

> I suggest closing the historical parentheses around the African post-colonial state, perhaps about 1990. The silent incorporation of many defining attributes of the colonial state in its post-independence successor for three decades validated the 'post-colonial' characterization. Nevertheless, by the 1980s a corrosive dynamic was visible, weakening most states, and by the 1990s eviscerating several. The state crisis became manifest by 1990 in the radically altered international environment of the collapse of the Soviet Union and irresistible pressures for liberalization.[35]

Young's argument is firmly situated within the neo-modernization paradigm and echoes the pervading triumphalism among neoliberal scholars after the collapse of the Soviet Union in the late 1980s. He rehashed the same charges of patrimonialism, prebendalism and the detrimental statist approach to development, among others, which modernist scholars leveled against the postcolonial state, and used to justify the introduction of the neoliberal political economy. He stated that based on these problems, "African recovery required not just the miracle of the marketplace, but the blessings of democracy. The now deeply enrooted structures of patrimonial autocracy were not reformable by economic tinkering; the post-colonial state required political surgery in order to make a liberalized economy possible."[36] He further noted that although the political and economic reform programs failed, they left the postcolonial state extremely weakened. According to him, this weakened form of the state as manifested in the spread of civil conflicts in many parts of Africa and various other challenges to the authority of the state in most African countries rendered the state considerably weakened. Thus, the state no longer resembled the inherited powerful and "hegemonic" colonial state, and so, the postcolonial state and "the post-colonial moment appears to have passed."[37] The examples used by Young to support his argument are rather dubious. Contrary to his claim, the neoliberal orthodoxy entrenched rather than weakened the authoritarian and, and in certain critical respects, interventionist nature of the African state. The label postcolonial, therefore, still applied to the African state after 1990.

Scope and Organization

This book examines the impact of modernization on Africa's development using Nigeria as a case study. The primary aim is to show the central role that the modernization paradigm played in creating and perpetuating the crisis of development. This is significant because the mainstream works have erroneously equated the "modernization" project as synonymous with promoting development. The modernist analysis of blaming internal irrationalities particularly on the part of the African state and other internal weaknesses as the main culprit for the development crisis have been continuously reproduced in these works. As a result, the central role of modernization in creating and fostering the crisis of development has not received adequate attention. This book, therefore, adopts a theoretical, analytical and empirical approach and critically interrogates the central role that modernization played in the development process. Special attention is paid to the dialectical relationship between modernization and the indigenous realities and culture, with a view to showing the impact of this pattern of relationship on the development process. In addition, the patriarchal orientation and the resultant gendered nature of the development policies are examined. Each chapter therefore incorporates the issues of state, culture and gender, which are anchored on a radical political economy approach, in analyzing the modernist development project.

The book is divided into ten chapters. Chapter 2 situates the discussion within the continental context by critically examining the role of modernization, as embodied in the received wisdom, on Africa's development trajectory. The theoretical issues that this book employs in the analysis of the Nigerian experience are fleshed out in this chapter. Chapters 3 to 9 examine different aspects of the Nigerian experience. Chapter 3 discusses the colonial antecedents and shows how the foundation for the development policies adopted in the postcolonial period were laid during this time. The next six chapters examine different aspects of Nigeria's development experience, namely, democratic experiments, technology transfer, agricultural transformation, oil and economic development strategies, economic crisis and structural adjustment programs, and student and women movements. Chapter 10, which concludes the discussion, discusses how to overcome the crisis of development in Africa. Among other things, it examines the significant issues of the roles that the state, culture and relevant indigenous non-governmental organizations should play in Africa's development as well as the need to adopt a pan-African approach to the development question.

Notes

1 W. W. Rostow, "The Take-off into Self-sustained Growth," *Economic Journal*, Vol. 66, 1956, 25-48; and idem., *The Stages of Economic Growth: A Non-Communist Manifesto*, Cambridge: Cambridge University Press, 1960.

2 These political scientists drew heavily from the work of the structural-functionalist school in sociology, especially the work of Talcott Parsons and his colleagues.

3 See G. A. Almond and J. S. Coleman eds., *The Politics of Developing Areas*, Princeton: Princeton University Press, 1960.

4 K. Deutsch, "Nation-Building and National Development," in K. Deutsch and W. Foltz, *Nation-Building*, Chicago: Atherton Press, 1963.

5 See G. Hyden, "Rethinking Theories of the State: An Africanist Perspective," *Africa Insight*, Vol. 26, No. 1, 1996, 28; and V. W. Ruttan, "What Happened to Political Development?" *Economic Development and Cultural Change*, Vol. 39, No. 2, 1991, 284.

6 J. Toye, *Dilemmas of Development: Reflections on the Counter-Revolution in Development Economics*, Second Edition, Oxford, UK and Cambridge, Massachusetts: Blackwell Publishers, 1993, 32.

7 See for instance, W. F. Stolper, *Planning Without Facts: Lessons in Resource Allocation from Nigeria's Development*, Cambridge, Massachusetts: Harvard University Press, 1966.

8 Indeed, the appointment of Charles Soludo as the Governor of Nigeria's Central Bank, marked a departure from the longstanding tradition of selecting people to this position from among the officials of the bank.

9 J. Ferguson, *The Anti Politics Machine: Development, Depoliticization and Bureaucratic Power in Lesotho*, Minneapolis: University of Minnesota Press, 1994.

10 K. Yankah, "Displaced Academies and the Quest for a New World Academic Order," *Africa Today*, Vol. 42, No. 3, 1995, 8.

11 See M. Mamdani, *Citizen and Subject: Contemporary Africa and the Legacy of Late Colonialism*, Princeton: Princeton University Press, 1996, 9-12.

12 O. Owomoyela, "With Friends Like These . . . A Critique of Pervasive Anti-Africanisms in Current African Studies Epistemology and Methodology," *African Studies Review*, Vol. 37, No. 3, 1994, 97.

13 P. T. Zeleza, "NOMA Award Acceptance Speech," *ISSUE*, Vol. XXIII, No. 1, 1995, 7. Also see idem., *Manufacturing African Studies and Crises*, Dakar: CODESRIA, 1997.

14 See J. I. Dibua, "The Idol, Its Worshippers, and the Crisis of Relevance of Historical Scholarship in Nigeria," *History in Africa*, Vol. 24, 1997, 117-137; A. O. Adeoye, "Understanding the Crisis in Modern Nigerian Historiography," *History in Africa*, Vol. 19, 1992, 1-11; and A. Temu and B. Swai, *Historians and Africanist History: A Critique*, London, Zed Books, 1981.

15 See W. Rodney, *How Europe Underdeveloped Africa*, Washington, D.C.: Howard University Press, 1982; D. Offiong, *Imperialism and Dependency*, Washington, D.C.: Howard University Press, 1982; and B. Onimode, *A Political Economy of the African Crisis*, London: Zed and IFAA, 1988.

16 A. Olukoshi, *The Elusive Prince of Denmark: Structural Adjustment and the Crisis of Governance in Africa*, Uppsala: Nordiska Afrikainstitutet, 1998, 21.

17 It should be stated that this idea of individuals using part of their illegally appropriated wealth for the material benefits of their kith and kin and their communal groups, should not be overemphasized and, in fact, represents a bit of a stretch. It is a rather simplistic explanation of a more complex situation nor did many people actually use the corruptly acquired wealth to satisfy the material needs of their communal groups.

18 G. Hyden, *Beyond Ujamaa in Tanzania: Underdevelopment and an Uncaptured Peasantry*, Berkeley: University of California Press, 1980.

19 See for instance, C. Clapham, *Private Patronage and Public Power*, New York: St. Martins Press, 1982; S. N. Eisenstadt and R. Lemarchand eds., *Political Clientelism, Patronage and Development*, Beverly Hills and London: Sage Publications, 1981; R. Sandbrook, "Patrons, Clients, and Factions: New Dimensions of Conflict Analysis in Africa," *Canadian Journal of Political Science*, Vol. 5, No. 1, 1972; and idem., *The Politics of Africa's Economic Stagnation*, Cambridge: Cambridge University Press, 1985.

20 In reality, Richard Joseph's prebendalism is not substantially different from the other Weberian theoretical constructs that he criticized. With the exception of differences in appellations and semantics, the basis and kernel of all the constructs are fundamentally similar.

21 R. Joseph, *Democracy and Prebendal Politics in Nigeria: The Rise and Fall of the Second Republic*, Cambridge: Cambridge University Press, 1987, pp. 63 and 68.

22 Ibid., 67.

23 Ibid., 56.

24 T. Forrest, *Politics and Economic Development in Nigeria*, Boulder, CO: Westview, 1993, 6-7.

25 E. E. Osaghae, *Crippled Giant: Nigeria Since Independence*, Bloomington and Indianapolis: Indiana University Press, 1998, 311-314.

26 See for instance, P. M. Lewis, "From Prebendalism to Predation: The Political Economy of Decline in Nigeria," *Journal of Modern African Studies*, Vol. 34, No. 1, 1996; and L. Diamond, "Postscript and Postmodern," in L. Diamond *et. al.*, *Transition Without End: Nigerian Politics and Civil Society Under Babangida*, Boulder, CO: Lynne Rienner, 1997, 471-472.

27 Yankah, "Displaced Academies and the Quest for a New World Academic Order," 8.

28 C. Ake, *Democracy and Development in Africa*, Washington, D.C.: The Brookings Institution, 1996, 2-3.

29 W. D. Graf, *The Nigerian State: Political Economy, State Class and Political System in the Post-Colonial Era*, London and Portsmouth, NH: James Currey and Heinemann, 1988, 224.

30 C. Ake, "The State in Contemporary Africa," in C. Ake ed., *Political Economy of Nigeria*, London and Lagos: Longman, 1985, 4.

31 B. Fine and C. Stoneman, "Introduction: State and Development," *Journal of Southern African Studies*, Vol. 22, No. 1, 1996, 19.

32 See B. Beckman, "The Liberation of Civil Society: Neo-Liberal Ideology and Political Theory," *Review of African Political Economy*, No. 58, 1993, 30.

33 Y. Bangura and P. Gibbon, "Adjustment, Authoritarianism and Democracy: An Introduction to Some Conceptual and Empirical Issues," in P. Gibbon, Y. Bangura and A. Ofstad eds., *Authoritarianism, Democracy, and Adjustment: The Politics of Economic Reform in Africa*, Uppsala: Nordiska Afrikainstitutet, 1992, 15-16.

34 On the continued relevance of the concept of postcolonialism and the postcolonial approach, see R. Abrahamsen, "African Studies and the Postcolonial Challenge," *African Affairs*, Vol. 102, No. 407, 2003, 189-210.

35 C. Young, "The End of the Post-Colonial State in Africa? Reflections on Changing African Political Dynamics," *African Affairs*, Vol. 103, No. 410, 2004, 24-25.

36 Ibid., 40-41.

37 Ibid., 49.

Chapter 2

Received Wisdom and Africa's Development Trajectory

The severe economic crisis that African countries faced by the 1980s once again helped to bring into sharp focus the issue of Africa's development trajectory. The discourse over Africa's development dilemma has largely centered on the role of the state, or what has been referred to as state versus markets, with another variant being the trial of development economics which is seen as the main culprit for Africa's economic crisis. This analysis, which became influential with the publication of the World Bank report of 1981,[1] has become the dominant neo-liberal paradigm that has been used to analyze Africa's development trajectory. At the core of the analysis is the linkage between development economics and the African state, with African states accused of promoting anti-market development policies prescribed by development economists.[2] Even then, African governments were criticized for poorly and irrationally implementing the state-centered anti-market development policies. Based on this linkage, the African economic crisis has been used to pronounce and even celebrate the "death" of development economics and, therefore, its influence on Africa's development process,[3] as well as the irrelevance, failure and collapse of the African state.[4] The prevailing dominant neo-liberal orthodoxy, championed by the International Financial Institutions (IFIs) – notably the World Bank and the International Monetary Fund (IMF), which promotes the peripheralization and minimization of the African state in favor of the ascendancy of the markets, is a product of this perceived state collapse.

Indeed, the collapse of the African state has been accepted as so indisputable and uncontestable, that on a rather celebratory note, Hyden stated "there is little evidence that state theories will make an imminent return to the field (of African studies)." Rather, it seems that "regime" "has largely replaced the state as a major focus of interest in the study of African politics." Furthermore, he asserted that, "with the state literally vanishing in much of Africa, scholarly interest is likely to be elsewhere, if not on regimes at least on institutions and the many informal ways in which cultural phenomena in Africa influence formal institutions."[5] Some of the areas that scholarly interest shifted to are: civil society, democratization and human rights.[6] Indeed, for some Africanist scholars, civil society has become "the new master concept that now conveys the site of efficacious human agency in the building of a new political life in the continent."[7] Perhaps more relevant is the fact that the definition and characterization of what constitutes civil societies in Africa are mainly derived from the Western concept of civil society and therefore Eurocentric.[8] Civil societies are, thus, defined from the point of view of the extent to which they approximate the Western experience. This neo-modernization paradigm has become the dominant hallmark of Africanist scholarship since the 1980s neo-liberal era.

Paradoxically, one of the greatest misconceptions that have been propagated about the influence of modernization on Africa's development trajectory is that the paradigm became irrelevant after the 1970s with the demise of development economics. It is pointed out that since development economics was the primary vehicle through which modernization was propagated in Africa, the failure of the development programs promoted by development economists resulted in the concomitant demise of both development economics and modernization. As a result, most scholars, including radical and non-radical scholars who are critical of the prevailing neo-liberal orthodoxy introduced into Africa under the guise of the SAPs and globalization, failed to realize that these neo-liberal policies are continuations of the modernization paradigm. Yet the policies represent a continuation of the modernization-dictated Orientalist philosophy of the unbridled promotion of Eurocentrism or Westernization in Africa.[9] R. L. Sklar described the prevailing neo-liberal orthodoxy as the new modernization,[10] which under the supervision of the IFIs, has been used to reinforce the dominance of the modernization paradigm in Africa's development trajectory.[11]

An important reason why the enormous influence of the modernization paradigm on the neo-liberal policies has not been subjected to more critical, wide-ranging and intense debate has to do with the fact that the agenda for the discourse has been disproportionately set by the IFIs and their neo-liberal collaborators. Some have attributed this situation to the so-called demise of the neo-Marxist-dependency paradigm, whose adherents were the most consistent critics of the modernization paradigm.[12] It is true that after the exhaustive debate of the late 1970s and early 1980s, on the relevance of the dependency paradigm for analyzing the African situation, as epitomized by the "Kenyan debate," the paradigm lost some of its vigor.[13] Even then, radical scholars operating from the neo-Marxist-dependency paradigm were among the earliest to seriously critique the neo-liberal policies and have remained some of the most consistent and incisive critics of the policies.[14] However, the neo-liberals have dismissed these individuals as ideologues while using their enormous material and institutional support to try to marginalize these individuals and their works. As observed by Colin Leys and Bruce Berman, mainstream (neo-liberal) development theorists have used their institutional power to marginalize these alternative viewpoints, dismissing "them as unscientific and impractical, while sustaining efforts to reproduce the paradigm of modernity in the face of persistent failure in country after country."[15] Furthermore, the IFIs and Western donor agencies exploited the increased impoverishment of African academics to influence the outcome of their research by granting them consultancy work that effectively undermined their independent assessments of Africa's economic development trajectory. Indeed, with research being increasingly "funded by donor agencies with research agendas heavily swayed by World Bank development discourse and carried out in the form of short consultancies by African researchers or foreign 'experts' who often had little country experience," the independence of the assessments of the researchers was compromised.[16] It is this use of institutional power to marginalize alternative viewpoints, rather than a mere "inclination to be applied and useful" thereby overlooking "the need for research that transcends the boundaries of the neo-liberal paradigm or discourse,"[17] that is responsible for the dominance of the modernization-inspired neo-liberal paradigm.

However, the dominance of the neo-liberal orthodoxy has been accepted as so hegemonic and uncontestable, that even some of the most ardent critics of the neo-liberal policies are quick to pronounce the irrelevance of the Marxist-dependency paradigm in terms of criticizing and recommending alternatives to the neo-liberal orthodoxy. As stated by Sklar, "if the critics of prevailing theories of development studies simply resurrect new versions of Marxist-dependency theory, their failure to influence the course of history would be predictable."[18] Another variant of this observation is that both the Marxist-dependency and the neo-liberal paradigms share a great amount of similarity in "their underlying assumptions," and analysis, that they both help to reproduce and reinforce the modernization paradigm.[19] On the basis of this perceived irrelevance of the Marxist-dependency paradigm, an eclectic mix of rational-choice, pluralistic and poststructuralist analyses, among others, have been recommended as the appropriate alternative approach to adopt in confronting the neo-liberal orthodoxy.[20] Yet, this recommendation constitutes a reformulation of the new modernization paradigm and represents a submission to the "all conquering" force of neo-liberalism. Furthermore, the recommendation rather unwittingly represents an acceptance of the so-called ideological triumphalism of neo-liberalism, a situation, which Francis Fukuyama arrogantly but inappropriately celebrated as "the end of history."[21] For Fukuyama and other Western celebrationists, the demise of the Soviet Union means that the only path to development for all non-Western societies lies in the promotion of unbridled Westernization or Eurocentrism in these societies.

This chapter examines the role which modernization played in Africa's development trajectory especially from the late colonial period. It states that in spite of the various reformulations of the modernization paradigm, a central and consistent goal among proponents of the paradigm has been to present it in a beneficial form, in what constitutes a variant of "the civilizing mission." As a result, the failure of modernization inspired programs has been blamed on poor implementation on the part of African states, rather than the paradigm itself, hence the nature and limitations of the African state has occupied a central position in the analysis of the proponents of modernization. But as has been aptly observed by

Berman, the African crisis should be seen "as a crisis of the paradigm of modernity itself and the various projects of national development that have been its concrete expression" in African and other Third World countries.[22] It is from this perspective that this chapter critically interrogates the role of modernization (which has constituted the received wisdom) in Africa's development process.

Concept of Modernization

Weber's theory of rationality and irrationality provided the basis for the modernization paradigm as popularized by Parsons, who interpreted and translated Weber's works into the English language. Writing in defense of, and celebration of, the Enlightenment, Weber characterized the Enlightenment model of Western societies as the rational, modern and ideal type societies, while non-Western societies were characterized as irrational, traditional and non-ideal type societies. The implication of Weber's analysis is that to attain the features of the rational and ideal type society, non-Western societies should discard the irrational features that characterize their traditional societies in favor of the instrumental rationality of modern Western societies. Of great significance is the fact that Weber's ideal type modern society, is one in which instrumental rationality is to be applied to all facets of the society. In other words, for non-Western societies to attain the features of the ideal type society, they have to imbibe all the features and characteristics of the rational, modern (Western) society.[23] It has been argued that Weber's theory of the rational society was neither deterministic nor evolutionary (as was the case with the Parsonsian modernization school), rather, the end result is the outcome of struggles and conflicts, and therefore indeterminate.[24] Biko Agozino has suggested that the general interpretation of Weber's rational/irrational ideal types might be misleading because Weber must have meant regular/irregular processes of doing things.[25] Even then, in line with Weber's binary characterization of societies, regular approximates the ideal modern Western type process of doing things while irregular approximates the non-ideal, traditional non-Western type process of doing things.

In any case, Weber's binary categorization of rational and irrational or ideal and non-ideal type societies, as well as modern and traditional societies, and the assumed superiority of the rational and modern Western societies over the irrational and traditional non-Western societies constitute the core of the modernization paradigm as applied to Africa. Using Weber's categorization as their reference point, Parsons and his colleagues in the modernization school, developed an Orientalist theory of development, which categorically stated that, African countries can only develop through the Westernization of their societies. Development theorists of the Parsonsian school who became very influential from the 1950s became the critical vehicles through which the modernization paradigm was transplanted into the African scene. A crucial aspect of the modernization paradigm was the denigration and devaluation of African cultures and indigenous practices while promoting the Euro-American culture as the epitome of civilization and the standard, which African and other non-Western cultures, should strive to attain.

Under the Parsonsian concept of "pattern variables" the idea of a hierarchy of cultures in which the Western culture was at the peak and African cultures at the lowest level was promoted.[26] African cultures were seen as primitive, backward, barbaric and cannibalistic and therefore incapable of promoting and sustaining development. In fact, African societies were presumed as so inherently backward and inferior that they were not capable of surviving "in competition with the rationality and efficiency of the technologically, scientifically, and organizationally superior societies of the West."[27] This position was justified by the claim that precolonial African societies consisted of the "unrewarding gyrations of backward and barbaric tribes" and therefore, peoples without history.[28] European colonization of Africa was therefore presented as a benevolent act of "civilizing mission" through which African societies finally joined the stream of world history.

The European development experience was universalized and it was stated that the only development path for African societies laid in the replication of this experience. The perceived monumental superiority of the Western culture over African cultures meant that development in Africa must be in the form of the reproduction of the so-called superior features of the Eurocentric culture in different aspects of the African societies. Thus, the degree to which the Eurocentric features replaced the indigenous features became the yardstick for measuring development. The universalization of the Western experience and the contention that the Westernization of African and other non-Western societies constitutes the only credible index of development has been described as a form of authoritarian high modernism.[29] Modernization therefore promoted a Eurocentric form of globalization, a phenomenon that has been continued by the IFIs-inspired neo-liberal policies. It thus, fostered a teleological notion of development, which for African societies entailed the replacement of an undesirable, traditional and irrational state of affairs with an ideal and rational state, unambiguously defined in terms of the characteristics of Western capitalist societies. The components of this development process and therefore what constitute the modernization paradigm include industrialization, mass production, rising per capita income, the dominance of science-based advanced technology, military hegemony, bureaucratization, secularization and urbanization.

Economic development and political development theorists were some of the most significant propagators of the modernization paradigm in Africa. Both groups regarded the development project in Africa as that of nation-building (replication of Western capitalist societies), a task that can only be accomplished through the modernization paradigm. Although economic development theorists were well known for their unabashed commitment to a linear development path for African countries under the auspices of an authoritarian developmental state, similar views, albeit in reformulated versions, were espoused by political development theorists. Vernon Ruttan has observed that prior to the mid-1950s; political development theorists measured the level of political development in non-Western societies in terms of the extent to which they approximated the attributes of Western, in particular, English and American liberal constitutional democracy. In other words, the level of political development of a non-Western country was "measured by its linear distance from the Anglo-American model."[30]

By the mid-1950s, acting under the auspices of the SSRC, the Committee on Comparative Politics (CCP) sought to move away from what it saw as the excessive parochialism and statism of the linear model of development. This school of comparative politics argued that irrespective of the level of development of any society, the political functions performed in each society are essentially the same. They however argued that the difference between societies are to be found at the level of social and political structures while implying that the ideal and rational types of social structures are those associated with the Western societies. They therefore emphasized the significance of changes in social structures and the erosion of traditional social institutions, for the attainment of the Western-type societies. This school believed that "changes in political culture, at both the level of beliefs and attitudes and the level of personality," were imperative for the process of political development which was still largely defined as the transition from traditionalism to Western-type liberal democracy.[31] Members of the comparative school were equally of the opinion that market exchange and economic development are crucial for the development of liberal democracy hence their belief that societies with more differentiated structures have greater chances of embracing liberal democracy. In any case, this school of comparative politics operated firmly from the Parsonsian structural-functionalist model of the modernization paradigm. Their primary preoccupation was how to make African and other non-Western societies move from their so-called traditional and irrational types of political systems to the rational and ideal type Western political system epitomized by liberal democracy.[32]

However, it was the economic development theorists that made the boldest and most far reaching attempt at ensuring that economic development in Africa and other non-Western countries result in the replication of the Western experience. The most influential work in this regard was Rostow's "stages of growth" theory.[33] Drawing primarily from empirical data of the historical experience of Western capitalist countries, Rostow identified five stages of economic growth that every economy must pass through: traditional society, preconditions for growth, take-off, drive to maturity, and age of mass consumption. Rostow's "stages of growth" became the catechism for economic development policy in Africa.

Development economics became a primary vehicle through which the modernization paradigm was foisted on African countries. The project of development was seen not just as catching up with the advanced capitalist countries of the West, rather, as the replacement of the irrational, backward and traditional economic characteristics of African countries with the rational, modern and ideal type economic features of the Western countries. National development planning was viewed, as the veritable instrument through which the attainment of these Western characteristics would be accomplished in African countries, hence planning became the most popular economic development tool in postcolonial African countries. According to Thandika Mkandawire planning came to attain the status of a national symbol such as a flag, national anthem, etc.[34] As a result, the development enterprise was portrayed strictly in terms of replicating the Western path of development. Indeed, under the auspices of development planning, the stages of economic growth theory assumed the position of authoritarian modernism in that it became the only acceptable path for promoting economic development in Africa. Adherence to this form of authoritarian modernism was ensured through an authoritarian (the so-called developmental) state that the development economists promoted.

The preoccupation with replicating Western institutions and norms resulted in the transplanting of Western patriarchal practices into African countries. Contrary to the significant role that women played in the precolonial African economies and societies, women were portrayed as obstacles to development and modernization under the new dispensation. Development was therefore regarded as a male-centered affair. The outcome was the marginalization and neglect of women in the development process.[35]

It has been pointed out that the Marxist paradigm share a fundamental similarity with the liberal paradigm which it ironically vehemently criticized, in that both were committed to a developmentalist and unilinear conception of history which is based on the Western experience while dismissing the traditional African societies as backward. In addition, both defined the goal of development in terms of the "backward" and traditional African societies succumbing to the features of the modern Western societies. According to Berman, there was an implicit "shared assumption in liberal and Marxist concepts of dual economies in Third World societies, consisting of a dynamic modern sector that would eventually absorb and transform a technologically stagnant and backward 'traditional' sector."[36] Furthermore, it has been claimed that although "dependency theory was at once a critique of both developmentalism and a mechanical Marxism, both variants of unilinear evolutionist thinking," dependency itself succumbed to another form of unilinear evolutionism. This is in the sense that dependency theory "collapsed into a sterile structuralism denying the possibility of a capitalist transition in any and every dependent country no matter what the historical circumstance."[37]

There are valid points in these criticisms but it would be wrong to conclude that Marxist and dependency theories were guilty of helping to reproduce or sustain the modernization paradigm. It is true that in practice the Marxist theory assumes a unilinear perspective and a similar track of development for each society. In addition, the observation of Karl Marx on colonialism in India tended to create the impression that he was a modernization theorist.[38] But a detailed examination of the Marxist position clearly shows that the Marxist and modernist perspectives had very little in common. Indeed, the Marxist model is based on a dialectical approach to development rather than clearly defined stages of development where each stage is unambiguously empirically linked with the Western experience as advocated by modernization theorists. As noted by Hyden, "modernization theorists wish to empirically certify their theory as a means of reaching consensus (i.e. of replicating the features of Western societies) while the Marxists assume that the laws of history exist out there and only need to be fully understood."[39] The significant point about dependency theory is not really the denial of the possibility of a capitalist transition in every dependent society: it recognizes such a possibility but points out that under the realities of the global economy the outcome would be a dependent capitalist system. The examples of the newly industrialized Asian and Latin American countries that are normally used to question the validity of the dependent capitalist development assertion of dependency theorists, paradoxically, helps in certain significant respects, to validate the claim of the dependencists.[40] Furthermore, contrary to the modernizationists goal of Westernizing African societies through a unilinear process, dependency theorists advocate an internally engendered dialectical development process that would promote self-reliance. According to Okwudiba Nnoli, such a dialectical development process is one in which the individual and the society interact with their physical, biological, inter-human environments, and transforming them for their own benefit and that of humanity at large while being transformed themselves.[41]

None the less, the state is central to the development project of the modernization school. Development economists, political development theorists and liberal/neo-liberal scholars, as well as their critics, have devoted much attention to the phenomenon of the African state. The next section will examine the modernization discourse on the African state.

Modernization and the African State

The state occupies a central position in the modernization paradigm's analysis of economic development in Africa. Given the teleological notion of development held by members of this school, the state was seen as the only institution capable of ensuring the mobilization of resources toward the attainment of the preconceived rational and ideal type development. As has already been pointed out, the goal of development was defined in terms of the replication of the characteristics of the Western capitalist societies. Development economists were in the forefront in proclaiming the centrality of the state for economic development. Since the goals and end of development were unambiguously defined, development economists argued that the role of the state was to ensure that resources for development were mobilized in such a way that there was no deviation from the prescribed ideational modernist path. As a result, right from the period of its emergence as a subdiscipline in the late 1940s and early 1950s, development economics theorists held the view that a strong and authoritarian developmental state is a *desideratum* for the promotion of economic development in Africa. In spite of various reformulations and variations, this view of the necessity of an authoritarian state for economic development has remained a constant factor in the modernization paradigm.

In line with the methodology of the modernization paradigm, the notion of an authoritarian developmental state was justified on the basis of the experience of European countries. Relying on Alexander Gerschenkron's studies of European economic history,[42] development economists argued that the examples of the late industrialized countries of Europe (notably Germany, Russia, and other eastern and southern European countries) demonstrated the incompatibility between the practice of democratic principles and development. Rather, the need for the African state to run roughshod over all sectors of the society in the mobilization of resources was viewed as crucial for the development project in Africa. On this basis, many development economists and political development theorists (particularly Western-based Africanists) have devoted much energy to finding parallels between the historical experience of the development of the state in Western societies and the situation in postcolonial Africa. They therefore equate the characteristics of postcolonial African states to specific stages in the development of the early modern European state, in particular the period from the sixteenth to the eighteenth century. This Eurocentric unilinear, evolutionary model is a common thread that runs through the works of the state-centrist Africanists. Thomas Callaghy is one of the most consistent apostles of this model as reflected in his writings, which are equally unequivocally Weberian. For instance, in his examination of the state and the development of capitalism in Africa, Callaghy noted that the similarity between the African state form and that of early modern Europe is striking. According to him:

> As in early modern Europe, the (African) state is authoritarian and extractive, but its control is ultimately limited, especially in regard to attempts to redefine existing relations of production. In Europe this was made very clear by the limited substantive impact of mercantalist efforts, just as in most of Africa today.

Furthermore, he stated that "like their early modern European predecessors, most African states today are centralizing, but distinctly limited, authoritarian patrimonial-bureaucratic states."[43]

This Eurocentric approach has therefore resulted in a situation where the terms that have been used to describe the postcolonial African state are not only neo-Weberian but amount to "caricatures" of the early modern European states.[44] Thus, among other terms, African states have been variously characterized as 'absolutist', 'Bonapartist', 'patrimonial', 'prebendal', 'clientelist and rent-seeking', 'predatory', 'overdeveloped or underdeveloped', 'weak' or 'soft', and 'corporatist.'[45] Other variants of these characterizations are those of 'state decay', 'state decline', 'sultanism' and 'statism'.[46] As a result, it is alleged that the once-impersonal, potent and efficient colonial state has in its postcolonial form been personalized, rendered inefficient, corruption-laden and therefore unable to effectively allocate public resources for the promotion of capitalist development (yet the postcolonial state retains the absolutism of the colonial state). These features are seen as similar to the patrimonialism of the early modern European states. The African state is therefore portrayed as primarily inefficient because of its propensity for the pursuance of irrational development policies.

Comparison of the role of the state in African development to specific stages in early modern Europe has resulted in a situation where emphasis is placed on the ability of the African state to foster a transition to capitalism as occurred in modern Europe. This preoccupation has in turn promoted the proliferation of a great amount of modernization scholarship. Since state intervention was crucial for the development of capitalism in modern Europe, as well as for the creation of a bourgeois social order and the protection of the capitalist class, state-centrist development theorists expected similar functions for the postcolonial state in Africa. Furthermore, since capitalism developed under the aegis of the powerful nation-states in modern Europe, capitalist development in Africa is seen as a national enterprise under the protection of a powerful state. As a result, development is perceived only from the perspective of national development hence the emphasis on national development planning while the core components of the development project are Western-style industrialization and large-scale capitalist farming.

The responsibility of the state, which is defined as ensuring an effective transition to capitalism therefore, involves the promotion and protection of a national capitalist class that would champion this transition. The nature and preconditions of the capitalist transition as well as the nature and effectiveness of African capitalism and the African capitalist class have generated a great deal of Eurocentric debates. For instance, basing his stand on Weber's definition of capitalism, Callaghy flatly asserted that "early modern Europe and Africa today cannot . . . be considered capitalist," rather, they are pre-capitalist because they lack the attributes of "modern, rational, productive or industrial capitalism," which are based on the "rational permanent enterprise."[47] Similar Eurocentric approaches are evident in the works of Paul Kennedy and the edited volume by Berman and Leys, on African capitalism. Kennedy's unilinear evolutionary approach equates postcolonial African capitalism to the stage of capitalist development in Europe in the 18th century and predicted the possibility of a gradual, evolutionary path for African capitalism, along the lines of the development of capitalism in Europe.[48] With the exception of the chapter by Berman, the collections in Berman and Leys edited work were preoccupied with how to establish the conditions that would promote rational, Western ideal type capitalism in Africa.[49]

The belief that the nature of the African state can only be meaningfully analyzed from the perspective of the extent to which it reflects a specific stage in the development of the modern European state, suffers from a number of shortcomings. The implicit universalization of the Western experience as the rational and ideal type amounts to Orientalism and Eurocentrism while at the same time promoting cultural imperialism. Even more significant is the fact that the analysis of the African state from the perspective of the modernization paradigm has resulted in speculative scholarship and the mystification and distortion of the concrete African realities. Furthermore, the unilinear evolutionist approach which presents the historical experience with state building and capitalist development of sixteenth to eighteenth century Europe as the universal path that African societies are fated to tread, has resulted in a scholarship of history by analogy rather than history as process.[50] Indeed, this approach represents a reactionary application of the Western epistemological-modernist project.

In any case, the general verdict among modernization scholars and international financial institutions is that the inept, authoritarian, corrupt and patrimonial African states are the primary culprits for the underdevelopment of African countries. The states, in particular their bureaucracies were accused of fostering underdevelopment through the stifling of the private sector thereby making it impossible for market forces to promote growth and prosperity. They therefore recommended the minimization of the state through the granting of ascendancy to market forces.

This neo-liberal orthodoxy, as embodied in SAPs, with the so-called emphasis on a peripheral and less authoritarian state, is usually seen as deviating from, and in fact, jettisoning the modernization paradigm in favor of a form of market liberalism. The contrary is however the case. The neo-liberal orthodoxy is squarely and firmly situated within the modernization paradigm. It is based on the perceived superiority of the "rational" economic mechanism and democratic systems of the Western societies as opposed to the irrational and primitive state regulated economy and authoritarian personal rule of African societies. Thus, the neo-liberal policies sought to construct African societies in the Western image through policies that emphasize the minimization of the role of the state, massive devaluation of national currencies, drastic reduction in state expenditures especially on social services, privatization of state-owned enterprises, liberalization of the trade regime and democratization.

The neo-liberal policies have been largely unpopular in African countries. Contrary to the so-called state minimization policy of the neo-liberals, only authoritarian states can forcefully implement the SAPs-induced policies in the face of massive opposition. Thus, in line with the modernization paradigm, the neo-liberals support and in fact, promote authoritarian regimes in Africa so long as these regimes are geared toward the forceful implementation of SAPs. It follows that in contrast to the claim of the neo-liberals, the state occupies a central position in the implementation of their policies. Indeed a central tenet of neo-liberalism, the need to reduce the role of the state, "has had the perverse effect of locating the state at the centre of the analytical stage, not least in the twin themes previously identified as success/failure which now command the field of development studies."[51]

Also, the binary division between rational and irrational sectors of society, which is the hallmark of the modernization paradigm, occupies a central position in the neo-liberal policies. Hence some of the jargons of the neo-liberal orthodoxy include the distinction between the formal (rational) and the informal (irrational) sectors, the state (irrational) and civil society (rational) sectors, among others. However, in spite of these distinctions and in spite of the fact that the neo-liberals claim that the civil society is the rational and robust sector for the rejuvenation of African societies, their approach to civil society is essentially state-centrist. They rely on the massive use of state power (on the part of the countries implementing SAPs), to construct civil society in the Western image.[52] It is apparent that the modernization paradigm in its various reformulations and reincarnations has remained a constant factor that has influenced development policies in Africa. The modernization policies therefore constitute the main culprit for the persistence of the crisis of development in Africa.

Modernization and Africa's Development Trajectory before the 1980s

The 1950s during which the Parsonsian modernization school developed coincided with the period of political decolonization in Africa. The prevailing notion among development scholars and colonial authorities during this period was that the most realistic way to promote the development of the then decolonizing African countries was by Westernizing them through a transition from their irrational backward and primitive state to a rational modern state. The tool to effect this transition at the economic level was provided by development economists who were uncompromisingly committed to the modernization of the economies of African countries through state development planning. The success of the post-World War II reconstruction efforts in Western Europe under the auspices of the Marshall Plan increased the confidence of the development economists in the ability of the modernization paradigm to effect the Westernization of African economies. Furthermore, political development theorists operating from the structural-functionalist perspective touted the modernization paradigm as the basis for establishing meaningful and sustainable political systems in the decolonizing African countries. They therefore used the paradigm to support and advocate the adoption of Western-style liberal democracy in African countries. In reality, both the economic and political development theorists used the modernization program to support a transition from colonialism to neocolonialism in Africa under the guise of transiting to modernity.

Nevertheless, in the immediate postcolonial period of the 1960s, development economists were the most uncompromising and most visible advocates of a state-sponsored development process that would be firmly based on the modernization paradigm. Development planning was perceived as the most important instrument through which the economic features of Western societies would be replicated in Africa. In this enterprise, the global political atmosphere especially the intensification of the Cold War resulted in a situation where development economists enjoyed immense influence and prestige among Western governments and international financial and aid agencies thereby resulting in increased financial sponsorship from these governments and agencies. In their desire for rapid economic development, the newly independent African countries were attracted to the Soviet Union's development planning model, which produced the rapid industrialization of the country within a short period. The desire to counter this attraction of the Soviet planning model made the Western capitalist countries to use their neo-colonial relationships with the African countries to ensure a continuation of their own version of development planning which they had introduced in the late colonial period.[53]

Western governments and international financial and aid agencies sent various Western-based "experts" to African countries to assist them in drawing up their development plans. The outcome was a thriving partnership between Western development economists and Africanist scholars on the one hand, and Western governments and international financial and aid agencies on the other hand, a situation that helped to imbue Africanist studies with a large dose of economism and developmentalism. But the economism and developmentalism were firmly rooted in the modernization paradigm.

Rostow's "stages of growth" theory had perhaps the greatest influence on development policies and greatly contributed to entrenching the modernization model in the economic development policies of African countries. As already pointed out, the empirical data for the "stages of growth" theory were based primarily on the historical experience of Western capitalist countries. The theory idolized the features of Western capitalist societies as the epitome of development to which all non-Western societies should strive.[54] Development economists stated that the route to the development of African countries laid in their passing through the Rostownian five stages thereby entrenching a teleological notion of development. Indeed in the 1960s and 1970s the "stages of growth" theory was the catechism for Africa's development policies. However, Rostow identified the take-off stage as the most important component or watershed in the process of economic development in that it helped to lay the foundation for the attainment of self-sustaining growth and development.[55] As a result of the prominence attached to the take-off stage, economic development planning in various African countries became primarily tailored toward establishing the conditions for take-off. Given this fact, economic development policies were preoccupied with attaining a certain amount of growth in the Gross Domestic Product (GDP), capital formation, industrialization, urbanization, population, and infrastructures, among others. A prime place was accorded to capital formation, perceived in the form of an increase in GDP per capita.[56] It was assumed that once the take-off stage was attained, the benefits of growth would automatically spread and trickle down to all levels of society. This growth-and-trickle-down approach made economic development to be viewed primarily in technical and bureaucratic terms while de-emphasizing human beings as the essence of development.

Among other things, the modernization paradigm, in line with the principle of comparative advantage, emphasized the production of raw materials for Western industries and discouraged the establishment of capital and intermediate capital goods industries. However, given the significant position that industrialization occupied in the economic development process of the Western capitalist countries, an industrialization strategy supposedly aimed at locally producing the consumer goods that were imported from Western countries was put in place. This Import Substitution Industrialization (ISI) only promoted the establishment of consumer goods industries. Under this industrialization strategy, the state was basically to provide a favorable environment in the form of the provision of infrastructures and various fiscal policies among others, for a private sector-led industrialization. The ostensible reason for this industrialization strategy was that it would enable African countries replicate the modern types of consumer goods industries that exist in the Western capitalist countries. The rationale for this position was that the indigenous technology and production system was backward, primitive and irrational, and therefore incapable of fostering development. In addition, the ISI strategy was expected to contribute to the conservation of foreign exchange since the imported consumer goods would now be produced locally. Moreover, the strategy was regarded as crucial for the development of industrial modernity in Africa through the transfer of the Western style industrial technology.[57]

In reality, the ISI strategy was very exploitative and turned out to be a monumental failure. The strategy resulted in the establishment of mainly medium-sized import substitute consumer goods industries in different African countries, with the vast majority of them owned by Western-based Trans-National Corporations (TNCs). As branches of TNCs, these industries were strategically dependent on imported raw materials and capital equipment mainly from the home industries. With the high import content of the industries, about 70 percent of the added value accrued to foreigners. Thus, a strategy that was supposedly aimed at helping to conserve foreign exchange ironically became a conduit pipe for foreign exchange leakage. An outcome of the highly dependent nature of the import-substituting industries was the failure to promote linkages between them and the rest of the African economies. The products of these industries could not effectively compete with similar imported products while the establishment of similar industries in other African countries meant that, as was the case with raw materials production, the industries could not export their products to fellow African countries. Furthermore, the capital intensive nature of the industries fostered by the ISI strategy made them to be out of tune with the realities of the African labor surplus economies. All these factors associated with the ISI strategy detrimentally affected African economies and significantly contributed to the African economic crisis.

By the second half of the 1960s, it had become apparent that growth in the GDP – the centerpiece of the stages of growth-induced economic development policies of the modernization paradigm – was not having any meaningful impact on the economic development of African countries in the sense that even with a consistent level of growth in the GDP for many of the countries, the problem of underdevelopment was becoming more intractable. The standard of living of the majority of Africans remained unchanged and in some cases worsened. There was therefore a great amount of disenchantment with the prevailing notion of development, in particular, the growth-and-trickle-down notion promoted by the modernization paradigm. The modernization paradigm and the economic development policies it championed therefore came under severe criticism, especially from dependency scholars. The dependency school criticized modernization for, among other things, having the penchant for sterile economism and developmentalism, and for promoting the integration of Africa's economies into the world capitalist system at a subordinate level, thereby promoting underdevelopment and neocolonial dependency. In contrast to the development economists unilinear conception of development, dependency theorists pointed out that the structural features of peripheral capitalism such as highly unequal trading relationship between African countries and the Western capitalist countries, high levels of monopoly and surplus leakage were promoting underdevelopment rather than development in Africa.[58]

Liberal scholars came to the defense of modernization and in line with the paradigm's method of blaming internal factors, in particular, poor implementation; they argued that African governments should rather be blamed for failing to effectively implement policies that would help to modernize their countries. However, some liberal scholars eventually came to acknowledge the fact that modernization and the attendant economic development policies had some deficiencies that needed to be addressed. They realized that the technocratic obsession with growth was misplaced since the growth in the GDP did not translate into meaningful improvement in the standard of living of the majority of the African peoples. Moreover, since man is the centerpiece of development, the issue should be viewed more in qualitative rather than in quantitative terms and more emphasis should be placed on the objectives of development as a basis for redefining the concept. These liberal revisionists stated that the modernization influenced development paradigm should go beyond the preoccupation with growth, and include issues like attacking poverty, reducing inequalities and removing the specter of rising unemployment in its conception of development. As a result there was a new emphasis placed on "redistribution with growth" and "meeting the basic needs" of African peoples.

The redistribution with growth model is based on the notion that growth is the centerpiece of development. However, in view of the increasing amount of inequality in income between the rich and the poor in African and other Third World countries, efforts should be made to promote economic equity through the redistribution of the benefits of growth.[59] In accordance with the developmental state policy of the modernization paradigm, the government was expected to put in place measures for achieving the desired state of growth in juxtaposition with policies for redistributing the benefits of growth. In essence, an authoritarian and paternalistic state was deemed better placed to determine what is good for the people. The failure of the redistribution with growth policy to make positive impact on the standard of living of the majority of the people led to the further reformulation of the notion of economic development. It was felt that African governments would more effectively serve the interests of African peoples by putting in place measures that would serve their basic needs. Basic needs were identified as adequate food, shelter and clothing, access to facilities such as potable drinking water, transportation, health, education, and employment, among others.[60] Thus under this new interpretation, development came to be conceived not only in terms of economic growth but also in terms of quantitative and qualitative changes in the standard of living of the majority of the peoples.

The basic needs conception of development did not mark a departure from the modernization paradigm, on the contrary, it was firmly situated within the paradigm, as a crucial role was assigned to the authoritarian state while the resources for meeting the basic needs were perceived as replication of Western resources. Indeed, the authoritarian state, international organizations, and Western governments and agencies were deemed to be better placed to determine for African peoples what their basic needs were as well as the most appropriate means of attaining them. As a result, rather than make use of the available local resources and indigenous knowledge, resources and the knowledge embedded in them were transplanted from Western countries to be used to satisfy African peoples basic needs because the transplanted resources were perceived as superior to the "backward" indigenous ones.[61] Thus, as was the case with the redistribution with growth model, the basic needs approach promoted an authoritarian and paternalistic state while equally helping to further entrench neocolonial dependency. In essence, the redistribution and basic needs approaches did not challenge the socio-economic matrix within which poverty, inequalities and underdevelopment were in the first place generated: they sought to alter the distribution of income and wealth without changing the neo-colonial and dependent structures within which they were produced.[62]

Development economists integrated the various reformulations of the modernization paradigm into the development plans of the respective African countries. The Nigerian experience will help to illustrate this point. In the 1960s and early 1970s, planning in Nigeria was primarily preoccupied with the growth-and-trickle-down approach. The main objective of the Nigerian First National

Development Plan, 1962-68 was to ensure a minimum GDP growth rate of 4 percent per annum as a means of creating the conditions for the attainment of self-sustaining growth.[63] In fact W. F. Stolper, the main architect of the plan, argued that "the only realistic aim of a plan ought to be to ensure that the economy will grow at a certain minimum rate or more."[64] Thus, "the whole purpose of the planning exercise (was) to aid Nigeria in mobilising as many resources as possible and allocating them for growth."[65] The Second National Development Plan, 1970-74, emphasized the attainment of "growth as a pre-condition for a meaningful distribution of the fruits of development." The plan stated that "the 'national cake' must first be baked before it is shared; and the bigger the cake, the more it can go round at each succeeding round of the sharing game."[66] Although the growth rate for the two plans exceeded the projected minimum (5.2 percent for the first plan and 8.2 percent for the second plan), the growth-and-trickle-down model clearly failed to result in any meaningful improvement in the standard of living of the majority of the people. As a result, the Third National Development Plan, 1975-80 was committed to translating "economic growth into meaningful development through income redistribution."[67] Furthermore, the Fourth National Development Plan, 1981-85 emphasized the provision of basic needs in order to promote "true development" which "must mean the development of man – the realisation of his creative potential, enabling him to improve his material conditions of living through the use of resources available to him."[68]

In spite of the new sentiment embodied to some extent in the redistribution with growth model and more specifically in the basic needs approach the development paradigm remained that of modernization. As observed by J. F. Ade Ajayi, the shift from the growth-and-trickle-down model did not remove the basic flaws in the method of planning because the redistribution and basic needs approaches with their vision of an egalitarian and individualistic society, conceived from above, were mere reformulations of the objectives of modernization.[69] Nevertheless, in the 1980s, the failure of the various versions of the reformulated modernization paradigm to promote meaningful development in Africa resulted in the intense criticism of development economists by their neoclassical counterparts. The neoclassical economists held development economists and their policies of a developmental state, which encouraged state intervention through the agency of planning as responsible for the worsening African crisis. With institutional and massive financial support from Western governments and the IFIs, the neoclassical economists became ascendant and were able to use the agency of the IFIs to compel African countries to adopt economic policies embodied in the SAPs. Particularly beneficial to the neoclassical economists was the emergence of Ronald Reagan as the US president and Margaret Thatcher as the British prime minister. The resultant Reaganomics and Thatcherism were very much hostile to development planning and the perceived welfare orientation of development plans. Essentially, SAPs repudiated the idea of a developmental state, and advocated the minimization of the state and the ascendancy of market forces for the promotion of economic development.[70]

Leopold Mureithi's study of development planning in Kenya shows that the planning process and economic development policies passed through a similar trajectory as that of Nigeria. The Kenyan first and second development plans, 1964-70 and 1970-74 respectively were based on the growth-and-trickle-down model while the third and fourth development plans, 1974-78 and 1979-83 adopted the redistribution with growth and the basic needs strategies respectively. Also, the worsening economic crisis in Kenya led to the adoption of the SAP in the second half of the 1980s. In summarizing the planning process Mureithi stated:

> First, there was a "growth-and-trickle-down" approach beginning in the 1950s and lasting until the late 1960s. Then came the strategy of "growth with distribution." When redistribution proved difficult due to the structural nature of poverty, the 1970s saw the "basic needs" approach of "who gets what." In the face of fundamental changes in the economic environment, the World Bank and the International Monetary Fund have sold the idea of structural adjustment, policy planning, institutional reform, privatization, etc., as canons for proper economic management. All these strands run through Kenya's economic policy and planning practice.[71]

In the 1980s, the SAPs with their emphasis on deregulation therefore replaced development planning as the new catechism for economic development policies in Africa.

Economic Crisis, Neo-liberalism and the New Modernization

The severe economic crisis that African countries experienced in the 1980s provided the neoclassical economists with an opportunity to reformulate the modernization paradigm although they tried to disguise the new approach embodied in SAPs as a departure from the modernization model. The reason for this disguise was the obvious unpopularity of the modernization paradigm and development economists who were the main theorists of modernization. However, although the development economists drew their inspiration from Keynesianism and therefore favored state interventionism while the neoclassical and supply side economists were more in favor of market forces, both were committed to modernization. Indeed, the neo-liberal policies of the neoclassical economists are strikingly similar to the modernization model of the development economists. The policies continue with modernization's binary division of African societies and institutions into irrational and rational sectors as in state versus markets, state versus civil society and informal sector versus formal sector. Furthermore, in spite of the professed hatred for the state, the neo-liberal orthodoxy relies on a strong and authoritarian state for the implementation of its unpopular policies. In addition, the neo-liberal policies merely seek to replicate or transplant Western institutions into Africa. Thus, although the neo-liberal theorists are supposedly from an opposing school they still operate within the paradigm of modernity.

As was the case with the development economists, the neoclassical economists blamed internal factors for Africa's economic crisis placing the major blame on the irrational domestic policies adopted by African governments as well as poor implementation of development policies. In this regard, the Berg report, which constituted the basis for the 1981 World Bank's influential publication blazed the trail and has become the "gospel" of the neoclassical school in explaining Africa's economic crisis. The publication unambiguously blamed inadequacies and deficiencies in African domestic development policies as the primary culprit for the economic woes of African countries.[72] The World Bank's sister institution, the IMF also placed the main blame for Africa's economic crisis on irrational domestic policies pursued by African governments. According to the IMF "external debt problems are generally symptomatic of underlying balance of payments difficulties arising . . . from the adoption of inappropriate economic and financial policies by the debtor country."[73]

Nevertheless, the centerpiece of the neoclassical explanation of the causes of Africa's economic crisis is the irrational excessive state regulation of African economies and the attendant overvaluation of African currencies. The neoclassical economists claimed that these factors did not create the conditions necessary for the rational operation of free market forces thereby hindering the ability of market forces to efficiently allocate resources. They alleged that the resultant patrimonialism bred widespread corruption and the inefficient allocation of resources, as the African ruling class saw the state as an arena of action and source of power, status, rents, and other forms of wealth.[74] However, some of the irrational state policies that were specifically singled out as being responsible for the crisis were the overvaluation of African currencies, abuse of the import licensing system, subsidization of petroleum products and various social sectors of the economy, inefficient state-owned enterprises, and corruption.[75]

It has been pointed out that the foreign exchange management policies adopted by African countries resulted in the extreme overvaluation of their currencies, a situation that in turn, introduced serious structural defects in the African economies. The outcome was that imports were cheaper than exports, thereby creating high demands for exports while discouraging local industries from producing export-oriented goods. The resultant import dependency did not promote industrialization and diversification of African economies. Furthermore, the import dependency created serious balance of payments deficits, which was continuously worsened by the excessive local demands for foreign exchange. This gave rise to an irrational elaborate system of foreign exchange controls such as import licensing, quotas, and tariffs, a situation that in turn, promoted patrimonialism and patronage in the foreign exchange system. This analysis fails to take into account the fact that the replication and transplantation of Western institutions into Africa, which the modernization-based development paradigm promoted, were highly culpable for entrenching import dependency since the resources had to be imported from Western capitalist countries. Furthermore, the modernization-inspired industrialization strategy which was based on import substitution, promoted import dependency, dependent industrialization and lack of diversification of African economies.[76]

Furthermore, the neo-liberals pointed out that excessive government subsidies of petroleum products and social services such as health, education, electricity, and piped water hindered the effective operation of the market forces and made these services available at uneconomic rates. They were therefore regarded as avenues of wastage of government resources. In terms of state-owned enterprises, they contended that since governments were bad economic managers, the enterprises were inefficiently managed, riddled with corruption and therefore ran at huge losses, thereby constituting a drain on government resources. On the whole, the neo-liberals contended that the excessive amount of corruption, rentierism, corporatism, prebendalism and inefficiency associated with excessive state regulation of African economies fundamentally contributed to the severe economic crisis of African countries. These factors certainly contributed to the emergence of the economic crisis but they amount to laying the blame primarily on factors internal to African countries. Yet the nature of the incorporation of African countries into the global economic system, the attendant machinations of the international monopoly capital and the acute limitations of the neocolonial political economy installed in African countries, are critical for explaining the emergence of the African economic crisis. Indeed, most of the internal factors listed as responsible for the development crisis were at best manifestations or symptoms of the paradigm of modernity on which African development policies were based.

Nevertheless, two of the most important manifestations of the economic crisis were balance of payments deficits and the debt burden. In view of the massive nature of the debts, which were owed mostly to Western countries and the IFIs, African countries needed to negotiate the rescheduling of the debt and other conditions of repayment with the Western creditor countries and the IFIs. At the same time, African governments needed both short-term and long-term loans from the IFIs to take care of their balance of payments deficits, debt repayments and to carry out other economic activities. This predicament of the African countries placed the Western creditor nations and the IFIs in the advantageous position of dictating the terms on which debt rescheduling and further loans would be extended to African countries. They used the opportunity to impose some conditionalities that African debtor countries should meet before their debts would be rescheduled and before they could obtain new loans. The conditionalities were presented in the form of stabilization and adjustment programs which African debtor countries were expected to carry out as a way of resolving the economic crisis. Although it was the IFIs that stated the conditionalities, the Western creditor countries made acceptance of the conditionalities by African debtor countries, a requirement for debt rescheduling. In any case, in view of the reasons, which the IFIs and the neo-liberals in general attributed for the crisis, the centerpiece of SAPs is the peripheralization of the role of the state through the ascendancy of markets. Thus, in line with the paradigm of modernity, the state occupies a central position in the analysis of the neo-liberals.

Furthermore, as is characteristic of the modernization paradigm, the conditionalities of the adjustment programs were mainly economistic and developmentalist, and various African countries were expected to uniformly and mechanistically apply the adjustment programs regardless of the prevailing situations in each country. The core of SAPs is hard neo-liberalism: the adjusting African countries were expected to put in place processes of achieving economic stabilization, long-term sustainable growth, and an unfettered operation of market forces. The common policies of SAPs, which have been uniformly applied to various African countries, include devaluation of national currencies, drastic reduction in state expenditures, privatization of state-owned enterprises, and liberalization of the trade regime.

Massive devaluation of African currencies occupies a central position in the adjustment policies. As already noted the perceived overvaluation of African currencies was said to have promoted a high amount of import dependency, a situation, which greatly contributed to the balance of payments deficits. The adjustment of exchange rate was therefore seen as crucial for Africa's economic recovery. Closely related to devaluation is the policy of trade liberalization. It was felt that by removing all the irrational bureaucratic control over the foreign exchange markets, African businesses would be able to import the necessary inputs for their industries. At the same time more foreign investments would be attracted into the continent. Furthermore, the abolition of governmental control and direct participation in the marketing of agricultural products would increase the income passed on to crop farmers, thereby increasing rural income. This would in turn encourage increased production for exports by the rural dwellers. Theoretically, the policies of massive devaluation and trade liberalization are situated within the neo-classical economic policy of comparative advantage which advocates that African countries should continue with the imperialist imposed international division of labor which consigns them to the position of producing raw materials for Western capitalist industries. It is stated that "the primary thrust of these economic reform efforts is to more fully integrate African economies into the world economy by resurrecting the primary-product export economies that existed at the time of independence and making them work right this time by creating a more 'liberal' political economy."[77] It should be noted that this integration of African economies into the world economy has historically been at a subordinate level while the so-called 'liberal' political economy implies the replication of the Western style 'ideal' liberal democratic system in Africa.

The policies of reduction in public expenditures and the privatization of public enterprises are interrelated. The reasoning behind the demand for cutting public expenditure is based on the argument that the huge spending on social sectors like health, education, social infrastructures and other services constitute large drains on the resources of African countries. At the same time the expenditure only benefit the urban elites to the detriment of the rural dwellers who need to be encouraged to increase their agricultural outputs. In the case of privatization of public enterprises, the argument is based on their poor performance necessitating regular subsidies, which constitute a further drain on government resources. It is stated that privatization would expose these enterprises to market determined competition and therefore make them operate more efficiently if they want to remain in business. The justification for privatization is normally cast in the modernization paradigm's contextualization of African states as corrupt, inefficient, patrimonial, corporatist and rent-seeking. Mkandawire has clearly summarized the neo-liberals case for privatization of public enterprises:

> Privatization is intended to achieve at least three things. First, it is supposed to contribute to the bridging of the fiscal budgets and rationalization of public finances by unburdening African economies of overextended and corrupt state and parastatal structures that have putatively wrought havoc on public finances . . . Second, privatization is expected to lead to greater efficiency in the allocation of resources, to generate less inflationary pressures, to stimulate more competitiveness of African economies, all of which are expected to contribute to greater total factor productivity in the economy. Third, privatization is expected to free both domestic and foreign private capital from the tentacles of corrupt and inefficient bureaucracies so that it can be productively engaged in those activities that have thus far been monopolized by the state or have been off-limits to the private sector.[78]

Although the core of the neo-liberal policies is the minimization of the state through the ascendancy of the markets the neo-liberal discourse has generated state-centrist analyses that are reminiscent of the modernization paradigm. Indeed, the neo-liberal agenda of minimizing the state in relation to the markets has elevated the state to a dominant position in the analysis and debate over the adjustment programs. Three broad analytical positions in terms of what should be the relationship between the state and markets have emerged. The positions are: belief in the supremacy of the markets and therefore the peripheralization of the state, belief in the supremacy of the state, and an understanding that both the state and markets should play equally important roles. Although at the superficial level there might appear to be some differences between the role assigned the state by the modernization paradigm of the 1960s and 1970s on the one hand and the IFIs since the 1980s on the other hand, in reality these differences are more apparent than real.

In the 1960s and 1970s the African states were expected to play developmental roles through authoritarian and interventionist policies, thereby giving rise to the concept of the developmental state which was usually authoritarian. It is rather ironic that while in theory the adjustment policies calls for the minimization of the

African state, in practice the neo-liberals and the IFIs rely on interventionist authoritarian states to promote the operation of the so-called free market forces. Furthermore, in view of the very harsh and anti-peoples policies of SAPs and the resultant massive opposition the adjustment policies generated all over Africa, the neo-liberals and the IFIs rely on authoritarian states to forcefully and mercilessly implement the adjustment policies. They mask this reliance on authoritarianism to ensure the implementation of the adjustment policies with such jargons as having the "political will" or creating the "enabling environment" for SAPs to succeed in Africa. But in reality, the "political will" and the "enabling environment" are euphemisms for the establishment of authoritarian regimes that can ride roughshod over internal opponents of SAPs by insisting that there are no alternatives to the program. It is therefore not surprising that the IFIs star adjuster in Africa, Ghana, and for sometime the "strong adjusters," Nigeria, Malawi and others, all earned this dubious distinction under authoritarian regimes. As far as the neo-liberals and the IFIs are concerned, the important thing is that these regimes use state intervention to ensure the implementation of SAPs.[79] This is reminiscent of the modernization-inspired authoritarian and developmental state policy of the 1960s and 1970s.

It is important to realize that in spite of the binary division promoted by the neo-modernization paradigm, state and markets are not separate entities existing independently of each other; on the contrary, they are interconnected institutional forms through which different economic and political interests are pursued. Indeed, they are terrains of struggles between conflicting interests for political and economic ascendancy. State intervention is therefore not a neutral affair but is conditioned and shaped by the political and economic interests of the ascendant groups.[80] Nevertheless, it should be realized that the neo-liberals claim of the existence of non-state intervention and the unfettered operation of market forces in the Western capitalist societies, in whose image they sought to cast African societies, is a myth. Thomas Biersteker has identified six ways in which the state intervenes in the economy: to influence, to regulate, to mediate, to distribute, to produce and to plan. He states that every state intervenes in its economy, and that nearly all states intervene in each of the six ways. Furthermore, even in the so-called self-consciously laissez-faire economy of the U.S., "with the exception of the of the planning function, each of (the) forms of state intervention has taken place in varying degrees since the end of the second world war."[81] Similarly, with reference to state intervention in the Western capitalist economies since the end of World War II, Callaghy noted:

> Contrary to popular assumption and official rhetoric, orthodox liberalism, especially its free-market core, has not been the dominant form of political economy in the industrial West since World War II. Instead, the dominant political economy has been a form of compromise called "embedded liberalism," which involves the use of quite extensive

> state power simultaneously in the interests of domestic political and social stability and wellbeing on the one hand and international economic adjustment on the other.[82]

Nevertheless, the imperialistic role of the IFIs and the extremely harsh effects of SAPs generated massive resentment against the adjustment programs in various African countries, as epitomized by large-scale and popular anti-SAP uprisings, which have youths, the urban unemployed and market women as their vanguard. Realizing the high level of resentment against SAPs and the fact that the success of anti-SAP uprisings could bring to power regimes that are anti-SAPs, anti-imperialists and anti-IFIs, the IFIs, particularly the World Bank, decided to seize the initiative by introducing "political conditionality" as an aspect of SAPs in Africa. This neo-modernization policy requires countries implementing SAPs to embark on democratic reforms. However, political conditionality is an extension of the neo-classical economic logic, which claims that for market forces to succeed, both free enterprise economies and multiparty democracies should be mutually reinforcing. The World Bank outlined this new position in its 1989 publication: *Sub-Saharan Africa: From Crisis to Sustainable Growth.*[83] The document emphasized what it called good governance, democratization, alleviating poverty and empowering the grassroots, thereby adopting and appropriating some of the ideological armor of the opponents of SAPs.

Bjorn Beckman's incisive critique of this publication has demonstrated that the document was primarily an attempt by the World Bank to subvert internal opposition to SAPs in Africa by adopting some of the opposition's ideological weapons. The document equally aimed at creating new bases of popular support for SAPs and the regimes implementing the programs in Africa, from among the rural dwellers who were regarded as not as hostile to SAPs as the urban dwellers.[84] Thus, in the face of massive internal opposition to SAPs, the need for the IFIs and Western creditor nations to control the character and direction of democratic change in Africa greatly contributed to their new stance regarding democratic reforms.[85] Indeed the World Bank had a pattern of trying to undermine opposition to the SAPs through the publication of preemptive reports. For instance, in 1989, the Economic Commission for Africa (ECA), prepared a report that harshly criticized the adjustment programs in Africa. The ECA report called for issues like popular participation in the political and economic affairs of African countries, rural and grassroots empowerment, subsidies for important social sectors that affect the lives of the majority of African peoples, state intervention in the economies of African countries, and the development of African alternatives to SAPs.[86] According to Carol Lancaster, in order to undercut the harsh criticisms in the ECA's report, the World Bank, without going through the usual internal bank clearances, rushed to publish its own report[87] at the same time that the ECA was presenting its draft report to a meeting of African finance ministers in Malawi.[88] R. H. Green has argued that the World Bank's report was not aimed at preempting the ECA's report though he agreed that the World Bank's report was based on "ill-digested" or deliberately "rigged" statistics.[89] However, the apparent shoddiness exhibited in the preparation of the report, clearly demonstrate that the World Bank's objective was indeed to preempt the ECA's report. The publication of the long-term perspective study in 1989 can be said to have marked the culmination of this exercise of preempting and undermining serious and credible criticisms of SAPs from within Africa.

This pattern of the World Bank trying to deflect attention from the disastrous social and economic consequences of SAPs on the vast majority of the African peoples and hijacking the ideological armor of the critics of the adjustment policies was reproduced in subsequent World Bank policy statements and publications.[90] As noted by Deborah Bryceson and Leslie Bank:

> Neo-liberal policies, championed by the World Bank and International Monetary Fund (IMF) ...have not secured 'economic take-off'. Rather there has been growing immiseration through livelihood displacement, physical infrastructural decay, and social service breakdown. In a bid to deflect criticism, the World Bank has co-opted a post-modernist perspective ... (supposedly aimed at) documenting the 'voices of the poor'.

Furthermore, the IFIs have tried to effect "a shift in African policy discourse from neo-liberalism, with its unshakeable belief in the benefits of market optimisation, to what might best be called 'post-modern liberalism' with a professed commitment to poverty-alleviating welfare measures and backpedalling on African prospects in world markets."[91] None the less, rather than see the new discourse as "post-modern liberalism" it can, in fact, be characterized as constituting part of the neo-modern discourse.

However, it should be noted that the progression from predominantly neo-classical economism and developmentalism to one that came to include political conditionality, political liberalization and good governance is a reflection or reincarnation of the kind of ideological summersault that the modernization paradigm carried out in the 1960s and 1970s when, in the face of criticisms, its theorists cashed in on International Labor Organization's (ILO) concern with basic needs to reformulate the modernization theory. Yet, the revision did not tamper with the essence of the paradigm, which continued to influence development policies in Africa. In fact, while advocating democratization, grassroots empowerment and rural development, the World Bank at the same time supported authoritarian states so long as this would lead to the replication of the features of the Western capitalist societies and the consolidation of SAPs at the end of the democratization process. Indeed, before the massive anti-SAP demonstrations compelled the World Bank to belatedly introduce political conditionality in the form of democratization, the neo-liberal orthodoxy held the view that authoritarian states were better placed to implement the adjustment policies.[92] Thus, this technocratic-managerial approach, masquerading as populism, encouraged pro-SAP state-sponsored democratization processes in various African countries.

Nevertheless, as was the case with the kind of developmentalism promoted by the modernization-inspired development economists in the 1960s and 1970s, the SAPs have worsened the problems of underdevelopment in Africa as their policies have resulted in the aggravation of the economic crisis, poverty and misery in the continent.[93] As is characteristic of the modernization paradigm, apologists of SAPs have argued that the adjustment policies were based on sound economic analysis while the major problem lies in the poor implementation of the policies.[94] However, a major contradiction of the neo-liberal analysis is that while they blame internal factors, especially the economic policies adopted by the African states as being primarily responsible for the economic crisis and therefore call for the minimization of the state, the adjustment policies promoted authoritarian and interventionist states. It has been asserted that the allegation of destructive irrational and patrimonial policies leveled by the neo-liberals against African states was "designed to justify the increasing interference by foreign powers in the economic and political affairs of Africa and the search for 'rational' bureaucratic authoritarian states."[95]

In any case, an important issue is whether the state *per se* is the problem. As noted by Abdi Samatar and Ahmed Samatar, while the African state in its inherited postcolonial form suffers from serious shortcomings, the problem is not with the state *per se*, rather, the problem lies in the shortcomings of the inherited postcolonial African states. They therefore noted that the development failure in Africa is not because of the state *per se*, but because the inherited postcolonial state is of the wrong kind.[96] There is no doubt that the state must play a significant role in Africa's development trajectory, but the problem is the form that the state should assume and the interests that it should serve.

Bringing the State Back into the Development Process

The aggravating effects of the state minimalism and the market ascendancy policy of the adjustment programs, has resulted in a new body of literature that demand a critical role for the state in the development process. This new demand for an activist, interventionist and developmental state started gaining prominence in the mid-1980s as epitomized with the publications of the edited work of Peter Evans *et. al.*, incidentally titled *Bringing the State Back In* and Alice Amsden's work on South Korea's industrialization.[97] This strong statist approach emphasized the need for the developmental state to be strong and enjoy autonomy vis-à-vis the interests of the social groups that make up a country in order for the state to be able to perform its developmental role. This new conception of an autonomous and dominant developmental state is clearly reflected in the title of Robert Wade's work, *Governing the Market*, in which he advocated a strong and authoritarian state that should be able to set economic policies and compel the private sector to adopt the policies.[98]

The developmental state theory was further refined and made more Weberian in the 1990s with the adoption of the concept of embedded or bounded autonomy. The concept of embedded autonomy, in a somehow contradictory manner, juxtaposes an autonomous state with specific internal social groups with which the state shares intimate and strategic relationships in the common goal of promoting development.[99] In the Weberian tradition, this concept advocates a rational, coherent and effective bureaucracy that is insulated from the pressures of special interest groups but maintains strategic relationship with specific social groups with which it shares the development agenda, as a condition for the developmental state to thrive. Specifically, it is stated that capitalism cannot thrive unless a state bureaucracy helps to provide the direction and the public goods for attaining the goals of capitalism.[100]

Nevertheless, the bulk of the empirical evidence for the new literature on the developmental state is drawn from the experience of the Newly Industrializing Countries (NICs) of East Asia, the so-called Asian Tigers. Like the earlier Japanese experience, the industrialization of the East Asian NICs is explained in terms of a strong activist and interventionist state thus contradicting the neo-liberal prescription of state minimalism and ascendancy of the markets.[101] However, the analyses on these NICs are in the main, squarely situated within the modernization paradigm: they adhere and accept the paradigm's binary division between state and markets. The analyses also tend to celebrate or at least condone the high degree of authoritarianism under which the industrialization of these countries occurred stressing the commitment of the states to development and their ability to run roughshod over various pressure groups. Furthermore, in the Weberian manner, the presence of a rational and efficient bureaucracy is celebrated.

Perhaps, more significant is the fact that in seeing development as a replication of the Western experience, undue emphasis is placed on industrialism. Yet while the state in the NICs have been able to suppress some categories of internal interest groups its industrialization process has accorded a prominent position to interest groups representing foreign capital working in alliance with local interest groups through the agency of the state. The outcome has been a high degree of inequality among the social groups within the countries while promoting dependence on foreign capital.[102] However, realizing that the NICs experience contradicts the neo-liberal demand for minimizing the role of the state, the World Bank attempted to explain the NICs situation on the basis that they used the state to adopt market-conforming policies.[103] But this explanation is a face saving devise on the part of the World Bank and its fellow travelers on the neo-liberal path for it does not correctly portray the East Asian experience.[104]

However, the disastrous failure of the adjustment policies in various African countries has resulted in the demand for activist and interventionist states in Africa. There are two schools of thought in this demand for activist and interventionist states. The first school, taking its cue from the industrialization success of the East Asian NICs, promotes the East Asian experience as the model that should be replicated in Africa if the quest for industrialization and capitalist development is to be successful. Adherents of this school therefore devote their efforts to trying to find out ways that the East Asian experience can be successfully replicated in Africa.[105] The starting point for this school in terms of the possibilities of replicating the East Asian experience in Africa is to descend heavily on the bureaucracies of African countries which are described as the greatest handicaps for the attainment of the development enterprise. Operating from the Weberian and modernization perspectives, they describe Africa's bureaucracies as suffering from instrumental irrationality, inefficient, patrimonial, swollen and bloated, and therefore the main roadblock to economic development.[106] Arthur Goldsmith has however pointed out that the charge of swollen and bloated bureaucracies in Africa is not correct because compared to other regions of the Third World; Africa has fewer bureaucrats per capita.[107] Furthermore, Toye has observed that although Third World countries as a group were blamed for over-extended public sectors, the size of their public sectors "are actually smaller proportionally than that of the US is to the size of its total economy."[108] Overcoming the perceived weakness of African states and bureaucracies are normally seen from the perspective of the eclectic juxtaposition of the political economy and rational choice model.[109] This kind of approach "explicates policy-making in terms of interest group pressures on the State, with the explicit or implicit hope that a bureaucratic-authoritarian regime will emerge to free the state from the instrumentalist exigencies of interest groups."[110]

The second school agrees that African countries need developmental states if they are to successfully transform their economies, but adherents of this school argue that this should not be the kind of developmental state promoted by the modernization paradigm which they see as responsible for the continent's economic malaise. They therefore contend that it is imperative to redefine the form of the African state and its role in the development process.[111] Mkandawire notes that the persistence of the problem of underdevelopment in Africa will invariably resurrect a nationalist "developmentalist" ideology that would demand for "planning" and greater state involvement in the economy.[112] However, adherents of this school maintain that although the East Asian NICs industrialization experience helps to demonstrate the salience or necessity of state intervention, the East Asian model is not a viable alternative for Africa. This is particularly so, because of the extremely dictatorial and authoritarian conditions under which the industrialization of these countries took place.[113] They therefore call for a form of developmental state that fits better the cultural traditions and unique experiences of African peoples and yet meet the developmental needs of African countries.[114]

Conclusion

The conventional discourse of Africa's development trajectory has tended to categorize the dominant influence on African development policies into two main phases: the modernization phase, which is said to have ended in the 1970s and the post modernization neo-liberal/neoclassical phase, which started in the 1980s. Development economists who dominated the so-called first phase were blamed for Africa's economic crisis as their state-centered development policies were seen as operating in opposition to the "appropriate" and rational market-led development policies. The neo-liberal orthodoxy championed by the IFIs, which became ascendant in the analysis of Africa's development crisis, was posited by its apostles as marking a break from the state-centeredness of development economics, by emphasizing policies that granted ascendancy to the markets. In addition, the new orthodoxy sought to distance itself from the discredited modernization paradigm by asserting that the paradigm lost its relevance with the demise of development economics. This assertion is however not correct for the neo-liberal orthodoxy is firmly situated within the tenets of the modernization paradigm and therefore constitutes the new modernization. For both the development economists and the neo-liberals the reference point remained the historical experience and characteristics of Western capitalist societies, which African countries are expected to replicate in order to develop.

However, as has been clearly demonstrated by Africa's development woes, the modernization inspired development policies promoted by both the development economists and the neo-liberals represent dead-end to Africa's development. The policies are out of tune with Africa's historical, social, cultural and material realities. Contrary to the claim of the neo-liberals, the state should play a critical role in Africa's development process but this role must be firmly situated within African socio-cultural and material realities. The development policies should be African-centered and clearly rooted in the African culture. A developmental state with the appropriate African-centered characteristics is therefore a necessity for the promotion of a self-reliant development in the continent.

Notes

1 World Bank, *Accelerated Development in Sub-Saharan Africa: An Agenda for Action*, Washington, D.C.: The World Bank, 1981.

2 For an interesting analysis of this perspective, see D. Eyoh, "From Economic Crisis to Political Liberalization: Pitfalls of the New Political Sociology of Africa," *African Studies Review*, Vol. 39, No. 3, 1996, 43-80.

3 A. Hirschman, "The Rise and Decline of Development Economics," in A. Hirshman, *Essays in Trespassing: Economics to Politics and Beyond*, Cambridge: Cambridge University Press, 1981; D. Seers, "The Birth, Life and Death of Development Economics," *Development and Change*, Vol. 10, 1979; T. Mkandawire, "The Crisis in

Economic Development Theory," *Africa Development*, Vol. XV, Nos. 3 and 4, 1990; and P. Krugman, "Toward a Counter-Counterrevolution in Development Theory," in World Bank, *Proceedings of the World Bank Conference on Development Economics*, Washington, D.C.: The World Bank, 1992.

4 See for instance, D. Rothchild and N. Chazan, eds., *The Precarious Balance: State and Society in Africa*, Boulder, CO: Westview, 1988; J. S. Wunsch & D. Olowu, eds., *The Failure of the Centralized State: Institutions and Self-governance in Africa*, Boulder, CO: Westview, 1990; and I. W. Zartman, ed., *Collapsed States: The Disintegration and Restoration of Legitimate Authority*, Boulder, CO: Lynne Rienner, 1995.

5 G. Hyden, "Rethinking Theories of the State: An Africanist Perspective," *Africa Insight*, Vol. 26, No. 1, 1996, 34.

6 See for example, E. Osaghae, ed., *Between State and Civil Society in Africa*, Dakar: CODESRIA, 1994; M. I. M. Abutudu, *The State, Civil Society and the Democratization Process in Nigeria*, Dakar: CODESRIA Monograph Series, No. 1, 1995; J. Harbeson *et. al.*, eds., *Civil Society and the State in Africa*, Boulder, CO: Lynner Rienner, 1985; B. Beckman, "The Liberation of Civil Society: Neo-Liberal Ideology and Political Theory," *Review of African Political Economy*, No. 54, 1993; M. Bratton, "Beyond the State: Civil Society and Associational Life in Africa," *World Politics*, Vol. 51, No. 3, 1989; J. F. Bayart, "Civil Society in Africa," in P. Chabal, ed., *Political Domination in Africa: Reflections on the Limits of Power*, Cambridge: Cambridge University Press, 1986; and E. Onwudiwe, ed., *African Perspectives on Civil Society*, New York: Tri-Atlantic, 1998.

7 Abdi I. Samatar and Ahmed I. Samatar, "Introduction," in idem. eds., *The African State: Reconsiderations*, Portsmouth, NH: Heinemann, 2002, 5.

8 M. Mamdani, "A Critique of the State and Civil Society Paradigm in Africanist Studies," in M. Mamdani and E. Wamba-dia-Wamba, eds., *African Studies in Social Movements and Democracy*, Dakar: CODESRIA, 1995, 602-615.

9 E. Said, *Orientalism*, New York: Random House, 1978; idem., *Culture and Imperialism*, London: Chatto and Windus, 1993; S. Amin, *Eurocentrism*, London: Zed, 1988; and Chinweizu, *The West and the Rest of Us*, New York: NOK, 1978.

10 R. L. Sklar, "The New Modernization," *ISSUE*, Vol. XXIII, No. 1, 1995, 19-21.

11 B. J. Berman, "African Capitalism and the Paradigm of Modernity: Culture, Technology, and the State," in B. J. Berman and C. Leys, eds., *African Capitalists in African Development*, Boulder, CO: Lynne Rienner, 1994, 252.

12 Sklar, "The New Modernization,"; and C. Leys, "African Capitalists and Development: Theoretical Questions," in Berman and Leys, eds., *African Capitalists in African Development*, 20-22.

13 For a summary of the "Kenya debate," see G. Kitching, "Politics, Method and Evidence in the 'Kenya Debate'" in H. Bernstein and B. Campbell eds., *Contradictions of Accumulation in Africa*, London and Beverly Hills: Sage, 1985, 115-151. Also see B. Beckman, "Imperialism and Capitalist Transformation: Critique of the Kenya Debate," *Review of African Political Economy*, No. 19, 1980, 48-62.

14 In this regard, the works that were carried out under the auspices of the London-based Institute for African Alternatives (IFAA) are very significant. See for instance, Onimode, *A Political Economy of the African Crisis*; and idem., ed., *The IMF, the World Bank and the African Debt*, 2 Vols., London: IFAA and Zed, 1989. Also see C. Ake, *Democracy and Development in Africa*.

15 C. Leys and B. J. Berman, "Introduction," in Berman and Leys, eds., *African Capitalists in African Development*, 9. Also see B. Hettne, *Development Theory and*

the Three Worlds, London: Longman, 1990; and T. J. Biersteker, "The 'Triumph' of Neo-Classical Economics in the Developing World," in J. N. Rosenau and E. O. Cziempiel, eds., *Governance Without Government: Order and Change in World Politics*, Cambridge: Cambridge University Press, 1992.

16 D. F. Bryceson and L. Bank, "End of an Era: Africa's Development Policy Parallax," *Journal of Contemporary African Studies*, vol. 19, No. 1, 2001, 9-10.

17 Hyden, "Rethinking Theories of the State," 31.

18 Sklar, "The New Modernization," 20. This observation failed to take into account the fact that it was the relentless criticism of the dependency scholars that helped to expose the severe limitations of the development policies that were anchored on the modernization paradigm. Their criticism did not only make modernization to be on the defensive, but equally prompted various reformulations of the paradigm and the attempt to mask the paradigm's influence on the neo-liberal policies.

19 Ley and Berman, "Introduction," and Berman, "African Capitalism and the Paradigm of Modernity," both are in Berman and Leys, eds., *African Capitalists in African Development*, 9 and 235-237. Also see B. J. Berman, *Control and Crisis in Colonial Kenya: The Dialectic of Domination*, London and Athens, OH: James Currey and Ohio University Press, 1990.

20 Sklar, "The New Modernization," 21; Leys, "African Capitalists and African Development," 26-27; and R. H. Bates, *Towards a Political Economy of Development: A Rational Choice Perspective*, Berkeley, CA: University of California Press, 1988.

21 F. Fukuyama, "The End of History?", *The National Interest*, No. 16, 1989; and idem., *The End of History and the Last Man*, Penguin, 1992. Also see T. van Lave, *The World Revolution in Westernization: The 20th Century in Global Perspective*, New York: Oxford University Press, 1987.

22 Berman, "African Capitalism and the Paradigm of Modernity," 238.

23 M Weber, *General Economic History*, Glencoe: Free Press, 1950; and idem., *The Protestant Ethic and the Spirit of Capitalism*, New York: Scribner, 1958.

24 T. M. Callaghy, "The State and the Development of Capitalism in Africa: Theoretical, Historical, and Comparative Reflections," in Rothchild and Chazan, eds., *The Precarious Balance*, 73; and Leys, "African Capitalists and African Development," 15. Indeed, Callaghy accused Talcott Parsons of contributing greatly to the misperceptions of Weber's views, due to his selective and misleading interpretation of Weber's works to the English-speaking scholars, 69.

25 B. Agozino, *Counter-Colonial Criminology: A Critique of Imperialist Reason*, London: Pluto Press, 2003, 24.

26 T. Parsons, *The Social System*, London: Routledge and Kegan Paul, 1951. Also see D. Apter, *The Politics of Modernization*, Chicago: Chicago University Press, 1965.

27 Berman, "African Capitalism and the Paradigm of Modernity," 236.

28 See H. Trevor-Roper, "The Rise of Christian Europe," *The Listener*, 28 November 1963; and E. R. Wolf, *Europe and the People Without History*, Berkeley, CA: The University of California Press, 1982.

29 J. C. Scott, *Seeing Like a State: How Schemes to Improve the Human Condition Have Failed*, New Haven: Yale University Press, 1998.

30 V. W. Ruttan, "What Happened to Political Development?," 271. Also see R. A. Packingham, *Liberal America and the Third World: Political Development Ideas in Foreign Aid and Social Science*, Princeton: Princeton University Press, 1973; and F. Tachau ed., *The Developing Nations: What Path to Modernization?*, New York and Toronto: Dodd, Mead and Company, 1972, 1-8.

31 Ruttan, "What Happened to Political Development?," 271.

32 Some of the influential works of this comparative school are, Almond and Coleman, eds., *The Politics of Developing Areas*; D. Apter, *Ghana in Transition*, Princeton: Princeton University Press, 1957; and idem., *The Politics of Modernization*.

33 Rostow, *The Stages of Economic Growth*.

34 Mkandawire, "The Crisis in Economic Development Theory."

35 See E. Boserup, *Woman's Role in Economic Development*, London: George Allen and Unwin, 1970; and D. Elson ed., *Male Bias in the Development Process*, Manchester: Manchester University Press, 1995.

36 Berman, "African Capitalism and the Paradigm of Modernity," 236-237.

37 Mamdani, "A Critique of the State and Civil Society Paradigm in Africanist Studies," 609.

38 K. Marx, "The British Rule in India," *New York Daily Tribune*, 25 June 1853, Reproduced in A. L. Macfie ed., *Orientalism: A Reader*, New York: New York University Press, 2000, 16-17. I am grateful to Musa Abutudu for drawing my attention to this issue.

39 Hyden, "Rethinking Theories of the State," 29.

40 See P. Evans, "Class, State, and Dependence in East Asia: Lessons for Latin Americanists," in F. C. Deyo, ed., *The Political Economy of the New Asian Industrialization*, Ithaca: Cornell University Press, 1987, 203-26; and Ake, *Democracy and Development in Africa*, 126-129.

41 O. Nnoli, "Development/Underdevelopment: Is Nigeria Developing?," in O. Nnoli, ed., *Path to Nigerian Development*, Dakar: CODESRIA, 1981, 35-36.

42 See A. Gerschenkron, *Continuity in History and Other Essays*, Cambridge, Mass.: Harvard University Press, 1968; and idem., *Economic Backwardness in Historical Perspectives*, Cambridge, Mass.: Harvard University Press, 1962.

43 Callaghy, "The State and the Development of Capitalism in Africa," 81 and 83. Also see T. M. Callaghy, *The State-Society Struggle: Zaire in Comparative Perspective*, New York: Columbia University Press, 1984; and idem., "The State as Lame Leviathan: The Patrimonial Administrative State in Africa," in Z. Ergas, ed., *The African State in Transition*, London and New York: Macmillan and St. Martins, 1987.

44 See Mamdani, "A Critique of the State and Civil Society Paradigm in Africanist Studies," 606-612.

45 Some of the works in which these characterizations can be found include, Callaghy, The State-Society Struggle; idem., "The State as Lame Leviathan,"; idem., "Absolutism, Bonapartism, and the Formation of Ruling Classes: Zaire in Comparative Perspective," in I. L. Markovitz, ed., *Studies in Power and Class in Africa*, New York: Oxford University Press, 1987; Hyden, *Beyond Ujamaa in Tanzania*; idem., *No Shortcuts to Progress: African Development Management in Perspective*, Berkeley, CA: University of California Press, 1983; R. H. Jackson and C. G. Rosberg, *Personal Rule in Black Africa: Prince, Autocrat, Prophet, Tyrant*, Berkeley, CA: University of California Press, 1981; R. Joseph, "Class, State, and Prebendal Politics in Nigeria," in P. Lewis, ed., *Africa: Dilemmas of Development and Change*, Boulder, CO: Westview, 1998; D. Rothchild, "Hegemony and State Softness: Some Variations in Elite Responses," in Ergas, ed., *African State in Transition*; N. Chazan, "Patterns of State-Society Incorporation and Disengagement in Africa," and idem., "State and Society in Africa: Images and Challenges," both are in Rothchild and Chazan, eds., *The Precarious Balance*.

46 See C. Young and T. Turner, *The Rise and Decline of the Zairian State*, Madison: University of Wisconsin Press, 1985; and G. B. N. Ayittey, *Africa in Chaos*, New York: St Martins, 1999, 49, 92-95.
47 Callaghy, "The State and the Development of Capitalism in Africa," 69.
48 P. Kennedy, *African Capitalism: The Struggle for Ascendancy*, Cambridge: Cambridge University Press, 1988.
49 Leys and Berman, "Introduction," 3.
50 Mamdani, "A Critique of the State and Civil Society Paradigm in Africanist Studies," 608; and idem. *Citizen and Subject*, 12.
51 Fine and Stoneman, "Introduction: State and Development," 7.
52 See Beckman, "The Liberation of Civil Society," 30.
53 Mkandawire, "The Crisis in Economic Development Theory."
54 Rostow, *The Stages of Economic Development.*
55 Ibid.; and idem., "The Take-off into Self-Sustained Growth," 25-48.
56 See B. I. Adelman, *Theories of Economic Growth and Development*, Stanford: Stanford University Press, 1962, 1.
57 G. P. Uwujaren, "The Political Economy of Nigeria's Dependent Industrialization via Import Substitution," *Nigerian Journal of International Studies*, Vol. 5-7, 1981-1983, 81-93.
58 Rodney, *How Europe Underdeveloped Africa*; and Offiong, *Imperialism and Dependency.*
59 H. Chenery, *et. al.*, *Redistribution with Growth*, New York: Oxford University Press, 1974; and M. S. Ahluwalia and N. G. Carter, "Growth and Poverty in Developing Countries," in H. Chenery, ed., *Structural Change and Development Policy*, New York: Oxford University Press, 1979.
60 International Labor Office, *First Things First: Meeting the Basic Needs of the People of Nigeria*, Addis Ababa, Jobs and Skills Program for Africa (JASPA), 1981.
61 B. Wisner, *Power and Need in Africa: Basic Human Needs and Development Policies*, London: Earthscan, 1988; F. Stewart, *Planning to Meet Basic Needs*, London: Macmillan, 1985; and M. B. Brown, *Africa's Choices: After Thirty Years of the World Bank*, Boulder, Colorado: Westview, 1995, 60.
62 J. F. E. Ohiorhenuan, "Some Critical Issues in the Theory of Development Planning," Paper Presented at the National Seminar on Innovative Approaches to Development Theory, Held at the Conference Center, University of Ibadan, Ibadan, Nigeria, 23-27 January 1984.
63 Federal Republic of Nigeria, *First National Development Plan, 1962-68*, Lagos: Federal Ministry of Information, 1962, 23-25.
64 Stolper, *Planning Without Facts*, 55.
65 W. F. Stolper, "The Main Features of the 1962-1968 National Plan," *Nigerian Journal of Economic and Social Studies*, Vol. 4, No. 2, 1962, 85.
66 Federal Republic of Nigeria, *Second National Development Plan, 1970-74*, Lagos: Federal Ministry of Information, 1970, 31 and 33.
67 Federal Republic of Nigeria, *Third National Development Plan, 1975-80*, Lagos: The Federal Ministry of National Planning, 1975, 29 and 33.
68 Federal Republic of Nigeria, *Guidelines for the Fourth National Development Plan, 1981-85*, Lagos: The Federal Ministry of National Planning, 1980, 20-23.
69 J. F. Ade Ajayi, *The Past in the Present: The Factor of Tradition in Development*, Lagos: Nigerian Institute of International Affairs, 1990, 12.
70 The World Bank, *Accelerated Development in Sub-Saharan Africa*; idem., *World Development Report*, 1983, New York: Oxford University Press, 1983; idem., *Toward*

Sustained Development in Sub-Saharan Africa: A Joint Program of Action, Washington, D.C.: The World Bank, 1984; and idem., *World Development Report, 1985*, New York: Oxford University Press, 1985.

71 L. P. Mureithi, "Development Planning in Kenya," in M. Urrutia and S. Yukawa, eds., *Development Planning in Mixed Economies*, Tokyo: The United Nations University, 1988, 207-208.

72 The World Bank, *Accelerated Development in Sub-Saharan Africa.*

73 International Monetary Fund, *Recent Multilateral Debt Reschedulings with Official and Bank Creditors*, Occasional Paper No. 25, Washington, D.C.: International Monetary Fund, 1983, 20.

74 For a summary of this position, see T. M. Callaghy, "Lost Between State and Market: The Politics of Economic Adjustment in Ghana, Zambia, and Nigeria," in J. M. Nelson, ed., *Economic Crisis and Policy Choice: The Politics of Adjustment in the Third World*, Princeton: Princeton University Press, 1994, 258.

75 For elaborate discussion of these factors, see J. I. Dibua, "Economic Crisis and Structural Adjustment Programs," in T. Falola, ed., *Africa: Volume 5: Contemporary Africa*, Durham, N.C.: Carolina Academic Press, 2003, 511-513; and idem., "World Bank, International Monetary Fund, and Structural Adjustment," in K. Shillington, ed., *Encyclopedia of African History*, Vol. 3, New York and London: Fitzroy Dearborn, 2005, 1664-1666.

76 Uwujaren, "The Political Economy of Nigeria's Dependent Industrialization via Import Substitution."

77 T. M. Callaghy, "Political Passions and Economic Interests: Economic Reform and Political Structure in Africa," in T. M. Callaghy and J. Ravenhill, eds., *Hemmed In: Responses to Africa's Economic Decline*, New York: Columbia University Press, 1993, 469.

78 T. Mkandawire, "The Political Economy of Privatization in Africa," in G. A. Cornia and G. K. Helleiner, eds., *From Adjustment to Development in Africa: Conflict, Controversy, Convergence, Consensus*, New York: St. Martins Press, 1994, 192-193.

79 J. I. Dibua, "Journey to Nowhere: Neo-Liberalism and Africa's Development Crisis," *Comparative Studies of South Asia, Africa and the Middle East*, Vol. XVIII, No. 2, 1998, 127.

80 B. Tsie, "States and Markets in the Southern African Development Community (SADC): Beyond the Neo-liberal Paradigm," *Journal of Southern African Studies*, Vol. 22, No. 1, 1996, 86-93. Also see A. Dutt, *et. al.*, *The State, Markets and Development: Beyond the Neoclassical Dichotomy*, Aldershot: Edward Elgar, 1994.

81 T. J. Biersteker, "Reducing the Role of the State in the Economy: A Conceptual Exploration of IMF and World Bank Prescriptions," *International Studies Quarterly*, Vol. 34, No. 4, 1990, 480-481.

82 Callaghy, "Political Passions and Economic Interests," 507.

83 World Bank, *Sub-Saharan Africa: From Crisis to Sustainable Growth, A Long-Term Perspective Study*, Washington, D.C.: The World Bank, 1989. Also see idem., *Adjustment in Africa: Reforms, Results and the Road Ahead*, Oxford: Oxford University Press, 1994.

84 B. Beckman, "Empowerment or Repression? The World Bank and the Politics of African Adjustment," *Africa Development*, Vol. 16, No. 1, 1991, 45-72.

85 See T. Mkandawire, "Adjustment, Political Conditionality and Democratization in Africa," in Cornia and Helleiner, eds., *From Adjustment to Development in Africa*, 155-173.

86 Economic Commission for Africa (ECA), *African Alternative Framework to Structural Adjustment Programme for Economic Recovery and Transformation (AAF-SAP)*, Addis Ababa: United Nations Economic Commission for Africa, 1989.

87 World Bank, *Africa's Adjustment and Growth in the 1980s*, Washington, D.C.: The World Bank, 1989.

88 C. Lancaster, "Economic Reform in Africa: Is it Working?," in O. Obasanjo and H. d'Orville, eds., *The Leadership Challenge in Economic Reforms in Africa*, New York: Crane Russak, 1991, 100-101.

89 R. H. Green, "The IMF and the World Bank in Africa: How Much Learning?," in Callaghy and Ravenhill, eds., *Hemmed In: Responses to Africa's Economic Decline*, 66.

90 See for instance, World Bank, *Adjustment in Africa*; idem., *Can Africa Claim the 21st Century*, Washington, DC: World Bank, 2000; and idem., *World Development Report 2000/1: A World Free of Poverty*, New York: Oxford University Press, 2000.

91 Bryceson and Bank, "End of an Era," 5-6.

92 See J. Toye, "Interest Group Politics and the Implementation of Adjustment Policies in Sub-Saharan Africa," in P. Gibbon *et. al.*, eds., *Authoritarianism, Democracy and Adjustment: The Politics of Economic Reform in Africa*, Uppsala: Scandinavian Institute of African Studies, 1992.

93 For an elaboration on the degree of economic crisis caused by the SAPs policies in Africa, see Dibua, "Journey to Nowhere,"; idem., "Economic Crisis and Structural Adjustment Programs," 521-527; and B. Founou-Tchuigoua, "Africa Confronted with the Ravages of Neo-Liberalism," *Africa Development*, Vol. 21, No. 2, 1996, 5-24.

94 See for instance, Green, "The IMF and the World Bank in Africa,"; D. E. Sahn, ed., *Adjusting to Policy Failure in African Economies*, Ithaca, NY: Cornell University Press, 1994; and J. M. Nelson, ed., *Economic Crisis and Policy Choice: The Politics of Adjustment in the Third World*, Princeton: Princeton University Press, 1994.

95 Mkandawire, "The Crisis in Economic Development Theory," 229.

96 Samatar and Samatar, "Introduction," 5.

97 P. Evans, *et. al.*, eds., *Bringing the State Back In*, Cambridge: Cambridge University Press, 1985; and A. Amsden, *Asia's Next Giant: South Korea and Late Industrialization*, New York: Oxford University Press, 1985.

98 R. Wade, *Governing the Market: Economic Theory and the Role of Government in East Asian Industrialization*, Princeton: Princeton University Press, 1990.

99 P. Evans, *Embedded Autonomy: States and Industrial Transformation*, Princeton: Princeton University Press, 1995.

100 See D. Seddon and T. Betto-Jones, "The Political Determinants of Economic Flexibility, with Special Reference to the East Asian NICs," in T. Killick, ed., *The Flexible Economy: Causes and Consequences of Adaptability on National Economies*, New York: Routledge, 1995, 326; and A. A. Goldsmith, "Africa's Overgrown State Reconsidered: Bureaucracy and Economic Growth," *World Politics*, Vol. 51, No. 4, 1999.

101 C. Johnson, *MITI and Japanese Miracle: The Growth of Industrial Policy, 1925-1975*, Stanford: Stanford University Press, 1982; and idem., "Political Institutions and Economic Performance: The Government-Business Relationship in Japan, South Korea and Taiwan," in Deyo, ed., *The Political Economy of the New Asian Industrialization*.

102 See P. Evans, "Class, State, and Dependence in East Asia,"; and W. Huff, "The Developmental State, Government, and Singapore's Economic Development Since 1960," *World Development*, Vol. 23, No. 8, 1995.

103 World Bank, *The East Asian Miracle: Economic Growth and Public Policy, A World Bank Policy Research Report*, Oxford: Oxford University Press, 1993.
104 For a critical review of the World Bank's publication, see A. Amsden, ed., "The World Bank's East Asian Miracle: Economic Growth and Public Policy," Special Section, *World Development*, Vol. 22, No. 4, 1994.
105 See for instance, H. Stein, ed., *Asian Industrialization and Africa: Studies in Policy Alternatives to Structural Adjustment*, New York: St Martins, 1994.
106 Hyden, *No Shortcuts to Progress*; R. C. Crook, "Patrimonialism, Administrative Effectiveness and Economic Development in Cote d'Ivoire," *African Affairs*, Vol. 88, No. 351, 1989; R. H. Bates, "The Impulse to Reform in Africa," in J. Widner, ed., *Economic Changes and Political Liberalization in Sub-Saharan Africa*, Baltimore: Johns Hopkins University Press, 1994; L. Diamond, "Class Formation in the Swollen African State," *Journal of Modern African Studies*, Vol. 25, No. 4, 1987; and D. Abernethy, "Bureaucratic Growth and Economic Stagnation in Sub-Saharan Africa," in S. K. Commins, ed., *Africa's Development Challenges and the World Bank*, Boulder, CO: Lynne Rienner, 1988.
107 Goldsmith, "Africa's Overgrown State Reconsidered."
108 Toye, *Dilemmas of Development*, 27.
109 Bates, *Towards a Political Economy of Development*; and idem., *Beyond the Miracles of the Market*, Cambridge: Cambridge University Press, 1989.
110 Mkandawire, "The Crisis in Economic Development Theory," 230.
111 See for instance, Ake, *Democracy and Development in Africa*; M. Mamdani, "State and Civil Society in Contemporary Africa: Reconceptualizing the Birth of State Nationalism and the Defeat of Popular Movements," *African Development*, Vol. 15, No. 4, 1990; M. Owusu, "Democracy in Africa: A View from the Village," *Journal of Modern African Studies*, Vol. 30, No. 2, 1992; and Samatar and Samatar, "Introduction," 5.
112 Mkandawire, "The Crisis in Economic Development Theory," 230.
113 On this point, see for instance, Ake, *Democracy and Development in Africa*, 126-129.
114 Samatar and Samatar, "Introduction," 5.

Chapter 3

Colonial Antecedents

Colonial imperialism was responsible for initially laying the foundations of, and in the late colonial period, consolidating the modernization paradigm in Nigeria. Since the primary reason for the imposition of colonial rule was the exploitation of Nigeria's resources, there was the need to put in place institutions and structures that would aid this exploitative end. However, in order to mask the exploitative reasons behind the subjugation of various Nigerian polities, the British imperialists sought to justify their violent intrusion into Nigerian societies based on some form of "a civilizing mission." This necessitated the characterization of precolonial Nigerian societies and culture as "primitive," "backward" and "barbaric." The colonial enterprise was therefore presented as a form of "Father Christmas" that bore the burden of helping to save the Nigerian societies from themselves. This "messianic" mission theoretically involved seeking to ultimately wipeout the "irrational," "backward" and "primitive" institutions of the indigenous societies and replacing them with transplanted "civilized" British/Western institutions. Herein lays the theoretical and epistemological background of the modernization paradigm in Nigeria, which portrayed various colonial policies and "reforms" as attempts at modernizing the Nigerian societies.

Various institutions and structures were put in place to aid the "modernization" project which itself was critical for the successful exploitation of Nigeria's resources. In the first instance, the Weberian model of the binary division of society was adopted; hence, the colonial sector was regarded as the modern (ideal/rational) sector while the indigenous sector was regarded as the traditional (non-ideal/irrational) sector. Missionaries and various educational institutions, the so-called "modernizing" agents/agencies were deployed to train and recruit a few individuals into the privileged colonial modern sector. Some of the educated individuals were accorded varying degrees of the civil rights available to those in the modern sector while the vast majority of the people who were not educated and therefore belonged to the traditional sector were treated as subjects belonging to the native administration sphere.[1] At the economic level, the myth of a dual economy was propagated: the indigenous African crops that were only relevant to the Nigerian people were categorized as irrelevant crops belonging to the irrational traditional economy. On the other hand, crops that were needed as raw materials by the colonial economy were regarded as cash crops belonging to the modern economy. Similar distinctions were made in the manufacturing and processing sector where indigenously produced goods were despised as products of backward and irrelevant artisan and craft knowledge, while imported mass-produced Western goods were regarded as modern and products of Western instrumental rationality. Underlying these categorizations was the desire to satisfy the exploitative interests of the imperial British administration.

Imposition of Colonial Rule

The territories that make up modern day Nigeria were brought under British colonial rule between 1851 and 1914 after various wars of conquest and resistance. Before the imposition of colonial rule, Nigeria was made up of diverse polities ranging from large centralized kingdoms to acephalous societies. In the north, there were centralized kingdoms such as Kanem-Borno, located around Lake Chad and the Hausa kingdoms such as Gobir, Kano, Kebbi, Katsina, Zamfara and Zaria which were brought together to form the Sokoto Caliphate as a result of the nineteenth century Islamic jihad led by Usman dan Fodio. There were a number of kingdoms in the West among which Oyo and Benin kingdoms were the most powerful. The East comprised mainly acephalous societies such as the Igbo, Ijaw and Efik. Acephalous societies were also present in the North and West, notably the Middle Belt, northern Edo and the Urhobo and Isoko.

The immediate impetus for the British colonization of the respective Nigerian societies was the desire to control and exploit the raw materials present in these territories. The abolition of the slave trade in the early nineteenth century and the introduction of the so-called "legitimate" trade in raw materials, which were needed by Western industries, introduced a new dimension into the relationship between Nigerian societies and European countries. The industrial revolution created a great appetite for raw materials from Nigeria and other African countries among the European nations, a situation that fostered intense competition among them for the control of the sources of raw materials. To ensure that the rush for African territories did not result in wars among European powers, the Berlin West African Conference (BWAC) of 1884-1885 was convened to establish the guidelines for recognizing the claim of a European nation over an African territory. In this regard, two of the most important decisions of the conference were the principles of "sphere of influence" and "effective occupation" which would help to convince other European countries of the validity of the claim of a European country over a specific African territory. These principles accentuated the scramble for African territories.

Although British imperial incursion into Nigeria started with the gunboat attack on Lagos in 1851 which resulted in the loss of sovereignty and subsequent annexation of Lagos as a Crown colony in 1861, the pace of conquest and annexation of Nigerian territories assumed a new intensity after the Berlin Conference.[2] Lagos became the base through which the British penetrated into the

Yorubaland. The prolonged Yoruba civil war which started after the collapse of Oyo empire left the various warring Yoruba kingdoms considerably weakened and therefore not in the position to put up stiff resistance against British imperial aggression. Indeed, the British who were interested in unhindered trade with the Yoruba hinterland used the opportunity of the internecine and exhaustive war to mediate in the conflict and facilitate the signing of a peace treaty in 1886. In 1892, the British attacked the Yoruba kingdom of Ijebu Ode over disagreements on access to missionaries and access to trade routes to the Yoruba hinterland, among other things. The defeat of the Ijebu made the other Yoruba kingdoms, which had been considerably weakened by the civil war not to be in the position to militarily resist the imposition of British colonial rule over their territories.

The Niger Delta was of immense significance to Britain and the other European nations because of the strategic role it played in international trade since the era of the slave trade. The Niger Delta states acted as intermediaries first, in the slave trade, and subsequently in the trade in raw materials after the abolition of the slave trade. The immense opportunity created by the new trade led to the rise of new leaders (merchant princes) like Jaja of Opobo and Nana Olomu of Itsekiriland. The desire to benefit from the opportunities created by this trade led to various levels of conflict in the Niger Delta. There were intra- and inter-state conflicts, conflicts between the Niger Delta city-states and European merchants, and competition among merchants from different European countries (mainly Britain, Germany and France) for privileged and ascendant position in the trade. A significant development during this period was the involvement of Europeans in domestic politics. In addition, European firms sought to bypass the Niger Delta intermediaries and increase their own profits by penetrating the hinterland. This further increased the conflict between them and the local Niger Delta leaders.[3]

The arrival of George Taubman Goldie, a consummate imperialist, in the Niger Delta in 1877 significantly affected trade and politics in the region. Goldie sought to preserve British commercial and imperial interests in the Niger Delta by putting an end to competition from German and French traders and imposing a trading monopoly in the region.[4] Toward this end, in 1879 he brought all the British trading firms together to form a single company, the United Africa Company (UAC). In 1882, he reorganized the company and changed its name to the National African Company (NAC) with the aim of putting an end to the remaining competition from French trading firms. By 1884, Goldie had signed about thirty-seven treaties with different chiefs, which enabled him to interfere in their internal politics. Based on the decision of the Berlin Conference and capitalizing on the threat that French and German colonial ambitions posed to British imperial interests in the Niger Delta, Goldie applied for a royal charter from the British government. The charter, which was granted in 1886, gave Goldie's company political and administrative authority over areas where treaties of "protection" were signed as well as the right to further British imperial interest by conquering new territories. With this charter, Goldie changed the name of his company to the Royal Niger Company (RNC).

The RNC established its headquarters at Asaba with its own administrative structures, High Court of Justice and constabulary. The company achieved monopoly over trade through the imposition of high import and export duties, the requirement that foreign firms and Nigerians pay high charges for permission to trade and the expulsion of firms from France and Germany. The RNC used force to maintain its monopoly in the Niger Delta, a situation that led to resentment among the indigenous people and the Brassmen's raid on its Akassa port in 1895. Furthermore, on the excuse of slave raiding into its territory, the company used force to impose treaties on the rulers of Ilorin and Nupe in the Middle Belt in 1897, thereby extending its control to these places. Thus by the time its charter was revoked at the end of 1899, the RNC had succeeded in securing a huge territory for Britain.

At the time the RNC was advancing British imperial interests in the Niger Delta, the British government was simultaneously doing the same thing through the activities of its consuls who were busy signing dubious treaties of "protection" with local rulers. The British wanted to keep the French and Germans out of this area while protecting the commercial interests of her citizens. A number of Niger Delta rulers were suspicious of the implication of these treaties for their sovereignty and trade and were therefore reluctant to sign them. For instance, King Jaja of Opobo only signed the treaty in 1885 after receiving assurance from Consul Hewett that the treaty would not threaten the sovereignty or trade of his kingdom but, rather, it was aimed at ensuring that another European nation did not colonize Opobo. However, when Jaja prevented British traders from penetrating the hinterland to trade, he was deceived into coming aboard a British ship to resolve the dispute but on getting aboard the ship, Jaja was seized and deported to the West Indies. In 1891, Britain furthered its imperial interest in the Niger Delta by proclaiming the Oil Rivers Protectorate over the area, and in 1893, the area was proclaimed the Niger Coast Protectorate. Nana of Itsekiri kingdom also clashed with the British over his refusal to allow British traders into the hinterland, which would undermine his lucrative intermediary position. The British accused Nana of hindering trade and a military confrontation ensued between them in August and September 1894, which the British won primarily because of their superior military power.

After completing the conquest of the Niger Delta, the British decided to turn their attention to the Benin kingdom whose king had steadfastly refused to sign a treaty of protection with them. Benin forces defeated a British expedition led by Acting Consul-General Phillips in 1897 but a second British attack defeated the Benin kingdom after Benin soldiers had put up stiff and heroic resistance. The triumphant British soldiers looted the treasures in the Benin palace while the king, Ovonramwen, was captured and banished to Calabar where he died after seventeen years in exile.

The British conquest of Southern Nigeria was completed with the defeat of Igbo villages in 1902.[5] Here the Aro put up stiff resistance against British encroachment but were finally defeated after a prolonged war that lasted from 1901 to 1902. However, given the non-centralized nature of the Igbo society, some Igbo groups continued to resist British imperialism up to the outbreak of World War 1.[6]

Having completed the conquest of southern Nigeria, the British turned its attention to the North most of which was under the control of the Sokoto Caliphate. The activities of the RNC had given the British a foothold in the Middle Belt from where they could stage their attack on the northern emirates. Toward this end, the charter of the RNC was abrogated in 1899 and Frederick Lugard who was appointed the High Commissioner for northern Nigeria proceeded to further British imperial ambition in the area through the creation of the West African Frontier Force (WAFF). The British conquest of the North started with the invasion of the emirates of Bida and Kontagora in 1901 and continued with the systematic attack of each emirate until the final conquest of Sokoto in 1906. Although each emirate put up stiff resistance to British aggression, they eventually lost their respective battles due mainly to the superiority of the British weapons. The British faced the greatest resistance in the Middle Belt particularly among the Tiv where the British had to fight wars among various non-centralized Tiv groups. Although by 1914, most parts of the Middle Belt had come under British control, resistance continued in parts of the area until the 1930s.

The period between 1900 and 1914 is crucial because it marked the historical beginnings of the factors that shaped Nigeria's history throughout the colonial period into the postcolonial period. It was during this period that various administrative, economic and social institutions that significantly affected Nigeria's history were put in place.[7] This period also marked the historical roots of the modernization project in Nigeria. By 1906, the territory that eventually became Nigeria comprised the Lagos Colony, the Protectorate of Southern Nigeria and the Protectorate of Northern Nigeria. In 1906, the Lagos Colony and the Protectorate of Southern Nigeria were merged with Lagos as capital. This development was largely based on economic considerations, as the funds from the larger and more endowed Southern Nigeria were needed for the construction of infrastructures like harbor and railway, which were crucial for the exploitation of Nigeria's resources.[8] In January 1914, the Southern and Northern Protectorates were amalgamated to form a single country under the administration of a governor-general. Again, economic considerations provided the primary motive for the amalgamation. The landlocked Northern Protectorate was experiencing severe economic crisis and the amalgamation was seen as providing the opportunity to use the resources of the more endowed Southern Protectorate to subsidize the administration of the North as well as finance large-scale public works.

The period between 1906 and 1914 witnessed the rapid imperial penetration of Nigerian societies and the intensification of the emphasis on the production of cash crops as opposed to food crops production. The missionaries who combined their mission of evangelization with the promotion of cash crops production ("the bible and the plow") played a very significant role in this regard. Furthermore, through their "cultural colonization" and educational activities, the missionaries helped to create a new class of people who would later play an important role in the modernization project.[9] Indeed, the missionaries were among the earliest propagators and champions of the modernization paradigm in Nigeria. In their bid to Christianize and "civilize" Nigerians, they idealized the Christian religion and Western culture while degrading the indigenous religion and culture as "pagan," "primitive," "backward," and "barbaric." In addition, their encouragement of cash crops production was predicated on the notion that this would help to advance the colonial enterprise of fostering "progress," "civilization" and "modernization" while food crops production was portrayed as "traditional," and not relevant to the progress of the Nigerian societies. Finally, the 1906 to 1914 period witnessed the creation of the outline of a colonial state and its administrative structures, all of which were concretized with the amalgamation in 1914.

Indirect Rule and the Colonial Policy of Divide and Rule

Indirect rule has traditionally been defined as "a system of local government that enabled the British to govern Nigeria through indigenous rulers and institutions." Under this system, contacts between colonial officials and the majority of the indigenous population were minimized as regulations and instructions were passed to the people through their chiefs and kings. It is claimed that under this system, indigenous institutions were retained after they had been purged "of their so-called excesses and inhumane practices," as well as "uncivilized" indigenous laws that were not conducive to the "civilizing" and "modernizing" goals of colonialism.[10] It is however debatable whether the institutions that were used by indirect rule can be said to be really indigenous. Such an assertion might amount to equating a façade to the real thing while ignoring the actual nature and purpose of the policy. Indeed, the *raison d'être* of indirect was the subversion of the indigenous culture in order to be able to achieve the exploitative ends of colonialism. Rather than make use of the traditional institutions to administer the people, indirect rule in practice was reduced to the use of "traditional" chiefs as the medium for administration at the local level even in acephalous societies where such chiefs did not exist in the precolonial period. Furthermore, even in the Northern Nigeria, which is usually "celebrated" as representing the success of the indirect rule system, the so-called traditional rulers were no longer defenders of the indigenous culture; rather, they became agents of exploitation and for subverting salient aspects of the indigenous culture and traditions.

Lugard, the architect of indirect rule in Nigeria, is credited with introducing the policy based on his experiences in the Sudan and India where he witnessed the operation of such a policy, and the problems he encountered in Northern Nigeria between 1900 and 1906. As the administrator of Northern Nigeria, he was faced with problems of personnel, revenue and absence of specific directives from London. In the midst of all these difficulties, Lugard saw in the North a comparatively well developed bureaucracy, which he could convert to serve the interests of British imperialism. He therefore decided to impose his authority on the emirs and to use their administration and officials as agents of British imperialism.

After the amalgamation in 1914, indirect rule was extended to Southern Nigeria where it faced many problems. The same argument of practical necessity has been advanced to justify the amalgamation and the extension of indirect to the South. Factors like the shortage of personnel, problems of communication within the vast Nigerian territory and financial considerations, especially the need to use southern revenue to subsidize the administration of the poorer Northern Protectorate were said to have made the adoption of indirect rule in the different parts of Nigeria inevitable.[11] However, in the West where the obas were not as powerful as the northern emirs, indirect rule turned the obas into autocrats thereby alienating many Yoruba people. A significant example was the new wide-ranging powers accorded the Alaafin of Oyo under the indirect rule system.[12] This creation of autocratic "traditional" rulers led to rebellions in parts of Yorubaland such as the Iseyin rebellion in 1916[13] and the Egba rebellion in 1918. This same kind of despotic rule was introduced in the Benin kingdom.[14] Indirect rule faced even stiffer opposition among the Igbo people in the east where there were no kings in the precolonial period. Lugard decided to create "warrant chiefs" who were mainly men who did not occupy any significant position in the traditional society. The wide-ranging powers given to these chiefs turned them into tyrants. They violated well-established traditions, and were corrupt and oppressive.[15] These factors led to widespread resentment and demonstrations against the warrant chiefs and the indirect rule system with one of the most notable demonstrations being the Igbo women's war of 1929.[16]

In reality, indirect rule was adopted because the system provided the most effective means of exploiting Nigeria's resources. The kings, who were appointed as Native Authorities, no longer represented the indigenous people's traditional institutions, culture and "customary laws." Rather they were mere agents of colonial imperialism and were therefore dependent on the colonial authorities rather than responsible to their own people. Thus, they represented the lowest ladder in the exploitative colonial administrative system. In order for them to effectively perform their role as the primary agents of exploitation and domination at the grassroots level, various coercive and administrative institutions were put at their disposal. Mahmood Mamdani notes that the Lugardian system of indirect rule was "a single and coherent edifice resting on three pillars: a Native Court, a Native Administration, and a Native Treasury." To these can be added the Native Police and the Native Prison that effectively concretized the coercive powers of the chief.

Thus rather than being a system of local government, indirect rule promoted "decentralized despotism." The chiefs exercised unfettered powers over their subjects so long as they were able to collect the amount of taxes assigned to them, ensure the constant supply of labor and the unhindered production of cash crops.[17]

This system of indirect rule enabled the colonial officials who dictated the policies implemented by the chiefs to exercise power without responsibility. Perhaps even more significant for the postcolonial history of Nigeria is the fact that this policy developed the tradition of local governments not being autonomous or responsible to their constituents.

In the pursuance of the modernization project, the native administration system set in motion the colonial policy of marginalizing women in the development process by defining development in patriarchal and masculinist terms. Under this notion of development, the role of men in the wage economy or in commercial agriculture, among others, was viewed as crucial for the attainment of modernity.[18] This patriarchal conception of development was a product of the transplanted Western notion of men as breadwinners and women as homemakers, which was at variance with the precolonial situation where women were active participants in the economies of various Nigerian societies.[19] As noted by Kathleen Staudt:

> With the imposition of European colonialism in Africa, groundwork was laid to conceive of work, its value and reward in ways already present in the highly differentiated and sex-segregated industrializing world. The best and the brightest of administrators selected for the colonial service were products of late-Victorian middle-class society in which women preserved the home refuge for men, who in turn insulated women from the pressures of public life. In this ideological model, men are the family breadwinners and men's work in the wage economy or in commercializing agriculture is viewed as necessary for 'modernization.'[20]

The emphasis on cash crops production which were mainly cultivated by men and the introduction of taxation to be paid by men, enhanced men's entry into the monetary economy while the food crops production sector which was dominated by women was regarded as traditional and largely remained non-monetized. Because cash crops were regarded as necessary for modernization, the sector benefited from various colonial agricultural researches while food production was ignored, and indeed, suppressed by the colonial administration.[21] According to Catherine Coquery-Vidrovitch:

> Generally, the colonial administration ignored women, and for a long time development "experts," African and foreign, did as well. The colonizers focussed on men, from whom they demanded a tax in silver and compulsory cash-cropping, privileging men's entry into the monetary economy. Cash-crop production was a determining factor in keeping men on the land while profoundly changing how the land was worked.

She added that, "their lack of money condemned . . . (women) to grow foodstuffs in their own fields . . . just as they had in the past, the only change being an increase in their work hours."[22] Furthermore, in the public realm, "former female-managed political responsibilities (such as judicial functions) were removed from their hands to be replaced with the now male-controlled administration, male-run Native Courts, or the private market, in which women participated but in increasingly marginal ways."[23]

Another significant negative development that emanated from indirect rule was the promotion of ethnicity, which adversely affected Nigeria's colonial and postcolonial politics. In line with the colonial policy of divide and rule, indirect rule was used to promote communal sentiments among Nigerians.[24] The ethnic group was defined as the unit of indirect rule administration with the belief that every Nigerian belonged to an ethnic group. In other words, ethnic citizenship rather than civic citizenship became the basis for defining a Nigerian thereby giving rise to a situation where Nigerians were "closeted in separate ethnic containers, each with a customary shell guarded over by a Native Authority."[25] In deploying this policy in Nigeria, deliberate and elaborate efforts were made to emphasize the differences between the different ethnic groups, in particular, the majority ethnic groups. Another dimension of the divide and rule policy of indirect rule was the deliberate emphasis on the religious and cultural differences between northern and southern Nigeria.

In spite of the amalgamation, the activities of the agents of the Western culture such as missionaries were severely curtailed in the north while they were allowed to operate freely in the south. Indeed, under the indirect rule system, the north was regarded as the land of the noble "savage" which should be preserved in its pristine nature untouched and unspoiled by the corrupting influences of western civilization.[26] In the same vein, the north was to be protected from the corrupting influence of people from southern Nigeria who had already imbibed western influence. This gave rise to the establishment of Sabogaris (strangers quarters) in northern towns and cities where people from the south could reside. Furthermore, the divide and rule policy of indirect rule was greatly aided by the emphasis on the use of vernacular. It is significant that indirect rule worked best in the north where the vernacular policy was more successful while the antithesis was the case in the south where the use of English had spread among the educated people. An outcome of this vernacular policy, which fit well with the colonial divide and rule policy, was the intensification of the gap between the north and the south in terms of exposure to western influence.

Furthermore, the restriction of the activities of traders, businessmen, and missionaries in the Muslim areas of the north resulted in the concentration of industries, commercial activities, and educational institutions in the south. This not only resulted in the widening of the educational imbalance between the north and the south but also widened the social distance between the peoples of the two parts of the country.[27] This would have profound negative effects on subsequent Nigerian politics.

In spite of the amalgamation, the north and the south were not brought under a uniform administration until 1946. There was no legislative body for the whole country and the Nigerian Council that was created in 1914 only had advisory responsibilities. The administrative reforms introduced by Hugh Clifford in 1922 did not bring the north and the south under a uniform administration. The Legislative Council, which he created, had powers to legislate for Southern Nigeria only, while the Governor legislated for the Northern Protectorate by decree. This development that maintained the sociopolitical particularism of the north and the south, tended to perpetuate the individuality and separateness of the two parts of the country.[28]

In 1939, Southern Nigeria was divided into two administrative areas while Northern Nigeria was left as a single administrative entity. The Richards Constitution of 1946 concretized this administrative division of Nigeria. The constitution divided the country into three administrative regions: North, West and East. The constitution strengthened the three regions by granting them greater political and budgetary powers. In line with the British colonial policy of divide and rule, the internal administrative division fostered ethnic particularism by ensuring that people from the same ethnic group were brought under one region while each region was controlled by one of the three dominant ethnic groups in the country. The bulk of the Igbo were in the Eastern region, the bulk of the Yoruba were in the Western region and the bulk of the Hausa-Fulani were in the Northern region. Nigerians were not encouraged to seek employment in regions other than their own region of origin while ethnic identity was promoted. Conscious attempts were made to discourage inter-ethnic cooperation.

Colonialism and the Nigerian State

The Nigerian state owes its origin to colonialism. As the conquest of the different Nigerian societies was proceeding between 1885 and 1906, the British imperialists were simultaneously creating and nurturing new territorial and authority units as well as establishing other institutions of colonial exploitation and social control. By the time of the amalgamation, the Southern and Northern Protectorates had been delimited into districts, divisions, and provinces. Two types of administration corresponding to the internal divisions emerged, namely, the colonial superstructure and the native authority system.

With the amalgamation in 1914, the colonial superstructure consisted of a governor-general, provincial commissioners, residents, divisional officers and district officers (all of whom were British personnel). Subordinate to the colonial superstructure was the native authority system, which was under the direct supervision of the district commissioner. As noted by Mamdani "the colonial state was a two-tiered structure: peasants were governed by a constellation of ethnically defined Native Authorities in the local state, and these authorities were in turn supervised by white officials deployed from a racial pinnacle at the center."[29] Because of this bifurcated nature of the colonial state, colonial officials, citizens of Britain and other Western nations as well as citizens from non-European countries and "assimilated" Nigerians who belonged to the colonial structure were accorded the civil liberties of citizens. On the other hand, the overwhelming majority of Nigerians who came under the jurisdiction of the native authorities were regarded as subjects and therefore not entitled to the civil liberties available to citizens. Coercive measures could therefore be used to make them produce the resources needed by the colonial economy. In a sense, it can be said that although colonial rule did not completely destroy precolonial social forces and pattern of authority in some Nigerian societies, it set in motion new forces and social relations of production. From this perspective, the colonial political economy consisted of a simultaneous articulation and organization of the precolonial and colonial forces and social relations of production, distribution and exchange.[30]

The primary function of the native authority was to ensure that the exploitative designs of the colonial administration were achieved. Toward this end, as already noted, they had at their disposal coercive institutions like the native treasury, native court, native police, native prison, etc. In addition, the introduction of taxation and the British currency as the legal tender ensured that the peasants were compelled by the native authorities to produce cash crops required by the British industries, while the construction of railways and ports promoted the easy evacuation of these goods from Nigeria. Thus, another peculiarity of the colonial state:

> was that the relation between force and market was not antithetical. It was not simply that force framed market institutions. It was more that force and market came to be two alternative ways of regulating the process of production . . . exchange (and exploitation). Within its (native authority's) parameters, market relations were enmeshed with extra-economic coercion.[31]

In fact, by the time of the amalgamation, the basic structures of the Nigerian colonial state had been established while all the precolonial state-systems had been completely subordinated to the exploitative designs of British imperialism. It has been rightly observed that rather than marking the beginning of the Nigerian colonial state the amalgamation marked the culmination of the state.[32]

This basic character of the early colonial state that has been sketched above remained essentially the same throughout the colonial period. The few changes that were introduced did not alter the character of the state: on the contrary, they helped to consolidate this nature and character of the state. Meanwhile, with all the administrative, economic and coercive institutions at its disposal, the colonial state became the primary instrument for surplus accumulation in Nigeria. In the same vein it became the primary instrument for the development or underdevelopment of the country. The control of the all-powerful colonial state guaranteed access to the surplus that had been accumulated by the state – thanks to the activities of the marketing boards. This kind of situation would eventually promote a dialectical relationship between politics and the Nigerian economy.

Moreover, in order to achieve the *raison d'être* of colonialism, that is, the ruthless exploitation of Nigeria's resources, the colonial state had the responsibility for providing the right atmosphere for the attainment of this goal. In this regard, the colonial state was responsible for providing the necessary infrastructures, technical assistance, loans and subsidies to British industries. All these were in line with the dictates of the modernization paradigm, which saw the colonial state as the primary instrument for the modernist transformation of the Nigerian economy and society. The desire to fulfill this modernist project made the colonial state to be absolute and arbitrary. Indeed, Ake aptly characterized the absolutist and arbitrary nature of the colonial state.

> To begin with, it (the colonial state) was unusually statist. The colonial state redistributed land and determined who should produce what and how. It attended to the supply of labor, sometimes resorting to forced labor; it churned out administrative instruments and legislated taxes to induce the breakup of traditional social relations of production, the atomization of society, and the process of proletarianization. It went into the business of education to ensure that workers could do the jobs they were required to perform and would remain steadfast in the performance of their often tedious and disagreeable tasks. It built roads, railways, and ports to facilitate the collection and export of commodities as well as the import of manufactured goods. It sold commodities through commodity boards. Indeed, it controlled every aspect of the colonial economy tightly to maintain its power and domination and to realize the economic objectives of colonization.[33]

This character of the colonial state was retained on the attainment of political independence hence the postcolonial state became a tool for serving the neocolonial project in Nigeria.

Thus, on the attainment of political independence, the basic character of Nigeria's colonial political economy, that is, its dependence on, and exploitation and domination by, international monopoly capital remained unaltered. The Nigerian state remained the primary and most important instrument for capitalist development and surplus accumulation. The state was authoritarian, and retained its masculinist and patriarchal-focused development process, which was regarded as crucial for the success of the modernization project. In addition, the state retained its character as an organ of capital accumulation, for both the domestic and foreign bourgeoisie. In essence, the Nigerian state remained an organ of international capital.[34] This is significant for understanding the political economy of postcolonial Nigeria.

Colonialism and the Nigerian Bourgeoisie

Just like the colonial state, the Nigerian bourgeoisie owes its origin to colonialism. The exigency of colonial rule created the need for a small group of Nigerians with varying levels of Western education to help in different aspects of the colonial project of exploitation. The native authority system was helping to subjugate and exploit the Nigerian people and their resources, but there was the need for some educated Nigerians to serve in lower bureaucratic and commercial exchange levels. Colonial rule therefore employed the services of Nigerians as clerks, teachers, interpreters, produce buyers, etc. This group of people, who were mainly members of the petty bourgeoisie, formed the nucleus of the Nigerian bourgeois class. They were essentially a subordinate and dependent class. As products of colonialism, they depended on the manipulation of colonial structures for their survival and continued relevance.

Although relatively speaking members of this class grew in status and wealth before the outbreak of World War II, they did not occupy important positions in the colonial scheme of things as more reliance was placed on the native authorities. The educated elite resented their exclusion from colonial administrative systems. However, the special circumstances of the post-World War II period made it inevitable that the British imperialist authorities should ditch the traditional rulers in favor of the newly emergent Western educated bourgeoisie. For instance, anti imperialist ferments in Nigeria and other African colonies as well as the desire by American industries to have unrestricted access to the markets of the African colonies created the need for some reforms in the colonies. Furthermore, Britain realized that in order to protect her economic interests in Nigeria she needed to rely more on the new social class which colonial rule had helped to create. However, members of this class resented the fact that they did not have equal access to economic opportunities as well as resenting the social discrimination they faced.[35]

From 1945, Britain introduced some measures that would help to improve the relative material conditions of the Nigerian bourgeoisie. To consolidate her control over Nigerian resources, Britain encouraged her TNCs to establish import-substituting industries in Nigeria. At the same time, British capitalist interests were encouraged to withdraw from merchant trading and the Nigerian bourgeoisie were given more access to this sector through the award of more import licenses and the guarantee of bank credit.[36] In addition, the Nigerianization of the civil service, which commenced in 1948, gave Nigerians more access to higher positions.

The setting in motion of the process of decolonization in the 1950s assured the Nigerian bourgeoisie access to the surplus that had been accumulated by the colonial state. This surplus had been tremendously increased by the exploitative activities of the commodity marketing boards. In addition, the regionalization of the marketing boards ensured that sufficient surplus accrued to the various regions. Part of the preoccupation of Nigerian politicians during the period of political decolonization was the desire to control the resources that had been accumulated by respective regional governments. This set in motion intense competition among the Nigerian bourgeoisie. The colonial administration was therefore able to manipulate the fragmented Nigerian bourgeoisie and ensure a programmed transition from colonialism to neocolonialism.[37] Furthermore, given the origin, nature and character of the Nigerian bourgeoisie, they did not question the modernist project of the colonial administration. On the contrary, they regarded the colonial modernization project as constituting the appropriate path for the economic, political and social transformation of Nigeria.

Colonial Reforms and Consolidation of Modernization, 1945-1960

The period between 1945 and 1960, the last phase of colonial rule in Nigeria, has been described as crucial in terms of launching the country on the path to "modernization." This period witnessed the introduction of various political, social and economic reforms aimed at promoting the modernization project.[38] It witnessed the birth of the Parsonian modernization school as well as the birth of development economics, both of which were the godfathers and primary propagators of the modernization paradigm. Through the activities of scholars and development policy "experts" associated with the modernization school, various colonial reforms aimed at entrenching the modernization paradigm in Nigeria's political economy were introduced.

Political Reforms

The Second World War had a great impact on the development of a more mass-based form of nationalism in Nigeria. Over 100,000 Nigerians were recruited to fight in the war on the side of the Allies. These Nigerians were exposed to the propaganda of the Allies that claimed that they were fighting for the cause of liberation, freedom, liberty and equality. The Nigerian servicemen and elites therefore expected that these principles would apply to Nigeria at the end of the war. The Atlantic Charter of 1941 and the formation of the United Nations both of which stated their commitment to self-determination for conquered and colonized peoples all over the world reinforced this belief. There was also the anti-colonial stance of the Soviet Union and the United States, which emerged as superpowers at the end of the war. The resolutions of the Manchester Pan-African Conference of 1945 equally contributed to the commitment to the eradication of colonialism in Nigeria and other African countries.[39] Moreover the serious economic problems caused by the war and the massive unemployment faced by the ex-servicemen at the end of the war, further contributed to the anti-colonial sentiment.[40]

The National Council of Nigeria and the Cameroons (NCNC – it was renamed the National Council of Nigerian Citizens in 1961) which was formed in 1944 championed the nationalist cause up to 1950. The NCNC was particularly active in the period from 1945 to 1947 when it championed the cause of various groups that had grievances against the colonial administration, such as the ex-servicemen. It was in the forefront of the demand for political reforms. The party took the lead in the opposition against the Richards constitution: it undertook a vigorous national campaign and sent a delegation to London in 1947 to protest the constitution. However, between 1948 and 1950, when the colonial administration in reaction to the nationalist activities took some concrete steps to address the political demands of the Nigerian politicians as well as satisfy their material and class interests, the pace of the NCNC's nationalist activities declined. The measures included the granting of more concessions to Nigerians in the merchant trading sector, setting in motion the process of the Nigerianization of the civil service[41] and the announcement of the beginnings of constitutional reforms that would eventually grant Nigerian politicians more access to legislative and executive authority.

The inactivity of the NCNC resulted in a void in the nationalist movement, which the Zikist movement sought to fill through radical and militant nationalism in the period between 1948 and 1950. The movement, which was formed in 1946 because of Nnamdi Azikiwe's inspiration, sought to undermine and bring about the downfall of colonial rule through strikes, boycotts, and the use of violence.[42] The Zikists hoped that their activities might lead to the imprisonment of Azikiwe; thus, turning him into the Nehru of Nigerian politics. He would therefore become the rallying point of all the Nigerian anti-colonial forces and many more politicians would probably be imprisoned thereby congesting the jails with political detainees. Given the increasing effectiveness of the militant activities of the Zikists, the colonial state reacted by violently repressing the movement. Since they were not prepared to become prison graduates on the altar of Nigerian nationalism, Nigerian politicians including Azikiwe dissociated themselves from the Zikists. In fact, Azikiwe described the Zikists as a group of hot headed and irresponsible youths. Thus, abandoned by Azikiwe and the other Nigerian politicians, the Zikist movement was proscribed in 1951.

Nevertheless, the cumulative effects of the various nationalist activities compelled the British colonial administration to set in motion a process of political decolonization in 1950. This process which was situated within the modernist paradigm and characterized as political modernization, entailed the phased transplantation of the "ideal", "rational" and "universally applicable" British Westminster model of liberal democracy into Nigeria.[43] The process completely discountenanced the indigenous culture and socio-historical experiences as irrelevant for the political administration of Nigeria. The Nigerian politicians who were mostly products of the colonial structure and who had been socialized into seeing Western liberal democracy as the epitome of civilization did not really quarrel with the character and nature of the political transition process. Rather, they were busy competing among themselves over access to, and control of, political power. Thus, at the various constitutional conferences that were held from 1950, Nigerian politicians were busy trying to secure their control over their respective regional governments, while arguing over the number of seats that each region would have in the central legislature and the formula for revenue allocation, among others. In the circumstance, the British colonial administration ironically became the referee and used this position to ensure that her vital interests were not threatened at the end of colonial rule.

The political decolonization movement was primarily male-dominated although a number of women participated in the process.[44] This was largely a product of the colonial policies that privileged men over women in the public arena and promoted domesticity and the private realm as the appropriate arena for women. Furthermore, colonial education, largely carried out under the auspices of mission schools, fostered an ideology and activities that "prescribed an extreme dichotomization of gender along the lines of antiquated Victorian norms." This ideology promoted an educational socialization process of women as "helpmates, appendages, and financial dependents on men as well as moral guardians of the home, family, and children." Women were therefore encouraged to confine themselves to the home and family life, which were considered important for "inculcating values" and "socializing children," while politics should be left to the men.[45]

In spite of these limitations, many women played very active roles in the decolonization politics. They were particularly active in protest politics and grassroots organizing. Of significance in this regard was the role of market women who through their economic activities were able to attain some degree of economic empowerment that facilitated their involvement in local and nationalist politics. The Lagos Market Women Association (LMWA), formed by the indefatigable Alimotu Pelewura in the early 1900s, played an active part in local and national politics from 1908 to the 1950s. The LMWA actively participated in the 1945 general strike that lasted for thirty-seven days and led by Michael Imoudu, one of the most militant and selfless labor activists in Nigeria's history. On June 2, Pelewura was one of the key speakers at a public reception for Imoudu upon his release from detention. Furthermore, as the strike progressed the LMWA decided to keep prices of foodstuffs low as a means of demonstrating the women's solidarity with the strikers. Large donations were also collected from the market women for the Workers' Relief Fund. In the 1950s, the LMWA was involved in local protest politics and grassroots mobilization of women in support of various nationalist causes.

The Abeokuta Women's Union (AWU), formed in 1946, comprised both elite and market women. Under the leadership of Funmilayo Ransome-Kuti the AWU played a very active role in local and national politics. Between 1946 and 1949, the movement waged a relentless campaign against the *Alake* of Abeokuta who as the Native Authority under the indirect rule system was the symbol of colonial sexism and oppression. The sustained protest movement eventually forced the *alake* to abdicate his throne in January 1949.[46] Based on the success of the AWU, it decided to transform itself into a national organization. It changed its name to the Nigerian

Women's Union and had branches in different parts of the country. By the 1950s, many of its members had become actively involved in the decolonization politics and joined two of the mainstream political parties – the NCNC and the Action Group (AG). Funmilayo Ransome-Kuti was part of the NCNC delegation (the only woman member of the delegation) that went to London in 1947 to protest the 1946 Richards constitution. While in London, she used the opportunity to publish an article in the *Daily Worker* on 18 August 1947 in which she pointed out the ways in which colonialism had worsened the status of women vis-à-vis their male counterparts. According to her:

> Before the British advent in Nigeria . . . there was division of labor between men and women; . . . women owned property, traded and exercised considerable political and social influence in society. . . . With the advent of British rule . . . instead of the women being educated and assisted . . . their condition has deteriorated. . . .

She argued that under colonialism Nigerian women had lost their traditional economic and political power and that they were oppressed by the colonial system and its agencies, such as the Sole Native Authority in Abeokuta. Not only were they denied suffrage and any voice in the government but in Abeokuta they were forced to pay taxes that they could not afford and in return did not receive even basic amenities, such as medical services. She maintained that women were poverty-stricken, disease-ridden, and malnourished. She held Britain responsible for this state of affairs and appealed to British women to help free the women of Nigeria from "slavery-political, social, and economic."[47]

Margaret Ekpo was also very active in the politics of decolonization and the fight for women's rights. Both Funmilayo Ransome Kuti and Margaret Ekpo were members of the NCNC.[48] Margaret Ekpo attended the 1953, 1957 and 1958 constitutional conferences as an adviser. She was a member of the Eastern region house of chiefs in the 1950s and won election into the Eastern region house of assembly in 1961.

Nevertheless, the various constitutional reforms that were introduced in Nigeria during the period of political decolonization promoted the regionalization and ethnicization of Nigerian politics. These centrifugal tendencies were deliberately fostered by the British colonial administration so that it would be able to "impose" its preferred type of constitution on Nigeria at the end of the political decolonization process. The Richards constitution set in motion the process of the regionalization of Nigerian politics. As noted by Graf, under the constitution:

> Each Region was given its own House of Assembly and was permitted to deliberate on Regional matters in consultation with the colonial Regional Governor. No comparable machinery existed at the centre. Therefore, the Regional assemblies, which were supposed to be harbingers of national unity by creating three systems of 'unity in diversity' at the subnational level, antedated the same process at the national level, thus in effect becoming agencies for the assertion of Regional interests as *against* the centre,

> and in this way setting in motion the process of the *regionalization of politics.* (Emphasis in the original)[49]

The 1951 constitution completed the centrifugal process by adding ethnicization to the regionalization of Nigerian politics. The constitution, which can be said to have marked the beginning of the political decolonization process, was based on the outcome of the constitutional conferences held in Ibadan and London in 1950 and 1951 respectively, under the "guidance" of British officials. Delegates were elected based on the three regions. The conferences revealed the sharp divisions among Nigerian politicians as the position they took on issues were influenced by the desire to secure the maximum gains for their respective regions. Some of the main areas of disagreement were the number of seats each region would have in the proposed central legislature, the formula for revenue allocation, ministerial responsibility, the size of each region and the status of Lagos.

The 1951 Constitution allocated half of the seats in the central legislature to the Northern region and, this concession to the North as A. H. M. Kirk-Greene noted, was to dominate the shaping of Nigeria's political culture until the First Republic exploded sixteen years later.[50] With this arrangement, the Hausa-Fulani elite assumed control over the political sector of Nigeria's political economy while the Yoruba and Igbo elites dominated the administrative, professional and business sectors. As already noted, since the Nigerian elites were largely products of the colonial structures, they depended on the manipulation of the structures for relevance and surplus accumulation. Thus, given the fact that political power was crucial for the accumulation of the surplus that accrued to the colonial state, the Hausa-Fulani elite came to occupy an advantageous position in this regard vis-à-vis the Yoruba and Igbo elites. They were determined to hold on to this advantage at all cost throughout the period of political decolonization.

Nevertheless, the 1951 constitution provided for the election of members of the unicameral central legislature (the House of Representatives) from among the members of the regional legislatures. In addition, the twelve Nigerian ministers who were members of the central executive council were made up of four ministers from each region, chosen from among the representative or elected members of the central legislature. The Governor appointed the ministers upon the approval of the legislative bodies of their respective regions of origin. This "ladder" method of electing members of the central legislature and appointing ministers emphasized the ethnic group and region of origin as the basis for political power. Furthermore, the arrangement of constituencies along ethnic lines gave expression to a clear-cut definition of the boundaries of each of the ethnic groups.[51] This resulted in the formation of two political parties along ethnic and regional lines – the AG by Yoruba elite under the leadership of Obafemi Awolowo and the Northern People's Congress (NPC) by Hausa-Fulani elite under the leadership of Ahmadu Bello, the Sardauna of Sokoto. The main reason behind their formation was the desire to gain control of the governments of their respective regions. Billy Dudley has pointed out that the 1951 constitution "marked the start of a full-scale swing towards regionalism" in that it enhanced the status of the regions by providing them with legislative and executive powers.[52] However, through some of its strong centralizing features, the constitution gave the central government considerable legislative and executive advantage over the regions. At the same time, some of the constitutional provisions, paradoxically, contained some features, which could undermine its centralizing features thereby enhancing the powers of the regions.[53] This contradiction would eventually lead to demands on the part of Nigerian politicians, for more autonomy for the regions.

The election held in late 1951 based on the 1951 constitution was a victory for regionalist and ethnic chauvinists. The AG came to power in the West, the NPC in the North and the NCNC in the East. One of the most unfortunate outcomes of the 1951 constitution was the regionalization and ethnicization of the hitherto national NCNC. The party began championing the cause of the Igbo Federal Union. This development was partly the outcome of Azikiwe's experience in the Western region's legislature. He was elected into the Western region's House of Assembly from one of the constituencies in Lagos but failed in his bid to get elected into the House of Representatives from the AG and Yoruba dominated Western House. Ebere Nwaubani has argued unequivocally that Azikiwe, an Igbo, failed in his election bid because of ethnic politics.[54] There certainly was the ethnic element in the obstacle that Azikiwe encountered but the greatest blame should go to members of his own party, the NCNC whose act of indiscipline was exploited by the majority AG members of the House to prevent his election into the central legislature. Azikiwe was therefore confined to the ineffectual position of opposition leader in the Western House. Because of this setback, he decided to resign from the Western House and go to his home region, the Eastern region. Here he became the head of government after precipitating a crisis in 1952/53 that led to the removal of Eyo Ita who was from a minority ethnic group in the East, from his position as the head of the Eastern regional government. With this act, the NCNC finally capitulated to the vastly growing forces of regionalism and ethnic chauvinism.

The issue of the formula for revenue allocation was equally addressed in 1951 with the setting up of the Hicks-Phillipson Commission. The Commission was the first to attempt to spell out the criteria on which revenue allocation should be based. The criteria included derivation, needs, national interest, population and even development. It gave great weight to derivation by providing that 100 percent of mineral rents and royalties be retained in the regions from where the minerals were derived.[55]

The constitutional reform of 1954 further enhanced the ethnicization and regionalization of Nigerian politics. At the constitutional conferences that were held in London and Lagos in 1953 and 1954 respectively, the contentious issues included the percentage of representation of each region in the central legislature, the formula for revenue allocation, the status of Lagos, and the question of self-determination for Nigeria. Based on these contentious issues and the fact that Nigerian politicians were not happy with the juxtaposition of regional autonomy and centralizing features in the 1951 constitution, the 1954 constitution firmly established federalism in Nigeria[56] while entrenching the regionalization of Nigerian politics. As noted by the Colonial Secretary, "it was clear that Nigeria, if it was to be a nation, must be a federation, with as few subjects reserved for the central government as would preserve national unity."[57] The constitutional conferences agreed that any region that so desired could become self-governing in matters of regional competence in 1956.[58]

The 1954 constitution assigned specific subjects to the federal government; there was a concurrent list on which both the federal and regional governments had equal jurisdiction while the regions had exclusive jurisdiction over the remaining subjects (the bulk of the subjects). Among other things, the public service, the judiciary and the police force were regionalized. As noted by Dudley, "in many different ways the Nigerian 'citizen' now found he (or she) had to live with the fact of regionalism."[59] With regionalization of the public service, many of the most experienced and versatile civil servants left the federal public service for their regional public services thereby depriving the federal government of the services of these experienced civil servants at the crucial moment when Nigeria was moving towards political independence.

The shift toward regionalism was further enhanced by the improvement of the fiscal base of the three regions. A new revenue allocation formula emphasizing derivation was introduced. The Chick Commission on revenue allocation, which was set up as part of the constitutional review process, "provided for the re-allocation of a substantial proportion of federally-collected revenues on the basis of regional derivation or consumption." In addition, the federal government was constitutionally required "to return one-half of general import, excise and export taxes, plus all revenue receipts from mining rents and royalties and import duties on motor fuel, to the regions of derivation." Thus, while "about 22 percent of federally-collected revenues devolved annually to the regions during the 1952-1954 period, the proportion increased to over 40 percent during the 1954-1958 period."[60] The regionalization of the commodity marketing boards further bolstered the financial base of the respective regions. The accumulated reserves of the marketing boards, which amounted to about 75.5 million pounds sterling, were divided among the regional governments based on derivation.

With the granting of regional autonomy, the securing of the fiscal base of the respective regions and the promise of self-government in 1956 for those regions that desired it, the locus of power shifted to the regions. The leaders of the ethnic-based political parties that captured the government of their respective regions preferred to remain in their regions as premiers while sending their lieutenants to participate in the federal government thereby tending to make the federal government function as an agent of the regional governments.[61] Thus, the 1954 constitution greatly fostered centrifugal forces in Nigeria through the entrenchment of regionalism. This constitution established the institutional framework that provided the basis for the independence constitution although it witnessed a number of amendments, which intensified the strains and divisions between the different ethnic groups.

Moreover, the 1954 constitution further strengthened the phenomenon of ethnicity in Nigeria. As observed by Ekeh, "the introduction of electoral process (in the form of 'one man, one vote') led to the power defining phenomenon of 'tribalism', which embittered the relations between various ethnic groups."[62] Indeed, with the introduction of the elective principle of "one man, one vote" where candidates for political office were chosen from constituencies defined along spatial lines rather than lines of specialization of production functions, ethnically salient parliamentary candidates emerged. For personal aggrandizement, these candidates constantly fanned the embers of ethnic identification.

The period between 1956 and 1960 marked the final phase in the movement toward political independence in Nigeria.[63] In 1957, the Western and Eastern regions became internally self-governing. In 1957 and 1958, constitutional conferences that were to prepare the final framework for Nigeria's independence were held in London. The conferences further exposed the divisions among Nigerian politicians as the stand taken on issues was determined by the vested interests of each region, and based mainly on their desire to retain control over their respective regional governments. However, the most contentious issue that confronted the conferences was the demand by ethnic minority groups for the creation of more states that would comprise ethnic minority areas. Ethnic minorities' agitation for state creation was vociferously made during the 1953 and 1954 constitutional conferences but the issue was not addressed because it was claimed that it was not included in the agenda of the conferences.[64] However, the 1954 constitution, which granted greater powers to regional authorities dominated by the respective majority ethnic groups, accentuated the agitation of the ethnic minorities. At the 1957 constitutional conference, the agitation by the minority ethnic groups for the creation of more states could no longer be ignored.

The Willink Commission was set up to examine the allegations and demands of the minority ethnic groups. The Commission was charged with ascertaining the facts about the fears of minorities in any part of Nigeria and to propose means of allaying the fears whether well or ill founded. It was also to recommend safeguards against the mistreatment of minorities that would be included in the independence constitution. The commission could only make detailed recommendations for the creation of not more than one new state in each region if no other solution could be found.[65] It is clear from the terms of reference that the colonial administration was reluctant to create any new states in Nigeria.

The report of the commission, which, expectedly, recommended against the creation of new states and merely recommended policies for protecting the interests of minority ethnic groups, was presented before the 1958 constitutional conference. The representatives of the minority ethnic groups were very critical of the report while the leaders of the NPC who all along had been firmly opposed to state creation were very pleased with the report. The leaders of the NCNC who would have liked to see more states created, largely supported the report. However, the leaders of the AG who had been advocates of states creation, and in fact, made it a campaign issue in the past, stridently criticized the report.[66] However, because the colonial administration threatened that the creation of new states would delay the granting of political independence, the AG dropped its opposition to the report. Thus, the colonial administration succeeded in manipulating Yoruba and Igbo politicians into sweeping under the carpet such a fundamental and sensitive issue that had serious implications for Nigeria's future stability and development.[67] This development was in line with the colonial administration's preference of handing over political power on the attainment of political independence, to an NPC-led or dominated federal government.

Nevertheless, with the attainment of consensus over the issue of state creation among leaders of the main political parties, the conference directed its attention to other issues. The North agreed to become self-governing in 1959 while it was agreed that Nigeria would become politically independent in 1960. The constitutional conference decided that representation in the central legislature should be based on population in place of the previous practice of parity between the North and the South. On this basis, the North had 174 seats in the legislature while the East, West and Lagos combined, had 138 seats. The constitutional and fiscal provisions increased the economic and police powers of the federal government,[68] which in line with the philosophy of the modernization paradigm was now expected, as a developmental state, to play the leading role in the country's development.

It is clear from the foregoing discussion that the decolonization process in Nigeria entrenched centrifugal federalism, as well as the regionalization and ethnicization of politics. Under the guise of political modernization, each stage in the process was used to transplant aspects of the British parliamentary system of government into the country. In the typical modernization practice of regarding the indigenous culture and socio-historical experience as irrational, primitive and backward, no attempt was made to integrate the indigenous experience into the process. This shortcoming would contribute substantially to the instability that characterized the First Republic eventually resulting in its demise. Graf aptly captured the modernist philosophy that underlined the decolonization process when he noted, "the 1960 Independence Constitution . . . established a governing structure whose origins and development lay outside the Nigerian socio-historical experience. In many ways, it was *an 'imposed' constitution*, a kind of extension of the British state structure (emphasis in the original)." Graf further observed that the transfer of sovereignty from British to Nigerian rulers "laid bare many structural problems of the Westminster model which had, hitherto, remained dormant, and set off a process of constitutional transformation whose result can be seen in the succession of military and civilian governments since 1960."[69]

Unfortunately, the Nigerian politicians who were largely products of the colonial structures could not see the acute limitations inherent in the transplantation of the alien Westminster model of government into the country. In fact many of them regarded the British system of government as the "epitome" of good governance and as supplanting the indigenous heritage. As stated by Abubaker Tafawa Balewa, Nigeria's Prime Minister in the First Republic, the British "system of democratic government has now become part of our own heritage and we should be wise to maintain our institutions on the British model."[70] Thus, the Nigerian politicians did not really quarrel with the British goal for the country: rather, they were busy competing among themselves over who would succeed the British colonial administration.

Indeed, the Nigerian politicians justified their desire to rule the country, on the basis that they were as qualified as the British imperial masters to operate the parliamentary system of government, which they uncritically regarded as the ideal form of government. Ekeh has therefore pointed out that the "fight" for Nigeria's independence was a "struggle" for power between two bourgeois classes – the British bourgeois class and the Nigerian bourgeois class. He contended that the intellectual poverty of the independence movement flows from the fact that what was involved was not the issue of differences of ideas regarding moral principles but, rather, the issue of which bourgeois class should rule Nigeria.[71] In the same vein, Aluko observed, "the nationalist parties were divided to such an extent that they expended more of their energy challenging each other than in challenging the colonial government."[72]

Economic Reforms

Economic reforms in Nigeria between 1945 and 1960 were carried out at the time when development economics and its ideological cousin, modernization, had become ascendant in colonial economic thought and, therefore, greatly influenced the economic development policies that were adopted in the country. Development economists and modernization theorists were of the opinion that state intervention was necessary for transforming the economies of the colonies from their so-called traditional, irrational and backward state to a modern, rational and ideal state. Colonial planning was the primary vehicle through which state-centered economic reforms were implemented during this period. Three colonial development plans, that closely followed the constitutional reforms promulgated as part of the political decolonization process, were launched in Nigeria.[73] Indeed, colonial planning was touted as the primary means of modernizing the country's economy and thus, transforming it from a traditional, primitive and backward state of underdevelopment to a preferred and ideal state of development. This ideal state of development was defined in terms of establishing the conditions for take-off, which euphemistically meant acquiring various characteristics and "artifacts" of Western societies. Colonial planning strategy was thus predicated on the conception of the Nigerian economy as a dual economy where the indigenous, that is, traditional economy was portrayed as backward and inimical to economic development while a modern Westernized economy was idealized as constituting the real index of development.

The origin of British colonial planning can be traced to 1929 when she launched the Colonial Development Act (CDA) aimed at ameliorating the depressed economic situation in Britain by increasing the volume of trade with the colonies.[74] However, it was only in 1945 that a Colonial Development and Welfare Act (CDWA) specifically devoted to Nigeria was launched. The CDWA made the sum of 120 million pounds available to the British colonies for a ten-year period. Based on the lessons learnt from the previous approach to preparing an overall plan for the entire colonies, the British government decided that it would be more useful for each colony to prepare its own separate plan. In this way, greater attention could be paid to the specific affairs of each colony. Each colony was therefore required to submit a detailed plan for a ten-year period, 1946-1956. In response to this requirement, the colonial administration in Nigeria produced a ten-year plan to cover the period, 1946-1956.[75] The plan envisaged the expenditure of 55 million pounds out of which 23 million pounds was expected to be in the form of allocation from the Colonial Development and Welfare Fund (CDWF). The sum of 15.8 million pounds was to be raised from loans while the remaining amount, was expected to be raised from internal revenue sources.

The ten-year plan and, indeed, the entire colonial plans were based on the modernization paradigm. As observed by J. M. Lee, development planning in the British colonies after 1945, tackled development issues from the assumption that Western skills and technical knowledge would gradually be transplanted to the colonies, but the pace of this transplanting was to be controlled by the colonial authorities in each colony.[76] The plan emphasized projects that were geared toward creating, expanding the scope, or serving the interest, of the "modern" sector of the Nigerian economy. Thus, the production of cash crops, the construction of communication facilities to help in transporting these cash crops to the coast, and construction of health facilities to ensure that the people were healthy enough to produce cash crops, were emphasized. At the same time, industrialization was discouraged. In fact, it was stated in the preliminary statement on development planning that it was not assumed "that Nigeria will become an industrial country as with its large population and area a great deal of its future must rest in agricultural development in its widest sense."[77]

The ten-year plan consisted mainly of a series of uncoordinated proposals and projects and lacked clearly defined goals or coherent statement of policy. No overall development strategy can be clearly discerned from the plan. Indeed the plan was more of an uncoordinated expenditure program than an actual development plan. A main philosophy of the plan was that the role of the government in the economy was to spend a minimal amount of money on social services, which would be enough to create a favorable environment for the exploitation of the country's resources by the private sector. Thus, the aim of the plan was "to improve the general health and mental condition of the people, and to provide those physical facilities which may be regarded as the minimum necessary for the general improvement of the country and its population."[78] The emphasis on health was justified on the ground that "a healthy body, reasonably nourished, is essential before further production effort can be expected."[79] The plan was therefore concerned with the promotion of a healthier population primarily because this would lead to an increased production of export crops. As a result, social facilities and infrastructures were concentrated in the parts of the country that produced the raw materials that were needed by British industries.

Two significant developments during the late 1940s were the decision by Britain to consolidate her hold over Nigerian resources by encouraging her TNCs to establish import-substituting industries in Nigeria and the establishment of commodity marketing boards. Both policies, which were aimed at maximizing the exploitation of Nigeria's resources, significantly contributed to the shaping of the character of Nigeria's economy in the late colonial and postcolonial periods. The decision on the part of the British colonial administration to encourage the establishment of import-substituting industries was essentially a market protection strategy. Before the Second World War, Britain was able to protect her colonial markets from cheaper imported goods from other industrialized countries with discriminatory tariffs and quotas. However, in the post World War II period, the United States, which became the leading capitalist power in the world championed an open door economic policy in the colonies so that her firms would be able to compete for the markets of the colonies. In response to this demand, Britain decided to protect her African colonial markets by encouraging her TNCs to establish a few strategic subsidiary import-substituting industries in the colonies.[80]

The origin of the marketing boards can be traced to the World War II period when the British colonial administration decided to intervene directly in the marketing of export crops produced from her West African colonies. Under this arrangement, private trading companies were obligated to sell the produce they purchased from West African peasant farmers and intermediaries to the British government, which had the responsibility of selling them in the world market. Toward this end, the West African Cocoa Control Board (WACCB) was established in 1940 to be specifically responsible for the purchase and marketing of cocoa. In 1942, the responsibility of the board was expanded to include the purchase and sale of other export crops such as groundnut (peanut) and palm produce thereby leading to the renaming of the board as the West African Produce Control Board (WAPCB). The establishment of the marketing boards was justified on the altruistic ground of helping to protect peasant farmers from economic ruin by stabilizing the prices paid for their crops thereby protecting them from the vagaries of the world market prices. In practice, the boards served the economic interests of Britain while they became avenues for exploiting the peasant farmers and taxing them in support of the World War II effort.[81]

Commodity marketing boards for cocoa, cotton, groundnuts, and palm produce were specifically established in Nigeria between 1947 and 1949. The boards were ostensibly supposed to help in securing the most favorable arrangements for Nigerian peasant farmers in the purchase, grading, export and marketing of the respective crops. The boards were expected to protect Nigerian farmers from the fluctuations in the world market prices of their products by underpaying them during periods of high prices and subsidizing their payments during periods of low prices. As stated in the policy statement establishing the marketing boards, the profits accumulated during periods of high prices were to constitute funds that would "be employed for the purpose of stabilising producer prices and of improving and developing production and the producing areas."[82] In practice, the marketing boards became veritable avenues for exploiting the peasant farmers and accumulating surplus by the colonial state.[83] For instance, between 1947 and 1954 when the prices for Nigerian produce were very high in the world market, the boards accumulated great surpluses by underpaying the farmers but in the late 1950s when produce prices declined, the boards continued to under pay the farmers while still accumulating surpluses. Thus in reality, the marketing boards were revenue earning agencies and instruments for exploiting the peasant farmers. This character and function of the marketing boards were carried into the postcolonial period until the boards were scrapped with the introduction of SAP in 1986.

In any case, by 1951, the weaknesses of the ten-year plan in addition to political developments in the country necessitated the revision of the plan. In fact, as early as 1948 the ten-year plan came under criticism by the Select Committee on Estimates of the British House of Commons, which criticized it for adopting "a wrong approach to development."[84] However, the official economic reasons given for revising the plan included the need to change the emphasis from the social services sector to the economic sector and the sharp increase in the cost of goods, services and labor. At the political level, it was stated that constitutional changes, which gave Nigerians majority representation in the regional and federal legislative bodies, rendered obsolete the ten-year plan's assumptions of a unitary system of government in which decision making, was dominated by colonial officials.[85]

The 1951-1956 revised plan of development and welfare proposed an expenditure of 34.2 million pounds made up of 16.2 million pounds – the balance from the Colonial Development and Welfare Grants; 9.95 million pounds to be raised from loans and 8.05 million pounds to be raised from Nigerian revenue sources. It was claimed that the plan was more than a mere review of the ten-year plan and that there was a shift of emphasis from the social sector to the basic equipment, and productive and revenue earning sectors. In reality, the shift was not fundamental. For instance, while the social services sector experienced a 7.7 percent reduction in the revised plan, the productive and revenue earning sector witnessed a 7.6 percent increase.[86] Indeed, the character and emphasis of the revised plan was not fundamentally different from that of the ten-year plan. The philosophy, content and form of planning as well as the implementation process were essentially the same. Thus, the years between 1946 and 1956 can be regarded as one of a single planning period. Nevertheless, the inability of the revised plan to make meaningful contribution to the promotion of economic development coupled with political developments in the country, which resulted in the introduction of a federal system of government in 1954, led to the premature termination of the plan in 1955.

In 1953, the British colonial authorities requested the International Bank for Reconstruction and Development (IBRD) to send a team of "experts" to Nigeria to report on the state of the country's economy. Specifically, the IBRD's mission was to assess the resources "available for future development, to study the possibilities for development in the major sectors of the economy, and make recommendations for practical steps to be taken, including the timing and coordination of developmental activities."[87] The IBRD's report, which was published in October 1954, criticized the existing approach to development planning in Nigeria and recommended a new approach to planning. In line with the existing notion of the role of the state in promoting economic development, the report recommended that the state should restrict its role to the provision of a conducive atmosphere, in the form of roads, railways and other relevant infrastructures, for a private sector led economic development.

The report helped to entrench the modernization paradigm in the development planning process in Nigeria. It completely devalued indigenous culture and institutions, which it regarded as irrational, traditional, backward, and inhibiting the development process. Thus, development could only be promoted through the discarding of the indigenous institutions and culture, and the transplanting of Western institutions into the country. The report therefore concretized the process of equating development to the Westernization of the Nigerian society and economy, an approach that dominated future economic policies in colonial and postcolonial Nigeria. Another aspect in which the IBRD mission influenced future development policies in Nigeria is the reliance on foreign "experts," particularly from the World Bank and other Western based international development agencies, in the formulation of economic development policies.

As already pointed out, the introduction of a federal system of government in October 1954 resulted in the need for a new constitution. The new constitution, which delegated increased powers to the regional governments while limiting the coordinating role of the federal government, rendered obsolete the continued implementation of the 1951-1956 revised plan that was formulated on the basis of a unitary system of government. Thus, in April 1955, a new five-year development plan, 1955-1960, was launched.[88] The plan closely followed the recommendations of the IBRD mission's report: it had a great degree of integration of the projects while emphasis was placed on economic considerations. However, the mission made separate detailed projections and recommendations for the federal and regional governments within the context of the new federal constitution. This resulted in a situation where five separate plans (one for the federal government, three for the regions and one for Southern Cameroon) were prepared.

The 1955-60 plan, fully entrenched the influence of the modernization paradigm on Nigeria's development trajectory. The plan was primarily concerned with growthmanship. Thus, the central preoccupation with growth in the GDP resulted in a situation where capital was considered more important than the human factor in the development process.[89] The programs placed the greatest emphasis on the production of cash crops to be used as raw materials by metropolitan industries. In line with the recommendations of the IBRD's mission, indigenous institutions were further denigrated as inhibiting development while emphasis was placed on the transplanting of Western institutions into the country. This was clearly demonstrated in the industrial sector where the import-substitution industrialization strategy promoted the transplantation of Western industries and technology into Nigeria while suppressing indigenous industrial activities and technological capacities. In fact this was the essence of the various industrial development policies of the 1950s. For instance, the 1956 industrial policy which stressed the importance of adequate infrastructures equally emphasized the "need for overseas capital and managerial and technical skills, if her (Nigeria's) resources are to be developed to the extent which the government and people of Nigeria desire."[90] Indeed, because of the deliberate policy of reliance on foreign enterprise for private sector led industrial development, all the colonial industrial policies favored foreign investors.[91] These kinds of industrial development policies that were biased toward foreign enterprises promoted the underdevelopment of indigenous entrepreneurship in Nigeria.[92]

The prevailing development economics preoccupation with creating the conditions for economic take-off that would result in the modernization of the economy, resulted in a situation where the state was assigned the critical role of massively expanding the required infrastructures for a private sector led development. Toward this end, the plan clearly ranked its priorities, with the highest allocation of 43.1 percent of the total planned expenditure for the entire country allocated to transport and communications (with the transport sub-sector receiving 38.7 percent). This pattern of allocation of funds was justified on the ground that "a cheap and extensive system of (transport and) communications is the greatest blessing which any country can have from the economic point of view," and that it "provides the greatest opportunity for a decisive advance in economic development."[93]

In any case, with the political independence of Nigeria fixed for 1960, the budget meeting of the House of Representatives in 1958 resolved to extend the duration of the 1955-60 plan to 1962 when the first postcolonial development plan would be launched. This extension would afford the federal and regional governments enough time to put together their first postcolonial development plans after the attainment of political independence. As a result, the federal and the Northern regional governments extended the duration of their plans to 1962 while the Eastern region launched a new five-year development plan (1958-1962). The Western region decided to stick to the duration of the existing regional plan and launch a new one in 1960 because by that year, the programs in the plan would have been "virtually fully implemented": thus, a new plan would ensure the continuity in the development of the region.[94] This not withstanding, the federal and all the regional governments agreed to terminate their plans in 1962 in order to permit the commencement of a national plan in that year.

Overall, the modernization paradigm, which influenced colonial economic reforms during the crucial period of decolonization, theorized that development could be more effectively promoted through the extermination of indigenous Nigerian institutions. Thus, indigenous institutions, which were portrayed as irrational, traditional, primitive and backward, were to be exterminated and replaced with transplanted Western "modern" institutions. In accordance with the modernization paradigm as propagated by development economists, a strong, patriarchal, authoritarian, developmental, and interventionist state was needed to effect this transition from tradition to modernity. As noted by Toyin Falola, since "the economy was regarded as 'too traditional,' the belief was that it would require the strong hands of the government to remove all the obstacles that tradition posed in the way of modernization."[95]

Moreover, the economic reforms during this period of political decolonization continued and, in fact, further consolidated the practice of marginalizing women in the economic development process. Even though the responsibilities of women increased in the so-called traditional sector of the economy, efforts were not made to improve this sector or address the "women issues" that were present in the sector. Rather, the reforms addressed those sectors of the economy like cash crops production, foreign trade, infrastructural development, and import-substitution industrialization that were considered as necessary for modernization. Incidentally, these sectors were male and foreign dominated. Furthermore, the products of the import-substitution industries and the importation of mass-produced consumer goods had more adverse effects on women since it was the consumer goods they produced that were largely displaced. In cases where the locally produced goods showed resilience and gave stiff competition to the imported goods, the colonial state deployed its coercive institutions to suppress the production of such goods. A good case in point was the local gin processed mainly by women, which was declared illicit, and people were arrested for producing, storing or marketing them.

Indeed, the colonial economic reforms implemented in Nigeria between 1945 and 1960 entrenched the dependence of the country's economy on foreign trade and foreign investment. These factors, which were supposedly aimed at fostering development and modernization were at the very best, marginally related to Nigeria's developmental requirements. Furthermore, in view of the continued dominant position of expatriate merchant firms in the Nigerian economy and the vital dependence of Nigerian merchants on them for supply of trading goods, for credit, and for other forms of patronage, Nigerian businessmen were not even in the position to establish manufacturing industries.[96] In the circumstance, rather than promote autonomous indigenous development, colonial economic reforms helped to institute a dependent capitalist system in Nigeria, a phenomenon that was aggravated by neocolonial dependency upon the attainment of political independence.

Conclusion

Colonial imperialism entrenched the modernization paradigm in Nigeria's development process. The so-called goal of "modernizing" the Nigerian society was advanced as a justification for the imposition of colonial rule, while at the same time; it was used to mask the exploitative aims that underlined colonialism. To effectively exploit Nigeria's resources, native authorities that had various coercive institutions at their disposal thereby creating a form of "decentralized despotism" were created at the local level. Although the creation of native authorities was justified in the name of tradition, these institutions actually amounted to a subversion of the indigenous culture and traditions. Rather than deriving their authorities from their people and indigenous traditions, they owed their position and loyalty to the colonial authorities from whom they derived their new powers and influence.

The political and economic reforms that were carried out during the period of decolonization were portrayed as aimed at launching Nigeria on the path of modernization. Under the guise of modernization, the reforms denigrated the indigenous culture and traditions as irrational, primitive and backward while helping to foster the exploitation of Nigeria's resources. Furthermore, they helped to promote a programmed transition from colonialism to neocolonialism. Moreover, colonial imperialism helped to transplant the patriarchal nature of Western societies into Nigeria, thus, greatly marginalizing women in the political, social and economic spheres. The colonial state laid the foundation for the "modern" sector "to conform with its cultural notions of appropriate gender relations in industrializing class society, in which women enable and stimulate male work force productivity through home labor . . . and consumer demand as well as serve as a low-skill reserve labor force."[97] Indeed, colonial imperialism laid the foundation for the critical role that the modernization paradigm played in postcolonial Nigeria's political economy.

Notes

1 For details on this bifurcated nature of the colonial administration, see Mamdani, *Citizen and Subject.*

2 The British conquest of Nigerian territories and indigenous resistance has been elaborately discussed in various works. See for instance, O. Ikime, *The Fall of Nigeria: The British Conquest*, London: Heinemann, 1977; and idem. ed., *Groundwork of Nigerian History*, Ibadan: Ibadan University Press, 1980.

3 For a detailed discussion of these developments in the Niger delta, see K. O. Dike, *Trade and Politics in the Niger Delta*, 1830-1885, Oxford: Oxford University Press, 1956.

4 On the imperial activities of George Taubman Goldie, See J. E. Flint, *Sir George Goldie and the Making of Nigeria*, Oxford: Oxford University Press, 1960.

5 For details on the British conquest of Southern Nigeria, see J. C. Anene, *Southern Nigeria in Transition, 1884-1906: Theory and Practice in a Colonial Dependency*, Cambridge: Cambridge University Press, 1965.

6 For a discussion of one of such resistance movements, see D. C. Ohadike, *The Ekumeku Movement: Western Igbo Resistance to the British Conquest of Nigeria, 1883-1914*, Athens: Ohio University Press, 1991.

7 M. Y. Mangwvat, "The Early Phase of Colonial Rule in Nigeria and the Beginnings of New Political Entities, 1885-1913: Some Reflections," Paper Presented at the Seminar on Historical Roots of the Contemporary Nigerian Nation, held at Durbar Hotel, Kaduna, Nigeria, 4-8 June 1986.

8 T. Tamuno, *The Evolution of the Nigerian State: The Southern Phase, 1898-1914*, London: Longman, 1972.

9 For details, see E. A. Ayandele, *The Missionary Impact on Modern Nigeria, 1842-1914: A Political and Social Analysis*, London: Longman, 1966. Also see idem., *The Educated Elite in Nigerian Society*, Ibadan: Ibadan University Press, 1974.

10 T. Falola, *The History of Nigeria*, Westport, Connecticut and London: Greenwood, 1999, 70.

11 I. F. Nicolson, *The Administration of Nigeria, 1900-1960: Men, Methods and Myths*, Oxford: Clarendon Press, 1975; and I. M. Okonjo, *British Administration in Nigeria, 1900-1950: A Nigerian View*, New York: NOK Publishers, 1974.

12 See J. A. Atanda, *The New Oyo Empire: Indirect Rule and Change in Western Nigeria, 1894-1934*, London: Longman, 1973.

13 J. A. Atanda, "The Iseyin-Okeiho Rising of 1916: An Example of Socio-Political Conflict in Colonial Nigeria," *Journal of the Historical Society of Nigeria*, Vol. 4, No. 4, 1969, 497-514.

14 P. A. Igbafe, *Benin Under British Administration: The Impact of Colonial Rule on an African Kingdom, 1897-1938*, London: Longman, 1979.

15 A. E. Afigbo, *The Warrant Chiefs: Indirect Rule in South-Eastern Nigeria, 1891-1929*, London: Longmans, 1972.

16 See F. K. Ekechi, "Perceiving Women as Catalysts," *Africa Today*, Vol. 43, No. 3, 1996, 243.

17 Mamdani, *Citizen and Subject*, 52-53 and 78.

18 Boserup, *Woman's Role in Economic Development*; and D. Elson ed., *Male Bias in the Development Process*, Manchester and New York: Manchester University Press, 1995.

19 On the active role women played in the precolonial economies of some Nigerian societies, see some of the contributions in B. House-Midamba and F. K. Ekechi eds., *African Market Women and Economic Power: The Role of Women in African Economic Development*, Westport, CT: Greenwood Press, 1995. Also see O. W. Ogbomo, *When Men and Women Mattered: A History of Gender Relations among the Owan of Nigeria*, Rochester, N.Y.: University of Rochester Press, 1997.

20 K. Staudt, "Women's Politics, the State, and Capitalist Transformation in Africa," in I. L. Markovitz ed., *Studies in Power and Class in Africa*, New York and Oxford: Oxford University Press, 1987, 196.

21 For details, see M. Lovett, "Gender Relations, Class Formation, and the Colonial State in Africa," in J. L. Parpart and K. A Staudt eds., *Women and the State in Africa*, Boulder, CO: Lynne Rienner, 1989.

22 C. Coquery-Vidrovitch (translated by B. G. Raps), *African Women: A Modern History*, Boulder, CO: Westview, 1997, 63.

23 Staudt, "Women's Politics," 197.

24 J. S. Coleman, *Nigeria: Background to Nationalism*, Berkeley: University of California Press, 1958, 210.

25 Mamdani, *Citizen and Subject*, 61.

26 U. O. Eleazu, *Federalism and Nation-Building: The Nigerian Experience, 1954-1964*, Ilfracombe: Stockwell, 1977, 80.

27 O. Nnoli, *Ethnic Politics in Nigeria*, Enugu, Nigeria: Fourth Dimension, 1980, 119; and B. Nkemdirim, *Social Change and Political Violence in Colonial Nigeria*, Ilfracombe: Stockwell, 1975, 30-34.

28 Coleman, *Nigeria: Background to Nationalism*, 322; and E. Nwaubani, "Constitution-Making and the Nigerian Identity, 1914-1960," in A. Oyebade ed., *The Transformation of Nigeria: Essays in Honor of Toyin Falola*, Trenton, NJ: Africa World Press, 2002, 76.

29 Mamdani, *Citizen and Subject, 287.*

30 Federal Republic of Nigeria, *Report of the Political Bureau*, Lagos: Federal Government Printer, 1987, 32.

31 Ibid.

32 Mangvwat, "The Early Phase of Colonial Rule in Nigeria."

33 Ake, *Democracy and Development in Africa*, 2.

34 B. Beckman, "Whose State? State and Capitalist Development in Nigeria," *Review of African Political Economy*, No. 23, 1982, 37-51.

35 E. A. Brett, *Colonialism and Underdevelopment in East Africa*, New York: NOK Publishers, 1973, 21-22. Brett argued that it is this blocked economic opportunities and social discrimination that greatly helped to foster the opposition to colonialism on the part of the Western educated elites.

36 P. Kilby, *Industrialization in an Open Economy: Nigeria 1945-1966*, Cambridge: Cambridge University Press, 1969; and G. Williams, *State and Society in Nigeria*, Idanre, Nigeria: Afrografika, 1980, 34.

37 S. Osoba, "Decolonization in Nigeria as a Programmed Transition to Neo-Colonial Dependence," Department of History, Obafemi Awolowo University, Ile-Ife, Seminar Paper, March 1977.

38 T. Falola, *Economic Reforms and Modernization in Nigeria, 1945-1965*, Kent, Ohio: The Kent State University Press, 2004.

39 On the contributions of the Manchester Pan-African conference to the promotion of radical nationalism and liberation from colonial rule, see J. I. Dibua, "Pan-Africanism," in T. Falola ed., *Africa: Vol. 4: The End of Colonial Rule: Nationalism and Decolonization*, Durham, NC: Carolina Academic Press, 2002, 36-38; and E. Kodjo and D. Chanaiwa, "Pan-Africanism and Liberation," in A. A. Mazrui and C. Wondji eds., *UNESCO General History of Africa: Vol. VIII: Africa Since 1935*, Paris: UNESCO, 1999, 744-746.

40 For a detailed discussion of the impact of the Second War on the intensification of nationalist activities in Nigeria, see G. O. Olusanya, *The Second World War and Politics in Nigeria, 1939-1953*, Ibadan: Evans Brothers, 1973.

41 G. O. Olusanya, *The Evolution of the Nigerian Civil Service, 1861-1960: The Problems of Nigerianization*, Lagos: University of Lagos Press, 1975.

42 For an incisive study of the activities of the Zikist movement, see E. E. G. Iweriebor, *Radical Politics in Nigeria, 1945-1950: The Significance of the Zikist Movement*, Zaria: Ahmadu Bello University Press, 1996. Also see M. Okoye, *A Letter to Dr. Nnamdi Azikiwe*, Enugu: Fourth Dimension, 1979; R. L. Sklar, *Nigerian Political Parties: Power in an Emergent African Nation*, Princeton: Princeton University Press, 1963, 72-83; and Olusanya, *The Second World War and Politics in Nigeria*, 112-123.

43 The theoretical justification for this modernist model was provided by political development/modernization scholars working under the auspices of the Social Science Research Council in the 1950s. See for instance, Almond and Coleman eds., *The Politics of Developing Areas*; G. A. Almond and B. Powell, *Comparative Politics: Developmental Approach*, Boston: Little, Brown, 1966; and G. A. Almond, *Political Development: Essays in Beuristic Theory*, Boston: Little, Brown, 1970.

44 For a comprehensive discussion of Nigerian women's nationalist activities and their involvement in decolonization politics, see N. Mba, *Nigerian Women Mobilized: Women's Political Activity in Southern Nigeria, 1900-1965*, Berkeley: University of California Institute of International Studies, 1982.

45 See Staudt, "Women's Politics," 197-199.

46 For details on the grassroots political activities of the LMWA and the AWU, see C. Johnson, "Grass Roots Organizing: Women in Anticolonial Activity in Southern Nigeria," *African Studies Review*, vol. XXV, Nos. 2 and 3, 1982, 137-157.

47 Cited in C. Johnson-Odim and N. E. Mba, *For Women and the Nation: FunmilayoRansome-Kuti of Nigeria*, Urbana and Chicago: University of Illinois Press, 1997, 135-136. Johnson-Odim and Mba argued that Funmilayo Ransome-Kuti's thesis which has been thoroughly documented by feminist scholars since the mid-1970s, shows that "she was way ahead of her time in making this point in 1947."

48 For detailed studies on the political activities of Funmilayo Ransome-Kuti and Margaret Ekpo, see ibid; S. A. Effah-Attoe and S. O. Jaja, *Margaret Ekpo: Lioness in Nigerian Politics*, Abeokuta: ALF Publications, 1993; and F. K. Ekechi, "Historical Women in the Fight for Liberation," in V. U. James and J. S. Etim eds., *The Feminization of Development Processes in Africa*, Westport, Connecticut: PRAEGER, 1999, 106-110.

49 Graf, *The Nigerian State*, 26.

50 A. H. M. Kirk-Greene, *Crisis and Conflict in Nigeria: A Documentary Source Book, 1966-1967*, Vol. 1, Oxford: Oxford University Press, 1971, 9.

51 P. P. Ekeh, "Citizenship and Political Conflict: A Sociological Interpretation of the Nigerian Crisis," in J. Okpaku ed., *Nigeria: Dilemma of Nationhood*, New York: The Third Press, 1972, 90.

52 B. Dudley, *An Introduction to Nigerian Government and Politics*, Bloomington: Indiana University Press, 1982, 52.

53 Nwaubani, "Constitution-Making and the Nigerian Identity," 93.

54 Ibid., 95-96.

55 Nigeria, *Report of the Commission on Revenue Allocation*, Lagos: Government Printer, 1951.

56 O. Awolowo, *Thoughts on Nigerian Constitution*, Oxford: Oxford University Press, 1966, 12.

57 Cited in J. P. Mackintosh ed., *Nigerian Government and Politics*, London: George Allen and Unwin, 1966, 26.

58 The decision to grant self-government in 1956 to those regions that so desired it, was a compromise between the positions of the delegates from the Western and Eastern regions who wanted self-government for Nigeria in 1956, and that of the delegates from the Northern region who opposed this move. The conflict over the self-government issue was generated by the motion for self-determination for Nigeria in 1956 that was moved in the central legislature, on 31 March 1953, by Anthony Enahoro, an AG member of parliament from the Western region. While the politicians from the East and the West supported the motion, those from the North vehemently opposed it and moved a counter motion that Nigeria should attain self-determination "as soon as practicable." The crisis that resulted from this disagreement led to the threat by the North to secede from the country, and was one of the crises that resulted in the constitutional conferences of 1953 and 1954 aimed at revising the 1951 constitution.

59 Dudley, *An Introduction to Nigerian Government and Politics*, 54.

60 R. T. Suberu, "The Politics of Fiscal Federalism in Nigeria," in W. Reno ed., *Nigeria After Military Rule: Federalism, Resource Allocation, and Ethnic Politics*, PAS Working Papers No. 12, Evanston, IL: Program of African Studies, Northwestern University, 2003, 15.

61 O. Arikpo, *The Development of Modern Nigeria*, Middlesex, England: Penguin Books, 1967, 82.

62 Ekeh, "Citizenship and Political Conflict," 91.

63 For details on developments during this period, see J. I. Dibua, "Nigeria: Conferences, Commissions, Nigerian Constitution: 1956-1960," in K. Shillington ed., *Encyclopedia of African History*, Vol. 2, New York and London: Fitzroy Dearborn, 2005, 1107-1109.

64 For an elaborate discussion of the ethnic minority agitation in Nigeria, see U. Okpu, *Ethnic Minority Problems in Nigerian Politics, 1960-1965*, Uppsala: Acta Universitalis Uppsaliensis, 1977.

65 Nigeria, *Report of the Commission Appointed to Enquire into the Fears of Minorities and the Means of Allaying Them* (Willink Commission), London: HMSO, 1958.

66 It should be noted that the AG's stand on state creation was not really based on progressive and selfless considerations: on the contrary, it was self-serving. In the 1954 federal election, the AG lost to the NCNC in the Western region mainly due to the votes from the minority Benin-Delta province of the region. The leaders of the AG therefore calculated that their support for state creation would increase their party's popularity among the minorities. Similar self-serving interests influenced the positions of the NCNC and NPC. The NCNC's lukewarm support for state creation was because the creation of the Middle Belt state from the North might weaken NPC's stronghold on the region while the NPC adamantly opposed state creation because it might weaken her advantageous position vis-à-vis the other regions.

67 See U. Okpu, "Nigeria's Dilemma: Development or New States," *Africa*, Revista trimestrale di studie documentazione dell' Istituto Italo-Africano, No. 38, 1983, 183-203.

68 Williams, *State and Society in Nigeria*, 76 and 81.

69 Graf, *The Nigerian State*, 27-29.

70 A. T. Balewa, *Nigeria Speaks: Speeches Made Between 1957-1964*, by Sam Epelle, Lagos: University of Lagos Press, 1966, 5, cited in Graf, *The Nigerian State*, 28.

71 P. P. Ekeh, "Colonialism and the Development of Citizenship in Africa: A Study in Ideologies of Legitimation," in O. Otite ed., *Themes in African Social and Political Thought*, Enugu: Fourth Dimension, 1978. 323.
72 O. Aluko, "Politics of Decolonisation in British West Africa 1945-1960," in J. F. A. Ajayi and M. Crowder eds., *History of West Africa*, Vol. 2, London: Longman, 1975, 636.
73 For details, see T. Falola, *Development Planning and Decolonization in Nigeria*, Gainesville: University Press of Florida, 1996.
74 United Kingdom, *Colonial Development Act, 1929*, London: HMSO, 1929.
75 Government of Nigeria, *A Ten-Year Plan of Development and Welfare for Nigeria*, Sessional Paper No. 24, Lagos: Government Printer, 1946.
76 J. M. Lee, *Colonial Development and Good Government: A Study of the Ideas Expressed by the British Official Classes in Planning Decolonization 1939-1964*, Oxford: Oxford University Press, 1967, 125.
77 Government of Nigeria, *Preliminary Statement on Development Planning in Nigeria*, Sessional Paper No. 6, Lagos: Government Printer, 1945, 5.
78 Ibid., 4.
79 Government of Nigeria, *A Ten-Year Plan of Development and Welfare for Nigeria*, 3.
80 For details, see Kilby, *Industrialization in an Open Economy*.
81 G. K. Helleiner, *Peasant Agriculture, Government, and Economic Growth in Nigeria*, Homewood, Illinois: Richard D. Irwin, 1966, 154.
82 Government of Nigeria, *Statement of the Policy Proposed for the Future Marketing of Nigerian Oil, Oil Seeds and Cotton*, Sessional Paper No. 18, Lagos: Government Printer, 1948, 5.
83 See P. T. Bauer, *West African Trade: A Study of Competition, Oligopoly and Monopoly in a Changing Economy*, Cambridge: Cambridge University Press, 1954, 283-299.
84 United Kingdom, *Fifth Report from the Select Committee on Estimates*, (Session 1942-48, Colonial Development, H.C. 181, 1948), viii, xiii, xviii-xix, cited in Lee, *Colonial Development and Good Government*, 85; and Stolper, *Planning Without Facts*, 36-37.
85 Government of Nigeria, *A Revised Plan of Development and Welfare for Nigeria 1951-56*, Sessional Paper No. 6, Lagos: Government Printer, 1951, 5.
86 Ibid., 4.
87 International Bank for Reconstruction and Development (IBRD), *The Economic Development of Nigeria*, Lagos: Government Printer, 1954, v.
88 Government of Nigeria, *The Economic Programme of the Government of the Federation of Nigeria, 1955-60*, Sessional Paper No. 2, Lagos: Government Printer, 1956, 3.
89 Falola, *Development Planning and Decolonization in Nigeria*, 140.
90 Government of Nigeria, *Federation of Nigeria: Opportunities for Overseas Investment: Joint Statement by the Federal and Regional Governments of Nigeria*, Lagos: Federal Government Printer, 1956.
91 See for instance, Government of Nigeria, *The Role of the Federal Government in Promoting Industrial Development in Nigeria*, Sessional Paper No. 3, Lagos: Federal Government Printer, 1958.
92 E. O. Akeredolu-Ale, *The Underdevelopment of Indigenous Entrepreneurship in Nigeria*, Ibadan: Ibadan University Press, 1975.
93 Government of Nigeria, *The Economic Programme of the Government of the Federation of Nigeria, 1955-60*, 43.

94 Government of the Western Region of Nigeria, *Western Nigeria Development Plan, 1962-68*, Ibadan: Government Printer, 1962.
95 Falola, *Economic Reforms and Modernization in Nigeria*, 102.
96 Akeredolu-Ale, *The Underdevelopment of Indigenous Entrepreneurship in Nigeria*, 43.
97 Staudt, "Women's Politics," 197.

Chapter 4

Democratic Experiments and Sustainable Democracy

A constant theme in the postcolonial history of Nigeria has been the quest to establish a democratic system that is sustainable and enduring. Since the country attained political independence in 1960, it has had two brief periods of unsuccessful democratic experiments, the First Republic (1960-66) and Second Republic (1979-83), an aborted third democratic experiment in 1993, and in 1999 a civilian administration came to power marking the inauguration of the Fourth Republic. Indeed, for the bulk of the postcolonial period, 1966-79 and 1984-99, Nigeria was under military rule. Most scholars on Nigeria's postcolonial political history have therefore understandably focused their attention on analyzing the nature of the democratic experiments and the reasons why they failed, while some attention have been paid to recommending processes through which an enduring democracy can be instituted in the country.

As is the case with the discussion of other facets of Nigeria's society and economy, the discourse on the democratic experiments has been disproportionately influenced by the modernization paradigm. While virtually all the analysis focus on the intense elite competition for the control of political power and the attendant material benefits, and corruption, as the bane of the democratic experiments, the explanation for these factors have been mainly Weberian and modernist. The few exceptions can be found in the works of those who adopt mainly the political economy, neo-Marxist, class and materialist perspectives.[1] In spite of differences in terminology and the claim to some differences in theoretical constructs, the explanation that most scholars have advanced for the intense competition for political offices and material benefits are primarily based on the Weberian construct of individual and group/collective values. The Weberian explanations include ethnicity, clientelism, patrimonialism and patronage,[2] the theory of the two publics,[3] conglomerate society and systems of reward,[4] and prebendalism.[5]

In adopting the typical Weberian binary division of societies, these analyses identified the existence of two realms in Nigeria: the "moral" private realm and the "amoral" public realm, which is subjected to the irrational practice of exploitation and corruption. Furthermore, it is argued that while moral values apply to the private realm, the amoral values associated with the public realm bred corruption, patrimonialism, clientelism, prebendalism, and in fact, the exploitation of public offices to satisfy private and communal ends. These factors have been used to explain the limitations of Nigeria's democratic experiments with prebendalism assuming an influential position in the analysis from the late 1980s.

This chapter argues that the fundamental factor responsible for the failure of the democratic experiments and the inability to establish sustainable democracy in Nigeria should be located in the modernization paradigm that underlined the liberal democracy model that was transplanted into the country. The intense struggle for the control of state power and the attendant material resources, and corruption, which had severe adverse consequences for the democratic experiments, can be more properly understood if situated within this paradigm of modernity. These factors were symptoms and products of the severe limitations of the paradigm of modernity that underlined the democratic experiments. The Weberian tradition that merely examine these factors as products of the inefficient, irrational and affective proclivities of the Nigerian society and therefore attribute them entirely to internal factors, in line with the paradigm of modernity, does not go deep enough. This pattern of analysis misses the fundamental factor responsible for the failure of democracy in Nigeria.

It should be noted that Western style liberal democracy, a product of the bourgeois triumphalism in the Western countries, is an aspect of the culture of capitalist Western societies and depends on Western institutional norms for its successful functioning. It is fundamentally wrong and in fact amounts to cultural imperialism, to transplant this type of democracy to the Nigerian and other African societies with entirely different cultural, democratic and administrative experiences. It is even worse in the sense that the transplanted Western style liberal democracy is based on the denigration of the indigenous experiences which are regarded as the non ideal type that need to be wiped out. Indeed, the transplanted Western style liberal democracy is portrayed "as being synonymous with civilisation, modernity and development."[6] Thus, a significant reason for the failure of the democratic experiments can be seen in the fundamental contradiction between the transplanted "imperial" liberal democracy and the indigenous culture and social realities.

The First Democratic Experiment, 1960-1966

The intense struggle among Nigerian politicians for control of political power and material resources during the decolonization process was carried into the postcolonial period and, in fact, shaped the nature and character of postcolonial Nigerian politics. Of significance are the accumulationist and authoritarian character of the Nigerian state, which was at the same time expected to play a developmentalist role. Furthermore, under the paradigm of modernity, the weak and fragmented Nigerian bourgeoisie was expected to play the historical role that the Western bourgeois class played, that is, the development of the productive forces and the capitalist transformation of the national economy. The situation was not helped by the neo-colonial system that was installed in Nigeria in 1960, a process that resulted in the Nigerian state serving as the primary instrument for accumulation for both the Nigerian and foreign bourgeoisie. The limitations and contradictions promoted by these factors greatly influenced the nature of the first democratic experiment.

These limitations and contradictions were clearly brought to the forefront by the 1959 independence elections. The campaigns for the elections were conducted mainly on the basis of regionalism and ethnicity, and therefore failed to produce a clear-cut winner at the federal level while the major political parties controlled the governments of the respective regions from which they drew their main support. Given the British type parliamentary system of government that was installed in the country and the provision that the political party with the majority seats in the legislature form the government it was imperative that a coalition government be formed at the federal level. The winner takes all parliamentary system of government and the weak material base of the petty bourgeois politicians who depended on access to state power as a means for controlling state offices and for accumulating wealth, made the stakes higher. This was particularly so since the party that finds itself in opposition would not have access to the resources controlled by the federal government. Furthermore, the departing British colonial administration, which still wanted to use a neocolonial relationship to continue to accumulate part of the resources controlled by the Nigerian state, had a stake in which political party formed the central government. Britain desired a coalition government in which the NPC (which was perceived as the more amenable party) occupied a dominant position: it therefore used subtle threats and manipulations to ensure the attainment of this goal. Indeed, even before the results of the 1959 elections were officially announced, James Robertson, the colonial governor-general of Nigeria, invited the leader of the NPC to form the government.[7] It was this self-serving interest on the part of Britain, rather than Osaghae's suggestion that the fear that the Northern leaders would not agree to independence if they did not control the federal government, or were not part of it,[8] that influenced Robertson's action. Indeed, this was consistent with the way Britain manipulated the decolonization process.

In terms of forming a coalition government, it would have been expected that the NCNC and the AG form such a government based on the similarities of their programs. The initial negotiation between the AG and the NCNC in this regard, did not result in any meaningful agreement not only because of the colonial administration's preference for the NPC, but also because of material considerations on the part of the party leaders. The NCNC eventually formed a coalition government as a junior partner with the NPC with the claim that it was done for national unity because a coalition government between the AG and NCNC would pitch the South against the North and therefore alienate Northern politicians. In reality, the NCNC entered into the coalition not for the stated altruistic reasons, but because such an arrangement afforded them more access to resources and state offices. For instance, they were assured of lucrative contracts, appointments into ministerial and ambassadorial positions, boards of federal parastatals, while people from the Eastern region were assured of senior positions in the civil service and armed forces. Furthermore, Azikiwe, the leader of the NCNC, became the first indigenous governor-general of Nigeria and the first president with the attainment of a republican status in 1963. The self-serving considerations behind the coalition agreement on the part of the NCNC, was clearly revealed when Azikiwe in reply to critics of the coalition government stated that "his personal 'future' had been well guaranteed in the bargaining leading up to the alliance."[9]

On its part, the NPC preferred an alliance with the NCNC as opposed to the AG, because of the perceived anti-Northern policies of the AG and the NPC's resentment of the AG's campaign stance on the creation of more states. This would have entailed the creation of the Middle Belt state from the Northern region, the Mid-West state from the Western region and the Calabar-Ogoja-Rivers state from the Eastern region, a situation that the NPC considered an anathema. At the superficial level, it could be argued that states creation would not affect the existing balance of power since states would be created from each of the three regions. However, the impact of such an exercise on the Northern region would have been more adverse since the loss of the votes of the ethnic minority middle belt people would mean the loss of the only advantage the North had over the other regions, i.e., political power. It should be noted that the AG's position on the creation of more states was not really based on "progressive" and altruistic reasons; rather, it was self-serving and opportunistic. Having failed to transcend its regional base by transforming itself into a national party, the AG's only hope of capturing power at the center was in championing the creation of more states, which would make the party appeal more to the minority ethnic groups in the other regions.

In any case, right from the beginning, the NPC/NCNC alliance was laden with tension and crisis. The transplanted Westminster system of government with its provision for dual headship of the executive branch in which only the prime minister had real executive powers while the governor-general (president after 1963) had only ceremonial powers, was out of tune with Nigeria's historical and social realities. This arrangement created tensions between the president and the prime minister. The same thing applied to the designation of a political party, the AG, as an opposition party, a role that was not really tolerated by the coalition partners. Furthermore, while the NPC and the NCNC formed a coalition government at the federal level, they did not collaborate at the regional level as each party held sway over their respective regional governments (NPC in the North and NCNC in the East). In addition, politicians from the other regions who were looking for ways to reverse this structural imbalance despised the structure of the federation, which guaranteed political power to the Northern region. In fact, in the midst of the tension between the alliance partners, the main reason that ensured the survival of the coalition government for a while was their shared antipathy toward their common rival, the AG.

The decision by the coalition partners to undermine the AG paradoxically set in motion events that eventually resulted in the collapse of the First Republic. In the quest to undermine the AG, the coalition government tampered with what had been a sort of a tacit agreement between Nigerian politicians since the era of decolonization, that is, the control of the government of each region by the dominant ethnic group in the region. The attempt to wrest the control of the Western region from the AG created two levels of crises in the country: within the Western region on the one hand, and between the coalition partners on the other hand. The opportunity to undermine the AG in the Western region was provided by the crisis within the party in 1962, which pitched S. Ladoke Akintola, the premier of the Western region and deputy leader of the party against Awolowo, the leader of the party and of opposition in the federal House of Representatives. J. O. Akintunde has pointed out that a major reason for the disagreement between Akintola and Awolowo was the struggle over the control of the vital sources of patronage and influence in the Western region.[10] A significant source of disagreement was the attitude to adopt toward the federal government: contrary to Awolowo's position, Akintola and some of his supporters wanted the AG to drop its opposition role and join the federal coalition as a means of granting the Yoruba elite access to federal patronage. Furthermore, Akintola disagreed with Awolowo's ideology of democratic socialism and the attempt by Awolowo to transform the party into a nationalist-democratic socialist party. The ideological split within the party came into the open at the party's 1962 congress in Jos, finally culminating in the attempt to remove Akintola from power in May 1962, which precipitated a parliamentary crisis that degenerated into violence. The federal government used this crisis as a pretext to undermine the AG by declaring a state of emergency in the Western region, suspending the AG-led regional government, and then appointing M. A. Majekodunmi as the region's administrator with considerable powers.

The coalition partners proceeded to eliminate their common enemy, Awolowo, with the setting up of the Coker Commission to probe the financial activities of public corporations in the Western region. The Commission found Awolowo guilty of gross financial misappropriation and of diverting funds from government-owned corporations to finance political activities and publish newspapers that supported the AG. At the same time that the Commission was indicting him, Awolowo and some of his close associates were tried for treason, for which they were found guilty, convicted and imprisoned.[11] The federal government created the Mid-Western region out of the Western region in 1963 as a way of further marginalizing the AG. This was in spite of the fact that the Western region was the smallest of the three regions. Yet the coalition partners disregarded the vociferous agitation of the ethnic minority groups in their respective regions: for the creation of the Middle Belt state from the North and the Calabar-Ogoja-Rivers state from the East.

The undermining of the AG government in the Western region and the creation of a new state out of the region, tended to upset the existing balance of power, a situation that made many Yoruba elites to feel cheated and therefore hostile toward the federal government. However, a more significant and perhaps unintended effect of this development was the hostility that emerged between the coalition partners. The NCNC had hoped that the weakening of the AG's hold on the Western region and the creation of the Mid-Western region would increase its influence in both regions thereby placing it in a favorable position to challenge the dominance of the NPC in Nigeria's politics. At the initial stage, it would appear as if the calculations of the NCNC were achieved because when Akintola was reinstated in power under the banner of the United People's Party (UPP), it formed a coalition government with the Western regional NCNC. At the same time, the newly created Mid-Western region fell under the control of the NCNC. The NPC, which was alarmed at the increasing influence of its coalition partner, decided to checkmate it. It encouraged Akintola to dissolve the UPP-NCNC coalition government, which was replaced with people drawn from a newly created political party, the Nigerian National Democratic Party (NNDP). In addition, the NCNC government in the Mid-Western region was favorably disposed to the NPC because it was not prepared to offend the dominant coalition partner.

The NCNC leadership was not happy with the fact that the developments in the Western region further strengthened the position of the NPC. In addition, the NCNC resented the fact that the NPC used its dominant position in the coalition government to allocate resources in favor of the Northern region: the rising share of oil (which came mainly from the Eastern region), in the federal revenue, heightened this resentment.[12] The NCNC and the governments of the southern regions saw in the 1962 census an opportunity to reduce the dominant position of the North, which was based on its perceived huge population. There was therefore a sharp increase in the population figures of the Eastern and Western regions which increased by 71 and 70 percent respectively, over the figures of the 1952-3 census while that of the Northern region increased by, a comparatively, moderate 30 percent during the same period. The NPC rejected these figures and a crisis almost developed. However, an open crisis was avoided with the conduct of another census in 1963, in which all the regions inflated their figures to retain the political status quo.[13] A significant factor that heightened the census controversy can be located in the emphasis on one-man-one-vote of the transplanted liberal democratic Westminster system of government, where the political party with the majority seats in the parliament controls the executive arm of government and therefore the resources controlled by the state. In a peripheral capitalist society like Nigeria's, where the state is the most important source of surplus accumulation and patronage, exercises such as census assumed greater political significance. Nevertheless, the immediate fallout of the census controversy was the heightening of hostilities between the coalition partners and indeed, the collapse of the coalition agreement.

The NCNC saw the 1964 elections as another opportunity to check the rapidly growing influence of the NPC while the latter saw in election an opportunity to further consolidate its hold on the North and extend its sphere of influence to the West and the Mid-West. The stakes were particularly high for the NCNC, which proceeded to enter into alliance with the weakened AG, the Northern Elements Progressive Union (NEPU), the United Middle Belt Congress (UMBC), the Kano People's Party (KPP) and the Zamfara Commoners' Party (ZCP), to form the United Progressive Grand Alliance (UPGA). On its part, the NPC entered into alliance with the NNDP, the Mid-West Democratic Front (MDF), the Niger Delta Congress (NDC) and the Dynamic Party (DP), to form the Nigerian National Alliance (NNA). The 1964 elections were contested under the auspices of these two grand alliances. At the superficial level, it might be argued that the formation of these alliances represented an attempt at transcending parochial ethnic interests; however, subsequent developments did not justify this optimism.

Given the high stakes involved in the elections, the electioneering campaigns were conflict-ridden. There were claims and counter claims of administrative coercion, intimidation, harassment and the use of thugs all over the country, while UPGA alleged that in the North, electoral officers refused to accept nomination papers from their candidates. In the circumstance, the UPGA declared a boycott of the elections, which was completely successful in the East, partially successful in the West and the Mid-West, and not successful in the North. Expectedly, the outcome of the elections considerably favored the NNA, but as Dudley has stated, "to say that the elections were contested is perhaps a misdirection of facts."[14] UPGA refused to accept the outcome of the elections. However, based on the results of the elections, Tafawa Balewa called on Azikiwe, the president, to reappoint him as the prime minister. The president who was sympathetic to the position of the UPGA refused to reappoint the prime minister thereby precipitating a constitutional impasse. The impasse was eventually resolved with the intervention of the chief justice of the federation, Adetokunboh Ademola and the chief justice of the Eastern region, Louis Mbanefo who worked out a compromise solution. The solution included the formation of a broad-based government, conduct of elections in areas where there were boycotts, grievances to be resolved through legal means and the setting up of a commission to review the constitution. In March 1965, fresh elections were held in some of the areas where the boycotts took place.

The compromise solution temporarily prevented the nation from being plunged into a cataclysm because a solution that assured sections of the various ethnic and regional elite' access to federal resources and patronage was arrived at. However, this was a short-lived respite. The very high stake Western regional election of October 1965 set in motion events that finally signaled the death knell of the crisis ridden first democratic experiment. The election witnessed large-scale victimization, intimidation and rigging mainly in favor of the NNDP, with the help of the NPC, which was bent on having its ally control the government of the region. The declaration of the NNDP as the victorious party was contested by the AG, which claimed that it actually won the election. The majority of the people rejected the so-called electoral victory of the NNDP and resorted to massive looting, arson, and destruction of lives and property. There was a complete breakdown of law and order making this an appropriate time to declare a state of emergency. Balewa refused to declare a state of emergency, stubbornly retaining Akintola in power while trying to use force to suppress the popular uprising in the region. While the West was in a state of total chaos and anarchy, the Balewa government was busy hosting the Commonwealth leaders' conference in Lagos. It was during this time that the military struck on 15 January 1966, ending the First Republic.

There is no doubt that the competition for the control of state power and therefore the resources associated with such control greatly contributed to the various crises that bedeviled the first democratic experiment in Nigeria. However, a significant shortcoming in the analyses of the intense competition and the phenomena of ethnicity and regionalism associated with them is the tendency to treat the factors as ends in themselves and as entirely internal problems associated with the irrationalities and affective politics of the Nigerian elites. Such analyses assume the form of blaming Nigerian politicians for their inability to practice the benevolent, civilized, rational and ideal type liberal democratic tradition handed over to them by the departing colonial administration. This Weberian and modernist viewpoint fails to get to the root of the matter. The British parliamentary system of government was an alien system that was transplanted into the country and depended on alien cultural, institutional and material practices to operate successfully. The supposed universality of such an alien democratic system of government is a myth. As a middle class system of government that grew out of Western bourgeois hegemony, it was at variance, and in fact, contradictory with Nigeria's cultural and social realities while the weak Nigerian bourgeois class lacked the strong material base of the Western bourgeoisie. Competition among the Nigerian elites can thus be seen as a pathetic case of "embourgeoisment" and, therefore, as symptoms and bye products of the transplanted, imperial liberal democracy.

In line with the patriarchal policies promoted by the colonial administration, the politics of the First Republic was male-dominated. Only one woman, Wuraola Esan was nominated from the Western region into the 36-member senate in 1960 while a second woman, Benice Kerry was nominated from the newly created Mid-Western region in 1964. No woman was elected into the 312-member House of Representatives while three women, Margaret Ekpo, Janet Mokelu and Mrs. Young (through a bye-election in 1963) were elected into the Eastern region's house of assembly.[15] There was no woman in the federal cabinet and no woman held a major office in the dominant political parties.

In any case, the first phase of military rule in Nigeria lasted from 1966 to 1979 during which time there were three military regimes. The regimes are, the short-lived Johnson Aguiyi-Ironsi regime, January 1966-July 1966; the Yakubu Gowon regime, 1966-1975 (during which period Nigeria fought a civil war, 1967-70); and the Murtala Mohammed/Olusegun Obasanjo regime, 1975-1979). The respective military regimes portrayed themselves as 'corrective' regimes that would hand-over power to civilians after restoring order to the polity.[16] However, only the Mohammed/Obasanjo regime successfully implemented a transition to civil rule program that resulted in the inauguration of the Second Republic in October 1979.

Mohammed/Obasanjo's Transition to Civil Rule Program, 1975-1979

Gowon's regime was bedeviled with a number of shortcomings, notably ineptitude, mismanagement and corruption, all of which made his administration to be very unpopular with the Nigerian populace. However, the greatest factor that adversely affected his popularity was his decision to renege on the promise he had made in 1970 to hand-over power to a civilian rule in 1976. Because of this promise, Nigerians were prepared to tolerate the acute shortcomings of his regime with the belief that he would quit the scene in 1976. But in his 1 October 1974 Independence Day broadcast to the nation, Gowon stated that the 1976 hand-over date was no longer realistic because of what he termed "a high degree of sectional politicking and intemperate utterances and writings," indicating that Nigerians had not learned any lessons from past events. This announcement brought the popularity of his regime to the lowest ebb and turned out to be the final nail on the coffin of his administration as it became clear that its days were numbered.[17] Most Nigerians who were disenchanted with the corrupt, bankrupt and inept nature of the regime welcomed the bloodless military coup d'etat of 29 July 1975, which ended Gowon's administration.

The new Mohammed/Obasanjo administration sought to distance itself from Gowon's regime by taking concrete steps to address the problems of corruption, ineptitude and indecisiveness that characterized the regime. One such step was the compulsory retirement of Gowon, and the retirement or dismissal of some top armed forces members of Gowon's regime. This was followed by the purging of other members of the armed forces and members of the civil service, considered as "deadwoods," on the bases of corruption, absenteeism, drunkenness and old age: an exercise, which lasted from August to November 1975. Although there were some misgivings over this "great purge," it was popular with many Nigerians as they felt that the exercise would make the civil service more efficient.[18] In addition, the regime decisively addressed some issues over which Gowon had vacillated: it cancelled the controversial 1973 census, set up the Aguda Panel to recommend a new federal capital for Nigeria and embarked on the much needed reorganization and demobilization of the armed forces.

However, it was clear right from the beginning that the credibility and legitimacy of the Mohammed/Obasanjo regime hinged on the initiation of a clear and decisive transition to civil rule program, a factor that greatly contributed to the erosion of the credibility of Gowon's regime. Indeed, right from the inception of the new administration, there had been calls for it to demonstrate its transitional nature by putting in place a credible program of handing over power to civilian rule. For instance, in its editorial of 1 August 1975, the *Nigerian Tribune* attributed the fall of Gowon's regime partly to its failure to hand-over power to civil rule. The editorial stated that "a military regime should be a transitional government and its tenure of office should be short and effective," and that "by their training and temperament, soldiers do not possess the qualities of politicians." It concluded that it is best to leave the act of governance to civilians "who have the necessary training, public confidence, temperament, experience, ability and the stomach for it."[19]

The Mohammed/Obasanjo regime showed its determination to hand-over power to civilians by announcing a five-stage, four-year transition to civilian rule program on 1 October 1975, thereby opting for the constitutional-evolutionary model of military disengagement from politics.[20] The credibility of the transition program was enhanced by the fact that it clearly spelt out specific dates for the completion of each stage of the program. The first stage of the program involved the creation of new states and the drafting of a new constitution to be completed by September 1976. The second stage, which involved local government reforms and the convening of the Constituent Assembly (CA), was to be completed by October 1978. The third stage involving electoral constituency delimitation, lifting of the ban on party politics and abrogation of the state of Emergency Decree was to be completed by October 1978. Both the fourth and fifth stages, which involved the holding of legislative and executive elections at the state and federal levels and the handing over of power to civilians, were to be completed by 1 October 1979. This elaborate process of constitutional engineering was justified based on the need to establish the conditions for an enduring democratic civilian administration.[21] Nevertheless, although the transition program received popular reception all over the country, there was initial skepticism over the regime's commitment to it or whether it was a mere ploy to win legitimacy and acceptance from the populace. However, the strict adherence to the timetable and the fact that the assassination of Mohammed in an unsuccessful coup in February 1976 did not lead to the abandonment or alteration of the transition program by Obasanjo who succeeded him, helped to win some measure of legitimacy for the regime.

In his address at the inauguration of the Constitution Drafting Committee (CDC), on 4 October 1975, Mohammed outlined the guidelines of what should be included in a new constitution as a way of ensuring a stable democracy in the Second Republic. Among other things, the guidelines endorsed the transplantation of the Western style liberal democratic system of government opting for the American-type presidential system of government as opposed to the British

Westminster system that was practiced in the First Republic. Specifically, he urged the CDC to examine ways of discouraging "institutionalised opposition to the government in power," but instead, develop "consensus politics and government." Furthermore, the committee was urged to suggest ways of establishing an executive presidential system of government in which the president and the vice-president would be elected, granted clearly defined powers and brought into office in a manner that reflected the "federal character of the country."[22] In line with Mohammed's guidelines, the CDC produced a draft constitution that recommended the presidential system of government and embodied the main features of the guidelines. However, Dudley who was a member of the CDC has argued that the fact that the draft constitution embodied Mohammed's guidelines does not mean that these guidelines, which were of course given "careful consideration" by the CDC, "dictated the main provisions of the draft." On the contrary, the draft constitution was a product of "a broad coincidence of view" between the military regime and members of the CDC.[23]

The preference for the presidential liberal democratic system of government was predicated on the belief that this would help in overcoming the shortcomings of the British-style Westminster system of government, which was considered inadequate for a federal and multiethnic country like Nigeria. The federal and heterogeneous nature of the United States was seen as similar to that of Nigeria, as a result, its system of government was regarded as more capable of promoting unity and democratic stability in the country. Indeed, given the increasing hegemony of American social science paradigms and the attendant spread of American-type high modernist models among Nigerian social scientists, many of them came to view Nigerian reality from the perspective of these high modernist models. They therefore viewed the replication of American political institutions as the panacea for the political instability in the country.[24] The Mohammed/Obasanjo regime, as was the case with other military regimes in Nigeria, relied heavily on Nigerian academics (mainly social scientists) and top bureaucrats for advice and for policy formulation. It is therefore possible as has been suggested by Osaghae, that Mohammed's inaugural address to the CDC could have been written by a Nigerian social scientist. This, he opines, could have been responsible for what Dudley described as the coincidence of view between Mohammed and members of the CDC.[25]

The composition of the all-male fifty-member CDC reflected the patriarchal orientation of the military regime. It also reflected the belief of the military administration and its advisers that a democratic republic predicated on capitalist accumulators, as was the case in the Western capitalist countries, was better placed to succeed. Thus, the 50 members of the CDC, who were handpicked by the military authorities (with at least two members from each state of the federation), were drawn from the domestic bourgeois class. However, given the influential position occupied by members of the bureaucratic bourgeoisie (intellectuals, members of the professions and top civil servants) under the military administration, they expectedly constituted the bulk of the membership of the CDC. In fact, the bureaucratic bourgeoisie constituted 80 percent of the members while the remaining 20 percent were drawn from the business-commercial bourgeoisie (businessmen, contractors, ex-politicians, etc).

On the other hand, members of the CA, who deliberated on the draft constitution prepared by the CDC, were elected indirectly through their local government councils. This indirect method of election favored members of the propertied class and former politicians who had the necessary resources to conduct campaigns hence the CA was dominated by members of the business-commercial bourgeoisie who constituted about 75 percent of the membership.[26] Twenty members of the CA were nominated by the federal military administration to represent special interests such as students and labor while the chairmen of the various CDC sub-committees were co-opted. No woman was elected into the 250-member CA. However, in response to the criticisms from women's groups and other sections of the society over the non-inclusion of women in the CDC, the military administration appointed five women to the CA. These women were largely responsible for the insertion of a clause in the constitution that made sex-based discrimination illegal. This clause automatically extended the right to vote to every woman in Northern Nigeria for the first time, in 1978.[27]

A few controversial issues such as the establishment of a federal *Sharia* court of appeal, rotational presidency and creation of states generated heated debates in the CA, with the *Sharia* issue almost paralyzing the work of the Assembly. However, the CA essentially agreed with the main provisions of the CDC's draft constitution. In fact, many members of the CA were more preoccupied with forging political alliances with a view to turning them into political parties once the military regime lifts the ban on politics. Given the composition of the CDC and CA, the 1979 constitution could be regarded as a product of a consensus between the bureaucratic bourgeoisie and the business-commercial bourgeoisie. It was therefore a constitution drawn up by the bourgeoisie for the bourgeoisie. According to Dudley, if "the CDC and the CA could be said to be representative of any group at all," that group would be the Nigerian bourgeoisie – the bureaucratic bourgeoisie in the case of the CDC, and the business-commercial bourgeoisie in the case of the CA.[28] With the modernist model that underlined the constitution making process, the military regime was not prepared to entertain any viewpoint that challenged the preferred American style liberal democratic system of government. Hence, the CA did not discuss a widely circulated minority report, prepared by two dissenting members of the CDC, Yusuf Bala Usman and Segun Osoba recommending a socialist constitution for Nigeria.[29]

The institutional structure of the Second Republic as designed by the 1979 constitution, was therefore biased in favor of the Nigerian elite, and thus against the interests of the overwhelming majority of the masses of the people such as workers, peasants, market women, students and the unemployed. The obsession with the American-style presidential system of government predicated on a strong capitalist class, the insistence on political parties with national spread and nation-wide presidential elections (to foster national unity), resulted in the adoption of policies that practically disenfranchised the subordinate classes from active participation in the political process. For instance, it was provided that before political parties could be registered to contest elections, they must be 'broad based' in the form of having functioning, well staffed and furnished offices in at least thirteen states of the federation. In addition, before contesting an election, a worker must resign his/her job while some election deposits were to be paid. The decision to make the political parties broad based and national probably aimed at avoiding the kind of ethnic and regional parties that fostered ethnicity and regionalism in the First Republic. Nevertheless, the effects of these policies, was the effective disenfranchisement of the subordinate classes. Ake noted that the 1979 constitution effectively disenfranchised the subordinate classes, discouraging the political involvement of organized labor, and including conditions, which ensured that only the wealthy or their surrogates could form political parties and contest elections.[30] Indeed, the only concession made to the masses of the people was the periodic ritual of voting.

Given the elite-biased nature of the constitution, it is not surprising that the five political parties that were approved by the Federal Electoral Commission (FEDECO) out of the over fifty political associations that applied for registration in 1979, were all led by frontline members of the domestic bourgeoisie. It is equally significant to note that apart from the Unity Party of Nigeria (UPN), led by Obafemi Awolowo who had declined an invitation to serve on the CDC, the other registered political parties had their genesis in the CA. In fact, seven of the nine members who constituted the initial national officers of the National Party of Nigeria (NPN) – excluding the president of the republic and the nine vice-chairmen of the party – were members of the CA. Four of these seven people became federal ministers in the Second Republic, one, the political adviser to the president and the other two became members of the national assembly.[31]

In any case, in an attempt to further promote elite consensus and promote democratic stability in the country, the 1979 constitution entrenched the "federal character" principle. This principle was a compromise between the demand for rotational presidency by mainly Southern delegates to the CA as a way of avoiding the domination of political power by the North and the strenuous opposition to rotational presidency by many Northern delegates. The federal character principle was characterized as "the distinctive desire of the people of Nigeria to promote national unity, foster national loyalty and give every citizen of Nigeria a sense of belonging to the nation." It should be noted that the search for national (elite?) consensus was based on the modernist model of transplanting features of the so-called national consensus of Euro-American nations that were seen as responsible for democratic stability in those countries, into Nigeria. The existence of "national consensus" was regarded as responsible for the effective operation of a government and opposition arrangement in many of these countries.[32] The principle was to be reflected in appointments to the federal executive council and other top government positions, and in the composition of the armed forces, public service, parastatals, and other government agencies. It was expected that the principle would help to "promote national unity," "command national loyalty," and ensure "that there shall be no preponderance of persons from a few states or from a few ethnic or other sectional groups" in government or any of its agencies.[33]

Many scholars have hailed this federal character principle as an important contribution to the search for national consensus and democratic stability in ethnically and religiously divided countries and societies like Nigeria. For instance, Obaro Ikime contended that "in providing for the principle of federal character at the center and making similar provisions at state and local government levels, the constitution clearly hoped to promote the development of a political culture in which every group and everyone would have stake in some commitment to the body politic in return for some lawful expectation from the nation irrespective of who is in power."[34] It should, however, be noted that the federal character principle, which in actuality is more of a power sharing exercise, erroneously equates elite unity with national unity. Furthermore, the principle contradicts the transplanted liberal conception of citizenship as enshrined in the constitution, in that this conception of citizenship emphasizes the primacy of individuality and competition as opposed to consensus, which the federal character sought to promote. The conception of federal character as a power sharing exercise resulted in a situation where members of Nigerian elite manipulated statism, ethnicity and regionalism to justify their competition for offices and the attendant resources controlled by incumbents. As observed by Ladipo Adamolekun, the fundamental contradiction in the 1979 constitution was the juxtaposition of consensual and competitive orientations as norms of political behavior.[35] Given the weak material base of the Nigerian bourgeoisie and the fact that the transplanted presidential variant of the bourgeois-democratic system of government is very expensive, it was inevitable that competition for offices and the attendant resources controlled by incumbents would assume precedence over consensus.

The liberal democratic presidential system of government is very expensive and relies on an advanced capitalist system, which can absorb the huge amount of capital and corruption associated with it, in order for it to operate effectively within the context of the bourgeois-democratic tradition. The neo-colonial intellectual orientation of the mainstream Nigerian social scientists and lawyers, who dominated the constitution-drafting process, imbibed in them the desire to transplant the American presidential model into Nigeria while seeking to create a strong class of indigenous capitalist accumulators who would ensure the success of the transplanted model. This was at variance with the realities of the Nigerian situation, in addition to the acute limitations of the indigenous bourgeois class, factors which as would soon be shown greatly contributed to the intra-elite conflict that eventually spelt the death nail of the Second Republic. The stringent conditions that political associations were required to fulfill before qualifying for registration as political parties and the conduct of nation-wide presidential election, as well as state-wide gubernatorial elections among others, were too expensive and out of tune with Nigeria's realities. More significant is the fact that the American-type presidential system of government breeds a high amount of corruption and abuse of the electoral process as even demonstrated by the United States experience.[36]

The Second Democratic Experiment, 1979-1983

The Second Republic was inaugurated on 1 October 1979, with the swearing in of Shehu Shagari, who won the presidential election on the platform of the NPN. However, Awolowo, the candidate of the UPN, who had the second highest numbers of votes, bitterly contested the swearing in of Shagari as president. He argued that Shagari did not satisfy the constitutional requirement of winning 25 percent of the votes cast in at least two-thirds of the states of the federation. Two-thirds of the states of the federation had generally been regarded as thirteen out of the nineteen states of the federation, a formula, which the federal electoral commission used in determining the national spread of political parties before registering them. Shagari won 25 percent of the votes in twelve states and about 19.4 percent of the votes in the thirteenth state. However, the electoral commission declared him the winner of the presidential election, basing its interpretation on 25 percent of the votes in twelve states and 25 percent of two-thirds of the votes in the thirteenth state, which it stated was the literary interpretation of two-thirds of nineteen. Awolowo's challenge of this interpretation before the election tribunal and the Supreme Court did not succeed as both upheld the declaration of Shagari as the winner of the election, although the Supreme Court stated that its ruling should not be regarded as a legal precedent.[37]

In spite of the elaborate process of constitutional engineering put in place to ensure that the second democratic experiment was more stable and more sustainable than the first one, the Second Republic lasted for only four years, a shorter period than the First Republic.[38] In analyzing the failure of the second democratic experiment, most scholars have adopted the modernist paradigm by focusing entirely on the irrationalism, prebendalism, patronage, corruption, ethnicity and clientelism (as epitomized in the intense and bitter competition for wealth and power), that characterized the Second Republic.[39] There is no doubt that this intense conflict adversely contributed to the collapse of the Second Republic.[40] However, to concentrate on them as ends in themselves, is to miss the more fundamental factor responsible for the collapse of the republic. This modernist approach is equally responsible for Osaghae's observation that although the 1979 constitution could be considered as "perfect," it failed to ensure democratic stability because of the character of the operators of the constitution and how they operated it.[41] Yet the constitution itself, which was based on the presidential variant of the liberal democratic tradition that was at variance with the country's cultural, social and political realities, was fundamentally responsible for the accentuation of the competition and conflicts that characterized the republic.

The highly expensive nature of the presidential system meant that political parties had to raise finance from the indigenous capitalist class and from interest groups that supported the policies of the respective political parties. However, the majority of the Nigerian bourgeoisie were materially weak while there was lack of well-established and financially endowed interest and advocacy groups to make financial contributions to the political parties. In the circumstance, Nigerian politicians intensified their use of state offices as sources for surplus accumulation, a factor that aggravated the bitter competition among them for political power. As Ake noted, Nigerian politicians resorted to "the use of legal and physical coercion to accumulate surplus and to institutionalize capitalism."[42] This situation accounted for the high incidence of inter- and intra-party conflicts during Nigeria's Second Republic.

Ake's incisive analysis of the composition of the five political parties has demonstrated that majority of their membership were from the "lower bourgeoisie" or petty bourgeois class and therefore more concerned with the use of access to state offices to accumulate surplus. The preoccupation of this class with using state offices for capital accumulation was reinforced by their realization that it was the huge amount of capital at the disposal of the powerful members of the business-commercial bourgeoisie that gave them advantageous and dominant positions in the formation of political parties. Ake notes that the core leadership of the UPN, were strong members of the business-commercial bourgeoisie who had a fairly well established base in commerce and industry while the leader and founder of the Great Nigerian People's Party (GNPP), Ibrahim Waziri, was a strong member of the business-commercial bourgeoisie. The ascendant leadership faction of the NPN was composed of feudal elements and members of the business-commercial bourgeoisie. On the other hand, the leadership and membership of the Nigerian People's Party (NPP) and the People's Redemption Party (PRP), were mainly from the lower or petty bourgeoisie (the PRP however, contained a significant group of young socialist-oriented radicals). Furthermore, a great segment of the business-commercial and the petty bourgeoisie were strongly disposed toward unproductive capitalism as they thrived on commerce, contracts and political access. For these people, capital came, "less from productive activity than the manipulation of social status and political power."[43]

On the other hand, there was a small faction of capitalist producers from mainly the ranks of the intelligentsia and bureaucratic bourgeoisie who were more disposed to what can be described as the development of productive capitalism. However, the unproductive capitalist faction of the domestic bourgeoisie gained ascendancy in the Second Republic, though there were some form of regular struggles going on between them and the capitalist producers throughout the duration of the republic.[44] Indeed, the NPN, the dominant political party in the

Second Republic, presents a typical example of this factional struggle with the nomination of Shagari as the party's presidential candidate marking the ascendancy of the feudal and business-commercial bourgeoisie faction of the party. The ascendancy of this faction was further reinforced with the gaining of more party offices as well as more gubernatorial and senatorial nominations.

The factional conflict among the Nigerian bourgeoisie and their desire to have access to state-controlled material resources were constant sources of conflict in the Second Republic. The issue of entering into an alliance with the NPN whose candidate won the 1979 presidential election and secured more seats in the national assembly, became a constant source of dissension and dispute within the other political parties. Although the NPN won more seats, it did not secure the required majority to ensure the passage and ratification of presidential bills and appointments in the national assembly. The party therefore needed a working majority in the national assembly particularly in the face of the strong challenge that the UPN mounted against the outcome of the presidential election and the determination of the UPN to frustrate bills and appointments sent to the assembly by the president. The NPP, which was predominantly composed of the petty bourgeoisie, readily reached an accord with the NPN after agreement on how to share offices, which resulted in the appointment of members of the NPP as federal ministers and to positions in federal government's corporations and parastatals. Significantly, the GNPP and PRP, with predominantly petty bourgeois membership, experienced serious dissension and crises over forming an accord with the NPN as a means of benefiting from federal patronage with the disagreements resulting in a split in both parties.[45] Even the opposition UPN was not immune from this dissension as a few prominent members of the party defected to the NPN, but the organizational efficiency of the party, its reputed strong discipline and the strong loyalty of many of its members to Awolowo, minimized dissension within the party.

In spite of the accord between the NPN and the NPP, many NPP members felt that they were not receiving enough federal patronage. They accused the NPN of discriminating against them in the award of contracts, import licenses and the distribution of offices, while the NPN accused the NPP of ingratitude, deceit, greed and blackmail. In July 1981, the NPP, in line with the terms of the accord served a six months notice to the NPN about its intention to terminate the accord but to their chagrin, the NPN chairman, A. M. A. Akinloye, waived the notice and terminated the accord with immediate effect. Given the petty bourgeois make up of the NPP, the six-month notice was only intended to be a bluff with the hope that the period would be used to secure more benefits from the NPN. As stated by Azikiwe, the presidential candidate of the NPP in the 1979 election, the notice was intended to serve as a cooling off period of fence mending during which the NPP was prepared to conduct a "conditional negotiated settlement" with the NPN.[46] However, the NPN could easily call off the NPP's bluff because it had succeeded in using the accord to consolidate its position and had been able to enter into working agreements with members of the breakaway factions of the GNPP and the PRP in the national assembly. Even then, when the accord came to an end some top NPP members including serving ministers disagreed with the leadership of their party and subsequently formed a break away faction of the party. The petty bourgeois nature of NPP's leadership and membership was clearly demonstrated by Ishaya Audu's (the vice-presidential candidate of the NPP in the 1979 election and appointed minister for external affairs under the accord), failure to resign his position with the termination of the accord. He stated that it would be suicidal for him to do so since he had no other job to fall back to.

Within the NPN, the ascendant feudal and business-commercial bourgeois faction engaged in internal struggles over sources of primitive accumulation, such as the award of contracts and the issuing of import licenses. The struggle over the award of contracts resulted in division and even intra-ethnic conflict within the party. For instance, a group of Yoruba politicians within the party opposed the re-election of Akinloye, a fellow Yoruba, as the chairman of the party because they felt that he did not use his position to influence the award of lucrative contracts to them. This prompted Akinloye to publish a list of multi-million naira contracts awarded to those Yoruba politicians who were seeking to dethrone him for "relegating Yorubas to the background." In addition, it is probable that the resentment of this group had its foundation in the 1981 cabinet reshuffle in which Yoruba ministers were dropped from what were regarded as lucrative ministries. Furthermore, politicians from non Hausa-Fulani ethnic group (the dominant ethnic group in the NPN), felt that the interpretation and implementation of the federal character principle discriminated against their ethnic groups in appointments into federal offices.

Nevertheless, the desire to satisfy the material interests of the dominant business-commercial bourgeoisie resulted in the massive award of contracts to members of this class. The two core programs of the NPN federal government, the "Green Revolution" and the housing policy, became veritable gold mines for the business-commercial bourgeoisie as they were awarded highly inflated and dubious contracts many of which were not executed.[47] The intensification of the unproductive primitive accumulation had by 1982, plunged Nigeria into serious economic crisis, which in turn resulted in a factional struggle within the Nigerian bourgeoisie that pitched the business-commercial faction against the capitalist producers' faction. The capitalist producers, many of whom were retired military generals and top civil servants, and were mainly large-scale capitalist farmers, called for the introduction of austerity measures and the ban on the importation of certain items as a way of solving the economic crisis. The business-commercial bourgeoisie disagreed with these recommendations but instead recommended that Nigeria should renounce its membership of the Organization of Petroleum Exporting Countries (OPEC), so that the country would be able to increase its oil exports.[48] The increasing economic crisis and the resultant increasing delegitimization of the NPN government made it resort to the use of coercion as a means of retaining itself in power.

In addition, other forms of crises notably religious conflict between Christians and Muslims in the Northern parts of the country, threatened the political stability of the Second Republic. The most notable of the religious conflicts was the Maitatsine riots, which started in Kano in 1980 and had by 1982 spread to other Northern states like Kaduna, Gongola and Borno.[49] Furthermore, there were various forms of disputes between the federal government and the states, particularly non-NPN controlled states over issues such as revenue allocation and the appointment of Presidential Liaison Officers (PLO) by the federal government to the states without consulting the state governments. Many state governors felt that the PLO did not only form parallel governmental organizations, but were there as spies of the federal government, and in the case of the non-NPN controlled states, were there to undermine the activities of the state governments.

In any case, by the time the 1983 elections took place, the country was bedeviled by various crises while the economic crisis had become worse. At the same time, the national assembly had become ineffective in checking the powers of the federal government because most federal legislators from the NPP, PRP and GNPP favored collaboration with the federal government as a means of benefiting from federal patronage. They therefore formed splinter groups from their respective political parties.[50] In the face of the emasculation of the national assembly, the governors from the twelve non-NPN controlled states became the vanguard of the opposition. They held regular meetings to fashion out their strategies. Unlike the federal legislators, the state governors were largely able to maintain their stand against forming accord with the NPN federal government because as chief executive of their respective states, they had access to state resources and therefore did not need federal patronage as much as the legislators. It was under the auspices of the governors meetings that the UPN and the non-legislators led factions of the NPP, PRP and GNPP came together to form the Progressive People's Alliance (PPA) in March 1982 with the aim of providing a formidable challenge to the NPN in the 1983 elections. Given the high stakes that were involved in the elections, the increasing delegitimization of the NPN federal government, and yet, the determination of the NPN to hold on to power, various acts of manipulation and intimidation particularly on the part of the NPN were put in place. The NPN so massively rigged and manipulated the results of the elections at both the federal and state levels that the outcome can more properly be described as an "electoral coup." In frustration, sections of the Nigerian populace particularly in Ondo and Oyo states (two UPN strongholds whose gubernatorial elections were declared as having been won by the NPN candidates), resorted to massive acts of arson and rebellion resulting in the loss of hundreds of lives and destruction of properties.

With the failure of the other political parties to accept the results of the massively rigged elections and therefore accept Shagari as validly reelected for a second term as president, and the apparent chaos and anarchy in various parts of the country, Nigeria was in a virtual standstill. There was also the likelihood that the festering situation would plunge the country into further anarchy. It was in this context that a group of retired military officers (from the faction of the capitalist producers) colluded with some serving military officers to end the Second Republic in a military coup on 31 December 1983. The coup, which brought Muhammadu Buhari to power, was presented as a form of messianic mission that was undertaken to save the country from self-destruction. However, in carrying out the coup, the military sided with the faction of the Nigerian bourgeoisie that sought to promote capitalist production. Thus, the collapse of the Second Republic was principally a form of realignment of the power structure within the Nigerian bourgeoisie in favor of the capitalist producers.

As was the case in the First Republic, the politics of the Second Republic was male-dominated. Although it might be said that women made a few gains in terms of elections into the federal and state legislatures, and ministerial and commissionership appointments at the federal and state levels, the gains were largely inconsequential and mainly restricted to a few elite women. In the 1979 elections, only three women were elected into the 450-member federal House of Representatives while no woman was elected into the senate. Only five women won elections into the houses of assemblies of the nineteen states. One woman, Franca Afegbua was elected into the senate in the 1983 elections, thus becoming the first woman to win a senatorial election in Nigeria. Three women, Ebun Oyagbola, Janet Akinrinade and Simi Johnson, were appointed as ministers at the federal level while many states appointed mainly one female commissioner. Women were largely not represented in the executive committees of the five political parties. Thus, the patriarchal orientation, which the Nigerian state inherited from the colonial period, was retained.

Nevertheless, as already noted the politics of the Second Republic was bedeviled with a great deal of corruption and intra-bourgeois struggle for access to state offices and the resources controlled by the state. There was therefore a great amount of primitive and unproductive accumulation. In analyzing these issues, most social scientists, operating from the modernist perspective have tended to portray them as emanating from factors internal to Nigerian politics and, indeed, as products of irrationalities in Nigeria's politics and governmental policies. As previously pointed out, various fancy terms and phrases such as patrimonialism, clientelism, politics of affection and prebendalism have been used to describe these phenomena. Underlying this modernist analysis is the notion of benevolence or even a reincarnation of the notion of "civilizing mission," which suggests that the internal irrationalities of the Nigerian polity made the operation of the transplanted "benevolent" and "civilized" American style presidential liberal democratic form of government difficult to operate. Yet the high level of corruption is a product of factors endemic in the transplanted presidential system of government.

The presidential system of government which emphasizes nation-wide political parties, nation-wide and state-wide elections into specific offices and the associated amount of electioneering campaigns, is very expensive and, therefore, promotes a great amount of corruption in raising funds to meet these goals. In the United States, political parties and individuals seeking elective offices raise funds through various measures, such as, donations by individuals, interest and advocacy groups. Special interest groups, who donate funds to individual politicians and the political parties that champion their causes, are usually euphemistically referred to as lobbyists. However, as demonstrated by the debates over the McCain-Feingold campaign finance reform bill the term lobbyist has been used to mask the immense corruption associated with this process in that most special interest groups are actually engaged in "bribing" politicians or their campaign organizations, to ensure the formulation of policies that favor their position. This amounts to buying influence and access. As American electioneering campaigns became more expensive and capital-intensive, politicians and political parties devised various unorthodox and corrupt ways of raising funds in a bid to out do each other. Indeed, the level of corruption associated with the process was such that after years of resistance, the US congress eventually passed a rather watered down version of the campaign finance reform bill, which was signed into law by the US president on 27 March 2002. Even the passing of the bill did not reduce the huge amount of money associated with American campaigns and the corrupt politics of special interest groups, who were still able to use their contributions to politicians' campaign funds to "buy" or gain influence and access. Indeed, American politicians devised various ways of circumventing the campaign finance law resulting, for instance, in the raising of much more money by the respective presidential candidates and their political parties in the 2004 elections than in the previous elections.[51] However, because of the advanced nature of the American capitalist system, the country has been able to absorb the huge capital and corruption involved in the operation of the presidential system without been plunged into debilitating economic crisis.

In a peripheral capitalist country like Nigeria, there are dearth of wealthy individuals, special interest and advocacy groups that can make substantial contributions to the campaign funds of politicians and political parties. In the circumstance, Nigerian politicians relied on the use of state offices to enrich themselves. This high level of corruption and its role in the collapse of the Second Republic has justifiably received great attention from scholars but operating from the modernist perspective, most scholars locate this phenomenon in the so-called internal irrationalities and affective politics that characterized Nigeria's politics and society. They placed the blame entirely on the political actors while ignoring the structures that fostered the so-called irrational acts. This kind of analysis ignores the fact that this pattern of corruption is largely inherent in the transplanted presidential system of government nor are the similar corrupt practices associated with the operation of the presidential system of government in the United States pointed out. To take the theory of prebendalism for instance, which has become rather influential in the analysis of Nigeria's politics by social scientists, the so-called prebendalistic qualities of Nigerian politics are present in the United States politics. This is clearly illustrated by the immense influence of special interest groups and "pork-barrel" projects in the United States politics.[52]

Joseph states that part of the legitimization of prebendal politics in Nigeria is that "an individual's *sectional support group* should obtain tangible benefits from the former's exploitation of his or her public office. (My emphasis)"[53] Furthermore, *an individual's exploitation of public offices does not just represent an act of individual ambition but concurrently represents the satisfaction of the interests of a subset of the general population* (my emphasis). The $275 billion transportation bill that was overwhelmingly passed by the United States House of Representatives in April 2004 clearly illustrates the prevalence of the so-called phenomenon of prebendalism in United States politics. The following extract from Dan Morgan's article in the *Washington Post* succinctly demonstrates the extent to which this bill was laden with selfish and sectional interests:

> ...the bill became a magnet for scores of parochial pork-barrel projects requested by lawmakers as the measure worked its way through the House. Republicans and Democrats divvied up an $11 billion pot of these 'high priority' projects, *with the majority going to senior members, committee chairmen and lawmakers serving on the Transportation Committee.* Such far-flung locations as Pago Pago, American Samoa islands, and North Pole, Alaska, were singled out for projects. *The bill channels $16 million to 'pedestrian walkway improvements' in Houston, hometown of House Majority Leader Tom DeLay (R-Tex).* (My emphasis)[54]

Perhaps the degree of corruption and 'prebendalism' associated with the highway bill was more clearly demonstrated by the $2.2 billion (two of the costliest of the highway projects in the bill) but economically irrelevant bridges that were approved for Alaska which have been described as "bridges to nowhere." Don Young, who represents Alaska in the House of Representatives, used his position as the chairman of the House's Transportation and Infrastructure Committee to ensure that the bridge projects were approved. An excerpt from Timothy Egan's article in *The New York Times* illustrates the "prebendal" practice in the United States polity:

> 'I'd like to be a little oinker, myself,' Mr. Young told a Republican lunch crowd here, taking mock offense at the suggestion that Ted Stevens, the Alaska Republican who is chairman of the Senate Appropriations Committee, directs more pork to their state than he does. 'If he's the chief porker, I'm upset.'
>
> When asked why a town with one main road, a dwindling population and virtually nowhere to drive to needs a bridge to rival the world's great spans, people here inevitably respond with two words: Don Young. *Mr. Young, mindful that the highway bill comes up for renewal only once every six years or so, and that the House Republican Conference imposes three-term limits on committee chairmanships, says the*

> *opportunity to pour so many federal dollars into his home state comes once in a lifetime, and should be seized* (my emphasis).
>
> 'If you don't do it now, when are you going to do it?' he said at the luncheon. 'This is the time to take advantage of the position I'm in, along with Senator Stevens.'
>
> ...'If I had not done fairly well for our state,' he said, 'I'd be ashamed of myself.'[55]

This excerpt is not fundamentally different from Joseph's "universe of understanding" which he claims sustains prebendal attitudes to politics in Nigeria.[56] Joseph's justification of this "universe of understanding" which is based on a write up by Haroun Adamu, a Nigerian political scientist and journalist, clearly illustrates this point.

> ...it is strongly believed in this country that if you do not have one of your kind in the local, state and/or national decision-making bodies, nobody would care to table your troubles before the decision makers, much less find solutions to them. Therefore, having someone in one of these bodies makes a community feel a part of the system since that community is vicariously participating in government, be it local, state, or federal.[57]

However, the existence of the so-called prebendalism in United States politics was clearly demonstrated by the fact that the normally contentious Republicans and Democrats came together to overwhelmingly pass the highway bill with a majority votes of 357 to 65. The margin assured them the required number of votes to override a presidential veto. Furthermore, the *New York Times* noted in an editorial, that "the congressional practice of dipping into the public trough to finance projects that benefit only a single legislator (and *his sectional group*) is so firmly established that most people yawn when they see the words 'pork-barrel spending.'" The editorial observed that the energy bill, which was passed by the congress, was equally laden with projects that benefited some special interest groups who were able to use their advantage with the Republican administration to satisfy their selfish interests.[58]

It is clear from the above examples that they fall into what Joseph describes as part of the legitimization of prebendal politics, that is, "an individual's *sectional support group*," obtaining "*tangible benefits from the former's exploitation of his or her public office*." It is true that while Nigerian politicians exploit offices for personal benefits (corruption, embezzlement, etc), they also appropriate offices for the satisfaction of the objectives of a subset (communal groups, ethnic groups, etc) of the general population. In the United States, although the degree of exploitation of offices for personal benefits on the part of politicians is not as high, such practices do exist as demonstrated by the scandals over trips for personal purposes sponsored by lobbyists, payment of family members from politicians' campaign funds, etc. More prevalent is the use of offices by politicians to satisfy the interests of *a subset* of the general population (interest groups who contribute to the campaign funds of politicians, constituencies, etc). These practices in the United

States go beyond patronage politics or clientelism: they are *prebendalistic* going by the distinction Joseph made between a patronage system and clientelism on the one hand, and prebendalism on the other hand.[59] They fit into Joseph's claim that a prebendal system is not just one in which offices are exploited for personal benefits but also one in "*which the appropriation of such offices is not just an act of individual greed or ambition but concurrently the satisfaction of the short-term objectives of a subset of the general population.*" The degree of personal corruption is higher in Nigeria and other African countries largely because of the existence of peripheral capitalism in these countries. It should be emphasized that my point here is not to justify any form of corruption whether in Nigeria, the United States or any other country: any form of corruption should be seriously condemned and should attract appropriate penalty/penalties. Rather, (although I do not believe in the analytic value of prebendalism) the aim is to show that features of what is described as prebendalism in Nigeria do also exist in the United States. Furthermore, these features are largely products of the capitalist system and are aggravated in the Nigerian situation by the existence of a peripheral capitalist system. In other words, these features are not just personal they are fundamentally structural.

Nonetheless, given the historical origin, nature and limitations of the Nigerian bourgeoisie, corruption serves as an important means for surplus accumulation for members of this class. The adoption of the extremely expensive presidential system of government in the Second Republic, the requirements and, even, corrupt practices necessitated by the process, intensified the degree of corruption among the Nigerian bourgeoisie. It was mainly through the massive accumulation of wealth through corrupt means that most members of this class hoped to be able to raise enough financial resources needed to meet the stringent and expensive conditions demanded by this system of government. From this perspective, the continuous adherence to the presidential variant of the liberal democratic system of government by subsequent constitutional and democratic experiments partly accounts for the further intensification of the degree of corruption.

Endless Transition to Civil Rule, 1986-1998

The Mohammadu Buhari military regime, which lasted from 1983 to 1985 was more concerned with resolving the country's economic crisis and did not commit itself to any program of transition to civil rule. The regime's belief that the economic crisis was caused mainly by the high level indiscipline and massive corruption in the Nigerian polity made it assume that economic recovery could be brought about through enforced ethical purification and regeneration. As a result, the administration launched an ethical campaign exemplified in the War Against Indiscipline (WAI) program, which sought to stamp out corruption. It equally introduced some austerity measures. The Buhari administration felt that these goals could only be achieved through authoritarian measures, hence it introduced an unprecedented scale of authoritarianism in Nigeria in the form of draconian decrees, brutal repression of any form of dissent and the curtailment of civil liberties. These draconian policies made the regime to be very unpopular, and this, combined with the failure to lay out a concrete plan for a return to civil rule (a measure which other military regimes in Nigeria adopted in order to win legitimacy), alienated most Nigerians.

With the overthrow of the Buhari regime in a military coup in August 1985, Ibrahim Babangida who came to power quickly cashed on the unpopularity of the Buhari administration by making respect for human rights and a promise to return the country to civil rule cardinal aspects of his administration's policies. In January 1986, Babangida took the first step in his program of transition to civil rule by inaugurating the 17-member Political Bureau that included two women.[60] The recommendations of the Bureau were expected to constitute the blueprint for the program of transition to civil rule thereby helping to lay the foundations for the establishment of an enduring democracy and sustainable development in the future Third Republic.[61] Given the enormity of the mandate of the Bureau, it organized wide-ranging consultations and debates in English and indigenous languages (for those people who could not speak English), all over the country among various interest groups, sections and classes of Nigerians. The Bureau submitted its report in March 1987 and the report supposedly constituted the basis of Babangida's transition to civil rule program. However, the transition program was to be eventually so manipulated by Babangida and Sanni Abacha who came to power after overthrowing the interim administration of Ernest Shonekan in 1993, that the country was subjected to endless transition programs.[62]

The Political Bureau's report, which was a thorough and comprehensive analysis of all aspects of Nigerian society, was divided into three parts. The first part blamed the problem of underdevelopment in Nigeria on colonialism and neo-colonialism, which created dependent structures in the country and subjugated Nigeria's economy and politics to the interests of international monopoly capital. The second part of the report dealt extensively with various aspects of the Nigerian society and recommended the establishment of a new political economy encompassing a new social, political and economic order for Nigeria. It recommended the adoption of a socialist ideology that emphasizes self-reliance and social justice, nationalization and socialization of the commanding heights of the economy, discontinuation of privatization, termination of the Structural Adjustment Program, and empowerment of the grassroots through local government reforms, public education and mass mobilization programs, among others. It should be noted that these recommendations, which were based on the wishes of the majority of the people as expressed in the political debates, marked a popular rejection of the policies associated with the modernization paradigm.

A significant aspect of the second part of the report was the attempt for the first time in Nigeria's postcolonial history, to make women and gender issues significant aspects of the "national" agenda by elevating them to a national level in the transition process. As noted by Kole Shettima, "the 'national' agenda has (always) been privileged over gender issues, as if gender issues are not matters of national concern."[63] The Bureau stated that women, as a group, were marginalized in social and public affairs. It attributed the marginalization to a number of factors such as the capitalist relations of production, the impact of colonialism and the prevalence of patriarchal attitudes. Furthermore, since "majority of the women fall within the under-privileged class" they "cannot be heard in the political system."[64] To rectify the situation and make women issues part of the "national" agenda, the Bureau made the following recommendations:

> Full involvement of women in politics is one method of defending and promoting women's interests in society. They can participate fully if they are members of the legislative and executive arms of government. For this reason, we recommend the allocation of 5 per cent of the legislative seats to women in all the three tiers of government. This 5 per cent seats allocated to women is to be filled by nomination through the political parties.

It equally recommended the formulation of a national policy on women and development.[65]

The third part of the report dealt mainly with the program of transition to civil rule. It stated that for the transition to civil rule program to be successful there was the need to democratize all the processes and institutions of government and that the majority of the people should be involved in the process. It called for a broadly spaced transition program in which democratic government can proceed with political learning, institutional adjustment and a re-orientation of political culture at sequential levels of politics and governance, beginning with local government and proceeding to the federal level.

The Babangida administration claimed that its transition program derived from the Bureau's report and therefore aimed at instituting a new political order and sustainable and enduring democracy in the Third Republic as recommended by the Bureau.[66] This claim is not correct and actually amounts to mere opportunism because the administration rejected key recommendations of the report that called for the abandoning of the prevailing modernization paradigm and neocolonial dependency while at the same time trying to use the report to legitimize its transition program. For instance, the government rejected the recommendations on the adoption of socialism claiming that this would amount to imposing an alien ideology on Nigeria: yet this recommendation was based on the wishes expressed by the majority of the people during the political debates.[67] Furthermore, the government rejected the recommendations on nationalization, the termination of privatization and the adjustment programs, arguing that SAP was vital for laying the basis of a self-reliant economy in the country.[68] Having rejected the kernel of the Bureau's report, the Babangida administration went on to institute other transition institutions, which were only relevant and meaningful within the context of the kernel of the report. As aptly noted by A. T. Gana, taken outside the context of the new political economy, "the entire corpus of activities and institutions articulated in the transition programme provide no more than an edifice whose foundations are as fragile as the materials used."[69] Furthermore, even the modest recommendation on the allocation of seats to women in the three tiers of government was rejected. While affirming the administration's belief in the equality of sexes, individuals and groups, it was stated that accepting the recommendation would amount to "reverse discrimination." Indeed, the transition to civil rule program was right from the beginning, fatally flawed.

Nevertheless, Babangida's transition to civil rule program was based on the neo-modernization paradigm promoted by the IFIs and Western creditor nations, which linked political liberalism with the SAP on the basis that the entrenchment of market forces can only succeed if free enterprise economies and liberal democracies are mutually reinforcing. As pointed out in chapter two, this neo-liberal orthodoxy encouraged authoritarian state sponsored democratization and false populist policies, so long as the democratization process ended up consolidating the structural adjustment programs. Two speeches by Babangida clearly illustrate the influence of the neo-liberal's neo-modernization paradigm on the transition program. In a speech delivered on the fifth anniversary of his administration on 27 August 1990, he stated *inter alia*:

> At this stage, it is time to forge ahead with the economic transition programme while taking note of the constraints and problems that hindered the full realisation of our goals in the past. Accordingly, it is imperative for us, in the last phase of our transition programme, to take new initiatives, in effecting such administrative changes as will consolidate the positive results so far achieved and prepare the grounds for the ultimate civilianisation of government and administration.[70]

The linkage between democratization and SAPs was perhaps more clearly demonstrated in Babangida's 1991 budget speech:

> The reform package of this administration is constructed on two pillars. The first is on the economy which some have seen as being concretised in SAP. The second is the political programme which we have articulated in the Transition to Civil Rule Programme. These two elements are mutually reinforcing; and both must be faithfully implemented for us to be able to construct a new social order that is democratic, viable and self-reliant.[71]

In the name of a transition to civil rule program, the Babangida administration set in motion an elaborate process of political engineering that aimed at reinforcing SAP at every stage of the process.[72] This was in spite of the massive opposition to SAP. Indeed, the overriding concern with consolidating the SAP at the end of the transition process,[73] made the regime state that opponents of SAP – dubbed as 'extremists' and 'radicals' – would not be allowed any say or participation in the transition process. Thus, in line with the modernization paradigm, the regime embarked on an authoritarian, carefully teleguided and "test-tube" transition program. The transition, which was expected to commence in the third quarter of 1987, had six schedules (stages) with the inauguration of an elected civilian president in October 1992, marking the final stage of the program.[74]

The first step in the transition program was the setting up of the Constitution Review Committee (CRC) in September 1987. The main task of the 46-member CRC was to review the 1979 constitution, an exercise that it completed in February 1988. In May 1988, the Constituent Assembly was inaugurated to deliberate on the CRC's report and make recommendations to the Armed Forces Ruling Council (AFRC).[75] The Babangida administration made sure that both the CRC and the CA were composed of conservative and pro-SAP individuals: indeed the National Electoral Commission (NEC), which supervised the process of electing individuals into the CA, disqualified known "radicals" and "extremists" from taking part in the election.[76] Furthermore, both the CRC and the CA were precluded from discussing SAP which was regarded as a "no go" area. In his inaugural address to the CA, Babangida made it clear that he would not accept any radical and "extremist" anti-SAP recommendations, stating, "extremism is fatally destabilizing to the political system."[77] Indeed, the extent of the teleguiding of the constitution drafting process was such that even a normally rabidly pro-government newspaper, the *New Nigerian*, on 9 May 1988, decried the "sordidly right wing" character of the CA whose members were "basically conservative in their beliefs."[78] Thus, the 1989 constitution was expectedly a conservative and pro-SAP document. It retained the American type presidential system of government.

An important stage in the transition process was the formation and registration of political parties. The stringent guidelines for the registration of political parties included the presentation of the passport photographs of all registered members and the establishment of well-manned and functioning offices in the federal capital, the capitals of all the states of the federation and in all local government headquarters. Furthermore, each political association was to pay a mandatory fee of 50,000 naira, workers must resign their jobs before belonging to political parties while the jobs of legislators were to be made part-time. These guidelines were such that the subordinate classes were not in the position to form political parties that would be registered. Even members of the domestic bourgeoisie found it difficult to fulfil these requirements. Oyovbaire's and Olagunju's attempt at rationalizing these stringent guidelines through the argument that they were deliberately made tough in order to eliminate frivolous, sectional and undemocratic political associations from the electoral process is not tenable.[79] Rather, this was designed to provide the regime an excuse to tightly control the affairs of the political parties in line with the authoritarian and self-serving nature of the transition process.

It is therefore not surprising that of the thirteen political associations that applied for registration as political parties, only six were deemed to have marginally met the conditions that were laid down by the NEC. Even then, the regime accused the associations of having been hijacked by "money bags." Furthermore, that they were unable to transcend ethnic, geopolitical, religious and class lines, while three of the four leading associations were said to be reincarnations of political parties of the First and Second Republics.[80] As a result, the AFRC did not approve any of the six associations for registration as political parties. The body went ahead to establish two "grassroots" political parties, the National Republican Convention (NRC), which was said to be "a little to the right," and the Social Democratic Party (SDP), which was said to be "a little to the left." The administration claimed that this would reduce the influence of the "money bags" as there would be no party founders and all members of the respective parties would be co-joiners. The NEC wrote the manifestos of the two political parties and chose the symbols of the parties. The federal government built the national, state and local government headquarters of both parties. For both parties, SAP was a *fait accompli*, which they had to accept uncritically. This type of intervention virtually turned the political parties into arms of the military administration and critics derisively referred to them as "test-tube" parties. It should be noted that since political parties are supposed to be made up of individuals with similar ideals who voluntarily come together, this authoritarian way of legislating them into existence is not only fundamentally wrong but equally negates and subverts the democratic order.[81]

It might be said that the establishment of the two parties was an attempt at empowering the new politicians who were not as wealthy as the older ones thereby reducing their dependence on the older politicians. The ban on politicians who had participated actively in the politics of the previous republics, referred to as the "old breed," from participating in the transition process would seem to support this view. However, in reality, the ban was self-serving hence the regular banning and unbanning of different categories of politicians depending on how these served Babangida's interest of perpetuating himself in office. If the transition program actually aimed at empowering the disadvantaged groups, there should have been meaningful attempts at empowering women, most of who constituted the most disadvantaged group. However, the manifestos of the SDP and NRC did not address the issue of gender inequality. In addition, men dominated the leadership positions in the two political parties. In fact, of the 20,503 executive positions at the ward, local government, state and national levels in the NRC the proportion of women who held executive posts was negative 4.23 (i.e. – 4.23) percent while in the SDP women accounted for about 4 percent of the 24,194 executive positions.[82]

Furthermore, a look at some of the transition measures, which were supposedly aimed at empowering the grassroots, would demonstrate that they were taken from the World Bank's playbook of pursuing deceptive populist and grassroots empowerment policies as a way of ensuring that democratization processes ended up entrenching economic liberalism. The World Bank's 1989 report advocated that the economic liberalization process should be accompanied by the promotion of grassroots democracy through measures such as promoting grassroots entrepreneurship, working through existing traditional leaders and strengthening local governments. Briefly, "a bottom-up approach that places premium on listening to people and on genuinely empowering the intended beneficiaries of any development programme" should be pursued.[83] At the superficial level, this is a noble idea but as has been pointed out by Beckman this was a false populist policy that was aimed at hijacking the ideological armor of the opponents of SAP while seeking to establish alternative basis of support for the adjustment programs.[84] It is from this perspective that we can understand the politics of "grassroots empowerment" policies such as local government reforms, the establishment of the Directorate of Food, Roads and Rural Infrastructure (DFRRI) and the Better Life Program (BLP) for rural women associated with the transition programs.[85] It is significant to note that the Political Bureau advocated the strengthening and democratization of local government institutions along with other measures that would promote the transformation of the rural areas. However, rural transformation was expected to be part of the general process of instituting a new political economy and social order in Nigeria that aims at terminating neocolonial dependency and promoting sustainable people-oriented democracy. However, the deceptiveness associated with these policies largely accounted for their failure to promote any meaningful grassroots empowerment.

In any case, rather than use the transition program to put in place structures that would promote an enduring democracy in the Third Republic, it became one for consolidating SAP and promoting Babangida's personal rule agenda. The NEC became a handy tool for Babangida's desire to perpetuate him in office. Its reports provided part of the subterfuge for shifting the hand-over to civil rule date (first from October 1990 to October 1992, later to 3 January 1993, and then to 27 August 1993) thereby plunging the country into an endless transition process. For instance, the cancellation of the first and second presidential primaries in 1992, which became an excuse for shifting the hand-over date, was based on the NEC's reports. In addition, Babangida employed the services of surrogate bodies like the shadowy "Third Eye" and the Arthur Nzeribe led "Association for Better Nigeria" (ABN) to campaign for the continuation of military rule. Although under the transition decree the activities of these organizations could be interpreted as capable of derailing the transition process therefore constituting an offense, the individuals behind these organizations were never taken to court for any offense. Yet critics of the authoritarian nature of the transition program who accused Babangida of having a "hidden agenda" to succeed himself were routinely taken to court and incarcerated for allegedly trying to "derail the transition."[86]

Having shifted the hand-over of power date so often on the basis of excuses like the transition being a learning process, the shortcomings of politicians and the desire to ensure the enthronement of a stable and enduring democratic Third Republic, Babangida had by early 1993 boxed himself into a corner. He ran out of excuses for further shifting of the hand-over date. In addition, the bloody and immensely popular military coup of April 1990[87] which the regime barely survived and the unrelenting criticism of pro-democracy groups over what they termed as Babangida's hidden agenda to perpetuate himself in office, compelled his regime to organize the 12 June 1993 presidential election. This election was to mark the final phase of the transition process. Agents of the federal military administration attempted to scuttle the election. For instance, just two days before the presidential election, the ABN obtained an order from an inexperienced and sympathetic Abuja high court judge, Bassey Ita Ikpeme, prohibiting the holding of the presidential election (it is significant that this order was issued at the most unusual time, 9.00 p.m.). Furthermore, working in concert with the NEC, the Babangida regime deliberately refused to build polling booths even though the election was substantially an open ballot one requiring voters to line up in the open before the ballot box of the candidate of their preference. The regime hoped that since this was the peak of the rainy season, rain would disrupt elections in parts of the country but June 12 turned out to be a very dry day.

The presidential election was generally hailed as very free and fair by both the local and international observers (in fact one of the freest and fairest elections in Nigeria's post-colonial history). The official results of the election released by NEC for sixteen states and thc unofficial results that were available to the press and the public for the entire country showed that M.K.O. Abiola, the presidential candidate of the SDP, clearly and decisively won the election. Yet in a final desperate move to scuttle the transition process, the ABN went to the same Abuja high court and obtained an order stopping further announcements of the election results.[88] This ruling was met with general disapproval by Nigerians, which resulted in a tense atmosphere in the country. Yet Babangida used the so-called "confusion" arising from the two court orders, the tense atmosphere, and other flimsy excuses to annul the results of the presidential election on 23 June 1993.[89] This decision was met with general disapproval as it threw the country into a very serious crisis which eventually resulted in Babangida hastily handing over power to a hand picked, concocted and inept Interim National Government (ING) under the leadership of Shonekan on 27 August 1993.

The authoritarian model of the Babangida regime's transition to civil rule program was based on the neo-modernization paradigm promoted by the neo-liberal policies of the IFIs which favored such authoritarian models so long as they result in the entrenchment of economic liberalism through SAP at the end of the process. In fact, as demonstrated by the case of the transition to civil rule in Ghana under Jerry Rawlings, the IFIs do not hesitate to support a military ruler using the transition process to perpetuate himself in office, so long as he is committed to the goals of economic liberalism. Indeed, the Ghana model, which earned praise from the IFIs for Rawlings commitment to SAP,[90] became the example that other African leaders like Babangida, sought to replicate. Bangura has aptly summarized the neo-modernization authoritarian model that underlined Babangida's transition program in Nigeria:

> The current policy makers are keen to develop a political framework that will allow for a smooth transition from state interventions to markets… Political reconstruction calls for strict control of the political process… The political programme was interlaced with the objectives of SAP, with the government calling for the latter's consolidation at every stage of the transition… There has been an attempt to weaken the militant leaderships of some of the groups considered to be critical of SAP and the transition programme, such as the academic unions, students movement and the fiercely independent national union of banks, insurance and financial employees.[91]

The turmoil that the annulment of the June 12 presidential election generated within Nigeria, the resultant national paralysis and the universal condemnation of the action by the international community, made it clear that Nigeria would for a long time remain ungovernable if Babangida remained in power.[92] The reasons Babangida advanced for annulling the election in his 26 June 1993 national broadcast, as well as those advanced by his surrogates were greeted with universal skepticism as various pro-democracy and sectional groups, and the international community insisted on the release of the results of the election. In the circumstance, Babangida was compelled to relinquish power, as he put it, to "step aside" by handing over power to a hastily concocted and handpicked ING headed by Shonekan.

As already noted Babangida's transition program did not address the marginalization of women and failed to make women an integral part of the transition process. The outcome was that the elections held under the program resulted in the election of very few women into various levels of government. For instance, in the local government elections of 1990, women won elections to only 206 out of the available 1,297 positions nation-wide while no woman was elected a governor in the governorship elections for the then thirty states of the federation. Also in the 1992 national assembly elections, only one woman was elected into the 90-member senate while only twelve women were elected into the 638-member House of Representatives. The only female presidential aspirant for the 1993 presidential election, Sarah Jubril, dropped out of the presidential primaries because she could not muster the 500,000 naira non-refundable deposit required for participating in the primaries.[93]

Meanwhile, the ING contraption was vigorously opposed by pro-democracy and human rights groups, labor and professional unions and some primordial groups, who regarded the setting up of the ING as an attempt to legitimize the annulment of the June 12 election. In addition, the ING was seen as a puppet body and a continuation of the Babangida administration. This view was reinforced by the fact that all its members were handpicked by the departing Babangida regime while Shonekan had previously been appointed by Babangida as the head of the Transitional Council (TC) that replaced the federal executive council, in January 1993. The TC, was supposedly set up to help to ensure a smooth transition to civil rule, thus, creating the impression that Babangida's transition program was in the final phase. However, in reality, the TC was a subterfuge and a powerless body that was not involved in the decision-making process,[94] but was in actuality designed to create the false impression that Babangida was committed to the successful implementation of the transition program. Shonekan's antecedent in this regard, therefore created the impression that his appointment to the headship of the ING was designed for him to play another puppet and ineffective role. This was reinforced by the fact that although Babangida retired the service chiefs and replaced them with his loyalists before his exit, he left Abacha in his position as the minister of defence and chairman of the Joint Chiefs of Staff. With his powerful position as the head of the military, Abacha did not regard himself as answerable to Shonekan, as he clearly demonstrated by unilaterally retiring and redeploying service chiefs and military officers deemed as loyal to Babangida.

Meanwhile large segments of the Nigerian society regarded the ING as an illegal government and called for the deannulment of the June 12 presidential election and the handing over of power to the winner of the election. The unpreparedness of Shonekan to deannul the election further incensed large segments of the Nigerian people and pro-democracy activist groups who resorted to various acts of protests, strikes and other forms of civil disobedience. There were calls on Abacha from different pro-June 12 activists, including Abiola, the presumed winner of the election, to intervene and restore the results of the presidential election. On 17 November 1993, Abacha led a group of military officers to force Shonekan and the executive members of government to "resign" from their positions while he assumed power as head of state to "save" the country from further descending into chaos and anarchy. Contrary to the expectations of those who expected him to release the results of the June 12 election, Abacha introduced full-scale military rule by abrogating the transition program, dissolving the two political parties, and all elected executive and legislative branches of government at the national, state and local government levels. In his inaugural address, he assured the country that the new military regime would be a brief and corrective one and that a constitutional conference with "full constituent powers" would be convened in January 1994. Some pro-democracy groups welcomed this announcement which they interpreted to mean the convening of a sovereign national conference that would provide the basis for a transition that would foster an enduring democratic order.

Given the belief among pro-democracy groups, and even Abiola, that the Abacha regime would deannul the result of the June 12 election and hand-over power to the winner of the election, these groups initially welcomed the regime. In fact, Abiola, who held meetings with Abacha immediately after the coup, sanctioned the participation of some of his close associates, including Babagana Kingibe, his vice presidential running mate, in the new government. However, when it became clear that Abacha was intent on holding on to power rather than revisit the June 12 election, his regime lost this initial goodwill of the pro-democracy and pro-June 12 activist individuals and organizations. They referred to

Abacha's regime as an illegal administration and called for the release of the results of the June 12 election. Their unease with Abacha was not helped by the fact that contrary to the promise he made in his inaugural address, he failed to constitute a constitutional conference with "full constituent powers" in January 1994.

Thus, there were persistent calls for the restoration of the results of the June 12 election in the first half of 1994. In fact, the year 1994 witnessed the largest scale of opposition by civil groups, labor and professional unions, among others, in Nigeria's postcolonial history. The period between May and August 1994 can be regarded as marking the pinnacle of civil society activism involving large-scale strikes, riots, arson and rebellion, virtually bringing the country to a standstill.[95] In response, Abacha adopted brutal and repressive measures to quell the pro-democracy activism and when Abiola proclaimed himself president on 11 June 1994, he was declared wanted and eventually arrested and detained. Nevertheless, the persistent activism of the pro-democracy groups forced Abacha to set in motion a so-called transition to civil rule program.

The first step in Abacha's transition program was the setting up of a nineteen member National Constitutional Conference Commission (NCCC) to draw up an agenda for the constitutional conference based on the opinions expressed in the memoranda submitted to it by members of the public. In late May 1994, elections of delegates to the National Constitutional Conference (NCC) were held but as a result of the opposition of pro-democracy groups, the turn out was abysmal while many prominent individuals especially from the Yoruba ethnic group declined to seek to be elected into the body. For the pro-democracy groups this exercise was a charade: they insisted on the release of the results of the June 12 election as the only viable way forward for the country. In spite of the abysmal turn out, the 273 delegates who were "elected" together with the ninety-six people nominated by the Abacha regime, constituted the NCC, which was inaugurated on 27 August 1994, under the chairmanship of Justice Adolphus Karibi-Whyte. The conference did not have constituent powers as Abacha had promised in the inaugural speech of his regime.

Right from its inception, the NCC suffered from credibility problem as most Nigerians regarded it as a powerless body designed to rubber-stamp Abacha's agenda. The rather feeble proceedings of the conference and the degree of patronage members received from the Abacha administration, helped to reinforce this notion.[96] The NCC submitted a draft constitution to the federal military government on 27 July 1995. A significant recommendation of the report was the adoption of a power-sharing system of rotational presidency (an issue that had previously been extensively debated by the CDC in 1975 and the Political Bureau in 1986/7) and multiple vice presidency. It is equally significant to note that the NCC did not recommend a terminal date for the military to hand-over power to civilians, yet this was perhaps the most significant task before the body. After deliberating on the draft constitution, Abacha's ruling military council settled on the "transplantation" of the French plural executive system of government into the country, comprising a president, vice president and prime minister. To enhance the power-sharing exercise, the country would be divided into six zones with each zone producing in rotation one of the six principal officials: president, prime minister, vice president, deputy prime minister, president of the senate and the speaker of the house of representatives. However, the respective powers of the president and the prime minister, were not clearly defined while no decision was made on which of the six zones would be the first to produce the president.[97] The issue of which of the zones would produce the first president was very significant since many Yoruba people who believed that they were robbed of the presidency by the annulment of June 12 election, felt that they should be compensated by producing the first president.

However, on 1 October 1995, the Abacha regime released the timetable for the transition to civil rule, which spanned October 1995 to October 1998. The duration of the transition program attracted criticism from both domestic groups and the international community. For instance, the Commonwealth called on the regime to return the country to civil rule within two years or risk having Nigeria expelled from the organization. Borrowing from the kind of argument that the Babangida regime used to justify the long duration of its transition program, the Abacha regime argued that as a learning process a transition program needs not be short. Rather, a long drawn transition program would enable the country to learn from mistakes in each stage, consolidate the gains of each stage and therefore ensure the installation of "a lasting and sustainable democracy" at the end of the process.[98] The transition timetable included the lifting of the ban on political activities and establishment of the National Electoral Commission (NECON), in the last quarter of December1995. It also included the conduct of two local government elections in 1996 (one on non-party basis and the other on party basis), the creation of more states and local governments and the registration of political parties, both in 1996. The program also provided for the holding of elections into the state and federal legislative and executive bodies in 1997 and 1998 with 1 October 1998 marking the termination of military rule with the hand-over of power to a civilian president.

The Abacha regime has remained the most corrupt, brutal, repressive and authoritarian regime in Nigeria's postcolonial history: factors, which subjected it to unprecedented internal opposition and international isolation. The internal and external opposition was heightened by events such as the execution of Kenule Saro-Wiwa, a writer and environmental activist, and other eight Ogoni activists on 10 November 1995 on the accusation of involvement in the murder of four prominent Ogoni men in 1994. This execution, which was carried out in spite of far reaching local and international appeals to spare their lives, resulted in the suspension of Nigeria from the Commonwealth. Another factor, which generated widespread opposition to the regime, was the crude authoritarian manner in which the transition program was used to try to ensure that Abacha succeeded himself in office. While Babangida's self-succession bid was subterranean, that of Abacha was brazen and farcical thereby draining the transition process of any form of legitimacy. As was the case with Babangida, the electoral commission became the primary tool for trying to ensure the self-succession bid.

Like previous transition programs, the guidelines stipulated by NECON for the registration of political parties were so stringent, even more stringent than that of Babangida's regime, that the subordinate classes and even many wealthy individuals were not in the position to form viable political parties. The guidelines which were to be met within two months, included the payment of 500,000 naira registration fees, a minimum membership of 40,000 per state and 15,000 in Abuja, maintenance of well staffed and functioning offices and branches at Abuja and in all the states and local governments. Other guidelines were a constitution, manifesto and clear articulation of issues. Of the twenty-three political associations that started the registration process, eighteen completed the registration formalities (the figure was later reduced to fifteen due to mergers between some of the associations). On 30 September 1996, five of the political associations were granted registration as political parties, namely, the Congress for National Consensus (CNC), the Democratic Party of Nigeria (DPN), the Grassroots Democratic Movement (GDM), the National Center Party of Nigeria (NCPN), and the United Nigeria Congress Party (UNCP).

The caliber of the registered five political parties fuelled the suspicion that Abacha was bent on succeeding himself in office. Political associations such as the People's Progressive Party (PPP) and the Social Progressive Party (SPP), which were made up of prominent politicians perceived as too powerful and prominent opposition figures capable of frustrating Abacha's self-succession bid, were not registered. Yet given the resources of the members, these associations were most likely better placed to meet the stringent requirements for registration.[99] Suspicions of Abacha's self-succession bid were reinforced by the proliferation of government-sponsored "Abacha-must-stay" rallies and demonstrations "urging" him to succeed himself in office since he was the only one capable of ensuring peace and stability in the country. Various traditional rulers and some other prominent Nigerians were coerced to join the "Abacha-must-stay" chorus. Even several leaders of the newly registered political parties started "urging" him to run as president on the ticket of their respective parties. The final script in Abacha's self-succession bid was written in April 1998 when all the registered five political parties were coerced into nominating him as their presidential candidate even though he was not a member of any of the party. This led to the complete loss of faith in the credibility of the transition process. As a so-called consensus candidate, there would be no need for presidential election (which Abacha feared he would not win because of his immense unpopularity) as he would be simply legitimized as the country's president.

Meanwhile, the increasing exposition of Abacha's transition program as a charade resulted in the intensification of domestic and international opposition to his regime. Domestically, and in spite of savage repression, there were intensified opposition to his self-succession bid by pro-democracy groups, labor, students, some market women associations and some professional unions. Nigeria's opposition groups based abroad such as the National Democratic Coalition (NADECO) intensified their mobilization of international opposition to the regime. An opposition group led by Wole Soyinka, the Nobel laureate, set up an underground radio station (Radio Kudirat – named after the assassinated wife of Abiola who was in the forefront of opposition to Abacha's regime), to wage a propaganda war against the regime. Internationally, the regime was further isolated as various countries and international organizations imposed sanctions on it. Abacha appeared unfazed by all the opposition as he repressively continued pursuing his self-succession bid but this enterprise ended with his sudden and mysterious death on 8 June 1998.

"Credible" Transition to Civil Rule, 1998-1999

With the death of Abacha, General Abdulsalami Abubakar, the Chief of Defence Staff under Abacha's regime, a self-effacing man, and generally regarded as a professional and apolitical military officer, was appointed by the ruling military council as the head of state. The immediate problems that confronted Abubakar were the restoration of the battered image of the military and the implementation of a transparent and credible transition to civil rule program. Abubakar immediately set about tackling these issues. He improved the human rights situation, released detained labor activists from jail, released political detainees (Abiola was still left in jail) and all those who had been detained in connection with the 1990, 1995 and 1997 coups and attempted coups and created a freer political atmosphere. To convince those who doubted his commitment to civil rule, he portrayed his regime as a caretaker one that would put in place a swift and short transition program that would result in the hand-over of power to a civilian administration on 29 May 1999. He repeatedly emphasized the point that he had no desire of succeeding himself in office.

Abubakar dismissed Abacha loyalists from the administration, retired some of them from the military and intelligence agencies while removing others from sensitive and powerful positions within the armed forces. Abacha's transition program was scrapped, the electoral commission scrapped and replaced with a new Independent National Electoral Commission (INEC), elections into local governments contested by the existing five political parties was nullified and the five parties, which had adopted Abacha as their presidential candidate, were dissolved. A major challenge, which Abubakar faced, was the demand by NADECO and various pro-democracy groups for the release of the results of the June 12 election and the release of Abiola from jail to head a national unity government that would oversee the final transition to democracy. Abubakar rejected these demands: the sudden death of Abiola while still in jail, under mysterious circumstances and in the presence of an official American visiting team on 8 July 1998, made the demand for his release to head a national unity government no longer tenable. However, even with Abiola's death, the call for a government of national unity from pro-democracy groups remained unabated. Abubakar insisted that such a government was not necessary. In a national broadcast on 20 July 1998, Abubakar argued that in view of "the strong desire of the overwhelming majority of (Nigerians) for a return to democratic governance … within the shortest practicable time, a Government of National Unity whose composition could only be through selection would be undemocratic."[100]

Abubakar's transition program was much more crowded and transparent than those of Babangida and Abacha – the program that commenced with the granting of provisional registrations to political parties on 24 September 1998 was to terminate with the swearing in of an elected president on 29 May 1999. Unlike previous transition programs, INEC would initially grant provisional registration to political associations that paid 100,000 naira and met other requirements, to function as political parties. A political party would only attain a permanent status if it attained 10 percent of the votes cast in each council in at least twenty-four states during the local government elections scheduled for 5 December 1998, and had offices in two-thirds of the states of the federation. Of the nine political parties that were granted provisional registration, only three did well enough in the local government elections to qualify for permanent status, namely, the All People's Party (APP), the Alliance for Democracy (AD) and the People's Democratic Party (PDP). The 5 December local government elections experienced some problems, such as conflicts and boycott in the Niger Delta area where the people were engaged in the struggle for the control of their natural resources and accusations of rigging and bribery in different parts of the country. However, the elections were better organized than those held under Abacha and had better turnouts. The relative success of this election helped to prepare the ground for the conduct of the other elections that would finally result in the termination of military rule.

Based on their performance in the local government elections, the PDP, APP and AD became the main contenders in the state and federal government elections. Elections into state legislative and executive houses were held on 9 January 1999 while those for the national assembly and the presidency were held on 20 February and 27 February 1999, respectively. The results of the state elections showed that the PDP had the most national spread while the AD was mainly a regional party as it captured virtually all the legislative and executive seats in the Yoruba speaking Western region of Nigeria. The APP did not have a specific solid base as it scored sprinkles of victories in different parts of the country. For the presidential election, the PDP, which had most of the prominent politicians and retired military generals in its membership nominated Obasanjo, a former military head of state, as its candidate. The AD and APP realized that the only way they could challenge the dominance of the PDP was through a working cooperation. For the national assembly elections only both parties would support a common candidate from the party that had more influence in an area while for the presidential election, Olu Falae from the AD was the candidate of both parties. Obasanjo, the PDP candidate won the presidential election and on 29 May was sworn in as the country's president, thereby marking the end to military rule and the commencement of the third democratic experiment (usually referred to as the Fourth Republic).[101]

Given the fact that the transition programs of the regimes of Babangida, Abacha and Abubakar were male-dominated, the performance of women in terms of winning elective positions in the various elections that inaugurated the Fourth Republic was not encouraging. Indeed the manifestos of the AD and the APP did not pay any significant attention to women. On the other hand, the manifesto of the PDP stated that:

> Women are an important group of Nigerians whose participation in national politics have been minimal due largely to cultural inhibition and barriers. The relevance of women, their numerical strength and their multiplier effects in the mass mobilisation of the Nigerian people for the attainment of education, health and socio-economic objectives are recognised by the party. Accordingly, the party government shall pursue policies and principles enshrined in the Beijing Declaration.[102]

In the 1998 and 1999 elections, only 631 women contested elections for the 11,108 available elective public offices in all levels of government and only 181 women actually won elections representing 1.63 percent of the available positions. Only three women won elections into the 109-member senate while 12 women were elected into the 360-member House of Representatives. At the state level no woman was elected as a state governor, two women were elected as deputy governors while only 12 women were elected into the state houses of assembly out of the available 990 positions. The situation was not different at the local government level where only nine women were elected as local government chairpersons out of the available 774 positions while 143 women were elected as councilors.[103] Furthermore, the promise made in the PDP manifesto to implement the Beijing Declaration affirmative action that provided for the setting aside of 30 percent of appointive positions for women was not observed in appointments into governmental positions. For instance, only six women were appointed into the 50-member federal executive council with only one of them occupying a full ministerial position. Furthermore, there was only one female special adviser to the president of the federation out of a total of fourteen and only one female special assistant out of a total of seven.[104] The poor performance of women in the transition process is particularly disappointing when it is realized that both the Babangida and Abacha regimes launched state-sponsored feminist movements (discussed in chapter 9) that were purportedly aimed at empowering the Nigerian women thereby enabling them to play more active roles in politics.

The Third Democratic Experiment and Sustainable Democracy

In his address during the inauguration of the civilian administration of Obasanjo, Abubakar stated that democratization is "a continuous and unfinished business," noting that one of the main challenges facing the new civilian administration was the entrenchment of sustainable democracy in the country.[105] On his part, Obasanjo pledged in his inaugural speech that his administration "will leave no stone unturned to ensure the sustenance of democracy" in the country.[106] In view of the adverse effects military intervention had on the entrenchment of an enduring democratic process in the country and the image of the military which sank to the lowest ebb under the Abacha administration, Abubakar and Obasanjo admonished the military to refrain from intervening in the country's politics. Abubakar advised the military "to return to its constitutional role of defending the country's territorial integrity and sovereignty (and that they) must, forever, resist and renounce the seduction and temptation of political power and office." To enable the military submit itself to civil authority, Obasanjo pledged to conduct far-reaching reorientation and "a re-definition of roles, re-training and re-education (would) be done to ensure that the military submit to civil authority and regains its pride, professionalism and tradition."

As would be expected, the civilian administration pledged to tackle those negative issues that have bedeviled the country and had, in fact, threatened to bring an end to the corporate existence of Nigeria. The agenda of the new administration included restoring the peoples' trust in their government, an end to arbitrariness and the respect for human rights, eradication of corruption, resuscitation of various infrastructures, social and economic institutions, tackling the debt and economic crisis, and resolving the crisis in the Niger Delta. Some of the attempts that were made to tackle these issues included the creation of a national human rights commission, an anti-corruption agency, a special body to tackle the development problems in the Niger Delta, and a number of social and economic policies. Space will not permit us to examine the extent to which the government successfully addressed these issues: rather, attention would be devoted to the extent to which the third democratic experiment has helped to lay the foundation for the entrenchment of sustainable democracy in the country.

The retention of the transplanted and very expensive American style presidential system of government has helped to worsen the issues of corruption, primitive accumulation and political instability. The plethora of offices associated with this system at the federal, state and local government levels has put much strain on the country's precarious financial position. For instance, a survey of the presidency and 27 states of the federation conducted in June 2004 showed that the presidency had 15 special advisers and the 27 states had 238 special advisers, and the total salary for these special advisers was 1.3 billion naira a year.[107] Furthermore, the huge amount of finance involved in party formation and the electoral process helped to intensify corrupt accumulative processes on the part of incumbents in preparation for future elections as well as the struggle for the control of state offices. As previously noted, in the absence of funding from special interest and lobbyist groups as is the in the United States, Nigerian politicians continue to rely on access to state offices as the main means for accumulation. The dominant role of ex-military generals and officers (who used access to state offices to corruptly enrich themselves under various military regimes), in the politics of the Fourth Republic, has further helped to intensify the desire for primitive accumulation among the new generation of politicians. This struggle over the control of the state organs and processes of primitive accumulation partly accounted for the conflictual relationship between Obasanjo and the national assembly during the first term of his presidency and almost resulted in his impeachment in 2002. Furthermore, the negative experience associated with political godfatherism where a candidate for an elective office relies on a financier for campaign funds in return for loyalty to the godfather, after winning the election, further helped to intensify the quest for primitive accumulation on the part of office holders. The feud between Chris Ngige, who won the 2003 governorship election in Anambra state, and Chris Uba, the political godfather who funded Ngige's campaign clearly exemplifies this point. Based on perceived disloyalty on the part of Ngige, Uba, also a major financier of the PDP, was able to use state coercive forces to humiliate Ngige and attempt to make him resign from office.

In any case, the experience with the third democratic experiment has shown that the conditions for the establishment of sustainable democracy in the country are most probably lacking, as the country has been crises-laden. Underlying the various crises are the issues of true and fiscal federalism, citizenship, resource control and the conditions for the existence of a harmonious and sustainable Nigerian federation. These are clearly reflected in the crises arising from religious issues primarily manifested in the adoption of the *Sharia* Islamic system of justice in most of the northern states, the contradiction arising from indigeneity and citizenship, inter-communal violence and the struggle over resource control. Alabi Williams has aptly summarized these issues and the challenges they pose to a sustainable democratic system in Nigeria:

> The challenges facing the present (democratic) structure are very glaring. These are the challenges of religion and its excess hazards, which are highly combustible, as witnessed in Kano and Kaduna over these years. There is the challenge of citizens' rights of abode as witnessed in the killings and lawlessness in Plateau. There is the challenge of appropriate fiscal federalism as witnessed in the demands by the people of the Niger Delta to control their natural resources. There is the challenge posed by the various ethnic nationalities wanting to assert themselves and subvert the federal authority.[108]

All these factors have proved inimical for the democratic process. Significantly, the intervention of the military in Nigerian politics and the distortion of the federal system in favor of a command type centralized system that was only federal in name accentuated these factors. The various efforts at constitutional engineering embodied in the respective transition to civil rule programs have not contributed to the resolution of these issues.

For instance, the *Sharia* controversy, which threatened to halt the work of the CA in April 1978, was not effectively resolved with the compromise solution arrived at. The issue remained a sore and divisive point in Nigerian politics, a situation that was aggravated by its manipulation for political ends as in the case of Babangida surreptitiously making Nigeria a member of the Organization of Islamic Conference (OIC).[109] The fact that a person born in a state outside that of the person's ethnic origin or has resided, worked and paid taxes in a state outside of his/her ethnic origin, is considered a non-indigene in the state of residence has tended to promote ethnic citizenship. This has created the feeling of second-class citizenship among those so discriminated against. Furthermore, the federal character and quota system principles, which emphasize indigeneity as the basis for appointment into offices, reinforce the phenomenon of ethnic citizenship.[110] An issue that has posed one of the greatest challenges to political stability in the Fourth Republic is the demand for resource control by the oil producing minority ethnic groups and the attendant conflicts that have accompanied this demand.[111] The resource control agitation raises crucial issues that border on the restructuring of the Nigerian polity to allow for the operation of true and fiscal federalism.[112]

These vexatious issues, which are at the heart of what is regarded as the national question in Nigeria, have led to demands for the convening of a national conference with sovereign powers. At the conference, the representatives of the different ethnic and other groups would discuss the terms of the corporate existence of Nigeria.[113] These demands became more pronounced with the manipulative and decadent policies of the Babangida and Abacha regimes that spurred various forms of crises in the country. The demands for a national conference not only intensified under the Fourth Republic, but also in fact, widened beyond the traditional advocates such as pro-democracy and resource control groups to include conservative elite and ethno-regional groups. In fact, conservative elite and ethno-regional groups such as The Patriots, *Afenifere*, the *Ohanaeze Ndiigbo* and the Northern Unity Forum (NUF) used the occasion of the celebration of the democracy day on 29 May 2004 to join the demand for a sovereign national conference.[114]

Most advocates of a sovereign national conference argue that such a conference would result in the crafting of a constitutional and political arrangement that is indigenously derived (homegrown) and based on the Nigerian reality – a situation that would help to promote political stability and sustainable development in the country. They largely reject the modernist paradigm under which alien institutions, which are out of tune with Nigerian realities, are transplanted into the country. On the other hand, critics of the sovereign national conference argue that such a conference would be a recipe for disaster since it would lead to the breakup of Nigeria into independent entities.

Successive Nigerian administrations have spurned the demands for a sovereign national conference. The national crisis that accompanied the annulment of the 12 June 1993 presidential election provided hope to the protagonists of a sovereign national conference that such a conference would be convened as part of the process of finding solution to the crisis. Abacha's promise of convening a constitutional conference with constituent powers further gave them hope, but after entrenching himself in office, Abacha became very hostile to the idea and repressively suppressed demands for a sovereign national conference. The immediate aftermath of the sudden death of Abacha witnessed a renewed demand for the convening of a national conference under the auspices of a civilian government of national unity, to come up with solutions to the multifarious problems impeding stability and socio-economic development in Nigeria. The Abubakar administration rejected this demand with the argument that the constitutional conference that took place between 1994 and 1995 adequately articulated the wishes of the Nigerian people and therefore came up with a good draft constitution. Rather, he sated that the draft constitution would be widely circulated and debated upon before a revised version, that would constitute the constitution of the Fourth Republic would be produced. This argument is not tenable because as already noted, many of the members of the 1994/95 constitutional conference were handpicked while the general apathy among the Nigerian populace toward elections into the NCC rendered it unrepresentative of the wishes of the overwhelming majority of the people. Furthermore, the NCC suffered from serious credibility problems in view of the amount of influence exerted on its members by the Abacha administration. In addition, the 1999 constitution cannot be regarded as emanating from the people in that given the short duration of the transition program of Abubakar and the fact that the 1995 draft constitution was not widely circulated, most Nigerians did not make input in the revision of the draft. Indeed, the 1999 constitution as was the case with the defunct 1989 constitution, is just a slight revision of the 1979 constitution.

The civilian administration of Obasanjo has steadfastly rejected calls for a sovereign national conference (although at a conference on 29 May 2004 to mark the democracy day, Atiku Abubakar, the Nigerian vice president stated that he was disposed to the convening of a constitutional conference before the 2007 elections). There is an element of opportunism in Atiku Abubakar's position because having realized the momentum that the demand for a national conference was gathering all over the country, he wanted to align himself with the demand as a way of winning more support for his presidential ambition in 2007. Nevertheless, Obasanjo based his rejection of a national conference on the argument that such a conference has been rendered unnecessary by the 1999 elections in which the people transferred sovereignty to the national assembly that is now better placed to devise solutions to the multifarious problems confronting the people. This argument is simply not correct and as is demonstrated by the enormity of the various problems and crises confronting the country, a sovereign national conference is imperative for sustainable democracy and development. Indeed, by February 2005, Obasanjo could no longer resist the widespread demand for a national conference. In order to undercut this demand and in the face of threats by some pro-national conference (PRONACO) groups led by Anthony Enahoro and Soyinka to convene a national conference, independent of the government, Obasanjo went ahead to convene a National Political Reform Conference (NPRC) on 21 February 2005. However, the agenda of the national conference clearly does not suffice for a sovereign national conference. The Enahoro and Soyinka group has therefore decided to go ahead with the convening of a national conference.

Conclusion

Between 1960 and 2005, Nigeria had two failed democratic experiments, an aborted one and the third experiment that started on 29 May 1999, which is largely crisis-ridden and does not hold the prospect for entrenching sustainable democracy in the country. In trying to account for the shortcomings and failures of the democratic experiments, most social scientists operating from the perspective of the modernization paradigm put the blame entirely on internal factors arising from the so-called irrationalities of the domestic Nigerian situation. These factors are couched in Weberian and modernist models such as patrimonialism, irrational affective politics, clintelism and prebendalism all of which emphasize excessive corruption and the exploitation of offices to serve individual, sectional and group interests. Underlying these analyses are a form of benevolence and "civilizing mission" perspective, which accuses Nigerian actors of being irrationally unable to operate the ideal type, transplanted Western liberal democracy that is considered the panacea for civilization and development. This analysis fails to take into account the fundamental defects of the transplanted liberal democracy and the fact that its contradictory relationship with the prevailing social and cultural realities are at the heart of the failure of the democratic experiments. In other words, although the political actors are undoubtedly highly culpable for the failure of the democratic experiments, the fundamental cause of the failure is structural. It is important to come to terms with the structural factor before any meaningful solutions can be devised.

It should be noted that liberal democracy is a product of the historical and cultural realities of Western societies and represents the triumphalism of the bourgeois culture and capitalist system. The various Western societies have therefore devised versions of bourgeois liberal democratic traditions that are more in tune with their own realities and therefore more capable of serving the requirements and interests of their respective dominant bourgeois classes. Transplanting any of the Western versions of liberal democracy into Nigeria and, indeed, other African countries with entirely different cultural, historical and social realities is bound to be problematic as clearly reflected by the shortcomings of the different forms of constitutional engineering in Nigeria. While the independence constitution was based on the parliamentary version of the bourgeois liberal democracy, the subsequent constitutions engineered by successive military regimes were based on the American presidential model of bourgeois liberal democracy. These transplanted models failed to reflect Nigeria's cultural reality and its history of diversity, among others.

Furthermore, the transplantation of the Western liberal democratic model into Nigeria involved entrenching the patriarchal system associated with this model and the attendant marginalization of women in political and public affairs, contrary to what obtained in many precolonial and traditional Nigerian societies. This involved transplanting the "single-sex" system that obtains in the Western societies into Nigeria. Under this system, "political status-bearing roles are predominantly the preserve of men," and "women can achieve distinction and recognition only by taking on the roles of men in public life and performing them well." On the other hand, although many traditional Nigerian societies are patrilineal and patrilocal, they practice the "dual-sex" political system within which "each sex manages its own affairs, and women's interests are represented at all levels." In theory, the transplanted Western political system is supposed to be "sex blind" since office holders are seen as representing a constituency of both sexes. However, in reality "the absence of women from meaningful political representation in . . . (postcolonial) Nigeria can be viewed as showing the strength of the legacy of single-sex politics that the British colonial masters left behind." [115]

Moreover, as bourgeois constitutions, both the parliamentary and presidential models require the presence of a strong capitalist class for the constitution to operate effectively, a situation that is lacking in Nigeria. The adoption of the very expensive American presidential version of liberal democracy with all the corrupt practices associated with it worsened the problem of corruption in Nigeria. In the United States, politicians rely on campaign contributions from lobbyists and special interest groups many of who use these contributions to corruptly buy access and influence legislation that favor their position. Indeed, the amount of corruption associated with this process led to the introduction of the McCain-Feingold campaign reform bill, which was strongly resisted, by many politicians, special interest, and lobbyist groups, before a diluted version of the bill was eventually passed. Even then, politicians and special interest groups have adopted creative ways of circumventing the campaign finance reform bill while the Democratic and Republican parties have sponsored advocacy groups, the 527 committees that can raise unlimited amounts of money in support of the political campaigns of their candidates.[116] In addition, the practice of politicians using their offices to dip into public funds to finance projects that benefit only their constituencies – pork-barrel projects – is a prevalent aspect of United States politics. These corrupt practices in the American system share some similarities with some of the practices in Nigeria, but while the Nigerian situation has been variously described as excessive corruption, patrimonialism, clientelism and prebendalism, similar practices in the United States are less disparagingly described. The reason for this difference in analysis can be located in the structure of production and dissemination of knowledge about Africa in the social sciences, which is dominated by Western-based Africanists.[117]

As a peripheral, neo-colonial capitalist formation, Nigeria lacks the capitalist class and organizations that would be able to contribute to the campaign finance of politicians. Nigerian politicians therefore have to rely on either using their own resources to finance their campaigns or rely on political godfathers for the financing of their campaigns. Both the politician and the political godfather expect to recoup the money they spent ("invested") in the campaign for political offices and in the case of the politician, accumulate much more money for future elections, while the political godfather expects some returns on his investment through lucrative contracts. Adolphus Wabara, Nigeria's senate president from May 2003 to April 2005 clearly illustrated this point in an interview with the *Sunday Punch* newspaper. According to him, "membership of the National Assembly is an investment" because most Nigerian politicians sold their houses and other property to get elected into the national assembly and once in office, they would need to "recoup" the money they spent in contesting the elections.[118] This situation therefore resulted in the intensification of corruption in Nigeria. Thus, the intensification of the various forms of corruption associated with the democratic process in Nigeria is largely symptomatic of the transplanted bourgeois liberal democratic system of government that is at the root of the corrupt practices.

The primary focus of various constitutional engineering processes on transplanting the Western liberal democratic model into Nigeria under the Orientalist philosophy that this model is the ideal type for every non-Western society irrespective of that society's cultural, historical and social realities is fraught with problems and crises. The failure to use the constitution making processes to reflect the historical, cultural, and social diversity of Nigeria through a homegrown constitution drawn up by the representatives of the different ethnic groups, classes, social groups, gender and religions, is at the root of the crisis of democracy in the country. Devising a constitution that accords a central position to the culture of the Nigerian peoples and adequately addresses the prevailing realities of Nigeria demands a sovereign national conference of the representatives of different ethnic and other sectional and interest groups that make up the country. The political arrangement that will emanate from such a conference will be better placed to promote the conditions for stability and sustainable democracy in Nigeria.

Notes

1 See for instance, Graf, *The Nigerian State*; B. Onimode, *Imperialism and Underdevelopment in Nigeria*, London: Zed Books, 1982; J. I. Dibua, "Competition Among the Nigerian Bourgeoisie and the Demise of the First Republic," *The Herodotian*, vol. 5, No. 1, 1982; idem., "Conflict Among the Nigerian Bourgeoisie and the Demise of the Second Republic," *Africa Development*, Vol. XIII, No. 4, 1988; and T. Falola and J. Ihonvbere, *The Rise and Fall of Nigeria's Second Republic, 1979-1984*, London: Zed Books, 1985.

2 L. Diamond, *Class, Ethnicity and Democracy in Nigeria: The Failure of the First Republic*, Syracuse: Syracuse University Press, 1988; idem., "Cleavage, Conflict and Anxiety in the Second Nigerian Republic," *Journal of Modern African Studies*, Vol. 20, No. 4, 1982; idem., "Social Change and Political Conflict in Nigeria's Second Republic," in I. W. Zartman, ed., *The Political Economy of Nigeria*, New York: Praeger, 1983; idem., "Nigeria: Pluralism, Statism and the Struggle for Democracy," in L. Diamond, *et al.*, eds., *Democracy in Developing Countries*, Boulder, CO: Lynne Rienner, 1988; and C. S. Whitaker, *The Politics of Tradition: Continuity and Change in Northern Nigeria, 1946-1966*, Princeton: Princeton University Press, 1970.

3 P. P. Ekeh, "Colonialism and the Two Publics in Africa: A Theoretical Statement," *Comparative Studies in Society and History*, Vol. 17, No. 1, 1975; and idem., "Citizenship and Political Conflict."

4 K. Post and M. Vickers, *Structure and Conflict in Nigeria*, London: Heinemann, 1973, 6-8, 58-60.

5 Joseph, *Democracy and Prebendal Politics in Nigeria*.

6 L. Olurode, "The Limits of Democracy," *The Guardian* (Lagos, Nigeria), 1 June 2004.

7 B. J. Dudley, *Instability and Political Order: Politics and Crisis in Nigeria*, Ibadan: Ibadan University Press, 1973, 61.

8 Osaghae, *Crippled Giant*, 33.

9 Dudley, *Instability and Political Order*, 62-63.

10 J. O. Akintunde, "The Demise of Democracy in the First Republic of Nigeria: A Causal Analysis," *ODU*, Vol. 4, 1967, 16.

11 For details on the treasonable felony trial, see O. Awolowo, *Adventures in Power, Book1: My March Through Prison*, Ibadan: Macmillan, 1985; and L. K. Jakande, *The Trial of Obafemi Awolowo*, Lagos: John West, 1980.

12 Williams, *State and Society in Nigeria*, 76.

13 Ibid.; and Post and Vickers, *Structure and Conflict in Nigeria*, 80-82.

14 B. J. Dudley, "Western Nigeria and the Nigerian Crisis," in S. K. Panter-Brick, ed., *Nigerian Politics and Military Rule*, London: Athlene Press, 1970, 97.

15 C. Ndujihe, "The Changing Story of Women in Politics," *The Guardian*, 5 August 2004.

16 In fact with the exception of the Mohammadu Buhari military regime (1983-85), every other military regime portrayed itself as a "corrective" regime that would hand-over power to civilians after restoring order to the body polity. This commitment to restoring civilian rule was made largely to win legitimacy and acceptance from the populace. In practice, only the Mohammed/Obasanjo and the Abdulsalami Abubakar's regimes put in place fairly credible transition to civil rule programs that actually resulted in the handing over of power to civilians.

17 For detailed studies on the Gowon regime, see J. I. Elaigwu, *Gowon: The Biography of a Soldier-Statesman*, Ibadan: West Books, 1986; and O. N. Njoku, "Era of

Misguided Good Feeling: Yakubu Gowon and the Birth of a New Nigeria, 1970-1975," in L. A. Nwachuku and G. N. Uzoigwe, eds., *Troubled Journey: Nigeria Since the Civil War*, Lanham, MD: University Press of America, 2004, 51-77.

18 Some people, particularly those affected by the purge in the civil service, have argued that the exercise led to subsequent decline in the morale of civil servants, while adversely affecting productivity, efficiency and the spirit of comradeship in the civil service. See for instance, P. C. Asiodu, "The Civil Service: An Insider's View," in O. Oyediran, ed., *Nigerian Government and Politics under Military Rule, 1969-79*, New York: St. Martins, 1979, 73-95.

19 *The Nigerian Tribune* (Ibadan, Nigeria), 1 August 1975, cited in Falola and Ihonvbere, *The Rise and Fall of Nigeria's Second Republic*, 21-22.

20 On this and other models of military disengagement from politics, see J. Adekson, "Dilemma of Military Disengagement," in Oyediran, ed., *Nigerian Government and Politics under Military Rule*, 212-234.

21 See J. I. Dibua, "Nigeria: Murtala Muhammed, Obasanjo and Return to Civilian Rule, 1975-1979," in Shillington ed., *Encyclopedia of African History*, Vol. 2, 1115-1117.

22 Federal Government of Nigeria, *Report of the Constitution Drafting Committee*, Vol. 1, Lagos: Federal Government Printer, 1976; and J. O. Ojiako, *Nigeria: Yesterday, Today, and ...?*, Onitsha, Nigeria: Africana Educational Publishers, 1981, 229-230.

23 Dudley, *An Introduction to Nigerian Government and Politics*, 129.

24 On the general hegemonic influence of Western social science paradigms over Nigerian social science paradigms, see C. Ake, *Social Science as Imperialism: The Theory of Political Development*, Ibadan: Ibadan University Press, 1982.

25 Osaghae, *Crippled Giant*, 88.

26 Dudley, *An Introduction to Nigerian Government and Politics*, 158-161.

27 Ndujihe, "The Changing Story of Women in Politics."

28 Dudley, *An Introduction to Nigerian Government and Politics*, 161.

29 O. Osoba and Y. B. Usman, "A General Report on the Work of the Constitution Drafting Committee: A Minority Submission," Lagos: August 1976, mimeo.

30 C. Ake, "Introduction," *Africa Development* (Special Issue on Nigeria), Vol. IX, No. 3, 1984, 7.

31 Dudley, *An Introduction to Nigerian Government and Politics*, 160-161.

32 L. Adamolekun, *The Fall of the Second Republic*, Ibadan, Nigeria: Spectrum Books, 1985, 6-7.

33 Federal Government of Nigeria, *The Constitution of the Federal Republic of Nigeria*, Lagos: Federal Government Printer, 1979, Section 14(3).

34 O. Ikime, *In Search of Nigerians: Changing Patterns of Inter-Group Relations in an Evolving Nation State*, Ibadan: Historical Society of Nigeria, 1985, 30.

35 Adamolekun, *The Fall of the Second Republic*, 30.

36 It is because of this high level of corruption and abuse of the electoral process, that the United States Congress passed the Campaign Finance Reform Bill in 2003.

37 See L. Bolaji, *Shagari: President by Mathematics*, Ibadan: Automatic Printing Press, 1980.

38 See J. I. Dibua, "Nigeria: Second Republic, 1979-1983," in Shillington ed., *Encyclopedia of African History*, Vol. 2, 1117-1118.

39 See for instance, Joseph, *Democracy and Prebendal Politics in Nigeria*; S. Mohammed and T. A. Edoh, *A Republic in Ruins*, Zaria: Ahmadu Bello University Press, 1986; Diamond, "Cleavage, Conflict and Anxiety in the Second Nigerian Republic,"; and idem., "Social Change and Political Conflict in Nigeria's Second Republic."

40 Dibua, "Conflict Among the Nigerian Bourgeoisie and the Demise of the Second Republic."

41 Osaghae, *Crippled Giant*, 110.

42 C. Ake, "The State of the Nation: Intimations of Disaster," Presidential Address to the Nigerian Political Science Association, 1982.

43 Ibid.

44 For details on the different factions of the Nigerian bourgeoisie and the struggles and conflicts among these factions, see Dibua, "Conflict Among the Nigerian Bourgeoisie and the Demise of the Second Republic," 75-87.

45 See U. Okpu, "Inter-Party Political Relations in Nigeria 1979-1983," *Afrika Spectrum*, Vol. 19, No. 2, 1985.

46 Ibid.

47 For details on the kind of abuse associated with these programs, see O. O. Ibeanu, "Class Interest and Public Policy in Nigeria: An Analysis of Government Policies on Agriculture and Housing," *The African Review*, vol. 16, Nos. 1 and 2, 1989, 29-39; and I. Nzimiro, *The Green Revolution in Nigeria or Modernization of Hunger*, Oguta, Nigeria: Zim Pan-African Publishers, 1985.

48 T. Turner and P. Badru, "Oil and Instability: Class Contradictions and the 1983 Coup in Nigeria," *Journal of African Marxists*, No. 7, 1985.

49 For details on the various religious riots, see Y. B. Usman, *The Manipulation of Religion in Nigeria, 1977-1987*, Kaduna: Vanguard Publishers, 1987; M. H. Kukah, *Religion, Politics and Power in Northern Nigeria*, Ibadan: Spectrum, 1993; and I. M. Enwerem, *A Dangerous Awakening: The Politicization of Religion in Nigeria*, Ibadan: IFRA, 1995.

50 The splinter factions that were led by federal legislators were the Senator Anah faction from the NPP, the Aminu Kano-Senator Sarbo Bakin Zuwo faction from the PRP, and Senator Mahmud Waziri faction from the GNPP.

51 For a sampling of the press reports on the record pace of fundraising for the United States 2004 elections, see "Campaign Money Flows Amok," *New York Times*, 8 July 2004; T. B. Edsall, "Fundraising Doubles the Pace of 2000," *Washington Post*, 21 August 2004; G. Justice, "Despite New Financing Rules, Parties Collect Record $1 Billion," *New York Times*, 26 October 2004; idem., "Even with Campaign Finance Law, Money Talks Louder Than Ever," *New York Times*, 8 November 2004; and L. Akande, "Bush, Kerry Campaigns Cost $400m as Polls Draw Near," *The Guardian*, 27 October 2004.

52 I do not believe that prebendalism is of much relevance to the analysis of the Nigerian situation because it is part of the attempt by modernist and Weberian scholars to state that Africa's reality is only relevant when equated to a stage in European history. I agree with Mahmood Mamdani that this kind of analysis constitutes "history by analogy" rather than history based on an accurate analysis of Africa's concrete realities. Nor do I believe that prebendalism is relevant to the analysis of the contemporary American situation. I make the comparison to show the double standard in the production and dissemination of knowledge on Africa compared to the production and dissemination of knowledge on the Western societies.

53 Joseph, "Class, State, and Prebendal Politics in Nigeria," 57.

54 D. Morgan, "$275 Billion Highway Bill Passes Easily in the House: Pork-Laden Measure Above Bush Spending Limit," *Washington Post*, 3 April 2004.

55 T. Egan, "Built With Steel, Perhaps, but Greased With Pork," *New York Times*, 10 April 2004.

56 Joseph, *Democracy and Prebendal Politics in Nigeria*, 67.

57 Cited in Ibid.

58 *New York Times*, 16 April 2004.

59 See Joseph, *Democracy and Prebendal Politics in Nigeria*, in particular 66-67.

60 Two members of the Bureau, Ola Balogun and Edwin Madunagu resigned in July 1986 and December 1986 respectively, for various reasons.

61 Federal Republic of Nigeria, *Report of the Political Bureau*, 4-6.

62 For a detailed discussion of Babangida's transition to civil rule program, see L. Diamond, A. Kirk-Greene and O. Oyediran, eds., *Transition Without End: Nigerian Politics and Civil Society Under Babangida*, Boulder, CO: Lynne Rienner, 1997; and J. I. Dibua, "Structural Adjustment Programme and the Subversion of Popular Will in Africa: The Case of the Transition to Civil Rule in Nigeria," in S. G. Tyoden, ed., *The Transition to Civil Rule: The Journey So Far – The Proceedings of the 19th Annual Conference of the Nigerian Political Science Association*, Lagos: The Nigerian Political Science Association, 1992, 158-169.

63 K. A. Shettima, "Engendering Nigeria's Third Republic," *African Studies Review*, Vol. 38, No. 3, 1995, 88. Also see H. Abdullah, " 'Transition Politics' and the Challenge of Gender in Nigeria," *Review of African Political Economy*, No. 56, 1993 27-41.

64 Federal Republic of Nigeria, *Report of the Political Bureau*, 152.

65 Ibid., 154-155.

66 See for instance, T. Olagunju, *et al.*, *Transition to Democracy in Nigeria, 1985-1993*, St. Helier, UK and Ibadan, Nigeria: Safari and Spectrum Books, 1993; and S. Oyovbaire and T. Olagunju, eds., *Foundations of a New Nigeria: The IBB Era*, London: Precision Press, 1989.

67 It is significant to note that only four of the sixteen members of the Political Bureau can be said to have had socialist leanings and so they could not have imposed their wish on the majority of the members. See A. T. Gana, *The Limits of Political Engineering: A Critique of the Transition Programme*, Jos: Covenant Press, 1990, 15. Indeed, a careful reading of the Bureau's report will show that the socialism it recommended for the country was a product of the extensive debates it conducted and its extensive examination of the peculiar Nigerian situation and was aimed at promoting democratization, social and economic justice, and self-reliant development. It is not quite correct as claimed by Tunji Olagunju, Adele Jinadu and Sam Oyovbaire, that the socialism recommended by the Bureau was "the socialism of social democracy" because, according to them, this was in line with the liberal political theory that underlined the entire report. See Olagunju, *et al.*, *Transition to Democracy in Nigeria*, 128-129.

68 Federal Republic of Nigeria, *Government's Views and Comments on the Findings and Recommendations of the Political Bureau*, Lagos: Federal Government Printer, 1987, 9-14.

69 Gana, *The Limits of Political Engineering*, 16.

70 T. Olagunju and S. Oyovbaire, eds., *For Their Tomorrow We Gave Our Today: Selected Speeches of IBB*, Vol. 2, St Helier, UK: Safari Books, 1991, 51.

71 Ibid., 107.

72 For elaborate discussion on the linkage between SAP and the transition to civil rule program, see J. I. Dibua, "The Structural Adjustment Programme and the Transition to Civil Rule in Nigeria," in L. A. Thompson, ed., *Democracy, Democratization and Africa*, Ibadan, Enugu and Abuja: Afrika-Link Books, 1994, 185-203; and A. Momoh, "The Structural Adjustment Programme and the Transition to Civil Rule in Nigeria (1986-1993)," *Africa Development*, vol. XXI, No. 1, 1996, 19-37.

73 The timetable for transition to civil rule stated that SAP would be terminated in the second quarter of 1988 while the third and fourth quarters of 1988 would be used to consolidate the gains of SAP. However, this turned out not to be the case as the entire transition program was devoted to reinforcing SAP. The claim that SAP would be terminated in 1988 was aimed at placating Nigerians who were overwhelmingly opposed to the program.

74 Federal Republic of Nigeria, *Transition to Civil Rule (Political Programme), Decree No. 9*, Lagos: The Federal Government Printer, 1987.

75 Federal Republic of Nigeria, *Constituent Assembly Decree: Decree No. 14*, Lagos: The Federal Government Press, 1988.

76 In fact, right from the moment of elections into the CA, NEC became a tool for justifying and supporting the Babangida regime's authoritarian attempts at constructing a new political (democratic?) order. See Abutudu, *The State, Civil Society and the Democratisation Process in Nigeria*, 19-20.

77 T. Olagunju and S. Oyovbaire, eds., *Portrait of a New Nigeria: Selected Speeches of IBB*, Vol. 1, London: Precision Press, 1989, 52.

78 *New Nigerian* (Kaduna, Nigeria), 9 May 1988. R. A. Akindele has however, argued that "to say that the 1988-89 Constituent Assembly had a right wing character is a mischievous exaggeration; it grossly overstates the implications of the situational reality of the absence of vocal radical elements in the Assembly." R. A. Akindele, "The Constituent Assembly, 1988-1989," Paper Presented at the Conference on Democratic Transition and Structural Adjustment in Nigeria, Held at Hoover Institute, Stanford University, California, 27-29 August 1990, 7. Akindele's contention represents a misrepresentation of the facts.

79 Oyovbaire and Olagunju, eds., *Foundations of a New Nigeria*, 28-31.

80 Olagunju and Oyovbaire, *For Their Tomorrow We Gave Our Today*, 5-9.

81 K. Amuwo, "Democracy by Fiat: Why it Will Not Work," *Africa Quarterly*, Vol. 35, No. 3, 1995, 19-31.

82 T. Olarewaju, "Fury of the Amazons," *The Guardian*, 9 July 1999.

83 World Bank, *Sub-Saharan Africa: From Crisis to Sustainable Growth*, 55, 59, 61, 191.

84 Beckman, "Empowerment or Repression?"

85 For a discussion of the so-called "grassroots empowerment" policies associated with the transition program, see J. I. Dibua, "Collapse of Purpose: Ibrahim Babangida, 1985-1993," in Nwachuku and Uzoigwe, eds., *Troubled Journey*, 212-220.

86 M. I. M. Abutudu, "Confronting Political Shock: Civil Society and the Annulment of the 1993 Presidential Election in Nigeria," Unpublished Research Report Submitted to the Social Science Research Council (SSRC), New York, 1996.

87 J. Ihonvbere, "A Critical Evaluation of the Failed 1990 Coup in Nigeria," *Journal of Modern African Studies*, Vol. 29, No. 4, 1991.

88 Justice Bassey Ita Ikpeme was appointed an Abuja high court judge barely six months before the presidential election. The manner in which she handled the ABN motions contravened clearly established procedural and institutional processes (for instance, her sitting late at night to rule over the ABN's motion). This tended to create the impression that the main reason for her appointment as a judge was to enable Babangida acting through surrogates to use her court to achieve his ambition of perpetuating himself in office.

89 Omo Omoruyi, a Professor of Political Science, former director-general of the Center for Democratic Studies, Abuja and a close confidant of Babangida has advanced six reasons that he categorized as the "primary real reasons" and the "secondary real

reasons" for the annulment of the results of the June 12 presidential election. See O. Omoruyi, *The Tale of June 12: The Betrayal of the Democratic Rights of Nigerians (1993)*, Lagos and London: Press Alliance Network, 1999, especially chapter 5; and idem., "Democratic Transitions in Africa: The Case of Nigeria," A Lecture Delivered under the auspices of the Dr. Sidney D. Redmond Lecture Series, Jackson State University, Jackson, Mississippi, USA, 24 February 2003.

90 C. Leechor, "Ghana: Frontrunner in Adjustment," in I. Husain and R. Faruqee, eds., *Adjustment in Africa: Lessons from Country Case Studies*, Washington, D.C.: The World Bank, 1994, 153-192.

91 Y. Bangura, *Crisis, Adjustment and Politics in Nigeria*, Stockholm and Uppsala: AKUT Group, 1989, 11-12.

92 For a detailed study of the turmoil generated by the annulment of the presidential election, see Abutudu, "Confronting Political Shock."

93 See Ndujihe, "The Changing Story of Women in Politics."

94 B. O. Nwabueze, *Nigeria '93: The Political Crisis and Solutions*, Ibadan: Spectrum, 1994, 22.

95 See J. I. Dibua, "Nigeria: Opposition, 1990s, to the Fourth Republic," in Shillington ed., *Encyclopedia of African History*, Vol. 2, 1123-1125.

96 See for instance, *Newswatch* (Lagos, Nigeria), 23 January 1995.

97 O. Okeke, "Legacy of National Paralysis: Ernest Shonekan and Sani Abacha, 1993-1998," in Nwachuku and Uzoigwe, eds., *Troubled Journey*, 243-244.

98 For a summary of this argument, see National Orientation Agency, *Abacha's Transition Programme*, Abuja, Nigeria: National Orientation Agency, 1995, 1-4.

99 See for instance, *Tell*, (Lagos, Nigeria), 14 October 1996; and *The News*, (Lagos, Nigeria), 14 October 1996.

100 A. Abubakar, "My Transition Agenda for Development," Text of a National Broadcast to the Nation by Head of State, General Abdulsalami Abubakar on 20 July 1998, reproduced in *Vanguard* (Lagos, Nigeria), 21 July 1998.

101 It is generally agreed that the Third Republic was aborted with the annulment of the results of the 12 June 1993 presidential elections.

102 Cited in Olarewaju, "Fury of the Amazons." The Beijing Declaration of 1995 recommeded that 30 percent of elective and appointive posts should be reserved for women.

103 See Y. Aderibigbe, "Women: Continued Search for Political Relevance," *The Guardian*, 8 April 2004.

104 Olarewaju, "Fury of the Amazons."

105 A. Abubakar, "Time to Break Cycle of Instability and Mistrust," Text of General Abdulsalami Abubakar's Address to the Nation, on the Hand-over of Government and Inauguration of the President-elect, 29 May 1999.

106 O. Obasanjo, "The New Dawn," Inaugural Speech of His Excellency, President Olusegun Obasanjo, Following his Swearing-in as President of the Federal Republic of Nigeria, 29 May 1999, reproduced in *Vanguard*, 30 May 1999.

107 See *The Punch* (Lagos, Nigeria), 21 June 2004.

108 A. Williams, "A Cross Nigeria Must Bear," *The Guardian*, 6 June 2004. Also see the editorial article, "Indigene/Settler Question," *The Punch* 23 June 2004.

109 Usman, *The Manipulation of Religion in Nigeria*; and Enwerem, *A Dangerious Awakening*.

110 D. C. Bach, "Indigeneity, Ethnicity and Federalism," in Diamond, *et al.*, *Transition Without End*, 333-349; A. Momoh, *Even Birds Have a Home: Explaining the Pathologies of the Citizenship Question in Nigeria*, EMPARC's Annual Lecture

Series, No. 7, Lagos: EMPARC, 2001; and P. P. Ekeh and E. E. Osaghae, eds., *Federal Character and Federalism in Nigeria*, Ibadan: Heinemann, 1989.

111 For details see, J. I. Dibua, "Conflict over Control of Natural Resources in Nigeria: The Case of the Oil-Producing Niger Delta Communities of the South-South States, 1990-2004," *Lagos Historical Review*, Vol. 4, 2004, 142-172; and idem., "Citizenship and Resource Control in Nigeria: The Case of Minority Communities in the Niger Delta," *Africa Spectrum*, Vol. 39, No. 1, 2005, 5-28.

112 B. Naanen, "Oil-Producing Minorities and the Restructuring of Nigerian Federalism: The Case of the Ogoni People," *Journal of Commonwealth and Comparative Politics*, Vol. 33, No. 1, 1995.

113 See A. Enahoro, "The National Question: Towards a New Constitutional Order," *The Guardian*, 5 July 2002; and G. Etakibuebu, "Future Uncertain Without a National Conference," *The Guardian*, 31 May 2004.

114 See P. Odiaka, "Many Questions as the Nation Celebrates Democracy Day," *The Guardian*, 28 May 2004; Y. Aderibigbe, "Rising Clamour for National Conference," *The Guardian*, 2 June 2004; and J. A. Ogbodo and L. Njoku, "Northern Govs, Ohanaeze, Others, Endorse National Conference," *The Guardian*, 6 June 2004.

115 K. Okonjo, "The Dual-Sex Political System in Operation: Igbo Women and Community Politics in Midwestern Nigeria," in Hafkin and Bay eds., *Women in Africa*, 45-58.

116 See for instance, G. Justice, "Republicans Rush to Form New Finance Groups," *New York Times*, 29 May 2004.

117 P. T. Zeleza, "The Perpetual Solitudes and Crises of African Studies in the United States," *Africa Today*, Vol. 44, No. 2, 1997, 193-210.

118 *Sunday Punch* (Lagos, Nigeria), 5 June 2004.

Chapter 5

Technology Transfer and the Crisis of Industrialization

The modernist conception of development perceives industrialization and the associated large-scale mechanized agriculture as constituting the core of development. Indeed, large-scale industrialization with the attendant mass production is accorded the crucial role in the project of transforming backward peasant societies into modern capitalist societies. For the proponents of the modernization paradigm, Nigeria and other African countries were so primitive and backward that they lacked the efficient rational base in science, technology and management to support any meaningful transformation of their societies through science and technology. The American model of development with its emphasis on advanced science, technology and managerial efficiency which became hegemonic in development discourse in the post World War II period, reinforced the notion of the attainment of industrial modernity along Western lines, as the main index of development.[1]

Furthermore, the dominant position that American social scientists and development theorists occupied in African studies from the 1960s and the fact that increasing number of African social scientists were trained in American institutions helped to foster the American model of industrial modernity among African social scientists and policy makers. This dominance was reinforced by the development and technical assistance provided to African countries by American based aid agencies. The centerpiece of this model was the belief in the universal applicability of the Western technological and industrial experience. This helped to lend intellectual weight to the perpetuation of the notion of technology transfer as the panacea for the attainment of technological and industrial modernity in Nigeria and other African countries.

Moreover, the instrumental rationality that underlined the technological development and industrialization process of the Western capitalist societies was idealized and universalized as the only credible means by which any society can attain development. Thus, the transplantation and replication of the Western technological and industrial development experience and trajectory were touted as the immutable path through which non-Western societies can attain development. From this perspective, some proponents of technology transfer have advocated the development of intermediate technology as the basis for creating the indigenous technological capacity for the absorption and replication of modern Western technology.[2] The notion of intermediate technology is based on the modernist linear conception of history: it advocates that Nigeria and other African countries should first revert to the 19th century technology of the Western industrialized countries and progress along the Western path to attain technological and industrial modernity. This recommendation is unrealistic and inappropriate because the 19th century socio-cultural and economic realities of Western countries were specific to those countries and different from the postcolonial realities of Nigeria and other African countries. Nevertheless, these perspectives provided the theoretical and epistemological bases for the policy of technology transfer that implemented in Nigeria and other African countries.

As is the practice with the modernization paradigm, the policy of technology transfer is based on the denigration of the so-called irrational, backward and primitive indigenous African production base, which was portrayed as consigning these societies to perpetual underdevelopment. The key to the development of African societies is therefore portrayed as lying in the transplanting of Western technology into Nigeria and other African countries because as a product of instrumental rationality, Western technology is universally applicable. This view fails to take into account the fact that Western technology is a product of concrete historical, social and material experiences of Western societies and therefore "bound up with concrete production processes and bears definite relations of production" of Western societies.[3] Technology is thus a cultural process and, so, it is not possible to talk of technology transfer in isolation of the cultural process to which it is intimately bound. The notion of technology transfer therefore amounts to cultural imperialism, which requires the denigration and suppression of the indigenous technology and culture, hence, the characterization of the indigenous Nigerian technology and culture as primitive, backward and irrational.

The denigration of indigenous Nigerian technology as backward and irrational was used to justify the notion that the indigenous technology was of no relevance to the industrialization and development process. Rather, the irrational and non-ideal type indigenous technology needed to be suppressed or even wiped out and replaced by the Western ideal type, rational and modern technology, thus, the imperative for technology transfer. As already noted, since technology is a cultural process, the technology that emanates from a people's socio-cultural realities is better placed to tackle the peculiar problems of the people concerned. In spite of this intimate relationship between technology and culture, the notion of the irrationality and backwardness or even absence of any meaningful indigenous technology has been uncritically accepted as an article of faith by Nigerian policy makers, mainstream social scientists and multilateral institutions. As a result, the discourse on technological development and industrialization in Nigeria is squarely situated within the modernization paradigm as epitomized by the strong commitment to the transplantation of Western technologies into the country, as the panacea for attaining development. Policy-making and mainstream scholarship are therefore mainly devoted to creating the so-called favorable conditions for the smooth transfer of Western technology into the country.

This chapter will interrogate the problematic and dialectics of technology transfer. It will discuss the evolution of the official Nigerian policy of technology transfer. Furthermore, the import substitution industrialization strategy and the establishment of joint industrial projects between Nigerian government and foreign TNCs, as well as the attempts at developing capital goods industry through the development of the iron and steel industry, as ways of ensuring technology transfer, will be examined. The role that the indigenous technological base should play in the industrial development of Nigeria will be highlighted.

Problematic and Dialectics of Technology Transfer

The location of the concept of technology transfer within the Weberian and modernist binary division of ideal type rational Western capitalist societies and the non-ideal type irrational Nigerian society provided the *raison d'etre* for the policy of transplanting Western technology into Nigeria as the solution to the country's development crisis. This policy of transplanting Western technology into the country was predicated on the supposed neutrality of science and the universal applicability of the instrumental rationality that underlined the process of capitalist development and the attainment of industrial modernity in Western capitalist societies. It should be noted that technological and capitalist development in the Western societies were closely intertwined with, and shaped by, the social, cultural, economic and political realities of these societies. Berman notes that the pursuance of profit, which is the primary factor that underlined these developments, engendered a profound cultural transformation that led to the emergence of definite relations of production and the reorientation of the "Western experience of time, space, labor, bodily life, and the production of knowledge." The result was "the mass production of uniform goods in large factory units that were components of even larger corporations combining capital and labor, production, and distribution in a single complex system."[4] This mass production model joined the Parsonian notion of "social differentiation, secularization and the move from ascription to achievement," as a defining characteristic of modern industrial society.[5] Unfortunately, this Western cultural transformation became so hegemonic and intimately bound up with the production and dissemination of knowledge in the Western dominated social sciences, that it formed the basis for the universalization of the Western experience and the rejection of non-Western cultures as primitive, backward and irrational.

From the preceding discussion, it is clear that the concept of the neutrality of science and technology is a myth, as is the case with the idea of technology transfer, which is based on this notion of neutrality. It follows that technology cannot really be transferred, at least, in isolation from the cultural context in which it is embedded, a factor that promotes a conflict-laden dialectical relationship between the supposedly transferred technology and the recipient culture. As pointed out by Berman, Western technology is an explicitly bureaucratic and capitalist technology that partly relied on the denigration of craft knowledge to promote the subordination of Western workers to the factory and technology-based control.[6] Thus, the denigration of the artisan technology as well as arts and crafts which constitute the foundation of the Nigerian indigenous technological base, has generated a number of contradictions that are at the root of the country's technological and industrialization crises.

The modernist conception of technology resulted in its conceptualization mainly in terms of Western type large-scale, centralized and capital-intensive technology that are used to support and promote mass production of goods. Technology is therefore perceived as relating to both the physical or chemical transformation of raw materials and the differentiation between similar outputs, where legal protection, trade names, or product differentiation play an important role. Furthermore, the technological content of any product includes the product design and differentiation, the process know-how or method of production, and the packaging.[7] This perspective promoted the commodification of technology in the sense that technology was seen as a commodity owned by the advanced capitalist countries that can be sold at the discretion of the owners to third world countries such as Nigeria. This viewpoint which underlies the whole notion of the transfer of technology from the West to non-Western countries has become the received wisdom hence the discourse centers on the form that the technology transfer should take. Yet it is not correct to see technology as only a Western phenomenon because technology, which can be defined as a body of knowledge (that is, the knowledge itself and the tangible embodiment of that knowledge) about techniques of production, is a phenomenon that is present in every society. Furthermore, technology can be regarded as the "productive knowledge required to transform materials into goods and services, create new or improved products, provide better and efficient services and generate further knowledge for production of goods and services."[8] Thus, given the utilitarian value of technology, various societies developed their own technology embodying specific skills and techniques, which they used in producing goods and services geared toward satisfying their basic and luxurious needs.

The conception of technology and industrialization as synonymous with the mass production of standardized goods model, precluded any alternative conceptualization of technology and industrialization that ran counter to this model. In fact, Western economic historians, development economists and other social scientists who defined the agenda of the discourse promoted the notion that the experiences of the Western industrial revolution and its aftermath, makes the mass production model the inevitable path to industrialization for non-Western societies.[9] As a result, non-Western societies were expected to adopt the technology and other features of the mass industrialization model in order to be able to industrialize their societies. Embedded in this concept of industrialization is the notion of irrational, backward, traditional and technologically stagnant African peasant societies whose economy of affection made it impossible for them to develop any form of worthwhile technology. As a result, indigenous African artisan technology was portrayed as backward and irrelevant to the industrialization process. Thus, the issue before African policy makers was conceived as not the form that industrialization would take, rather, it was the means for the attainment of the Western-style mass production model of industrialization. Technology transfer was therefore portrayed as the most viable means for attaining industrial modernity.

As a result, most of the discourse and policy instruments were preoccupied with how to put in place, the fastest means for effecting the transfer of Western technology to African countries. Various modernist scholars noted that less developed countries, such as African countries, were advantageously placed in this regard, in that there were readily available "the general fund of knowledge accumulated in the technically advanced countries," that could be easily transferred to them.[10] Technology transfer was therefore conceived as a "short-cut" toward technological "leapfrogging" or "catching-up" with the industrialized countries.[11] As noted by B. F. Johnston and P. Kilby:

> The most fundamental factor conditioning structural transformation in contemporary underdeveloped countries is the existence of a large stock of proven technical innovations in the more-developed countries. The existence of this technology backlog, much of which is transferable, creates the possibility for late-developing countries to bypass the vast investments of time and resources that the accumulation of the knowledge involved.[12]

Although technology transfer has been variously described as "replicative engineering," "indigenization of production processes," and "transfer of skills and resources,"[13] the respective viewpoints conceive of technology transfer in the form of buying and selling of commodities. Indeed, Cardinal Warde described it as:

> The process by which one nation acquires hardware and the technical skills and training necessary to operate that hardware from another nation. The process of technology transfer is not complete until the buying nation is, in addition, able to manage, maintain, replicate and improve that technology through research and without assistance from the selling nation.[14]

With this commodification view of technology transfer, much emphasis was placed on the methods and processes of effecting the transfer. Y, Hayami and V. Ruttan identified three stages in an effective transfer process: material transfer, design transfer, and capacity transfer.[15] In essence, the effective transfer of technology involves mastering the design of the technology, replicating the imported technology and adapting the technology to meet local needs.[16]

M. N. B. Ayiku has however pointed out that "the phrase 'transfer of technology' is not only vague but imprecise and misleading." He notes that this phrase and the related view of technology as a commodity make it appear as if there are "transferrors" and recipients of technology, and also that there is a fixed price for a particular technology or a "transfer" process. Furthermore, there are no "transferrors" and "recipients" of technology. There "are only buyers and sellers in a market which is highly imperfect since the seller of technology always aims at concealing the details of the technology even if the technology is not protected in order to increase his bargaining power when dealing with a buyer with low technological capability." Ayiku concluded that the notion that technology can be 'transferred' from a transferror to a recipient has no meaning: it is simply misleading.[17]

In any case, advocates of technology transfer have argued that an essential component of the process is the building of absorptive capacity within the recipient countries. As noted by A. S. Bhalla, mere reproduction or use of the transferred technology "is unlikely to strengthen the technological capabilities" within the recipient developing countries. Rather, effective technology transfer requires "a capacity to improve and adapt imported technologies and develop new ones."[18] Thus, transfer of technology should include the incorporation of features that will help in building the capacity to adapt and manufacture the technology by the recipient countries. It is therefore necessary to organize sufficient research on a wider scale that would enable the recipient countries "to keep abreast of modern trends and developments in world science and technology," in order to be able to efficiently adapt the imported technology to local conditions.[19]

The issue of capacity transfer was a major preoccupation of the United Nations Conference on Trade and Development (UNCTAD) in the 1980s and 1990s. However, the various negotiations between the advanced capitalist countries and the developing countries in this regard did not yield any meaningful result as the advanced capitalist countries persistently insisted that technology should only be transferred in their fixed final form.[20] The advanced capitalist countries insisted on this form of technology transfer because it guaranteed their continued dominance of the economies of the developing countries. It is apposite that even in the case of the newly industrialized non-Western countries such as Brazil, India and South Korea, the nature of the so-called technology transfer agreements, ensured that the structure of control of the manufacturing sector was highly skewed in favor of the advanced capitalist countries.[21] Typically, some clauses in such agreements promoted technological dependence by providing that major decisions, such as investment, pricing and sources of inputs, take place outside the country, at the headquarters of the transnational corporations. In addition, restrictions might be placed on exports, prices, sales volume and the sale of technology.[22]

Nevertheless, the discourse on capacity building is squarely situated within the framework of the modernization paradigm. It is argued that compared to other Third World countries, African countries are particularly worse off because of the very low level of scientific and technology research, which means that they have a very low or rudimentary level of technical capacity. However, the discourse on capacity building does not advocate the endogenous development of the existing indigenous scientific and technical knowledge, which are often dismissed as unscientific and irrelevant artisan and craft knowledge. Rather capacity building is seen from the perspective of creating the ability on the part of indigenous scientists and engineers among others, to operate, adapt and replicate the transplanted technology. The replication of imported technology, which is regarded as an indication of the success of the policy of technology transfer, is based on the modernist viewpoint in that it takes the imported technology as the point of reference. Thus, replication involves the production of technologies that are closely similar to the imported ones and fails to take into account the fact that the imported technologies are largely products of cultural, scientific and economic realities that are specific to their countries of origin.

The capacity building model, of technology transfer that emphasized, large-scale, capital-intensive heavy industrialization was refined by some scholars in the 1970s with a view to overcoming the perceived failure of this model. These scholars came up with the concept of relevant technology or appropriate technology. As exemplified by the title of E. F. Schumacher's work, *Small is Beautiful*,[23] this approach emphasized the adoption of small-scale, simple, low-cost and labor-intensive technology that are adapted to suit the specific realities and factor endowments of the locations where they are to be used. The underlying premise of the concept of relevant or appropriate technology is the perceived limited relevance of the advanced countries capital-intensive technologies to the different factor endowments of the developing countries.[24] In a sense, this concept questioned the prevailing belief in the unbridled universal application of Western large-scale capital-intensive technologies. Thus, technologies that are transferred should be adapted to suit the different social, cultural, economic and other conditions of the recipient societies while attempts should be made for the technologies to use locally available materials, resources and manpower. It was claimed that this approach would encourage and stimulate indigenous initiative and innovation by helping to build local capacity to adapt and manufacture the imported technology. Briefly, this approach emphasizes simplicity and practicability while providing many opportunities for the exercise of scientific and engineering talents in the recipient countries.[25]

It should be noted that the relevant or appropriate technology approach to the issue of technology transfer was based on the "basic needs" reformulation of the modernization paradigm in the 1970s. Thus, although the approach was more focused on micro technology issues, small-scale producers and recognized the need for technology to be ecological relevant to the areas of application, its reference point remained the imported Western technology. Its emphasis on capacity building was to the extent that non-Western peoples would be able to replicate imported technologies and adapt them to suit their respective ecological realities.

This modernist approach therefore failed to recognize the fact that the existing indigenous technology base which are products of the peoples culture and their ecology, should constitute the cornerstone of technological development. Furthermore, the approach was based on the linear or stages of growth conception of economic development as evident in studies of China's industrialization process, which is seen as the most significant example of the success of the relevant or appropriate technology model. Most of the studies state that the small-scale low level technology used by China replicates the type of technology used by the Western advanced capitalist countries at an earlier stage in their development.[26] Implicit in this analysis is that African countries revert to the type of technology used by the advanced capitalist countries at an earlier stage in their industrialization process and then progress along the industrial development path of these countries toward the attainment of industrial modernity.

In any case, the relevant or appropriate technology model has been criticized for its narrow interpretations of self-reliance and for having an attractive rhetoric but only made dubious or questionable contributions to national development.[27] Furthermore, in the 1980s, the model was criticized for placing too much emphasis on micro issues whereas the issues of technology choice and transformation of non-Western countries needed to be placed in a macro perspective. Thus, there was a shift of emphasis to issues pertaining to "the macroeconomic and political economy of technology decisions, intersectoral linkages to promote technology improvements and reduce technology gaps between modern and informal sectors, and the emergence of new technologies."[28] Even then, in spite of various negotiations conducted by UNCTAD, the advanced capitalist countries disowned the micro technology emphasis of the relevant and appropriate technology model while continuing to insist on the transfer of large-scale, capital intensive technologies to African and other developing countries.

Nigerian Government's Policy on Technology Transfer

The Nigerian government did not develop any clearly articulated policy on technology transfer until the mid-1970s. Indeed, in the 1960s and early 1970s, the primary preoccupation was the development of human capital, which was seen as crucial for the industrialization process. The development of human capital involved the strengthening of scientific and technical education in order to be able to build up aspects of technological infrastructure.[29] The function of technology transfer was peripherally accorded to the import substitution industrialization strategy with the hope that the importation of capital goods would eventually help to raise the level of intermediate and capital goods production. However, as noted by Akin Adubifa, the importation of foreign technology was mainly for the purpose of manufacturing goods rather than for the acquisition of skills.[30] The federal government realized this fact when it noted in the Second National

Development Plan, 1970-1974, that "import-substitution brought in its wake a rise in the importation of raw materials, intermediate and capital goods," thereby making the manufacturing sector to become highly dependent on import. The solution it proffered to the situation was "the upgrading of local production of intermediate and capital goods for sale to other industries."[31]

It was in the Third National Development Plan, 1975-80 that the Nigerian government for the first time clearly laid out its policy on technology transfer. This plan was drawn up during the period that some United Nations agencies, such as UNCTAD and the United Nations Industrial Development Organization (UNIDO), as well as some other multilateral organizations were preoccupied with controlling the unbridled importation of technology into Nigeria and other developing countries. They saw the uncontrolled influx of foreign technology into these countries as resulting in the dumping of many inappropriate technologies into the countries, under exploitative terms of contract. As part of the industrial development policy, the third national development plan aimed at exposing Nigerians to advanced technology through the transfer of industrial technology that would eventually result in the indigenization of technology.[32] The National Science and Technology Development Agency (NSTDA) was established in 1977 to promote science and technology research and oversee the process of technology transfer. In 1979, a separate federal Ministry of Science and Technology was created to replace the NSTDA. Among other things, the ministry was responsible for formulating a national policy for science and technology, promoting science and technology research, promoting, and administering programs for technology transfer.

Perhaps the most significant step that was taken with regard to technology transfer during the plan period was the establishment of a National Office of Industrial Property (NOIP) in 1979. This agency, which was created at the urging of UNIDO and UNCTAD, was specifically charged with scrutinizing and approving technology transfer contracts. The functions of the NOIP included "the development of the negotiating skills of Nigerians with a view to ensuring the acquirement of the best contractual terms and conditions by Nigerian parties entering into any contract or agreement for the transfer of technology." However, the NOIP could only approve or deny technology transfer contracts based on conditions that relate only to the fairness or otherwise of the terms of the contracts and not to the technology content of the contracts. Indeed, the NOIP could only exert peripheral influence on technology transfer: it could not determine a firm's technology choice, "rather it only ensures that the contractual terms and conditions for a transfer of technology contract are not unduly unfavourable to the country and to the Nigerian contracting party." Thus, the onus for the selection of technology to be used in Nigeria rested with the supplier of the technology.[33]

Furthermore, the Nigerian government as was the case with the governments of most developing countries, realized that the strategy of relying on investments by foreign-owned transnational corporations as a means of effecting technology transfer did not produce positive results. The corporations were primarily concerned with the maximization of profits and were usually unwilling to employ Nigerians in the technical departments of their branches in Nigeria. To overcome this shortcoming and ensure the transfer of technology, the Nigerian government decided to place more emphasis on joint ventures involving private indigenous capitalists, federal or state governments, and foreign technical partners. Joint venture agreements, especially those involving the federal government included clauses that specified that within a specific period, Nigerians should have been trained to take over full operational management of the joint projects. In the case of industries such as cement, textiles, sugar, fruit canning and other consumer goods industries, the process of training Nigerians to take over full operational control was expected to be completed within three years. However, in spite this provision, Nigerian engineers and other technical staff were usually employed in the joint ventures "either for glorified administrative duties, or for routine operations," while "the expatriates are given full control over technical operations."[34] In the joint venture motor-vehicle assembly industries, it was specified that 30 percent of all the component parts should be locally manufactured within ten years. In addition, the government promoted product standardization for various consumer goods with the belief that compliance with these standards would eventually help to promote the development of certain technical capabilities among Nigerians.

The Fourth National Development Plan, 1981-85 stated that emphasis would be placed on science and technology, which for the first time in Nigeria's planning exercise, was made a distinct sector with its own financial allocation. This development was influenced by the recommendation of the 1980 Organization of African Unity (OAU) Lagos Plan of Action for the Economic Development of Africa, which was adopted by member states. The recommendation urged member states to "take steps to improve existing and create new funding mechanisms to provide funds on a predictable and continuous basis at the national level, with a view to substantially increasing the resources available for the development of their scientific and technological capabilities." To achieve this objective, member states were expected to spend an annual amount of not less than one percent of the GDP on science and technology.[35]

The fourth national development plan noted that to develop indigenous technical capacity, more emphasis would be placed on scientific and technical research in tertiary institutions and relevant research institutes. Furthermore, new institutions (National Technology Development Center; National Institute for Chemicals Research; Research Products Development Corporation; and Technology Potential Data Bank and Documentation Center) that were expected to help in strengthening indigenous technology acquisition would be established. However, none of these institutions was established by the end of the plan period. It has been noted that the failure to adequately fund research in science and technology in spite of the creation of a separate ministry to handle these issues thwarted technological adaptation and innovation thereby creating a technological quagmire in the country.

> At its peak in 1982, capital budget allocation to the nation's Science andTechnology system was 98 million (Naira) representing under one per cent of the federal budget and less than 0.2 per cent of the GNP. In 1983, this was reduced to 68 million (Naira) and in 1984, it took a calamitous dive to 14 million (Naira). The 1985 draft budget (made) a provision for mere 7.5 million (Naira) for Science and Technology. Surely, these figures are far below the one per cent of GDP which the Lagos Plan of Action recommended as the minimum level of funding for Research and Development activities.[36]

With the marginalization of science and technology research and innovation, Nigeria joined other developing nations in resorting to "pious exhortation" to the advanced capitalist countries under the Paris Convention, to consider renegotiating the legal and juridical basis of technology transfer under "fair and reasonable terms and conditions."[37]

The first comprehensive official national policy on science and technology was published in 1986. Among other things, the policy stated that imported technology for major government projects would be procured in an "unpackaged" form; strategic capital goods industry would as far as possible be controlled by Nigerians; and that important national development projects would not be based on unproven foreign technologies. It stated that the primary objective of the technology policy was "to ensure the continuous and sustained upliftment of (the) general quality of life and national security, through self-reliance, in the shortest possible time, compatible with the nation's cultural patterns and optimal utilization of (the) nation's resources." Technology generation would involve "initiating, promoting and sustaining programmes that will engender technology generation through copy technology by unpackaging, analysing and adapting imported technology to complement technology development from local research activities." It would also involve "ensuring the involvement of local scientific and technical personnel in the planning, design, construction, installation and maintenance in national development programmes and projects." Furthermore, indigenous technology capability acquisition would be promoted through the initiation of programs that would ensure the "development of local capabilities through the incorporation of imported 'unpackaged' (component) technologies into appropriate areas of industry."[38]

With specific reference to technology transfer and diffusion, the National Science and Technology policy stated six goals that the government aimed at achieving.

1. Developing simplified manuals and liaison services to guarantee widespread dissemination and assimilation of research findings.

2. Controlling the mode of foreign investments in industries with a view to ensure technology acquisition within a specified time frame.
3. Encouraging personnel mobility as a key element in internal diffusion of technology.
4. Establishing an up-to-date Science and Technology data bank and technical journals for project reports and other statistical information with links to national and international network of information centers and libraries.
5. Initiating, promoting and supporting relevant and appropriate technology diffusion to rural areas.
6. Establishing a comprehensive inventory of local technology and initiating improvement of these through the incorporation of high-level technology for enhancing efficiency.

In order to promote technological capability through local research and development activities, incentives would be provided to manufacturing industries that set up such facilities within the country. Furthermore, tax write-offs and other financial incentives would be provided to groups that commission local small-scale industry technology research for the purpose of manufacturing goods.[39]

The science and technology policy provided for the setting up of a National Council for Science and Technology to promote the "effective infusion of science and technology to and from all the States of the (Nigerian) Federation." In addition, the federal government would allocate between 2.5 and 5 percent of its total annual budget to the development of science and technology while the state governments were expected to contribute a minimum of one percent of their annual budgets for the same purpose. Furthermore, the private sector, individuals and organizations would be encouraged to contribute to the science and technology development fund. The funds accruing to the sector would be managed by a new agency, the National Science and Technology Fund (NSTF), which would disburse the funds for the implementation of science and technology programs "in accordance with the national policy, guidelines, and strategies."[40] However, with the introduction of the SAP in July 1986 and the subsequent liberalization of the country's economy as well as the severe economic crisis caused by SAP, the policies enunciated in the national policy on science and technology were not implemented.

Nonetheless, based on the continued pressure on the federal government by members of the scientific community and other interest groups for the promulgation of a more meaningful science and technology policy, Babangida inaugurated the National Committee on Engineering Infrastructure (NCEI) in July 1990. The committee had the responsibility for surveying the state of development of Nigeria's technological capacity and recommending a blueprint for the speedy establishment of a national engineering infrastructure.[41] Based on the recommendations of the committee, the Nigerian government created the National Agency for Science and Engineering Infrastructure (NASENI) in 1992. Among other things, NASENI was expected to formulate policies and advise the government on the establishment of a national science and engineering infrastructure. In addition, it was to undertake relevant applied research and development activities, as well as the development, motivation and utilization of scientific and engineering manpower. In essence, NASENI was expected "to foster Nigeria's scientific and technological advancement through the development of the fundamental scientific and engineering infrastructure."[42]

To be able to perform these functions, NASENI was to be funded by the federal government and the private sector. The agency was to receive 1 percent of the federation account and this was expected to rise progressively until it reached 3 percent of the federation account by the year 2000. In addition, all commercial enterprises with a turnover of over 4 million naira were to contribute 0.25 percent of their annual income to the agency. However, the federal government and the private companies regularly defaulted on their financial obligations. Furthermore, some transnational corporations operating in the country whose interests were threatened by the functions assigned to the agency used their connections in government to try to undermine the agency.[43] The autonomy of NASENI was challenged by successive ministers in charge of the ministry of science and technology who advocated either the scrapping of the agency or the bringing of the agency under the jurisdiction of the ministry. Given these developments, the agency was not able to effectively carry out its activities.

It is clear that the Nigerian government's policy of technology transfer was anchored on the modernist notion of the backwardness, irrelevance and, indeed, absence of any worthwhile indigenous technology. As a result, technology was viewed mainly as a commodity owned by foreigners, mainly Western capitalist countries hence the government's preoccupation with how to promote the transfer of these technologies into the country. Thus, a major preoccupation was which of the foreign sources Nigeria should import technology from, in addition to the constant platitudes through multilateral agencies for fair and just terms and conditions for the transfer of technology by the advanced capitalist countries. As noted by Adubifa, "the overall approach to managing the technological dimensions of industrial development (in Nigeria) seems oriented against, rather than towards, the use of local sources of technology.[44] In the circumstance, the immense indigenous technological knowledge that was readily available and more relevant to the developmental needs of the country was completely ignored.

Import Substitution Industrialization and Technology Transfer

Based on the development experience of the advanced Western capitalist countries, development theorists advocated the view that industrialization is central to the modernization and development of the economies of Third World countries. The mass production of standardized manufactured goods model was prescribed as the fastest means through which these countries would attain industrial modernity. Furthermore, the deteriorating performance of primary products in the world market due to over production of these products, manipulation of the prices of primary products by the advanced capitalist countries and the development of synthetic alternatives created the impetus for industrialization. Industrialization was therefore seen as a means of ending the economic dependency on the capitalist countries while simultaneously promoting development in the Third World countries. The industrialization strategy of import substitution was adopted as a means of conserving foreign exchange through the domestic production of previously imported goods while at the same time speeding the pace of industrialization since the domestic market for such goods already existed. The import substitution industrialization strategy was first adopted in Latin America in the 1930s and in Africa in the 1950s during the period of decolonization.

However, an important factor that influenced the establishment of import substituting industries in Nigeria in the 1950s was the desire on the part of the colonial administration to preserve its Nigerian market for British transnational corporations. The import of cheaper manufactured consumer goods from Japanese and American firms were providing stiff competition to those produced by British firms. Thus in other to protect the Nigerian market against these competing cheaper imports, British TNCs were encouraged to establish import substituting industries in Nigeria: the ISI was therefore partly a market protection strategy.[45] Nigerian politicians, who had started playing more roles in the affairs of the country during the political decolonization process of the 1950s, embraced the notion that industrialization would help to speed up the process of development. They felt that industrialization through import substitution was capable of helping to transfer technology to Nigerians while at the same time contributing to the diversification of the economy and employment generation.

Although the policy of import substitution did not become official Nigerian government's policy until the first national development plan, it had been implicit in the various industrial policies of the 1950s. Also implicit in these industrial policies was the belief that the establishment of import substituting industries would automatically lead to the transfer of the technology embedded in these industries. Thus, all the industrial policies of the 1950s were aimed at creating a favorable climate for the establishment of import substituting industries by foreign private investors. For instance, the 1956 industrial policy recognized "the need for overseas capital and managerial and technical skills, if (Nigeria's) resources are to be developed to the extent which the government and people of Nigeria desire."[46]

With the attainment of political independence, Nigerian rulers remained committed to promoting the development and diversification of the country's economy through the ISI strategy. As a result, various incentives were put in place to encourage foreign investors to establish import substituting industries in Nigeria. The incentives include the provision of tax relief, provision of infrastructure, tariff protection and favorable terms of credit. In addition, there was the promise not to nationalize industries and, in the event of nationalization, fair compensation assessed through independent arbitration would be paid. As a result of the generous incentives, many import substituting industries were established in Nigeria but these were mainly low-technology consumer goods industries that specialized mainly in the production, packaging and assembling of items such as textiles, cement, alcohol, beverages, batteries, radios, shoes, etc. In fact, majority of the industries concentrated on the packaging, assembling and bottling of end products from parts imported from their parent companies. No technology was transferred to Nigerians who were employed in these kinds of activities.

Indeed, the various incentives and protectionist policies accorded the TNCs ironically helped to reinforce the kind of market protection strategy, which as already noted partly underlined the decision by the colonial administration to encourage import substituting industries in the 1950s. Realizing that their technology are the source of their market power the TNCs were bent on retaining this decisive advantage hence they paradoxically used the government incentives to promote measures that were antithetical to the transfer of technology to Nigerians. Rather than transfer technology, the TNCs promoted technological and economic dependence through the adoption of capital-intensive technology and the import of machineries, plants, chemicals, raw materials and other inputs from their home countries. As noted by Lynn Mytelka, "as a result of their product and process choices, multinational corporations from the advanced industrial countries tend to have fewer backward and forward linkages within the domestic economy than national firms, source locally less frequently for knowledge inputs such as engineering services, and rely heavily on external sources of technology than on the building of indigenous technological capabilities."[47] In fact, it can be said that since all the significant items needed in the import substituting industries were imported and in most cases what occurred were mere packaging of the finished products, it is a misnomer to refer to these enterprises as import substituting industries. In reality what obtains in these industries are not quite different from importing the products in their finished forms.

The partnership and licensing agreements between the TNCs and their Nigerian partners, as well as trademarks, patents and royalties, among others, were used to further entrench technological dependence. According to G. P. Uwujaren, these factors gave the TNCs the right to decide whether local personnel should be granted access to the imported technology, at what rate and to what extent. He further noted that the ability of the TNCs "to prohibit exportation or to require importation of machinery, spares or intermediate inputs from specified sources effectively limits (indigenous) ability to pursue an independent policy in the development, acquisition or adaptation/modification of technology."[48] This form of technological dependence and exploitation is clearly illustrated by the partnership agreements for the assembly of cars from Completely Knocked Down (CKD) parts and components which the Nigerian government signed with Volkswagen AG of Germany (VAG) and Peugeot of France in 1972. Among other things, VAG and

Peugeot of France were given the exclusive rights to plan the car assembly plants and the Nigerian subsidiaries – Volkswagen of Nigeria (VWON) and Peugeot Automobile of Nigeria (PAN) – were to procure the necessary assembly equipment from their parent companies. From the point of view of technology transfer, the non-involvement of the Nigerian assembly plants and Nigerian personnel in the planning process implies that they did not make much significant input over how to ensure the attainment of the goal of technology transfer.

The agreements also stated that the parent companies would assist the local assembly plants to achieve the incorporation of local parts and "in making use of locally manufactured parts when available, provided that the quality is acceptable." The plants were expected to achieve 30 percent of local content by value of the CKD, consisting of 15 percent through in-plant manufacture and 15 percent through purchases from local manufacturers, achieve 50 percent of local content after five years and then 100 percent of local content after thirteen years. In addition, the plants were not to pay any royalties and license fees until "the deletion value on the CKD pack of a car exceeds 30 percent of its ex-factory price," at which time the royalties would be negotiated between them and their parent companies. Furthermore, indigenous managerial and technical staff were to be recruited and trained in Nigeria in essential activities such as "design and procurement of equipment, planning, installing and maintaining assembly machinery, tools, and rigs."[49]

On the face value, it might be argued that the agreements made provisions for the development of some degree of indigenous technological capacity. However, as noted by John Ohiorhenuan, when the original joint venture agreements are read along with the licensing agreements, the degree of exploitation and technological dependence promoted by the assembly plants becomes clearer. The licensing agreements included several restrictive clauses. For instance the licensing agreement with VAG limited the assignment to third parties of technology acquired by VWON and also limited the production and sale of goods outside Nigeria. Furthermore, the agreement included several tie-in clauses that obliged VWON to purchase parts, materials, and spare parts from VAG unless under the incorporation-of-local-parts clause and to purchase only from VAG and its designated affiliates all assembly jigs, welding tongs, gauges, and templates as well as measuring and testing equipment. Thus, VAG retained control of the "sources, prices, and quality of the capital and intermediate goods, the hiring of key personnel, and the type and quality of the technology to be used," in VWON.[50] In the specific case of technology transfer, Ohiorhenuan noted:

> There is nothing in the arrangements at the Nigerian plant, nor in the legal documents on which the arrangements are based, to suggest that Nigerians would or could acquire effective knowledge of how to make engines or transmissions, for instance. Rather, the license agreement specifies the assembly of certain vehicle models and the possible incorporation of locally manufactured miscellaneous materials and parts. The

> manufacture of engines, gearboxes, and axles involves high-level technology in which only certain members of the Volkswagen group specialize. Thus the complete and effective transfer of automobile technology remains a long-term problem.[51]

Moreover, although the vehicle assembly plants were expected to achieve a 30 percent level in the incorporation of local materials in the first three years (i.e. 1978), the official records of the plants placed the average level of local contents at about 10 percent as at 1980. Even then, Nigerian experts who examined the records of the companies argued that the local content achievement level was overstated: they put the real local content level at less than 5 percent.[52] It should be noted that no meaningful technology can be acquired in arrangements involving the mere assembly of imported CKDs because Nigerians were not exposed to the technology involved in the making of these large components.

As already noted, a significant feature of the import substituting industries was the capital-intensive nature of the industries. The prevailing notion among development scholars promoted the pace of the establishment of capital-intensive consumer goods industries because it was assumed that this represented the fastest means through which technology would be transferred since "technology is to a large extent embodied in capital goods."[53] This was used to legitimize the package approach to the importation of capital goods while transnational corporations were touted as the primary channel through which this kind of technology transfer would occur. The outcome was a very high level of importation of capital goods by the import substituting manufacturing industries, a situation that further entrenched technological dependence. For instance between 1974 and 1985, the importation of capital goods averaged over 70 percent in relation to the importation of consumer goods in terms of end-use materials.[54] The fact that other inputs such as raw materials and chemicals were largely imported by the import substituting industries meant that Nigeria was plunged into a high degree of economic dependence. To worsen the situation, in spite of the optimism modernist scholars placed on capital goods importation as a primary avenue for technology transfer, empirical studies have shown that this was not the case in Nigeria. For instance, A. Ihuoma's study of ten import substituting industries in the period between 1962 and 1978, showed that Nigerians did not acquire any significant skills in seven of the industries through the use of imported technology.[55] Indeed the imported capital goods technology package suffers from a number of inappropriate characteristics such as "excessive scale, excessive capital intensity, skill intensity and excessively sophisticated products resulting in and requiring unequal income distribution."[56]

Nevertheless, most development literature operating from the modernist perspective continued to regard imported capital goods technology as critical for technological diffusion and economic development. They portrayed capital goods as crucial for the development and diffusion of technical change while contributing significantly to the process of technological innovation. Furthermore, the central role of the capital goods industry in the development and diffusion of technical change is generally associated with the development of new products and new processes, which generally require new machines. As a result, it is claimed that without capital goods production, many new ideas would remain on the drawing board. In addition, there is considerable technological feedback within the machine-making sector, with developments at one stage stimulating and requiring developments in that sector and elsewhere in the economy.[57] Thus, given the underdeveloped nature of the capital goods industry in developing countries such as Nigeria, it is opined that the viable channel for attaining industrial modernity lies with relying on external innovations through the agency of transnational corporations.[58] This therefore resulted in the perpetuation of technological and economic dependence while depriving the country of much needed foreign exchange.

The solution to this technological dependence has been seen in the form of the development of a viable capital goods industry within the country. However, the policy discourse regarding the development of the capital goods sector as is in fact the case with the general discussion on capital goods, are firmly situated within the modernization paradigm. It is argued that since capital goods were crucial in the industrial revolution process of the advanced capitalist countries, Nigeria and other developing countries need to reproduce the 19th century experience of the Western capitalist countries with intermediate and capital goods industries before advancing toward the attainment of industrial modernity. This linear conception of industrialization was justified on the ground that the underdeveloped nature of Nigeria's capital goods industry meant that the country lacked the basic skills, knowledge, organization and other factors necessary for the attainment of the mass production model of industrial modernity.

The development of an iron and steel industry was regarded as crucial for the development of the capital goods sector. The project was conceived from the point of view of import substitution, and was seen as a means of acquiring technological capacity and promoting self-reliant development. The idea of establishing an iron and steel industry in Nigeria was first conceived in 1958 and was included in all the national development plans. However, it was only in the third national development plan, 1975-80 that concrete steps were taken toward actualizing the establishment of the industry. This resulted in the establishment of a blast furnace steel plant at Ajaokuta by the Soviet Union and a direct reduction steel plant at Aladja by a German/Austrian consortium, as well as the establishment of steel rolling mills at Oshogbo, Jos and Katsina.

The implementation of the iron and steel project was patently faulty and did not result in the attainment of the proposed objectives. The design, supply of equipment, engineering and construction of the iron and steel plants were exclusively handled by foreign firms thereby making it impossible for Nigerians to acquire some of the technical skills associated with the industry. The plants produced materials that were not of strategic importance to the development of the manufacturing industries. The items produced include round and ribbed bars, equal and unequal angles, tees, channels, flat bars and beams. These items are needed in the building and construction industry while flat sheets which are critical for the manufacturing industries were neglected (the promise that these would be produced in the second phase did not materialize). In the circumstance, the import substituting manufacturing industries continued to rely on the importation of flat sheets, which in 1984 for instance, accounted for about 58 percent of the country's annual import of steel products.[59] In fact, right from inception the iron and steel industry was bedeviled with many problems, so that the plants and rolling mills never effectively took off and by the 1990s, they were in a state of comatose.[60]

The case of the iron and steel industry is particularly pathetic because the modernization paradigm that underlined its implementation made the planners to ignore the immense indigenous knowledge and technology that already exist in iron technology in the country. Various studies have demonstrated that respective Nigerian communities had developed sophisticated and culturally adaptive iron technology right from the precolonial period.[61] R. A. Olaoye has pointed out that the indigenous iron culture; with the people's knowledge of iron-ore, smelting is very much relevant to the success of the iron and steel industry. According to him:

> For Nigeria to achieve self-reliance in this (iron and steel) sector, greater and still greater attention should be paid to the involvement of local skills and techniques. The indigenous iron workers, black-smiths and related skills should be brought within the mainstream of production processes so as to update their local environment. The local artisans, for instance, would be useful in foundry, rolling mill, extrusion and fabrication. They could engage in the manufacture, repair and assemblage of components in the automobile, electrical and hardware industries, thereby providing an indigenous base for the technical-industrial development of the country.[62]

However, with the modernist mindset of viewing indigenous practices as irrational, primitive and backward, and, the devaluation of artisan knowledge by the mass production industrialization model, the indigenous reservoir of knowledge and skills were not tapped.

The ISI strategy failed to promote linkages between different sectors of the indigenous economy as well as promote indigenous technological capability through the conduct of Research and Development (R&D) in Nigeria. For reasons of maintaining their advantageous position and ensuring their continued dominance and exploitation of the Nigerian economy, the import substitution industries preferred to conduct their R&D in their parent companies located in their home countries. Ludicrously, research for solutions to problems emanating from production conditions in Nigeria was conducted abroad. A good example is the case of the fast deterioration and corrosiveness of cars assembled in Nigeria compared with those manufactured in France, Germany or Brazil. The solution to this problem was sought not in the assembly plants in Nigeria but in the parent companies "even though the end product will benefit mainly the Nigerian market."[63]

Generally, in order to maintain their economic and technological dominance, TNCs largely concentrated their R&Ds in their home countries. However, even in cases where they conducted their R&Ds abroad, Nigeria and other African countries received the least attention. Nagesh Kumer's study of the location of overseas R&D by transnational corporations has shown that they were overwhelmingly concentrated in a handful of advanced capitalist countries. For instance, between 1966 and 1989, developing countries only accounted for an average of 5 percent of the overseas R&D by subsidiaries of United States transnational corporations and the bulk of this percentage were conducted in Brazil, Mexico, Israel and Taiwan.[64] It has been argued that the low level of technological resources and technological capability of the developing countries, account for the low R&D activities conducted in these countries by transnational corporations. This excuse is not valid because, to maintain their economic and technological advantage over developing countries and therefore maximize the economic benefits they derive from these countries, the transnational corporations deliberately promoted policies that would ensure the technological and economic dependence of developing countries. Indeed, by concentrating their R&D investments in advanced capitalist countries, the TNCs helped to widen the technological gap between the industrialized countries and the developing countries.[65]

It is clear that the import substitution strategy merely promoted technological and economic dependence, did not contribute in any meaning way to the building of indigenous technological capability through technology transfer and is in fact at the root of the crisis of industrialization in Nigeria and other African countries. Mytelka has however argued that an import substitution strategy is crucial for technological development and industrialization in Africa and that what was pursued in African countries was an import *reproduction* rather than import *substitution* strategy. Given the significance and rather novel nature of Mytelka's argument, it is necessary to reproduce it in detail:

> Import reproduction strategies such as those implemented throughout Africa take "product" as their point of departure, rather than "purpose." They thus ignore the extent to which products incorporate concepts of functionality, cost, quality and aesthetics that correspond to the producer's principal market of sale. An import substitution strategy reverses this process by first identifying the purposes embodied in imported products, then determining their relevance to the local environment, and lastly by designing a product that conforms most closely to domestically available inputs, material and non-material. Within the context of an import substitution strategy, there is no automatic assumption that given product categories are homogenous either in the characteristics of the product – its quality, size, color, material inputs and design – or in the processes through which it is produced. The reduction of imports as a share of domestic consumption thus occurs without requiring that the locally made product be identical to

> the formerly imported one. Not only is the practice of import substitution different from that of import reproduction, but its teleology differs as well. Thus, in a process of import substitution "production" is not the sole end. Rather, it becomes part of a more complex process of technological learning that encompasses product specification and design, process choice and change, and the social organization of production. In this fashion technological mastery becomes part of the process of industrial deepening and the qualitative changes in the structure of production that this implies. In contrast to import substitution, import reproduction shifts our attention away from these dynamic learning effects and towards quantitative indicators of output growth.[66]

Mytelka's argument is attractive but the distinction between import reproduction and import substitution, is in certain respects, more apparent than real. The distinction lies mainly in the fact that the imported "product" is taken as an end in itself and needs to be replicated in the local production process in the import reproduction model. While the imported "product" is regarded as a purpose, in the import substitution model, involving learning the processes involved in its production and locally producing "a product that conforms most closely to domestically available inputs." However, the point remains that both models privilege the imported products over those that have been indigenously produced over time: they grant the prime place to exogenous technology for the development of technological capability and industrialization. The models are therefore situated within the modernist paradigm of devaluing indigenous technological knowledge in relation to exogenous technology.

Furthermore, by concentrating overwhelmingly on the production of consumer goods and the attendant massive importation of capital goods, the import substitution strategy promoted the underdevelopment and in certain respects, extinction of indigenous technology and industries. For instance, indigenous iron technology, which was developed in the precolonial period and contributed greatly in revolutionizing indigenous agriculture, manufacturing and warfare, was pushed into virtual extinction by the ISI strategy. Indigenous consumer goods industries such as textile, alcohol, pottery, beverages and food processing which had been deliberately repressed by the colonial administration so that they would not offer stiff competition to imported consumer goods were further undermined by the import substitution strategy. The process of undermining these indigenous consumer goods industries was facilitated by the promotion of tastes for imported consumer goods, which were characterized as modern and civilized, among the elites, and urban dwellers while simultaneously devaluing the indigenous ones as backward and primitive. The mass production of these goods and the various generous incentives granted the import substituting industries made their products to be cheaper than the indigenously produced ones which were therefore not in the position to effectively compete with them.

Women who dominated indigenous manufacturing sectors such as textile, alcohol and food processing[67] were particularly more adversely affected by the ISI strategy of concentrating on consumer goods production. In the specific case of alcoholic brewing, M. A. Onwuejeogwu noted, "indigenous brewing is generally a woman's task, because beer is a local drink which goes with food." He further stated that:

> The Westernized elites were introduced to drinking imported, western beer. Between the nineteen sixties and eighties, Nigeria was flooded with beer factories. The domestically brewed beer died out gradually. . . . The position now is that the old generation of women have not been able to transfer the brewing technology to the new generation of girls. Some transfer that might have taken place are in the rural areas. The multi-nationals, brewers of western beer, have taken over from our women brewers. The multi-national brewers now control Nigerian taste. They determine what we drink.[68]

Thus, the ISI strategy promoted a process of marginalizing women in terms of the economic power they hitherto derived from the indigenous manufacturing of various consumer goods while simultaneously promoting a general state of technological and industrial anarchy and disorder in Nigeria. Indeed, since technology is intimately bound with a people's culture and ecology, endogenous technology should constitute the basis of technological development and industrialization in Nigeria.

Indigenous Technology and Industrialization

As noted by Adubifa, "the issues of choice of technology in the Nigerian context are not about the legitimate choice between foreign and domestic technology; the latter hardly enters the picture." This is so "because the nation's dependence on foreign imports and foreign technology is so strong that the development of endogenous technology is usually not contemplated."[69] Yet for technology to be relevant to the needs of a society, it needs to originate from the cultural and ecological realities of that society. In fact, technological development is an autonomous process of growth from below that is intimately bound with the socio-cultural and ecological realities of a society. Technological development is therefore a cultural process. Thus, technologies are first of all developed in their basic forms, which respond to the realities of the local environments and make abundant use of the indigenous natural resources. These basic and simple technologies constitute the basis for further technological advancement, innovation, adaptation and replication, as the needs and realities of society develop and become more complex. Indeed, a technology that does not originate from within the socio-cultural environment of a people can hardly be useful in dealing with the people's peculiar problems. There is therefore the need for a close identity between technology and the ecology in which it exists,[70] a phenomenon that has been referred to as ecodevelopment.[71] This is not to say that technology cannot be borrowed from external sources; but such borrowed technologies can more relevantly contribute to development if they are adapted, internalized and embedded in the indigenous culture. It is under this kind of situation that a sustainable form of development, that is, a "development that meets the need of the present without compromising the ability of future generations to meet their own needs,"[72] can be promoted. From this perspective, technology must be rooted in a people's culture and ecology. In fact, the relationship between technology, culture, ecology and sustainable development cannot be overemphasized. As noted by A. I. Okpoko sustainable development is "concerned with the establishment of a system of economic growth and advancement that puts into serious consideration the cultural background of the people and the environmental impact of technological development and application."[73]

Indeed, the complementary interaction between technology and culture constitute the basis for the development of technology among different societies in the world. In the case of the Western experience for instance, Berman noted that the major technological innovations developed out of the existing indigenous knowledge and practice. Furthermore, "the major technological changes were shaped by and influenced in turn the cultures and social relations within which they were created, and interacted with each other to produce yet further changes."[74] It thus follows that indigenous knowledge and practice should constitute the basis of technological development and innovation in Nigeria and other African countries. Indigenous knowledge, which is the product of indigenous peoples' direct experience of the workings of nature and its relationship with the social world, includes the cultural traditions, values, belief systems and worldviews of local peoples.[75] Indigenous knowledge therefore constitutes the basis for the development of appropriate technology that is adaptable to the culture and ecology of the society while promoting sustainable technological development and industrialization.

Given the intimate relationship between technology, culture and development, indigenous technology, which involves the exploitation of local resources and the application of local methods in the production of goods and services, should form the cornerstone for technological development and industrialization in Nigeria. It should form the basis for creating the capability for adapting, modifying and replicating relevant foreign technology to suit the Nigerian environment and realities. It has been noted that:

> Indigenous technology embodies all the concepts of technology. In addition, it is a technology which is developed by or with active participation of the indigenous people through the harnessing and utilization of local materials and natural resources. It is based on the skill and techniques that make the heaviest use of the most abundant indigenous resources and locally produced machine and equipment. Indeed, it is a self-reliant technology which is capital-saving and one that could be easily operated, controlled, repaired and maintained locally.[76]

Various studies have demonstrated the relevance, versatility and immense contributions of indigenous technology and manufacturing to the development of Nigerian communities' right from the earliest times. The studies have demonstrated that sophisticated, dynamic and appropriate indigenous technology which have responded to various internal stimuli have existed and continue to exist in different sectors ranging from iron and other metals to consumer goods, building and transportation, among others.[77] Contrary to the modernist perception of the devaluation of indigenous technology, making indigenous technological knowledge and skills the centerpiece of contemporary technological development and industrialization constitutes the most viable means of promoting Nigeria's technological development and industrialization. This is because indigenous knowledge and skills are based on more acute understanding of the local environment and are therefore in the position to champion technological development and industrialization processes that are more attuned to the realities and specificity of the local environment. This point becomes more relevant when it is recalled that technological development and industrialization are cultural processes.

The crisis of industrialization confronting Nigeria and other African countries is largely a product of the denigration of indigenous technological knowledge and culture in favor of Western technology under the misguided belief that the associated technology transfer would promote Nigeria's industrialization. An important dimension of the technological and industrial crisis lies in the fact that the process and institutions through which technology is supposedly transferred do not seriously take into account the nature and general rules of the social environments in which the technology is supposed to be used. In fact, the principle of technology transfer is predicated on the so-called irrationality and backwardness of the indigenous technologies and values: any indigenous value or resistant force that may negate the transplantation of Western technology should therefore be crushed.[78] In spite of these coercive measures, significant aspects of the indigenous technology and culture remained resilient and the dialectical relationship between them and the imported technology helped to aggravate the crisis of industrialization. Indeed:

> the attempt by African states, spurred by international and bilateral aid donors, international corporations, and development experts, to replicate aspects of the historically and culturally specific experience of Western industrialization, is a major component of the social upheaval and economic decline that has overtaken much of Africa .... Western plants and equipment, and the instrumental rationality and models of reality underlying them, have little connection with indigenous culture and social conditions in Africa and rarely operate in the same way ... as in their place of origin.[79]

It thus follows that a critical step toward resolving the crisis of industrialization in Nigeria is for indigenous technology to play a vital role in the industrialization process.

Conclusion

The policy of technology transfer aggravated the crisis of industrialization in Nigeria and other African countries largely because of the modernization paradigm on which it was based. This paradigm failed to take into account the fact that technologies are products of concrete historical, social and material realities specific to the societies from which they originate and therefore intimately bound to the socio-cultural realities and relations of production of those societies. It is therefore not possible to transfer technology in isolation of the socio-cultural processes to which it is intimately bound. Furthermore, the paradigm of modernity failed to realize that technology is not just a Western phenomenon but that every society has developed its own form of technology that responds to the ecology, requirements and concrete realities of each society. It is therefore wrong to equate technology and industrialization to the large-scale capital-intensive Western style technology and mass production of standardized goods that devalue and disregard artisan and craft knowledge as irrational, primitive and backward. However, it was this denigration of indigenous technological knowledge and practices, and the supposed belief in the superiority and universal application of Western technology and mass production model that created the basis for the introduction of the policy of technology transfer. Yet the instrumental rationality and concrete realities underlying Western technology are at variance with the indigenous culture, social and material realities in Nigeria and other African countries.

The import substitution industrialization strategy which was the primary agency for the expected technology transfer, promoted the technological and economic dependence of Nigeria on the Western capitalist countries. The concentration of these industries on the production of consumer goods promoted a process of deindustrialization in Nigeria and fostered the collapse of indigenous consumer goods industries while simultaneously worsening the status of women who dominated the indigenous production of consumer goods. Moreover, the import substituting industries imported technologies in their packaged forms while most of the goods were merely assembled in Nigeria so that Nigerians were not really involved in the production process. In addition, these industries carried out their R&Ds in their parent companies. In essence, the import substituting industries merely exploited Nigeria's resources while promoting industrial chaos and crisis within Nigeria.

However, given the fact that technology is a cultural process and a product of the socio-economic and ecological realities of a people, indigenous knowledge, technology and practices should constitute the basis for industrialization. Thus, contrary to the devaluation and denigration of indigenous knowledge and technology by the modernist paradigm, indigenous technology should constitute the cornerstone of the industrialization process in Nigeria. In this regard, ecodevelopment "which differs radically from conventional (development) strategies with their universal elements: capital, labour, investment, etc" but rather, emphasizes decentralized small-scale industries that are adapted to the local culture and ecology, should constitute the foundations for industrialization in Nigeria. As noted by Bjorn Hettne, ecodevelopment "consists of specific elements: a certain group of people, with certain cultural values, living in a certain region with a certain set of natural resources." Furthermore, "ecodevelopment means that the local community and the local ecosystem develop together towards a higher productivity and a higher degree of needs satisfaction, but above all that this development is sustainable in both ecological and social terms."[80]

In essence, the modernist viewpoint that technological development and industrialization in Nigeria and other African countries should be based on the transplantation and rigid reproduction of Western technology and mass production model is not tenable. This perspective has only resulted in a harvest of technological and industrial anarchy and crisis in various African countries. In fact, endogenous technology and skills should constitute the basis for technological development and industrialization in Africa. As noted by Ake:

> In so far as our historical experiences are unique in Africa, we cannot rely on the transmission of scientific ideas from other continents to solve our problems. Until we stop thinking along the lines of transfer of technical and scientific know-how and think rather of internally generating it, we cannot begin to master our destiny or to develop our creativity.[81]

A viable model for technological development and industrialization in Nigeria and other African countries should be one that is flexible, decentralized, culturally and ecologically adaptive, relies less on imported technology while effectively mobilizing indigenous natural resources, knowledge and skills for the building of indigenous technological capacity and industrialization.

Notes

1 Berman, "African Capitalism and the Paradigm of Modernity," 236; and Scott, *Seeing Like a State*.

2 See E. P. Reubens, "Appropriate Technology for Nigerian Development," in M. Amoda and C. D. Tyson, eds., *Technological Development in Nigeria*, Lagos and New York: Third Press International, 1979, 240-248.

3 Onimode, *A Political Economy of the African Crisis*, 140.

4 Berman, "African Capitalism and the Paradigm of Modernity," 242-243.

5 L. K. Mytelka, "The Unfulfilled Promise of African Industrialization," *African Studies Review*, Vol. 32, No. 3, 1989, 77.
6 Berman, "African Capitalism and the Paradigm of Modernity," 244.
7 United Nations Conference on Trade and Development (UNCTAD), *Transfer and Development of Technology in Developing Countries: A Compendium of Policy Issues*, New York: United Nations, 1990, 24.
8 United Nations Economic and Social Commission for Asia and the Pacific (ESCAP), *Technology Atlas Project*, Bangalore, India, 1989, cited in M. N. B. Ayiku, "Science and Technology in the Development Process," in S. Rasheed and S. Tomori eds., *The Political Economy of Development: An African Perspective*, Vol. 1, Nairobi: ICIPE Science Press, 1996, 367.
9 Mytelka, "The Unfulfilled Promise of African Industrialization," 78.
10 V. Trickovic, "Science Policy and Development Strategy in Developing Countries," in B. R. Williams ed., *Science and Technology in Economic Growth*, London: Macmillan, 1973, 291.
11 L. Soete, "Opportunities For and Limitations To Technology Leapfrogging," in United Nations Conference on Trade and Development (UNCTAD), *Technology, Trade Policy and the Uruguay Round*, New York: United Nations, 1990, 3-24.
12 B. F. Johnston and P. Kilby, *Agricultural and Structural Transformation: Economic Strategies in Late-Developing Countries*, London and New York: Oxford University Press, 1975, 76.
13 G. E. Schweitzer, "Technology Transfer: The Nigerian Model," M. Amoda and Tyson eds., *Technological Development in Nigeria*, 251.
14 Cited in A. O. E. Animalu, "Models for Technology Transfer between Nigeria and the United States of America," in Amoda and Tyson eds., *Technology Development in Nigeria*, 241.
15 Y. Hayami and V. Ruttan, *Agricultural Development: An International Perspective*, Baltimore: The Johns Hopkins University Press, 1985, 256.
16 A. K. Bagchi, "Technological Self-Reliance, Dependence and Underdevelopment," in A. Wad ed., *Science, Technology, and Development*, Boulder, CO and London: Westview and IT Publications, 1988, 74-80.
17 Ayiku, "Science and Technology," 379-380.
18 A. S. Bhalla, *Facing the Technological Challenge*, London and New York: Macmillan and St. Martin's, 1996, 1.
19 Trickovic, "Science Policy and Development Strategy in Developing Countries," 291; and R. W. Hammond, "Relevant Technology and the University," in Amoda and Tyson eds., *Technology Development in Nigeria*, 271.
20 Soete, "Opportunities for and Limitations to Technological Leapfrogging"; and R. Ricupero, "Trade and Technology: Issues at Stake for Developing Countries," UNCTAD, *Technology Trade Policy and the Uruguay Round.*
21 See for instance, UNCTAD, *The Implementation of Laws and Conventions on Transfer of Technology: The Experience of the Republic of Korea*, New York: United Nations, n.d.
22 Bhalla, *Facing the Technological Challenge*, 171.
23 E. F. Schumacher, *Small is Beautiful*, London: Sphere, 1973.
24 Bhalla, *Facing the Technological Challenge*, 26.
25 Hammond, "Relevant Technology and the University," 270-274; and Reubens, "Appropriate Technology for Nigerian Development," 287-293.
26 See for instance, R. F. Dernberger, "The Relevance of China's Development Experience for Other Developing Countries," *Items* (Social Science Research

Council), September 1977, 29 and 31, cited in Reubens, "Appropriate Technology for Nigerian Development," 296-297; and Bagchi, "Technological Self-Reliance, Dependence and Underdevelopment," 80-83.

27 A. Wad, "Introduction," in idem, ed., *Science, Technology, and Development*, 11.

28 Bhalla, *Facing the Technological Challenge*, 23.

29 Federal Republic of Nigeria, *Second National Development Plan*, 235, 238-239.

30 A. Adubifa, *Technology Policy in Nigeria*, Ibadan: Nigerian Institute of Social and Economic Research, 1990, 26.

31 Federal Republic of Nigeria, *Second National Development Plan*, 141 and 143.

32 Federal Republic of Nigeria, *Third National Development Plan*, 154.

33 Adubifa, *Technology Policy in Nigeria*, 73-75.

34 Onimode, *Imperialism and Underdevelopment in Nigeria*, 194.

35 Cited in Federal Government of Nigeria, *National Policy on Science and Technology*, Lagos: Federal Ministry of Science and Technology, 1986, 26.

36 Ibid.

37 Onimode, *Imperialism and Underdevelopment in Nigeria*, 194.

38 Federal Government of Nigeria, *National Policy on Science and Technology*, 16-17.

39 Ibid., 18-19.

40 Ibid., 25-28.

41 E. E. G. Iweriebor, *Nigerian Technology Development Since Independence: The State of Development and the Strategy of Transformation*, Ibadan: BookBuilders, 2004, 33. My discussion of the activities of this committee as well as the steps taken to implement its recommendations relies heavily on Iweriebor's book, 33-46.

42 Ibid., 37-39.

43 A significant example is Ernest Shonekan, a former Chief Executive Officer of the United African Company (UAC) and head of the short lived Interim National Government in 1993, who was lukewarm toward the agency. See Ibid., 41-42.

44 Adubifa, *Technology Policy in Nigeria*, 178.

45 For details on this market protection strategy, see Kilby, *Industrialization in an Open Economy*, 53-80.

46 Federation of Nigeria, *Opportunities for Overseas Investment.*

47 Mytelka, "The Unfulfilled Promise of African Industrialization," 87.

48 Uwujaren, "The Political Economy of Nigeria's Dependent Industrialization via Import Substitution," 86.

49 The provisions of the assembly plants agreements are cited from Adubifa, *Technology Policy in Nigeria*, 93-95; and J. F. E. Ohiorhenuan, *Capital and the State in Nigeria*, Westport, Connecticut: Greenwood Press, 1989, 104-106.

50 Ohiorhenuan, *Capital and the State in Nigeria*, 107-108.

51 Ibid., 116.

52 Ibid., 113; and Adubifa, *Technology Policy in Nigeria*, 95.

53 Mytelka, "The Unfulfilled Promise of African Industrialization," 86.

54 B. U. Ekuerhare, "The Theory and Concepts of Capital Goods and Technology Development in Nigeria," Paper Presented at the Annual Conference of the Nigerian Economic Society, Held at Minna, Nigeria, 22-25 May 1990, 22.

55 A. Ihuoma, "Economic Implications of Underdeveloped Capital Goods Industry in Nigeria," M. Sc Thesis, Ahmadu Bello University, Zaria, Nigeria, 1983.

56 S. O. Uniamikogbo, "The State of the Capital Goods Industry in a Developing Economy: The Case of Nigeria," *The Indian Journal of Economics*, Vol. LXXII, No. 286, 1992, 321.

57 Ibid., 320-321; and Ekuerhare, "The Theory and Concepts of Capital Goods."

58 F. Stewart, "Capital Goods in Developing Countries," in I. Livingstone ed., *Development Economics and Policy: Readings*, London: George Allen and Unwin, 1976, 199.
59 *Newswatch* (Lagos, Nigeria), 8 June 1985, 12-13.
60 For a detailed discussion of the problems faced by the iron and steel industry, see J. I. Dibua, "The Post-Colonial State and Development Planning in Nigeria, 1962-1985," *Journal of Eastern African Research and Development*, Vol. 24, 1994, 219-221. Also see G. Ukpevo, "Still-Born: Nigeria's Steel Industry, Dogged by Mismanagement and Corruption, is, According to Critics, a Steal Industry," *Newswatch*, 5 October 1992, 39-41.
61 See for instance, R. A. Olaoye, "Intrinsic Values of Traditional Arts and Crafts to the Development of Modern Science and Technology in Nigeria," in S. Bello and Y. Nasidi eds., *Culture, Economy and National Development: Proceedings of the National Seminar Events of NAFEST '89*, Lagos: National Council for Arts and Culture, 1991, 53-54; and A. I. Okpoko and A. M. Ibeanu, "Early Metal-working in Nigeria," *West African Journal of Archaeology*, Vol. 29, Nos. 1 and 2, 1999, 34-46.
62 Olaoye, "Intrinsic Values of Traditional Arts and Crafts," 54.
63 Uwujaren, "The Political Economy of Nigeria's Dependent Industrialization," 88 and 93.
64 N. Kumer, "Intellectual Property Protection, Market Orientation and Location of Overseas R and D Activities by Multinational Enterprises," *World Development*, Vol. 24, No. 4, 1996, 673-688.
65 Ibid., 685-686.
66 Mytelka, "The Unfulfilled Promise of African Industrialization," 79.
67 See for instance, J. A. Byfield, *The Bluest Hands: A Social and Economic History of Women Dyers in Abeokuta (Nigeria), 1890-1940*, Portsmouth, NH: Heinemann, 2002; and M. A. Onwuejeogwu, "The Place of Indigenous Technology in Present-day Africa," *West African Journal of Archaeology*, Vol. 29, Nos. 1 and 2, 1999, 23.
68 Onwuejeogwu, "The Place of Indigenous Technology in Present-day Africa," 23.
69 Adubifa, *Technology Policy in Nigeria*, 67.
70 Olaoye, "Intrinsic Values of Traditional Arts and Crafts," 51.
71 B. Glaeser, *Ecodevelopment: Concepts, Projects, Strategies*, Oxford: Pergamon Press, 1984; and Hettne, *Development Theory and the Three Worlds*, 186-189.
72 World Commission on Environment and Development, *Our Common Future*, New York: Oxford University Press, 1987, 8 and 43.
73 A. I. Okpoko, "Indigenous Technology and Sustainable Development," *West African Journal of Archaeology*, Vol. 29, Nos. 1 and 2, 1999, 3.
74 Berman, "African Capitalism and the Paradigm of Modernity," 248.
75 G. J. S. Dei, "Sustainable Development in the African Context: Revisiting Some Theoretical and Methodological Issues," *Africa Development*, Vol. XVIII, No. 2, 1993, 105.
76 Olaoye, "Intrinsic Values of Traditional Arts and Crafts," 52.
77 For details, see Ibid., 40-60; and Onwuejeogwu, "The Place of Indigenous Technology in Present-day Africa," 7-26.
78 N. Assie-Lumumba and T. Lumumba-Kasongo, "The 'Silent Crisis' in the International Transfer of Knowledge in African Societies and Their Education Systems: A Theoretical Perspective," *CODESRIA Bulletin*, No. 4, 1994, 10.
79 Berman, "African Capitalism and the Paradigm of Modernity," 248-9.
80 Hettne, *Development Theory and the Three Worlds*, 188-189.

81 C. Ake, "The Social Sciences in Africa: Trends, Tasks and Changes," Paper Presented to CODESRIA for Discussion on the Social Science in Africa, April 1985, 11, cited in Assie-Lumumba and Lumumba-Kasongo, "The 'Silent Crisis' in the International Transfer of Knowledge," 13.

Chapter 6

The Dialectics of Agricultural Transformation

The crisis of development is perhaps more acutely manifested in the agricultural sector. This pathetic situation need not be so given the high amount of Nigeria's factor endowments. However, Forrest has argued that there is no acute agricultural crisis in Nigeria and that the crisis has been exaggerated. He pointed out that in the face of the chronic absence of reliable statistical data that characterize Nigeria's development efforts spurious data have been invented to create the picture of a serious agricultural crisis. Furthermore, while there probably is a crisis in the labor-intensive export crops especially with regard to the southern states of the country, the same is not true of the food sector. He noted that one of the reasons why the food crisis in Nigeria was exaggerated in the 1970s and 1980s was the desire to justify many different forms of intervention in agriculture, both domestic and foreign.[1] Contrary to the argument of Forrest, there is no doubt that Nigeria has experienced a severe agricultural crisis since the 1970s: indeed, most scholars on Nigeria's agriculture, irrespective of their intellectual or ideological orientations, agree that the sector has experienced a severe crisis.

The agricultural crisis is partly manifested in the huge decline in the performance of the agricultural sector over the years.[2] In 1964, agriculture accounted for 70 percent of Nigeria's GDP and 70.8 percent of the total exports, but in 1970, it accounted for 33.2 percent of the GDP and 9 percent of the total exports. In spite of the various forms of government intervention in the agricultural sector from the 1970s, the performance of agriculture did not improve. For instance in 1992, it accounted for 38.5 percent of the GDP and 1.4 percent of the total exports, and in 1999, it accounted for 41 percent of the GDP and 1.4 percent of the total exports. The crisis is also reflected in the decline in food production as reflected in the rising level of food imports, which rose from 46 million naira in 1965 to 2,115 million naira in 1981. At the same time, the percentage of food imports in relation to the total imports into the country rose from 7.6 in 1970 to 19, in 1982.[3]

Table 6.1 Basic indicators of agricultural performance in Nigeria, 1970-1992

GDP (1984 Factor Cost)	1970-74	1975-79	1980	1981	1982	1983	1984	1985
Total (in Billion Naira)	58.2	73.7	73.2	70.4	70.2	66.4	63.0	68.9
Agriculture	19.3	22.3	22.5	24.4	25.1	25.0	23.6	27.8
Agriculture as % of Total	33.2	30.2	30.8	34.7	35.8	37.7	37.8	40.3
Exports								
Total (in Million Naira)	2237.2	7242.3	19186.7	11023.5	8206.4	7502.5	9088	11720.8
Agriculture	200.8	357	339.3	178.4	177.6	259	208	193.6
Agriculture as % of Total	9	4.9	2.4	1.6	2.2	3.5	2.3	1.7
Imports								
Total (in Million Naira)	1157.4	6334.2	9095.6	12719.8	10770.5	8903.7	7178.3	7062.6
Agriculture	113.9	742.3	1564.6	1964.8	1810.1	1415.4	955.4	1003.7
Agriculture as % of Total	9.8	11.7	17.2	15.4	16.8	15.9	13.3	14.2
Food Consumption Per Caput								
Calories Intake	1896	1761	1762	1500	1600	1750	1790	1863
Deficit/Surplus (%)	-21	-27.2	-27.2	-38	-33.9	-27.7	-26	-23

GDP (1984 Factor Cost)	1986	1987	1988	1989	1990	1991	1992
Total (in Billion Naira)	71.1	70.7	77.8	83.5	90.4	94.5	98.4
Agriculture	30.4	29.3	32.3	33.9	35.3	36.9	37.9
Agriculture as % of Total	42.7	41.5	41.5	40.6	39	39	38.5
Exports							
Total (in Million Naira)	8920.5	30360.6	31192.8	57971.2	109886.1	121533.7	205613.1
Agriculture	407.4	2032.1	2532.6	2255.9	2248.13	2941.76	2895.9
Agriculture as % of Total	4.6	6.7	8.1	3.9	2.0	2.4	1.4
Imports							
Total (in Million Naira)	5983.6	17861.7	21445.7	30860.2	45717.9	89488.2	143151.2
Agriculture	941.3	1731.2	1844.3	2252.8	4080.9	8680.4	13742.7

Agriculture as % of Total	15.7	9.7	8.6	7.3	8.9	9.7	9.6
Food Consumption Per Caput							
Calorie Intake	1924	2146	2039	2146	2200	2200	2200
Deficit/Surplus (%)	-20.5	-11.3	-15.7	-11.3	-9.1	-9.1	-9.1

Source: Adapted from M. O. Ojo, *et al.*, "Sustaining Agricultural Development in a Deregulated Economy," *Central Bank of Nigeria: Economic and Financial Review*, Vol. 31, No. 2, 1993, 73.

Table 6.2 Agriculture as percentage of total of GDP and of exports, 1993-1999

Year	GDP (1984 Factor Cost) (in Million Naira)	Agriculture (in Million Naira)	Percentage of GDP	Percentage of Exports
1993	100,015.1	37,780.8	37.8	1.6
1994	101,040.1	38,692.4	38.3	1.9
1995	103,502.9	40,110.0	38.8	1.6
1996	107,020.0	41,750.0	39.0	1.3
1997	110,400.0	43,500.0	39.4	1.6
1998	112,950.0	45,250.0	40.1	2.2
1999	116,140.0	47,600.0	41.0	1.4

Source: Computed from Central Bank of Nigeria, *Statistical Bulletin*, Vol. 13, 2003, 114; and E. U. Ukeje, "Productivity in the Agricultural Sector," Central Bank of Nigeria, Occasional Paper, No. 8, 2000.

The agricultural crisis has led to the prevalence of the received wisdom in the analysis of the causes, nature and solutions to the crisis. The major blame for the poor performance of agriculture has been placed on the so-called conservative nature of peasant farmers, their primitive agricultural practices like the land tenure system, scattered land holdings, poor storage facilities, primitive technology and lack of innovative approach to farming.[4] In another variant of this argument, Hyden in his highly polemical work on the "uncaptured" African peasantry saw the conservative nature of African peasants, which makes them to be irrationally attached to "the economy of affection" as a major obstacle to the transformation of agricultural production.[5] This blame of the peasant farmers is rather unfortunate and constitutes a misreading of the significant role they have played in Nigeria's agriculture. They were responsible for the high level of agricultural production, especially the imperialist induced export crops production during the colonial period and the 1960s, and in spite of their marginalization by agricultural development policies from the 1970s[6] have remained the backbone of Nigeria's agriculture. Gerald Helleiner has noted that by the mid 1960s, Nigeria's economic growth was led by peasant agriculture, which accounted for over 70 percent of the total Nigerian exports and 95 percent of the total Nigerian food consumption.[7]

The perceived shortcomings of peasant agricultural practices has not only become an article of faith in the agricultural development discourse but more importantly became the justification for propagating modernization as the solution to the agricultural development crisis.[8] This wholesome belief in the messianic effects of modernization resulted in the wanton pursuit of what has been described as "high-modernist" agricultural development policies.[9] Essentially, agricultural modernization entailed the complete jettisoning of all the features associated with peasant agriculture including indigenous knowledge, all of which were seen as backward and primitive, and replacing them with transplanted modern, that is, Western or Euro-American agricultural practices. Significant aspects of this agricultural modernization include large-scale highly mechanized capitalist farms and irrigation schemes, and various inputs embodied in the "new technology" associated with the green revolution. This imperial knowledge became the received wisdom that has been accepted as the panacea for agricultural development and therefore underlies all the agricultural transformation policies in Nigeria, especially from the 1970s.

Since the catechism of modernization as the solution to Nigeria's agricultural crisis has been uncritically accepted by many scholars, most works on the crisis have not questioned the detrimental role played by the modernist agricultural development policies. Rather, the validity of the philosophy underlying modernist agricultural transformation policies has been accepted as fundamentally sound, while analysts of the agricultural crisis have concentrated on other issues. Peasant farmers continue to share a major blame in the analysis. Echoing Robert Bates, a number of analysts have emphasized the structural issues of the entrenched interests that agricultural development policies serve. They stated that the influence of the elite and the need to satisfy the tastes of urban dwellers made agricultural development policies to be elitist and urban-biased while neglecting the peasant farmers who ironically constitute the backbone of Nigerian agriculture.[10] While agricultural development policies were clearly elitist,[11] the argument about the urban-biased nature of the policies should be made with some caution.[12] Indeed, successive governments were not really concerned with serving the collective interests of the urban dwellers but saw the production and massive importation of food as ways of dousing urban riots, which were perceived as capable of bringing about the downfall of the respective regimes.[13]

Other arguments that have been advanced for the poor performance of agriculture include poor implementation of otherwise fundamentally sound agricultural development policies[14] and that agricultural development policies served as means of surplus accumulation for both the domestic and foreign bourgeoisie.[15] Furthermore, the policies merely promoted agricultural dependency on foreign inputs and consequently, underdevelopment.[16] Some other scholars have emphasized the degrading effects of the modern agricultural inputs on the Nigerian environment and the resultant significant decrease in agricultural production.[17] These factors are symptomatic of the poor agricultural performance and helped to aggravate the agricultural crisis, but they do not explain the fundamental factors responsible for the crisis. Scott described the factors as systemic failures that would have occurred under the best assumptions about administrative efficiency and probity.[18]

My argument in this chapter is that the pervasive influence of modernization on the agricultural transformation policies is fundamentally responsible for the poor performance of agriculture. By completely discountenancing the cultural, social, material and scientific bases of indigenous agriculture, as well as its complexity, the transplanted modern agricultural practices were destined to fail. It should be noted that indigenous agricultural practices developed overtime and through constant adaptation, experimentation and innovation, complex agricultural processes suitable to the different ecological zones were developed. These helped to ensure meaningful and sustained agricultural production. Thus, a great body of indigenous knowledge, as well as the material and cultural bases of indigenous agriculture were developed over a very long period. It follows that failure to situate agricultural transformation policies on the indigenous foundation or the desire to obliterate the indigenous agricultural foundation through the transplanting of Western agricultural practices will have negative effects on agricultural development. Such measures would amount to the cultural and intellectual imperialism.

Jim Scott and Paul Richards have drawn attention to the debilitating effects of modernization on agricultural transformation in non-Western societies.[19] Scott's work is highly theoretical and broadly devoted to the entire Third World while that of Richards is devoted to West Africa, with some examples from Nigeria. No significant attempt has been made to conduct an in-depth theoretical and empirical analysis of agricultural transformation policies in Nigeria from a perspective that focuses on the principal role of modernization. Furthermore, although the analyses of Richards and Scott are very useful, their liberal and postmodern approach made it impossible for them to more concretely come to terms with the dialectics and dynamics of agricultural crisis in Third World countries. They failed to take into account the intersection between modernization, and other factors such as imperialism, international finance capital, state, class, accumulation, dependency, and gender, among others, in creating and aggravating the agricultural crisis. This chapter will adopt a radical political economy approach in analyzing the dialectics of agricultural transformation. The analysis will accord a central place to modernization and show how it intersected with factors like imperialism, dependency, state, class, gender and the environment to create and sustain the agricultural crisis.

Polemics of Agricultural Modernization

The basic philosophy that underlined agricultural transformation is hinged on the liberal discourse of development, which echoing the "stages of growth" theory sees development as the complete modernization of a peasant society, with large-scale industrialization and massive mechanization of agriculture constituting the core of the transformation. In the case of agriculture, it was assumed that the attainment of the take-off stage would launch Third World countries on the path to agricultural modernity.[20] However, for the transformation of the peasant society to be successful, it should entail a change in their "whole way of life, in expectations and motivations, and even the physical environment of daily life itself."[21] As a result, agricultural modernization in Nigeria was perceived in the form of transplanting the new agricultural technologies developed mainly in the United States and other Western capitalist countries into the Nigerian agricultural scene. These technologies were touted as the panacea for rapid agricultural development in the country. The merchants of agricultural modernization justified it based on "the superior technical efficiency of large-scale farms, the importance of mechanization to save labor and break technical bottlenecks, the superiority of monocropping and hybrids over polycropping and landraces, and the advantages of high-input agriculture, including commercial fertilizers and pesticides."[22]

Briefly, the main characteristics of agricultural modernization are monocropping, mechanization, hybridization, fertilizers and pesticides, and large-scale and capital-intensive farms. Under the guise of universalism, the process seeks to promote a form of agricultural standardization that virtually disregards the diversity of local environments, ecology, and implements, among others. In line with the classical modernization policy, proponents of agricultural modernization believe that transplanting the new technology into Nigeria under the policy of technology transfer would promote rapid agricultural development. As noted by Johnston and Kilby "the most dramatic example of development research which achieved a new embodiment of existing scientific knowledge in a uniquely appropriate form for underdeveloped countries is to be found in the domain of agriculture."[23] Implicit in this perspective is that agricultural modernization should be viewed in the form of an import substitution strategy: but to what extent are the associated technologies actually relevant and transferable to a Third World country like Nigeria?

In addressing the issue of the transferability of the modern agricultural technology, Hayami and Ruttan noted that:

> The effective transfer of technology is critically important to the agricultural development process. Although there exist a few ready-made technologies (for example, particular machinery or seeds) for international diffusion, transfer of knowledge and the development of indigenous capacity to generate an ecologically adapted and

> economically viable agricultural technology are vital to the progress of less developed countries.[24]

Although this technology transfer process envisages the development of local capacity, it is still couched in the form of modernization. It discountenances indigenous knowledge and the indigenous basis of agricultural practices, and gives primacy to the modern technology. In practice, this would result in adapting the Nigerian environment to suit the imported technology rather than adapting the technology to suit the indigenous environment. More significant is the fact that since the primary motive behind the modern technology is the maximization of profit and therefore the monopolization of knowledge, it amounts to wishful thinking to expect this knowledge to be transferred to Third World countries. Rather than relying on the modern technologies that were developed for temperate conditions, the core of agricultural technology in Nigeria should be the indigenous knowledge.

The agricultural modernization program that was exported to Nigeria is exemplified in the "green revolution" and characterized by the notion of production and profit. An important feature of this productionist strategy is its "package" approach. Although distinctions are usually made between the forms of technologies involved in this system: biological technology involving the use of high-yielding seeds, fertilizers, herbicides and pesticides, and mechanical technology involving the use of tractors and harvesters, it is more reasonable to see the two as constituting a package. This is because it is the interdependence of all the factors that foster the successful operation of the new technology. To this package can be added infrastructural development, which is regarded as crucial for the timely delivery of the various components of the package to farmers.

However, those who argue for a distinction between the biological technology and the mechanical technology state that the former emphasizes the supply of seeds, pesticides and herbicides to small-scale farmers and therefore accessible to a broader range of farmers. On the other hand, the latter's emphasis on mechanized cultivation, which by its nature is very expensive, makes it biased in favor of large-scale farmers. In any case, given the interdependency between both technologies, this distinction is rather tenuous. Proponents of the broader accessibility of the biological technology would argue that the issue of mechanization is resolved through the setting up of machine hiring units where small-scale farmers can lend these machines at subsidized rates.[25] However, with the emphasis of the biological technology on capitalist farming and the non-affordability of the various inputs to small-scale farmers, both technologies in practice promote large-scale farming.

The core of the new technology is the miracle seed, which is highly responsive to fertilizer input.[26] The vulnerability of the seeds to pest attacks and the growth of weeds occasioned by the heavy fertilizer input necessitate the use of pesticides and herbicides. The shorter maturing period of the new seeds which makes possible the cultivation of two or more crops a year, means that harvesting must be completed on time in order to leave room for the preparation of land for the following crop. This in turn necessitates the use of combine harvesters, and since land preparation has to be completed on time, tractors have to be used. In short, without fertilizers, the new seeds would not achieve their potential, and without pesticides and herbicides their output would be highly variable, while without mechanization their potential for multiple cropping would remain underutilized.[27]

A significant issue that needs to be addressed is the extent to which the modern agricultural technologies took into cognizance varying environmental factors. How compatible were the technologies to the ecology and factor endowments of the respective and complex Nigerian vegetation zones? To what extent were they in the position to promote sustainable agricultural development in Nigeria? Rather than seriously ponder these issues and consider them, proponents of agricultural modernization simply regarded the transplanting of the new technology as the magic wand for Nigeria's agriculture especially in view of the perceived primitive and backward nature, and therefore, irrelevance of the indigenous agricultural practices. They justified their position based on the universality of science and the perceived superiority of Western science over indigenous knowledge.

Nevertheless, it was the desire for profit maximization rather than the belief in the universality of science and a genuine scientific commitment on the part of Western scientists, agricultural engineers and agronomists that fueled the relentless marketing of agricultural modernization to Nigeria and other Third World countries. The period between 1945 and 1975 witnessed the development and consolidation of an agricultural-industrial complex during which agricultural modernization under the guise of the green revolution was aggressively marketed to Third World countries. The American version of agricultural modernization, patterned along the Tennessee Valley Authority (TVA), was "absolutely hegemonic" and became the prevailing "export model" during this period. Agronomists, engineers, other scientists, economists and planners who had served in the TVA and the United States Department of Agriculture went on to work in the United Nations, the Food and Agricultural Organization (FAO), and the United States Agency for International Development (USAID).[28] They used their privileged position to influence the policies of these organizations under the guise of the neutrality and universality of science.[29]

At the same time, various agri-business industries in the West started developing and patenting different inputs of the modern agricultural technology ranging from seeds to machinery. In alliance with Western governments, and international agricultural and aid organizations the agri-business industries sought to influence and control the agricultural development process in the Third World. The denigration of indigenous agricultural practices and knowledge, which were seen as posing a threat to this exploitative design, was a significant aspect of the strategy of dominating the agricultural development process in these countries. Agricultural modernization therefore became a veritable tool for profit maximization and exploitation of the Third World countries by the emergent agricultural-industrial complex. It is significant to note that agricultural development policies in Nigeria were greatly influenced by the FAO and the World Bank. They used this opportunity to champion high-modernist agricultural development strategy.

A significant feature of the agricultural modernization policy was the perception of Nigerian and other African women as obstacles to the agricultural transformation process. The notion of women as inferior, backward and obstacles to the attainment of modernity, a product of the transplanted Western patriarchal ideology, resulted in the conception of agriculture as primarily a male activity. This was a complete misreading of the indigenous agricultural system in which women played a central role. The negative conception of the role of women in agriculture, made the different agricultural modernization policies to be directed to men.[30] According to Diane Elson:

> The picture of farmers as men disadvantages women farmers and hinders attempts to improve agricultural productivity. When there is an implicit assumption that farmers are men, it is not surprising if new agricultural technology and inputs flow mainly to men – and there is a wealth of evidence that this is what has happened in developing countries over the last three decades. . . . Governments still fail to collect comprehensive, reliable and unbiased statistics on the contribution women make to agricultural production.[31]

The agricultural modernization process in Nigeria therefore marginalized women and sought to remove them from the crucial role they had played historically, in the food production process. The gender-biased nature of the modernist-influenced agricultural development policies was therefore at variance with the cultural foundations of the indigenous agricultural system. This contradiction was bound to have adverse effects on the agricultural development process.

Modernization and Agricultural Development Trajectory

Modernization influenced Nigeria's agricultural development trajectory from the colonial period but became much more pronounced from the 1970s. The colonial agricultural policy emphasized the production of cash crops, which were needed as raw materials by Western industries. In order to make Nigerian farmers take to cash crops production measures such as taxation and the de-emphasis of indigenous food production were put in place. The cash crops sub-sector was seen as dynamic and modern, and was integrated into the colonial economy albeit at a subordinate level. However, the British colonial administration's primary concern with the maximization of the extraction of Nigeria's resources with minimal financial commitment made it decide against the establishment of plantations. Instead, it relied on male peasant farmers who through various fiscal, administrative and coercive measures were made to abandon food production in favor of cash crops. This set in motion the process of denigrating indigenous agricultural practices as backward and primitive, as a result, traditional agriculture did not receive support and encouragement from the colonial administration. Furthermore, since colonial agricultural policies privileged men over women and disparaged women's productive functions thereby marginalizing their crucial role in agriculture, particularly as food producers, there was a decline in food production. The beginning of Nigeria's food crisis can therefore be traced to the colonial period.

Thus, although the conventional wisdom has been to regard the colonial and immediate postcolonial periods as periods of agricultural boom because of the sector's contribution to the GDP and the total amount of exports, the origin of Nigeria's agricultural crisis can be located in the colonial period. Implicit in the so-called colonial agricultural boom was a latent crisis, which became manifest with the poor performance of export crops from the late 1960s and the alarming decline in productivity of the food sector occasioned by years of neglect and hostility toward indigenous agriculture.

The influence of modernization on Nigeria's agricultural development strategy became more pronounced in the late 1950s, which coincided with the high mark of modernist agriculture in the West, especially the United States. This period witnessed an increased emphasis on agricultural transformation through the introduction of large-scale plantations, the adoption of new agricultural techniques and high yielding seeds, and the establishment of more capital-intensive farms. In addition, the FAO became the major player in terms of advising on the agricultural development strategy to adopt. Although plantations were established in the Western and Eastern regions of Nigeria in the 1950s, the main significant step that was taken to transform agricultural production through large-scale farming, was the establishment of farm settlement schemes particularly in the Western and Eastern regions in the 1960s. The farm settlement scheme, which was patterned along the lines of Israel's Moshav form of agricultural organization, was touted as a revolutionary step that would make it possible to introduce modern agricultural practices into the country. The scheme, it was claimed, would help to overcome the limitations of the primitive and backward indigenous agricultural practices such as scattered small land holdings, primitive technology, lack of capital and lack of adequate marketing strategies. In short, the farm settlement scheme was portrayed as a direct attempt to transform traditional agriculture into a modern one. This involved the introduction of coherent land holdings, common processing and marketing facilities, more capital-intensive methods, a mixed farming pattern involving a higher proportion of production directed to marketed crops, as well as higher income for the participating farmers.[32] The FAO had the responsibility for implementing the scheme.

The objectives and principles underlying the farm settlement schemes were imbued with high modernist philosophy: because the peasant farmers were regarded as conservative, primitive and backward, they were not made part of the schemes. Rather, the farm settlements would comprise people with a minimum of elementary school leaving certificates, who, after attending state created farm institutes for two years where they were taught modern farming methods, will be sent to the respective farm settlements. Each settler was allocated between twenty-six and twenty-eight acres of land of which sixteen to eighteen acres were devoted to cash crops and ten acres to arable crops and livestock.[33] The farm settlements were expected to bring about rural progress through the modernization of agriculture and increase in productivity, profit and income. Furthermore, in line with the high modernist simple "production and profit" model of agricultural extension services[34] the farm settlements were expected to serve as extension centers to the surrounding peasant farmers with a view to accelerating agricultural production and profit. To perform these tasks successfully, the farms were to be mechanized, while modern inputs like seedlings and fertilizers would be applied.

In line with the inherited colonial patriarchal agricultural policies, the agricultural innovations that were expected to be brought about by the farm settlements were only directed at males who were considered the only group with the progressive perspective to accept and implement modern farming techniques. As a result, only males who had completed at least a primary (elementary) school education were accepted as settlers.[35] This again was at variance with the traditional agricultural system in which women played crucial roles. Thus, the masculinist ideology behind the farm settlement schemes further marginalized women in the agricultural sector.

The farm settlements failed mainly because the underlying modernization principles behind their establishment did not take into account the prevailing cultural, social and material realities on which indigenous agriculture was based. In adopting a paternalistic approach and failing to understand the complexities of the indigenous agricultural system, the schemes could not tap from the indigenous knowledge and practices that are vital for the success of such an enterprise. As noted by Chima Korieh:

> The (farm) settlement projects, which amounted to forced villagization and relocation of peasants, failed because they disrupted local social and production patterns. They operated under a labor arrangement which limited settlers' ability to call upon traditional forms of labor procurement. Under the traditional forms of labor arrangements, a household relied on the labor of the immediate family, the lineage and various work groups to carry out its farming tasks. This labor was often provided free. But the settlement schemes often took settlers away from their immediate locality, which tended to sever kinship-based labor networks.[36]

Furthermore, the imported machines, which were not suitable for the Nigerian environment constantly broke down and suffered from lack of adequate spare parts. Moreover, the machines created a number of environmental problems while the capital-intensive nature of the farms did not recommend them to the surrounding peasant farmers. A combination of these and other factors such as the failure to provide adequate social amenities and reduction in government subsidies led to disenchantment among the settlers, many of whom deserted the settlements within the first decade of their establishment. In spite of the failure of this comparatively modest modernist approach, the Nigerian government was even more committed to the implementation of full-scale agricultural modernization as the panacea for the worsening agricultural crisis from the 1970s.

As already noted in order to prepare the ground for the introduction of a full-scale agricultural modernization program, the 1970s witnessed a massive assault on peasant farmers. Their agricultural practices, described as traditional, primitive, conservative, backward and non-innovative, were castigated and blamed for all the woes bedeviling the agricultural sector. The attack on peasant farmers got to its peak in the Third National Development Plan (1975-1980) which identified certain "well known" characteristics of peasant agriculture as the main culprit for the poor performance of agriculture.[37] This attack as well as the supposed inadequacies of indigenous agriculture set the stage for the marginalization of peasant farmers and indigenous knowledge in favor of imperial knowledge and agricultural practices under the guise of agricultural modernization.

Under the auspices of the World Bank and the FAO, the solution to Nigeria's agricultural crisis was portrayed as the modernization of the agricultural system through the transplanting of Western agricultural practices as embodied in the "new technology" and the "green revolution." Emphasis was placed on large-scale capital-intensive farms and irrigation schemes, mechanization, massive injection of imported high yielding varieties of seeds, chemicals, pesticides and fertilizers. This phase of agricultural modernization was characterized by the massive importation of machines, chemicals, fertilizers and seedlings. It also witnessed a dominant position for foreign "experts" and the complete de-emphasis of indigenous agricultural knowledge. This has equally been the most prolific phase in terms of both the number of agricultural transformation programs launched and the amount capital devoted to the sector. The agricultural modernization programs launched under this phase, fall into three categories, namely, integrated rural development programs, establishment of private and state-owned large-scale mechanized capital-intensive farms, and the construction of large-scale irrigation schemes. A common feature of these programs was their gendered nature. All the innovations, new technologies, inputs and extension services associated with the programs, were directed at men because as already noted, they were considered as progressive. Thus, the programs continued the practice of discriminating against women. Although it is usually claimed that the integrated rural development programs were directed at small-scale farmers,[38] in actuality all the agricultural modernization programs were aimed at promoting the establishment of large-scale capital-intensive and mechanized farms. The rest of the chapter will be devoted to examining the respective programs.

Integrated Rural Development Programs

The integrated rural development programs were squarely situated within the paradigm of agricultural modernization. The worsening food crisis in Nigeria in the 1970s at a time when the country was making much money from crude oil exports provided the impetus for the launching of the programs. The petro-dollars were to be used to transform the agricultural sector with the twin purpose of solving the food crisis and diversifying the export base of the economy. The major influence behind the launching of integrated rural development programs was the World Bank, which directed the bulk of its lending policies in Africa to projects purportedly aimed at small-scale farmers.[39] The launching of these programs reflected a shift in the World Bank's approach to agricultural development in Africa. As stated by Gibbon *et al.*:

> The World Bank's approach to African agriculture has gone through a series of phases. In the 1960s and 1970s, World Bank loans to African agriculture were concentrated on large-scale development schemes seeking to introduce 'modern' and off-the-shelf agricultural technologies for livestock, cereals, tree crops, oil seeds, cotton, etc., based on packages of high yielding variety seeds, fertilizer, chemical pesticides, and credits. In the 1960s the emphasis was on the delivery of such packages to large-scale, low density farming, usually accompanied by mechanisation and/or irrigation. After a famous speech given by then World Bank head Robert McNamara, in Nairobi in 1973, the emphasis turned to smallholders and to rural and/or regional integrated development programmes, in which agricultural modernisation was combined with provision of local physical and social infrastructure. In both phases the state was seen as playing a key development role. . . .[40]

The launching of the SAPs in the 1980s was accompanied by a further shift in the World Bank's approach to agricultural development. The adjustment programs emphasized deregulation of the agricultural sector and the increased production of raw materials, among others (this issue is discussed in chapter 8).

The integrated rural development programs were normally products of collaboration between an African state and external financiers, usually the World Bank with the use of imported skills been a critical aspect of the agreement.[41] In theory, the programs placed emphasis on extension services to farmers who were expected to adopt the new agricultural inputs while operating within their own traditional milieu. However, in practice this was not the case as farmers were expected to discard their own cultural and agricultural practices in favor of the cultural and agricultural practices associated with the new inputs.[42] Furthermore, as will become clear later, the paradox of the integrated rural development programs is that while they were supposedly directed at small-scale farmers, the policies associated with them were more favorable to large-scale farmers.

Without taking into account the realities on which indigenous agricultural practices were based, the programs emphasized the uniform application of the transplanted "biological package" of improved seedlings, fertilizers, herbicides and pesticides, by farmers. Roads and other means of communication were to be developed so that these inputs can be sent to the farmers. In addition, realizing the need for mechanization in order for the inputs to perform well, the programs recommended the setting up of machine hiring centers where farmers would have access to machines at subsidized rates. Thus, while the core of this approach is the biological technology, the other two components of the programs are mechanization and infrastructural development.

Implementing the biological package alongside mechanization means that in reality the programs were only favorable to large-scale farmers. Indeed, the integrated rural development approach discriminated between farmers and concentrated on those who were regarded as "progressive" farmers (usually large-scale farmers) on account of their willingness to adopt the new inputs as well as their ability to purchase them. The approach delineated farmers into three categories: large-scale, progressive, and traditional. A major weakness of this approach is that it completely disregarded indigenous agricultural practices and marginalized the peasant farmers while fostering imperial knowledge and imperial agricultural practices under the rubric of modernization. In addition, although the integrated rural development programs were mainly aimed at increasing food production, the extension services were primarily directed at men, thus, ignoring women who occupied a crucial position in food production. Nevertheless, the transplanted agricultural technologies, which were at variance with the realities on which indigenous agriculture was based as well as subversive of the indigenous environment, failed to accomplish any meaningful success. Furthermore, the emphasis placed on the supply of imported inputs greatly increased the dependence of the Nigerian farmer on foreign seed banks, transnational corporations and various agro-businesses thereby strengthening their subordination to market forces. This had adverse consequences for self-reliance.[43]

The five major integrated rural development programs that were launched in Nigeria are the National Accelerated Food Production Program (NAFPP), the Operation Feed the Nation (OFN), the Green Revolution (GR), the Agricultural Development Projects (ADPs), and the DFRRI. Nevertheless, it was the ADPs and to some extent DFRRI, that more closely exemplified the main features of the integrated rural development strategy. However, DFRRI, as was the case with NAFPP, OFN and GR, was regime specific and therefore had rather limited impact. The ADP launched under the auspices of the World Bank, was the only program that transcended various regimes. This program has attracted a number of studies. This section will therefore briefly examine the other programs while devoting more attention to the ADPs.

National Accelerated Food Production Program

The NAFPP was launched in 1973 by the Gowon regime. It had as its aim the bringing of modern farm practices "like high-yielding varieties (of seed), fertilisers, pesticides, credit and management to farmers through a coordinated package approach."[44] The program emphasized the distribution of packages of information, imported inputs like seedlings, fertilizers and pesticides to small-scale farmers with a view to improving their production of items like wheat, maize and cassava. Agro Service Centers (ASC) was set up to handle the sale of seeds, fertilizers and insecticides to farmers while also teaching them how to use these inputs. Under its paternalistic approach, the practices of peasant farmers were dismissed as backward and irrelevant and so, they were to discard them in favor of the new practices. Thus, it was claimed that the NAFPP "integrated the technology information component (teaching and extension) with the technical service component (inputs and credit) in a total food crop technology transfer package for farmers."[45] This amounted to transplanting imperial knowledge, a factor, which along with other factors adversely affected the success of the program. The inability to distribute the inputs to farmers on time, and more importantly, the fact that the program was out of tune with the realities of the indigenous agricultural practices, meant that the NAFPP had very minimal impact on agricultural development. In the face of the lack of meaningful gains, the government ceased funding it and so it collapsed, but the problem of food scarcity remained.

Operation Feed the Nation

The OFN was launched in April 1976 by the Olusegun Obasanjo regime with the aim of curbing the increasing food imports and food scarcity in the country, especially in the urban centers. The program aimed at mobilizing Nigerians, particularly the urban communities toward contributing to the attainment of self-sufficiency in food production by cultivating their own food.[46] As was the case with the NAFPP, the emphasis was on the massive application of modern inputs like seedling, fertilizers and pesticides, which were to be provided at subsidized rates. Since urban dwellers were the target group, emphasis was placed on the use of media to urge them to embrace farming. Students in tertiary institutions were paid to distribute the agricultural inputs during their summer vacation. As it turned out, 6.5 million naira out of a total budget of 9.5 million naira for the program in the first year, representing about two-thirds of the entire budget was spent on the payment of student wages.[47] In the second year, the distribution of inputs was limited to a selected number of students, and in subsequent years, the program concentrated on the establishment of OFN farms mainly in schools and prisons.

The OFN failed mainly because of the modernization paradigm that underlined its philosophy. The denigration of peasant agricultural practices made them to be marginalized in favor of urban dwellers that it was felt would be more receptive and capable of establishing high modernist farms. Thus, right from the beginning, the program was destined to fail because it attempted to mobilize everyone with the exception of the peasant farmers who constituted the backbone of Nigeria's agriculture.[48] Yet the primary target of the program, the urban dwellers, was, and has remained marginal to Nigeria's agriculture. It is therefore hardly surprising that between 1976 and 1978, when the OFN was at its peak, the total estimated land under cultivation declined from 18.8 million hectares to 11.05 million hectares, while food imports rose phenomenally from 353.7 million naira to one billion naira.[49] In fact, the program can be seen as more of an attempt to "bribe" the increasingly restive student population and douse urban riots.

Green Revolution

This program, conceived along the line of the integrated rural development projects, was launched by the Shagari regime in 1980. As the name suggests, the program was operated on the Green Revolution principles[50] and it emphasized the massive use of new varieties of seeds, fertilizers, pesticides, tractors, as well as irrigation. The core of the program is the supply of the biological package to farmers at subsidized rates, the provision of extension services and infrastructural development. The National Council for the Green Revolution was created to run the program and this was accompanied by a high amount of publicity. According to Michael Watts, each Green Revolution project was expected to cater "to 60,000-80,000 farmers through a subsidized package of improved practices – fertilizers, insecticides, ploughs, tractors, and new seed varieties – administered through a phalanx of federal parastatal organizations." He added that the program's emphasis on the new technology "contributed to the import boom, notably through infrastructural investment (roads and construction) and fertilizers (whose import increased from 34,000 tons in 1970 to 513,000 tons in 1980)."[51]

In spite of the elaborate administrative system and publicity associated with the program, the Green Revolution did not record much achievement. The conventional explanation advanced for the failure of the program, are bureaucratic inefficiencies, corruption and the politicization of the program.[52] However, these factors do not get to the core of the reasons for failure of the program. The fundamental factors for the failure center on the serious limitations of the modernization policy. For instance, the inputs that were imported into the country could not adapt to the environment and so performed poorly. Furthermore, apart from having adverse effects on the indigenous environment, the practices associated with these inputs were at variance with the socio-economic milieu within which indigenous agriculture was based, hence the program could not have any meaningful impact on the country's agriculture. Moreover, apart from the fact that the reliance on the importation of the inputs promoted serious economic dependence, all the components of the package did not normally arrive at the same time thereby making it impossible to apply them in the recommended manner. The problems associated with the importation of these inputs call into question the adequacy of a strategy that relies on transplanting agricultural technologies developed elsewhere for the purpose of promoting self-reliance and self-sufficiency in food production.[53]

Directorate of Food, Roads and Rural Infrastructures

The perceived shortcomings of previous agricultural transformation programs, which regarded agricultural development as the cornerstone for rural development, provided the rationale for the creation of DFRRI by the Babangida regime. The previous approach linked rural infrastructural development to agricultural development. However, the Babangida regime saw this approach as constituting a misguided interpretation of what integrated rural development entails. The regime regarded agriculture as a major occupation of rural dwellers but in order to encourage more young people to take to farming as well as develop other aspects of the rural economy, rural infrastructures like housing, health care, industries and roads, among others, should be provided. It was argued that this new approach, which removed agriculture as the core around which rural infrastructural development revolved, represented a more meaningful integrated rural development program.[54]

Nevertheless, a significant place was accorded to agriculture since DFRRI was launched during the period when SAP had already been introduced. It was reasoned that the development of these infrastructures would encourage many youths to remain in the rural areas and contribute to the production of more food and cash crops. Indeed, a major objective of DFFRI was the promotion of food self-sufficiency in Nigeria and the promotion of the export of cash crops, with the belief that under the SAP-induced deregulation and drastic devaluation of the national currency, these would help to increase rural income.[55] DFRRI adopted the modernization approach to agricultural development as it castigated the practices of the peasant farmers and promoted the implementation of the biological package and the use of tractors. The program therefore neglected the rural farmers who ironically were said to be its primary target and actually concentrated more on the award of contracts to construct infrastructures in the rural areas. Most of these projects were either shoddily done or not even completed. In addition, the great amount of hardship promoted by SAP worsened the economic and material conditions of the rural dwellers with the peasant farmers adversely affected by these hardships. In fact, the program's agricultural development strategy did not result in any tangible improvement in agricultural production. Indeed, the continued implementation of SAP made the agricultural situation become pathetic.

Agricultural Development Projects

The ADPs, which are World Bank-sponsored projects, reflect the Bank's approach to integrated rural development. The projects are joint federal-state schemes mainly in the sense that the federal government acted as guarantor for the state governments in connection with the loans provided to the states by the World Bank. The loans were granted on "hard" World Bank terms. Under the terms of the loans, the World Bank would provide the management staff who were to be autonomous vis-à-vis the state governments and their ministries of agriculture. The program emphasized full-scale modernist agricultural practices with its core been the biological package and the inputs were to be imported by the management team. The program also provided for the setting up of special service centers where farmers could hire tractors, as well as the construction of rural roads. Nevertheless, given the nature of the agreement, which provided the project, its own command system autonomous of the Nigerian government, the World Bank operated "a characteristically neo-colonial organization (as) Nigerian state capital (was) brought under the control of international finance capital."[56]

ADPs were first introduced in Northern Nigeria during the 1975-80 plan period. The original three pilot schemes were located at Funtua, Gombe and Gusau: the program was subsequently extended to other parts of the country. Emphasis was placed on extension services and each project was expected to cater for 60,000 to 90,000 farmers through a subsidized package of inputs. However, the target group was those defined as "progressive" farmers, meaning those farmers willing to cooperate with the project. Nevertheless, farmers were categorized into three: large-scale (farmers with more than 100 acres), progressive (farmers with less than 100 acres but willing to cooperate with the project), and traditional (farmers unwilling to cooperate with the project). Preferential treatment was given to the first two groups, with special support to the large-scale ones under the belief that their success will have a demonstration and "trickle down" effect on all the other farmers.[57] Thus, although this program absorbed a lion's share of state resources, the only beneficiaries were the tiny group of large-scale and so-called "progressive" farmers while the vast majority of the small-scale farmers were neglected. Tina Wallace has pointed out that of the "83,332 small farmers on the Funtua Agricultural Development Project (96.33% of all farmers on the project) 67,932 received *no* visits from an extension officer, i.e. 79.5% had no extension advice."[58] Yet this was a project, which devoted a great deal of resources to extension services and had a high concentration of extension workers. Even worse was the gendered nature of the project. As was the case with the other integrated rural development projects, extension services were targeted at male farmers' thereby further marginalizing women in the agricultural production process.

The initial plan of the pilot schemes was the cultivation of high-yielding varieties of cotton and sorghum, but these failed. It should be noted that these projects were supposed to promote food production; however, cotton is not a food crop. Maize then became the main crop emphasized. Furthermore, although sorghum and millet were the most important indigenous food crops produced in the area, the program did not include the production of millet. Even then, the encouragement of maize production was because of its commercial value, particularly in Southern Nigeria, rather than the food needs of the people. In addition, the project officials felt that maize had the greatest potential of been produced along the high modernist lines of monocropping, and massive application of fertilizers and pesticides. Indeed, although in theory the World Bank claimed that its agricultural development projects was motivated by the need to increase food production, in practice the Bank was more preoccupied with the cultivation of "tradeable" and exportable crops such as oil seeds, maize and cottons. These crops would be cultivated through the application of "improved" technical packages and the raising of "management skills."[59]

Although the ADPs constitute the most elaborate attempt at providing extension to farmers, the program did not make much meaningful impact because of the emphasis on transplanting Western agricultural practices into Nigeria while completely disregarding the indigenous practices. Furthermore, the concentration of efforts on large-scale farmers shows that although on paper the ADPs emphasized serving the interests of small-scale farmers, the logic of the techniques associated with the transplanted farming practices only favor large-scale farming. Indeed, rather than serve the interests of the vast majority of small-scale farmers, the preference given to large-scale farming resulted in land appropriation from peasant farmers by the tiny group of large-scale farmers. The outcome was the creation, for the first time in the northern parts of the country where the program was initiated, a class of pauperized and landless peasant farmers.[60] This significant contradiction, which was out of tune with the realities on which indigenous agriculture was based negatively, affected the impact of the ADPs.

The adverse environmental impact caused by the new inputs and the emergence of new weeds and pests that were resistant to the fertilizers and pesticides and therefore negatively affected the output of the farms, made even the so-called "progressive" farmers abandon the new techniques and revert to the indigenous practices. For instance, the introduction of a sorghum package, which discouraged the use of the tested local varieties in favor of new unproven varieties of sorghum, fertilizer use, and monocropping, adversely affected the yields of the farms. This made the farmers to abandon the new varieties and the practices associated with them in favor of the ecologically tested, adapted and more productive local varieties. The farmers realized that the indigenous practices, which were adapted to the local ecology, were superior to imported practices associated with the new seeds. They therefore reverted to the traditional practices of farm management and intercropping which made better use of the nutrients of the soil, produced yields that are more balanced, and minimized their risks.[61] In fact, studies by the FAO have shown that the main condition under which some of the imported inputs contributed to increased production was when they were combined with the traditional inputs and subjected to traditional methods of management.[62] The disenchantment by farmers with the imported practices and the preference for the tested, more ecologically adapted and productive indigenous practices was clearly illustrated by the findings of Sumit Roy in his study of the ADP schemes in parts of northern Nigeria.

> Project findings in Funtua in 1980-81, 1981-82, 1982-83 show the dominance of traditional cropping patterns: sole and mixed. Thus, in 1980-81 about 34 per cent of the cropped area was under sole cropping while 41.1 per cent was under double cropping. In 1981-82 crop mixtures covered 66 per cent of the cultivated area while in 1982-83 sole cropping covered 32 per cent of the area, double cropping 48 per cent, and triple cropping 36 per cent. The peasants had adopted a risk minimalisation strategy.

He further noted that the "peasants in Batarawa undertook limited cultivation of maize (HYV). It was grown even without fertilser. Traditional crops and some root crops dominated their cropping patterns."[63] This clearly attests to the unsuitability of the transplanted technologies to the Nigerian environment.

The ADPs were supposed to exemplify the World Bank's professed commitment to integrated rural development, which had as its central focus the improvement of the productive capacity and quality of life of small-scale farmers. Paradoxically, the outcome of the program was antithetical to this commitment, as the main beneficiaries were large-scale farmers. A fundamental problem with the ADPs was the inadequacy of the premise on which the projects were based. However, some other factors that contributed to the poor performance of the ADPs include, the adverse environmental impact, policies that in reality favored large-scale farmers, technological dependence, and, worst of all, the huge capital flight out of the country. As noted by Gavin Williams, "the record of the World Bank projects and the texts of its policy documents reveal an incapacity to understand the conditions and constraints under which most farmers produce their crops or to learn from experience." He added that the huge amount of capital associated with the World Bank's ADPs "have certainly contributed to Nigeria's debts."[64] These factors gave rise to a sharp disagreement between the Balarabe Musa-led government of Kaduna state (where one of the pilot schemes was started) and the World Bank between 1980 and 1981.[65] The Kaduna state government questioned some of the main features of the projects, namely: the focus on non-staples; the bias in favor the so-called "progressive" farmers; the emphasis on the massive application of fertilizers and other chemicals; and the use of foreign skills at cost, which was considered exorbitant. With regard to the massive application of fertilizers, the government observed that:

> (T)he expatriates who controlled the Funtua project encourage the massive application of chemical fertiliser by the farmers, as if this is all that modern farming methods mean. This is certainly in the interest of the big foreign corporation who derive huge interest from the sale of fertiliser. But this is not in the long term interest of the farmers of this

> state, because this massive application of chemical fertiliser will in the long run damage the soil and cause other serious ecological distortion, which may render the whole area into an acidic wasteland in the not too distant future.[66]

This disagreement led to the withdrawal of the World Bank from the Kaduna state's ADP in 1981, although it was invited back in 1984 by the new military regime in Nigeria.[67]

An examination of the provisions of the agreement between the World Bank and the federal and state governments of Nigeria clearly reveals the highly exploitative nature of the ADP. The program resulted in considerable outflow of capital and helped to serve the financial interests of Western based agro-industrial complex by increasing Nigeria's dependence on their products. As noted by Williams:

> The World Bank appears to dismiss the prospects of crops for which it cannot offer yield-enhancing technologies. . . . The policies recommended by the Bank would increase Nigeria's dependence on imported fertilizer and foods, despite the uncertain prospects for Nigeria's capacity to maintain its foreign exchange earnings and to service its debts.[68]

The degree of exploitation associated with the ADP was clearly exemplified by the provisions of the agreement, which the federal government signed with the World Bank on behalf of the Kwara state government. The agreement stated that the World Bank would "lend the Federal Government (as guarantor of Kwara State) the sum of $27 million in various currencies." This loan would be used to pay "the salaries and allowances of internationally recruited staff and to settle the bills for equipment and farm inputs such as tractors, fertilizers, insecticides, improved seeds, etc."[69]

Table 6.3 IADP expenditure on selected items, 1979-1982

Items of Expenditure	Amount 1979-82 in Naira	Percentage of Total
Building	1,009,245	6.25
Vehicles: Heavy and Light	4,244,700	26.28
Vehicle Operation	1,100,699	6.81
Civil Works	1,870,860	11.58
Commercial Services	463,400	2.87
General Expenses	1,913,817	11.85
Land Development	121,748	0.75
Salaries: International and Local Staff	4,370,266	27.06
Research	145,980	0.90
Training	122,650	0.76
Evaluation	124,520	0.77
House and Office Furniture and Equipment	148,724	0.92
Management and Administration	455,380	2.82
Seed Multiplication	60,480	0.37
Total	16,152,469	

Source: Oniemola, *The World Bank and Capitalist Agricultural Development: The Ilorin Agricultural Development Project in Nigeria*, Nr. 22, Berlin: Das Arabische Buch. KnesebeckstrBe 16, 1989, 10.

The Kwara state government was responsible for the payment of the operational costs of the project, like housing for the foreign staff and offsetting bills for locally recruited staff.[70] Indeed, apart from importing all the physical materials used for the construction of the physical structures, the bulk of the money involved in the Kwara state ADP was spent on importing "vehicles, office materials including pins, and for settling of the high costs of the internationally recruited staff."[71] By June 1983, after spending over 20 million naira without any discernable improvement in production or in the social conditions of the farm families in the areas of operation, works at the Ilorin ADP office stagnated and actually stopped in the field. Table 6.3 clearly shows some of the frivolities on which most of the money was spent.

The table clearly illustrates the exploitative nature of the ADP as well as the fact that through the agency of the World Bank, the program was used to serve Western capitalist interests. The bulk of the expenditure went into the payment of salaries mainly of the international staff (27.06%) and for the importation of vehicles (26.28%), among others, while more relevant issues like seed multiplication (0.37%), research (0.90%), training (0.76%) and program evaluation (0.77%) received the least amount of money.[72] This promoted a great degree of dependence on Western-controlled international agribusiness as well as capital flight out of the country. Thus, a combination of the adverse environmental impact of the projects, the gender-biased nature of the projects, the fact that the program was out of tune with the material and socio-cultural setting on which indigenous agriculture was based, and its highly exploitative nature, militated against its success.

Large-scale Capital-intensive Farms

The establishment of large-scale capital-intensive farms is a critical requirement of agricultural modernization. Such farms were touted as the panacea for agricultural transformation in Nigeria, as they would phenomenally contribute to increase in food and raw materials production thereby helping to solve the problem of food scarcity while at the same time contributing to the diversification of the export base of the economy. To realize this goal, large-scale farming was to be made attractive to Nigerians by putting in place relevant institutional and fiscal measures. The period of the Third National Development Plan, witnessed the implementation of various measures that were aimed at making large-scale farming more attractive. One of the most significant measures was the promulgation of the land use decree in 1978.

Advocates of agricultural modernization constantly pointed to the land tenure system as a major culprit hindering efforts at agricultural transformation. They pointed out that the system encouraged scattered landholdings, promoted unproductive small-scale peasant agricultural practices, and importantly, made it impossible for individuals and private organizations to acquire large tracts of land for large-scale capitalist farming. The solution was therefore seen in the government takeover of land ownership, which would enable it to allocate land to large-scale farmers, a situation that will eventually result in a massive increase in agricultural production. This provided the justification for the promulgation of the land use decree in 1978. The decree vested state ownership of land on state governments thus vitiating the existing practice of communal ownership of land. Much work exist on the necessity or otherwise of the land use decree and its impact on small scale-farmers.[73] The decree led to massive alienation of rural land by top government officials, retired civil servants and military officials most of who acquired their wealth illegally, as well as businessmen, among others. It is significant to note that Obasanjo and Shehu Yar Adua, the head of state and chief of staff supreme headquarters (vice head of state) whose administration promulgated the land use decree, used their position to acquire large tracts of land and retired into large-scale capitalist farming. Thus, while urban-based influential individuals used the decree to acquire massive amount of land rural dwellers became increasingly landless with some of them reduced to the position of laborers on the farms of these absentee landlords and farmers.

The Nigerian government equally attempted to compel privately owned branches of transnational industries operating in the country and locally owned industries to take to large-scale capitalist farming. As a result, industries operating within the country were required to source a given percentage of their raw materials locally. This, it was believed, would make these industries establish large-scale capitalist farms where they would grow raw materials. In response, some private industries either established their own farms or purchased farms that had already been established by private individuals or state governments. However, many of these industries were not actually interested in large-scale capitalist farming but merely established large-scale farms as a façade to demonstrate that they were adhering to government policies. In fact, in a number of cases, farming did not proceed beyond land clearance, yet this land clearance resulted in the destruction of soil structures and erosion.[74] In addition, some state governments established state-owned large-scale capitalist farms with the twin purpose of solving the problems of food production in their states and making large-scale capitalist farming more attractive to private individuals through the success of the state-owned farms. Thus, it was intended that the state-owned farms would through their success, have demonstration effects on the surrounding people thereby resulting in the widespread adoption of large-scale capitalist farming by private individuals and organizations. These state-owned farms were normally established in partnership with foreign agribusiness capital, which had the responsibility of providing technical advice based on the biological and mechanical technologies – the "new technology." Since the farms were organized around the new technologies, no attempts were made to incorporate the indigenous agricultural practices. On the contrary, as already pointed out, it was believed that the success of the farms would make the surrounding peasant farmers embrace the new technology. Furthermore, as was the case with the other agricultural modernization programs, the innovations and demonstration effects of these farms were only targeted at the male farmers.

However, in spite of the various institutional and fiscal measures that were put in place to promote large-scale capitalist farming, it did not become popular among individuals and organizations. This was largely because of the serious shortcomings and failure of large-scale capitalist farming. The case of two Bendel state-owned large-scale capitalist farms will help to illustrate the serious limitations of these farms.

The Bendel state government established two large-scale, mechanized and capital-intensive farms at Agbede and Warrake in the northern part of the state in 1973. The main objective of the farms was to substantially increase food production "in the state within the shortest possible time through the use of modern farm machinery and the latest cultural techniques."[75] These farms, which were established in partnership with the United States-based Tiffany Industries Inc., that had the responsibility for providing the technical advice and management, were to produce maize and rice. Large tracts of land were alienated from the Agbede and Warrake communities to establish the farms. Unlike the other projects that have been examined, the farms fulfilled all the requirements for the establishment of high modernist large-scale capital-intensive farms. They were well financed, adequately supplied with improved varieties of seeds, the operations of the farms right from plowing through planting, fertilizer application, weed control and harvesting, were fully mechanized. The most sophisticated machines were introduced into the farms. For instance, the Agbede farm had "up to date workshop capable of handling all repairs and servicing demands of the project."[76]

One would expect that since the farms were established in line with the prescription of the protagonists of high modernist agriculture, they would perform very well but the antithesis turned out to be the case. It was expected that at optimum production, 4,000 hectares of land would be cultivated at the Agbede farm. However, in the 1973/74 planting season, the total hectares of land cultivated for both rice and maize was 568 while the figure for the 1978/79 planting season was 191. The highest hectareage cultivated in the first six planting seasons was 1,240 in the 1975/76 planting season.[77] The situation at the Warrake farm was similar. At optimum production, 5200 hectares of land was expected to be cultivated. In the 1974/75 planting season, a combined total of 370 hectares was cultivated with rice and maize while the figure for the 1979/80 planting season was 150 hectares. The highest hectares cultivated between 1974 and 1980 were in the 1976/77 and 1977/78 planting seasons, when 800 hectares were cultivated for the respective seasons.[78]

In spite of the fact that the farms were established in accordance with the recommendations of modernist agriculture, they failed to achieve the objectives for which they were established. Yet the vastness of the land occupied by the farms meant that the state had alienated large amounts of communally owned land, thereby depriving the surrounding peasant farmers access to valuable plots of land on which to farm. The resultant shortage of arable land, especially at Warrake, tended to create the problem of landlessness among some members of the community.[79] The official reason given for the poor performance of both farms was the constant breakdown of machines, which within a few years made many of them unserviceable. Watts has pointed out that the farms performed poorly because of the astronomical costs of the projects, technical difficulties, inoperative administration, and widespread corruption.[80] Nevertheless, the critical reason for the failure of the farm projects was the unsuitability of the "new Technology" (mechanical, biological, and chemical) for the Nigerian environment. Thus, the projects were right from the beginning doomed to failure.

In line with the recommendations of the apostles of high modernist agriculture, a core element of the Agbede and Warrake farm projects was the machines but they were constantly breaking down. The primary reason for this constant breakdown of the machines was their unsuitability for the tropical soil of the areas. In fact, the continuous use of machines in the farms resulted in the washing away of the fertile levels of organic matter in the surface soil, thereby rendering them much less suitable for farming. The outcome was a high incidence of soil erosion. The corrosive effects of erosion further increased the problem of shortage of arable land for the surrounding communities. Similarly, in the process of opening up large expanse of land for cultivation, trees, which functioned as wind breaks, and controlled the amount of evaporation, were destroyed. The consequence was a reduction for rainfall in the areas.[81] The environmental problems caused by such machines in African tropical areas made the Kenya-based United Nations Environment Program (UNEP), in June 1985 advise against their use in the tropics. It pointed out that the increased use of tractors without regard to the nature of the soil would lead to crop yield reductions because of soil compaction.[82]

Moreover, unlike the time and environmentally tested local varieties, the new seed varieties cultivated in the farms were not resistant to the local weed, *striga*, and diseases. They therefore required the application of large amounts of herbicides and pesticides, which caused great damage to the soil and resulted in the emergence of resistant strains of local weeds. As observed by UNEP, although estimates of crop losses due to pests and other parasites were alarmingly large in such large-scale capital-intensive farms, the number of pests no longer affected by pesticides was even more alarming.[83] In addition, the large amount of fertilizers used in the farms resulted in increased acidification of the soil. The immense problems associated with the large-scale capital-intensive farms, which in turn were products of the modernization paradigm, and the mediocre level of their yields made such farms, unattractive to Nigerian investors. In fact many of the large-scale capital-intensive farms that were established folded up while the much maligned peasant farmers continued to remain the backbone of food production. Nevertheless, as bad as these projects were, an even worse case of the failure and environmentally catastrophic effects of large-scale, modernized capitalist farming was the large-scale irrigation schemes associated River Basin Development Authorities (RBDAs).

River Basin Development Authorities and Large-scale Irrigation Schemes

RBDAs were touted in the 1975-1980 plan as one of the critical ways through which the country would attain the goal of self-sufficiency in food production. As a result, the number of RBDAs in the country was significantly increased – nine new ones were created in 1976 bringing the total number of RBDAs to eleven. The RBDAs are large-scale capital-intensive projects that were expected to perform a variety of functions, including flood control, irrigation, watershed management, pollution control, fisheries and navigation, and food cultivation and production. In practice, the RBDAs sought to create environments conducive for year-round large-scale capitalist farming. Some of them went into direct food production. The cultivation of wheat, rice and maize, which would provide food and raw materials for agro-allied industries, was emphasized. In order to achieve the objective of food and raw materials production, large-scale irrigation schemes became the centerpiece of the RBDAs.

The proponents of large-scale, capital-intensive, irrigation schemes justified the projects based on their helping to contribute to the attainment of food self-sufficiency in the country. The irrigation schemes not only represent a classic example of the immense limitations and shortcomings of high modernist agriculture but also demonstrate how agricultural modernization was manipulated to serve the interests of international agro-industrial complex. The land and water surveys that were carried out by international agricultural and development agencies like the FAO, the USAID and the Commonwealth Development Corporation in the 1960s, provided the initial justification for the establishment of the irrigation schemes. The increased revenue that the country derived from oil in the 1970s and the worsening food scarcity provided an ideal opportunity for international agencies and consultants, who wanted to get their share of the oil boom, to lobby for the construction of large irrigation schemes. Irrigation and large-scale capitalist farming were presented as the panacea for the problem of food scarcity. The Sahelian drought of 1972-1974, and the increased importation of wheat for the production of bread, provided the excuse that the international lobby used to present irrigation as the magic wand for the cultivation of wheat. They argued that this would help to end the dependence on wheat imports.[84] In addition, members of the Nigerian ruling class saw large-scale, capital-intensive irrigation schemes as providing the opportunity for primitive capital accumulation and for political patronage.[85] International agencies and foreign consultants whose services were engaged by the Nigerian government, provided fraudulent feasibility studies and reports, which exaggerated the benefits of the irrigation schemes thereby helping to provide the legitimization for the schemes. Thus, the convergence of the external and internal interests led to the launching of large-scale irrigation schemes.

The irrigation schemes, which were carried out along the lines of the high modernist prescriptions involved large capital-intensive schemes with high import components, centralized control over the type of crops to be planted, water management and massive land alienation. Furthermore, the project managers sought to exercise authoritarian control over the peasants whose land had been alienated and who were expected to become contractual tenants on the schemes. This was done under the guise that such a centralized and authoritarian power was critical for the apportionment of water between upstream and downstream users, and for ensuring the attainment of the objectives of the irrigation schemes. However, Steven Lansing's study of a large-scale irrigation scheme in Asia has demonstrated that these claims are not correct.[86] Nevertheless, the coercive arm of the Nigerian state viciously repressed the peasants who resisted this authoritarian control and exploitative relationship. In fact, the heavy foreign exchange component involved in the irrigation schemes, rather, than the provision of food sufficiency was the main attraction for the international agro-industrial complex. As a result, the schemes were unnecessarily mechanized while the foreign companies in charge of executing them used every opportunity to manipulate the process in such a way that they maximized their fraudulent accumulation of the country's resources. The Bakolori irrigation scheme clearly exemplifies the abuse associated with these irrigation projects, as well as their immense shortcomings. The rest of this section will be devoted to conducting an examination of the Bakolori irrigation scheme.

The Bakolori irrigation project marked the first phase of the Sokoto River Basin Development plan as identified by the FAO in 1965.[87] The FAO had recommended an irrigation project at Bakolori, in the Sokoto-Rima Basin with the first phase to cover about 27,000 hectares. Based on this recommendation, an Italian firm, IMPRESIT of Milan, a subsidiary of FIAT, was commissioned in 1972 to produce the design for the project. It submitted its report in 1974 and equally won the contract for the construction the irrigation project. The first contract for the project was signed in 1975. It involved the building of a dam at Bakolori on the Sokoto River with a storage capacity of 450 million cubic meters. The main contract was for 110.32 million naira but it did not include the provision of hydraulic and electro-mechanical equipment as well as land leveling. A subsidiary contract of 44.78 million naira was signed in 1977 to cover these aspects. By 1980, the total amount for the contract had been revised upwards to 300 million naira.[88] This arrangement where the same company was awarded the contract to design and construct the project was, of course, manipulated by the company to its own advantage. Eventually, the Nigerian government belatedly decided to check this exploitative arrangement by awarding a contract to a British firm, MRT, to act as supervisors and consultant engineers for the project.

The Bakolori project, which was to irrigate 25,000 hectares of land, was based on double cropping of wheat and rice, with wheat as the main dry season crop. In fact, wheat was the central crop that was expected to be cultivated in the various irrigation schemes that were constructed by the RBDAs in the northern part of Nigeria.[89] Emphasis was also placed on the production of rice for which 6,000 hectares was allocated and sugar cane for which 4,500 hectares was allocated. Other crops to be grown included tomatoes and tobacco. Yet none of these crops were central to the food system of the people in the area: the staples were millet and sorghum. The project primarily aimed at providing land for large-scale capitalist farming. The displaced farmers who were allocated land in the scheme were to sign an agreement making their continued tenure dependent on the adoption of project directives (a euphemism for adopting large-scale mechanized capitalist farming and cultivating the crops dictated by the project management).[90] However, the Bakolori project turned out to be a monumental failure. In fact, given the unrealistic modernist principles that underlie the project, it was right from the beginning destined to fail because it was based on a wrong premise and displayed a poor perception of the environmental issues involved.[91]

In line with the high modernist principles behind the Bakolori irrigation scheme, the project was constructed to fit into the predetermined pattern designed along lines suitable to Western environments rather than along lines suitable to the peculiarities of the indigenous environment. The project therefore caused a great amount of environmental degradation. Contrary to the opinion of soil experts, sprinkler pipes were laid in Jankarawa where they had to dynamite the rocks, and about five booster-pumping stations to take water from the dam were built. Yet this area was usually waterlogged and was traditionally avoided by the indigenous farmers as unsuitable for farming. Even then, when it came to using the more environmentally suitable sprinkler system for most of the other parts of the project that actually needed them, IMPRESIT opted for the construction of canals on 23,000 of the 25,000 hectares of the project.[92] A sprinkler system would have eliminated the need for costly land leveling, which flood irrigation involves, and it would have expanded the area that could be cultivated by reaching higher elevations and by sparing land that would have been occupied by canals. Indeed, the resident consultant engineer of MRT suggested in November 1979 "that the irrigation system at Bakolori should be changed from the flood system to that of using buried low-pressure pipe system that would leave the land, the trees and the present land tenure system undisturbed and unlevelled."[93]

The Bakolori irrigation scheme not only had a devastating effect on the environment of the project area: the adverse effect, indeed, extended far beyond the area. Abba *et al.* succinctly observed that dam construction in tropical semi-arid environment like that of the Sokoto-Rima area is not the best way for developing river basins because apart from having a very high rate of evapo-transpiration, such areas need constant flow of surface water to enable greater land area and populations to be adequately served by the water systems. They added that the Bakolori dam severely affected the flow of river water to the lower Rima thereby threatening the survival of over a million people by causing ecological degradation, and social and economic disruption.[94]

Indeed, the Bakolori irrigation scheme caused an unprecedented ecological degradation, and social and economic disintegration in the project area. The project deprived the peasant farmers of suitable land for the cultivation of local staples by withholding water from the downstream thereby retarding local agricultural output. In an apt summary of the negative environmental impact of the project, Okello Oculi noted:

> It has disorganized the farming lives and systems of 60,000 well-established farmers at Talata Marafa and drowned under water the homes, farms and fruit trees of another 13,000 people at Old Maradun in an area covering about 4,200 hectares. It has also disrupted water supply to 200,000 hectares of land that was traditionally farmed by river-bed irrigation (*fadama*), down stream from Talata Marafa to Sokoto.[95]

Moreover, the peasant farmers on whose land the project was constructed were moved from their homes and farmlands to so-called modernized villages (constructed at a cost of over 10 million naira), where the conditions were not conducive for their traditional pursuits.[96] The new "modernized" villages to which the people were moved were barren, open, deforested land. They were left without trees needed for firewood, for shade, and for various types of fruits and medicines. They had to travel eight to ten kilometers away for farming. Good and potable drinking water was not available since there was just one watering source, a dirty pool fed by a pump on the river, and even then, some of them had to walk three kilometers to get to this pond. In short, the project "deprived the peasant farmers of land for cultivation of local staples by withholding water from downstream . . . (and) dislocated the peasant farmers - the backbone of Nigeria's agriculture - and thus retarded local agricultural output."[97] Furthermore, with the ecological and salinization problems, as well as poor drainage, the yields from the project were very low. For instance, in 1983, the project produced only 9000 tons of poor quality grains. This was in spite of the fact that the federal government heavily subsidized wheat - the centerpiece of the project - at $300 per ton under the misplaced belief that it would become a highly profitable undertaking.[98]

In the face of all the problems that confronted the peasant farmers, in particular the forcible takeover and destruction of their environmental resources, the state government went ahead to destroy their guinea corn when it was almost ready for harvest in October 1979, without any warning, and without any compensation. This callous act became the final blow that led to violent resistance by the farmers: they started protesting and blocking work on the project. When an attempt by the government to bribe them failed, the police and paramilitary police forces were dispatched in April 1980 to violently suppress the resistance. In the ensuing confrontation, at least 19 farmers were killed, and hundreds of men, women and children were maimed and injured, while their villages were razed to the ground.[99]

The Bakolori project was right from the beginning destined for failure largely because it failed to take into account the indigenous realities and the lessons from previous experience with dam construction in the area. With the high modernist principles behind the construction of the project and the desire to serve the interests of Western-based agro-industrial complex, IMPRESIT opted for a capital-intensive import dependent project involving the importation of very expensive and unsuitable equipment. It failed to take into account the strengths and shortcomings of previous experiments with the construction of low cost, less capital-intensive dams in the same area between 1917 and 1921. According to William Adams, these less capital-intensive dams were more attuned to the environmental, economic, and social realities of the area. They had a great potential for success but failed because there was far too little technical information about flooding patterns in the valley, and the fact that the approach to the construction of the dams was amateur. He noted that the scheme contained many of the characteristics of "bottom-up" development and that the conservation project depended on an approach to cropping that was familiar to the floodplain farmers.[100] Rather than take this previous experience into account, IMPRESIT opted for a capital-intensive, centralized, "top-bottom" development approach that completely discountenanced the prevailing realities and practices of the people, and failed to make use of more appropriate technology. While the modernization of agriculture and the attainment of food self-sufficiency provided the justification for this approach, the actual reason for this preference was the need to create more opportunity for capital accumulation for Western-based agro-industrial complex. This was achieved through the purchase of vehicles, equipment and spare parts, and the payment of highly inflated expatriate salaries, among others. For instance, the main contract for the Bakolori project provided that 43 percent of the amount would be used locally while 57 percent would be spent on "imported equipment, plants, machinery and materials and services procured from abroad." In addition, the cars, jeeps, and trucks used by the project staff were FIAT products.[101] Moreover, in order to increase the opportunity for more capital accumulation, the prices for these imported inputs as well as the salaries and allowances for the expatriate personnel were highly inflated. In fact, although the costs of all the irrigation schemes in Nigeria were highly inflated that of Bakolori was scandalously over inflated. The ministerial committee that looked into the excessively high cost of government contracts in Nigeria noted that in the period between 1977 and 1978, the average unit cost per hectare of irrigation schemes in Liberia, Côte d'Ivoire and Ghana were 250 naira, 500 naira and 1,068 naira respectively. Yet while the costs were relatively low in these neighboring West African countries, the average cost for all irrigation schemes in Nigeria was 2,470 naira per hectare and for Bakolori the average cost was 7,540 naira per hectare.[102]

In spite of the huge amount of capital that was spent on the Bakolori irrigation scheme, the project turned out to be a monumental failure. It did not result in any significant increase in agricultural productivity; on the contrary, it left behind a legacy of massive land alienation, social and economic dislocation of the lives of the indigenous people, coercive and authoritarian disposition toward the indigenous farmers, and the wastage of Nigeria's capital. Indeed, in aptly dubbing the scheme "a classic example of development failure," Adams stated that the project could be criticized on a number of grounds:

> its implementation in ignorance of the environment (the downstream impact), ignorance of local socio-economic conditions (land tenure and land occupancy problems), an unrealistically rapid implementation schedule, ineffective communications and coercive relations with farmers related to the scale and speed of operations, unrealistic economic appraisal and unrealistic predictions about other essential related developments.[103]

In fact, in spite of the huge amount that was spent on all the irrigation schemes in Nigeria, they all turned out to be unmitigated failures mainly because the modernization premise on which they were based was patently faulty. Although between 1976 and 1982 the sum of 2.78 billion naira was spent on establishing irrigation projects in the country, their agricultural output were woefully infinitesimal.[104] Furthermore, although wheat production provided a main justification for the irrigation schemes in Northern Nigeria, very little wheat was produced, on the contrary, the volume of wheat import continued to experience a phenomenal increase.[105] The failure of the irrigation schemes was more clearly demonstrated by the fact that by 1987 the total area under double cropping in all the irrigation projects combined, was no more than 30,000 hectares.[106]

Conclusion

In spite of the number of agricultural modernization programs that were launched in Nigeria from the 1970s and huge amount of money involved, the performance of the sector did not improve. On the contrary, agricultural production stagnated. For instance, between 1992 and 1999 agriculture accounted for less than 2 percent of Nigeria's total exports for each of the years (the only exception was 1998 when it accounted for 2.2 percent of the total exports). The unbridled pursuance of agricultural modernization under the guise that this imperial knowledge, propagated in the form of received wisdom, which dictated the transplanting of Western agricultural practices into the Nigerian scene, was primarily responsible for the poor performance. By deciding to transplant alien agricultural technologies into the country without taking into account the environmental realities and the socio-economic matrix on which the indigenous agricultural practices are based, the programs ran into contradictory relationships with these factors and turned out to be counter-productive. The various inputs associated with the "new technology" caused different forms of environmental problems.

In addition, the gendered nature of agricultural modernization, which fostered a masculinist view of agriculture that directed the "innovations", embodied in the "new technology," and extension services at men, resulted in the marginalization of women in the agricultural production process. This patriarchal nature of agricultural modernization, which was at variance with the indigenous agricultural practices in which women played a crucial role, especially in food production, was subversive of the agricultural system and therefore greatly contributed to the poor performance of agriculture. Indeed, the sexist notion of women as obstacles to agricultural development is at variance with the empirical evidence showing women as effective innovators in the indigenous agricultural system.[107] On this basis, it has been observed that it is when resources are directed at both men and women, that agricultural productivity and efficiency increases.[108]

Moreover, by emphasizing the development of large-scale, mechanized, capital-intensive farming, the modernization process further entrenched the penetration of international finance capital into Nigeria. The import dependency that the "new technology" promoted created markets for the agricultural inputs of the TNCs and various agribusinesses. While the oil boom of the 1970s created the desire on the part of international capital and the Nigerian ruling class to accumulate the country's surplus, the worsening food scarcity created the perfect opportunity for this to be done. Under the guise of the modernization of agriculture and the universality of science, international agricultural and financial agencies like the FAO and the World Bank used the excuse of transplanting the agricultural practices developed in the West into Nigeria, to serve the interests of the international agro-industrial complex. Indeed, the World Bank, which had the dominant influence on Nigeria's agricultural development policies, served as an agent of international capital, as clearly demonstrated by the case of the ADP. The neo-colonial nature of the Nigerian state as well as the dominance of imperial knowledge among most Nigerian scientists and policy makers greatly facilitated this process of exploitation. Thus, imperial self-serving knowledge was marketed as scientific and impartial solution to Nigeria's agricultural crisis. The accumulative interest that underlined the agricultural modernization programs made the process to be fraught with a great deal of corruption as clearly exemplified by the emphasis on highly inflated imports and the award of highly inflated contracts, such as the Bakolori irrigation project.

Furthermore, by emphasizing large-scale capitalist agriculture, which involved the use of technologies and inputs beyond what the majority of peasant farmers could afford, and which had serious adverse effects on the environment, the agricultural modernization programs were not in the position to promote sustainable agricultural production in Nigeria. As B. N. Okigbo noted, agricultural sustainability can only be achieved "when resources, inputs, and technologies involved are within the capabilities of the farmer to own, hire, maintain, and orchestrate with increasing efficiency to achieve desired levels of productivity in perpetuity, without adverse effects on the resource base and environmental quality."[109] In this regard, peasant agriculture possesses immense superiority over the transplanted modern agricultural practices. A significant advantage of peasant agriculture is that through centuries of experimentation and adapting their agricultural practices to the environment, peasant farmers have been able to develop ways of both promoting environmental sustainability and sustainable agricultural production.

Although the received wisdom as embedded in imperial knowledge portrays peasant agricultural practices as backward, primitive and static, the antithesis is actually the case. Peasant farmers are constantly experimenting on their farms, which constitute their laboratories and provide avenues for pragmatic and realistic experimentation, and through a process of trial and error and cross-referencing with the results of neighboring farmers, they are able to come up with practices that are more relevant. Thus, peasant agricultural practices are not static but very responsive and dynamic. In fact, as already pointed out, innovation has been the hallmark of peasant agriculture in Africa for centuries. Furthermore, "the genetic improvement of crops depended entirely on (peasant) farmers' selection from local material, using visual characteristics: thus, (African peasant) farmers have for many centuries been actively involved in plant breeding and breeding skills within many community seed systems are highly developed."[110] It has been demonstrated that Nigeria's peasant farmers have developed unique ways of managing their agricultural practices in order to promote agricultural sustainability while deriving the best possible yields. The practices are not uniform but vary according to the different ecological and vegetation zones. In particular, they have been very successful in maintaining the biodiversity of their soil: techniques such as crop rotation, mixed cropping or intercropping and polyculture, among others, have been used effectively. For instance, crop rotation "is based on the knowledge that crops do not all use the same soil nutrients and that their roots occupy different soil layers." In addition, "the deep tree and crop roots that are grown in alternating years ensure that nutrients are brought up from the sub-soil." Also mixed cropping "represents a careful adaptation of cropping pattern to topographic features and it allows a fuller use of light and favourable distribution of carbon dioxide."[111] In fact, scholars have demonstrated the versatility of the indigenous agricultural practices and point out that some of them, such as management and sustenance of soil nutrients and biodiversity, show that "modern" agricultural experts have a lot to learn from African peasant farmers.[112]

The Nigerian experience shows that foreign technologies developed to suit alien environments cannot be relied upon to promote agricultural development in a very different environment such as that of Nigeria. Furthermore, it brings into sharp focus the acute limitations of the modernization paradigm in terms of promoting Nigeria's development. For agricultural development to be meaningful and sustainable, it must be embedded in the indigenous culture – after all, development is a cultural process. It has been pointed out that traditional agricultural practices in Nigeria are "rooted in the socio-culture of Nigerian peoples: that is, in the economic, social, cultural and (religious) settings," and that traditional practices should form the bases for agricultural development.[113] Indeed, given the fact that peasant farmers have remained the backbone of Nigeria's agriculture, and have developed ways of adapting their agricultural practices to the environment over time, in order to promote its sustainability, they should form the cornerstone of any attempt at improving the country's agriculture.

Notes

1 Forrest, *Politics and Economic Development in Nigeria*, 181-187. Also see idem., "Agricultural Policies in Nigeria 1900-78," in J. Heyer, P. Roberts and G.Williams eds, *Rural Development in Tropical Africa*, London: Macmillan, 1981.

2 M. O. Ojo *et. al.*, "Sustaining Agricultural Development in a Deregulated Economy," *Central Bank of Nigeria: Economic and Financial Review*, Vol. 13, No. 2, 1993; N. O. Uwadibie and A. Luma, "Decentralization and Agricultural Policy: The Case of Nigeria, 1976-1993," *The Journal of African Policy Studies*, Vol. 3, No. 1, 1997; and E. U. Ukeje, "Productivity in the Agricultural Sector," Central Bank of Nigeria, Occasional Paper, No. 8, 2000.

3 M. I. Obadan, "Agricultural Development Strategies and Performance in Nigeria: From OFN to DFRRI," *IRORO*, Vol. 3, Nos. 1 and 2, 1990, 41.

4 See for instance, S. Tomori, "Agriculture, Forestry and Fishing," in F. A. Olaloku *et. al.* eds., *Structure of the Nigerian Economy*, New York: St. Martins, 1979, 10-28; and Federal Republic of Nigeria, *Third National Development Plan*, 342-349.

5 Hyden, *Beyond Ujamaa in Tanzania*; idem., *No Shortcuts to Progress*; and idem., "The Anomaly of African Peasantry," *Development and Change*, Vol. 17, No. 4, 1986.

6 O. Ibeanu, "The Deteriorating Condition of the Nigerian Peasantry," in O. Nnoli ed., *Deadend to Nigerian Development: An Analysis of the Political Economy of Nigeria, 1979-1989*, Dakar: CODESRIA, 1993, 124-150.

7 Helleiner, *Peasant Agriculture, Government, and Economic Growth in Nigeria*, 44-45. Reacting to the attack on peasant farmers, S. Anyang, in a perceptive article, noted that the attack was unwarranted and that it is the peasant farmers that have, in fact, prevented the country from experiencing an unmitigated disaster on the agricultural front. See S. Anyang, "In Defence of the Small Farmer," *National Concord* (Lagos, Nigeria), 15 May 1985, 3.

8 See for instance, A. C. Nwosu, *Agricultural Mechanization in Nigeria (Assessing the Strategies and Technologies for Land Preparation)*, NISER Monograph Series, No. 2, Ibadan: Nigerian Institute of Social and Economic Research, 1989.

9 Scott, *Seeing Like a State*, 262-306.

10 R. Bates, *Markets and States in Tropical Africa: The Political Basis of Agricultural Policies*, Los Angeles: University of California Press, 1981; and idem., "The Politics of Agricultural Pricing in Sub-Saharan Africa," in Z. Ergas ed., *The African State in Transition*, London: Macmillan, 1987.

11 J. I. Dibua, "Government's Agricultural Policy and Rural Development in Nigeria: The Case of Bendel State, 1964-1988," *The African Review*, Vol. 16, Nos. 1 and 2, 1989, 40-53.

12 Bryceson and Bank, "End of an Era."

13 Tom Forrest has disagreed with the notion that government's agricultural policies neglected the peasant farmers. He points out that there is no history of widespread and persistent government intervention in domestic food production in Nigeria. He states that the policy of nonintervention by the government coupled with the inflationary situation in the urban centers caused by the Udoji wage increases of 1973 and the oil boom, led to a sharp increase in food prices. Peasant farmers responded by increasing aggregate food production and this led to strong increases in real wages in the rural areas, thus, while there was loss of labor in the export crops production sector, the same was not applicable to food crops production. See Forrest, *Politics and Economic Development in Nigeria*, 181-187. There is, however, no valid empirical evidence to support the claim of Forrest. On the contrary, available evidence suggest a general decline in food production as a result of the neglect of peasant farmers and the rural areas hence a high amount of migrations from the rural areas to the urban areas with the attendant adverse effects for food production. The high increase in food import bills clearly epitomizes this situation.

14 K. M. Baker, *Case Studies in the Developing World: Agricultural Change in Nigeria*, London: John Murray, 1989; and Obadan, "Agricultural Development Strategies and Performance in Nigeria."

15 M. J. Watts, "Agriculture and Oil-Based Accumulation: Stagnation or Transformation?" in idem. ed., *State, Oil and Agriculture in Nigeria*, Berkeley, CA: University of California Press, 1987; and Ibeanu, "Class Interest and Public Policy in Nigeria," 29-39.

16 A. Abba *et al.*, *The Nigerian Economic Crisis: Causes and Solutions*, Zaria, Nigeria: Academic Staff Union of Universities, 1985, 16-51; and Onimode, *Imperialism and Underdevelopment in Nigeria.*

17 See S. Roy, "Agrarian Crisis and Technology in Nigeria," *Africa Quarterly*, Vol. XXV, Nos. 1 and 2, 1988; and idem., *Agriculture and Technology in Developing Countries: India and Nigeria*, New Delhi and London: SAGE Publications, 1990.

18 Scott, *Seeing Like a State*, 263.

19 Ibid.; and P. Richards, *Indigenous Agricultural Revolution: Ecology and Food Production in West Africa*, London and Boulder, CO: Hutchinson and Westview, 1985.

20 Rostow, *The Stages of Economic Development.*

21 Tomori, "Agriculture, Forestry and Fishing," 13.

22 Scott, *Seeing Like a State*, 271.

23 Johnston and Kilby, *Agricultural and Structural Transformation*, 92.

24 Hayami and Ruttan, *Agricultural Development*, 260-262.

25 World Bank, *Sector Policy Paper on Rural Development*, Washington, D.C.: World Bank, 1975.

26 E. Cromwell, *Governments, Farmers and Seeds in a Changing Africa*, London: CAB International and Overseas Development Institute, 1996.

27 B. Dasgupta, *Agrarian Change and the New Technology in India*, Geneva: United Nations Research Institute for Social Development, 1975, 51.

28 Scott, *Seeing Like a State*, 270.

29 Ferguson, *The Anti-Politics Machine.*

30 See Boserup, *Woman's Role in Economic Development.*

31 D. Elson, "Male Bias in the Development Process: An Overview," in idem ed., *Male Bias in the Development Process*, Manchester and New York: Manchester University Press, 1995, 9-10.

32 J. C. Wells, *Agricultural Policy and Economic Growth in Nigeria*, Ibadan: Oxford University Press, 1974, 244.

33 D. Olatunbosun, *Nigerian Farm Settlements and School Leavers' Farms: Profitability, Resource Use and Social Psychological Considerations*, Report 9, East Lansing, Michigan: Consortium for the Study of Nigerian Rural Development (CSNRD), Michigan State University, n.d., 34. However, Helleiner put the acreage of land of each settler at between twenty and twenty-five while Oluwasanmi put it at thirty. See Helleiner, *Peasant Agriculture, Government and Economic Growth in Nigeria*, 304; and H. A. Oluwasanmi, *Agriculture and Nigerian Economic Development*, Ibadan: Oxford University Press, 1966, 192.

34 Scott, *Seeing Like a State*, 262.

35 My examination of the records of the four farm settlements in the former Bendel State of Nigeria (Ekpoma, Iguoriakhi, Mbirri and Utagba-Uno farm settlements) and interviews with some of the settlers in 1985 clearly showed that only males were recruited as settlers.

36 C. J. Korieh, "Agricultural Transformation, State Policy, and Agricultural Decline in Eastern Nigeria, 1960-1970," in A. Oyebade ed., *The Transformation of Nigeria: Essays in Honor of Toyin Falola*, Trenton, NJ: Africa World Press, 2002, 241.

37 Federal Republic of Nigeria, *Third National Development Plan*, 342-349.

38 See for instance, World Bank, *Sector Policy Paper on Rural Development*.

39 Ibid.

40 P. Gibbon, K. J. Havnevik and K. Hermele, *A Blighted Harvest: The World Bank and African Agriculture in the 1980s*, Trenton, NJ: Africa World Press, 1993, 7.

41 Roy, "Agrarian Crisis and Technology in Nigeria," 7.

42 Dasgupta, *Agrarian Change and the New Technology in India*, 52.

43 See Ibid. 56; and Cromwell, *Governments, Farmers and Seeds in a Changing Africa*, 10-11.

44 Federal Republic of Nigeria, *Third National Development Plan*, 72. Also see S. Famariyo, "Food Production Policies in Nigeria," *Food Policy*, February 1978, 56.

45 M. Connolly and T. Arokoyo, "Alleviating Fertilizer Technology Transfer Constraints," in A. U. Mokwunye ed., *Alleviating Soil Fertility Constraints to Increased Crop Production in West Africa*, Dordrecht, Boston, London: Kluwer Academic Publishers, 1991, 22-23.

46 Obadan, "Agricultural Development Strategies and Performance in Nigeria," 32; and A. Olorunfemi and O. C. Adesina, "Politics and Nigerian Agriculture in the First Decade of 'Oil Boom,' 1970-1980: A Preliminary Assessment," *The Nigerian Journal of Economic History*, No. 1, 1998, 62.

47 T. Wallace, "The Challenge of Food: Nigeria's Approach to Agriculture 1975-80," *Canadian Journal of African Studies*, Vol. 15, No. 2, 1981, 253; and Baker, *Case Studies in the Developing World*, 16.

48 Onimode, *Imperialism and Underdevelopment in Nigeria*, 35.

49 Dudley, *An Introduction to Nigerian Government and Politics*, 115.

50 The Green Revolution is usually showcased as the high mark and one of the greatest achievements of Western high modernist agriculture. It constitutes the core of the kind of agricultural modernization that is marketed to Third World countries like Nigeria.

51 Watts, "Agriculture and Oil Based Accumulation," 78 and 80.

52 See Baker, *Case Studies in the Developing World*, 16; and Obadan, "Agricultural Development Strategies and Performance in Nigeria."

53 Wallace, "The Challenge of Food: Nigeria's Approach to Agriculture," 249-253. Also, see Nzimiro, *The Green Revolution in Nigeria or Modernization of Hunger*, 25-44.

54 L. D. Koinyan, *Integrated Rural Development*, Lagos: Federal Government Press, 1987; and J. B. Idode, *Rural Development and Bureaucracy in Nigeria*, Lagos: Longman, 1987.

55 L. D. Koinyan, *Food Self-Sufficiency and Much More*, Lagos: Federal Government Press, 1988.

56 B. Beckman, "Public Investment and Agrarian Transformation in Northern Nigeria," in Watts ed., *State, Oil and Agriculture in Nigeria*, 112-113.

57 World Bank, *Accelerated Development in Sub-Saharan Africa*, 53.

58 Wallace, "The Challenge of Food: Nigeria's Approach to Agriculture," 248. Also see G. Williams, "The World Bank and the Peasant Problem," in Heyer *et. al.* eds., *Rural Development in Tropical Africa*, 25.

59 G. Williams, "The World Bank in Rural Nigeria, Revisited: A Review of the World Bank's Nigeria: Agricultural Sector Review 1987," *Review of African Political Economy*, No. 43, 1988, 42.

60 Kaduna State Government, *Report of the Land Investigation Commission*, Vols. 1 and 5, Kaduna: Government Printer, 1982, cited in Abba *et al.*, *The Nigerian Economic Crisis*, 29; and Watts, "Agricultural and Oil-Based Accumulation," 80.

61 Roy, *Agriculture and Technology in Developing Countries*, 180-183; Richards, *Indigenous Agricultural Revolution*, 63-81; and Scott, *Seeing Like a State*, 273-282.

62 K. G. Steiner, *Intercropping in Tropical Smallholder Agriculture with Special Reference to West Africa*, Eschborn: Deutsche Gesellschaft fur Technische Zusammenarbeit (GTZ), 1982, 135, cited in Richards, *Indigenous Agricultural Revolution*, 71-72. Also see K. G. Steiner, "Overcoming Soil Fertility Constraints to Crop Production in West Africa: Impact of Traditional and Improved Cropping Systems on Soil Fertility," in Mokwunye ed., *Alleviating Soil Fertility Constraints to Increased Crop Production in West Africa*, 69-89.

63 Roy, *Agriculture and Technology in Developing Countries*, 180-181.

64 Williams, "The World Bank in Rural Nigeria, Revisited," 62.

65 Balarabe Musa, the civilian Governor of Kaduna State during the Second Republic (1979-1983) until he was impeached in 1982, was a highly nationalistic, patriotic and anti-corruption crusader. He won the governorship election even though his party (the Peoples Redemption Party) was in the minority in the State House of Assembly. His failure to compromise with the majority party (the National Party of Nigeria) that had more than two-thirds of the seats in the House, his dogged adherence to principles, and his anti-corruption posture contributed to his impeachment.

66 Kaduna State Government, *The Struggle for a New Social Order in Kaduna State: The Policies and Programmes of the P. R. P. Government, 1979-1981*, Kaduna: Government Printer, 1982, 271-274, cited in Abba *et al.*, *The Nigerian Economic Crisis*, 49.

67 Roy, *Agriculture and Technology in Developing Countries*, 67.

68 Williams, "The World Bank in Rural Nigeria, Revisited," 62.

69 See D. Oniemola, *The World Bank and Capitalist Agricultural Development: The Ilorin Agricultural Development Project in Nigeria*, Nr. 22, Berlin: Das Arabische Buch. KnesebeckstrBe 16, 1989. The Kwara state ADP is named after Ilorin, the state capital; hence, it is referred to as the Ilorin Agricultural Development Project (IADP).

70 This agreement is a typical example of how the World Bank serves the interests of international capitalism. The Bank was mainly preoccupied with providing market for the products of Trans National Corporations, particularly the agro-industrial complex, and providing employment at outrageously favorable terms to foreign "experts." In fact, it has been estimated that the foreign exchange component of the respective ADPs in the country was over 40 percent. See Abba *et al.*, *The Nigerian Economic Crisis*, 28.

71 Oniemola, *The World Bank and Capitalist Agricultural Development*, 11.

72 The Kaduna state ADP clearly exemplifies the enormity of the amount spent on the payment of salaries, fringe benefits and allowances of the international staff. By 1981, the salary, benefits and allowances of the expatriates in the Kaduna state ADP were as follows: salary for each staff, 40,000 naira per annum, tax free and paid in foreign currency; 78 percent of the salary as cost of living allowance; 733 naira per annum as allowance for each dependant; 25 percent of the salary as "post allowance"; 75 percent of children's school fees paid abroad in foreign currency; a free air-conditioned chauffeur driven motor vehicle; a free air-conditioned and furnished-to-taste house; free electricity and water supply; a free return ticket to anywhere in the world for annual vacation; and forty working days leave per annum. See Kaduna State Government, *The Struggle for a New Social Order in Kaduna State*, 271-274, cited in Abba *et al.*, *The Nigerian Economic Crisis*, 49.

73 See for instance, P. Francis, "For the Use and Common Benefit of All Nigeria: Consequences of the 1978 Land Nationalisation," *Africa*, Vol. 54, No. 3, 1984; D. C. Williams, "Measuring the Impact of Land-reform Policy in Nigeria," *Journal of Modern African Studies*, Vol. 30, No. 4, 1992, 587-608; and D. A. Ogirri, "An Empirical Study of the Effects of State Land-reform Policies on Agricultural and Socioeconomic Developments in Nigeria from Colonial to Military Rule: A Macro Perspective," *The Journal of African Policy Studies*, Vol. 3, No. 2, 1997, 71-100.

74 Forrest, *Politics and Economic Development in Nigeria*, 199.

75 Mid-Western State Government, *The National Council for Agriculture and Natural Resources, Fifth Meeting, June 20-22, 1974, Benin City, Mid-Western Nigeria*, Benin City: Ministry of Home Affairs and Information, Information Division, 1974, 18.

76 Mid-Western State Government, *Agricultural Newsletter*, Vol. 2, No. 1, 1973, 20-21.

77 P. O. Agbonifo, "State Farms and Rural Development: A Case Study of the Agbede and Warrake Farm Project in Bendel State of Nigeria," Unpublished Ph.D Dissertation, University of Wisconsin, Madison, 1980, 30.

78 Ibid., 32.

79 Ibid., 242.

80 Watts, "Agriculture and Oil-Based Accumulation," 78. In fact, as was revealed by two panels of inquiry, there was a great amount of fraud associated with these farms on the part of the technical partners and some officials of the Bendel State government. The technical partners saw the farms as a means of massively exploiting and defrauding the state. The degree of exploitation and fraud on the part of the technical partners was such that the new military administration that came to power in the state in 1984 resolved that in future, technical partners would not enjoy such wide powers as were entrusted to the ones associated with these projects. In addition, the expatriate managing director of the farms was declared a *persona non grata* in the state because of the scale of fraud in which he was involved. See Bendel State Government, "Pree Release," Military Governor's Office, Benin City, Nigeria, 21 August 1984; and *The Nigerian Observer* (Benin City), 10 January 1985, 1 and 4.

81 Agbonifo, "State Farms and Rural Development," 242.

82 See "UN Agency Lists Dangers of Modern Farming Techniques," *The Guardian* (Lagos), 8 July 1985, 11.

83 Ibid.

84 See G. Andrae and B. Beckman, *The Wheat Trap: Bread and Underdevelopment in Nigeria*, London and Uppsala: Zed Books and Scandinavian Institute of African Studies, 1985, 80-85.

85 R. Palmer-Jones, "Irrigation and Politics of Agricultural Development in Nigeria," in Watts ed., *State, Oil and Agriculture in Nigeria*, 145-149.

86 See J. S. Lansing, *Priests and Programmers: Technologies of Power in the Engineered Landscape of Bali*, Princeton: Princeton University Press, 1991. Also, see *Scott, Seeing Like a State*, 286.

87 In 1962 the FAO was commissioned to carry out investigations on the Sokoto-Rima River Basin in order "to determine and map the natural resources of the area and develop plans for the stabilisation, diversification and increase of agricultural production." However, the study turned out to be primarily concerned with the location of specific areas for irrigation. The Bakolori irrigation scheme was one of those recommended. See W. M. Adams, "Approaches to Water Resource Development, Sokoto Valley, Nigeria: The Problem of Sustainability," in D. Anderson and R. Grove eds., *Conservation in Africa: People, Policies and Practice*, Cambridge: Cambridge University Press, 1987, 311-312.

88 O. Oculi, "The Political Economy of Planning the Bakolori Irrigation Project: 1974-1980," in Y. B. Usman ed., *Political Repression in Nigeria, Vol. 1: A Selection of Basic Documents 1979-1981*, Zaria, Nigeria: Gaskiya Corporation, 1982, 99-100.

89 In spite of the fact that the Nigerian environment is not suitable for wheat production and that wheat production is a highly capital-intensive enterprise, the cultivation of this crop remained the primary aim of Bakolori and other irrigation schemes in the northern part of Nigeria. It was claimed that this would help to reduce the dependency on the import of wheat. Yet wheat was not a significant part of the diet of the indigenous people on whose land the crop was to be planted. The emphasis on wheat production was mainly to satisfy the taste of urban dwellers. However, in the final analysis, the wheat production project turned out to be an unmitigated failure and huge waste of capital. See Andrae and Beckman, *The Wheat Trap*. Also see E. Nwaubani, "For Bread Alone: A Postscript on Nigeria's Wheat Entrapment," *Scandinavian Journal of Development Alternatives and Area Studies*, Vol. 18, Nos. 2 and 3, 1999, 47-58.

90 Beckman, "Public Investment and Agrarian Transformation in Northern Nigeria," 127.

91 Adams, "Approaches to Water Resource Development," 307-325.

92 In spite of the fact that sprinklers were used in unsuitable areas at very high costs, when it came to using them in more favorable parts of the project area at ultimately more favorable cost and better environmental consequences, the project contractors refused to do so. They opted for the more expensive and more environmentally unsuitable canal construction. This was probably because this involved more capital, which would be to their own financial benefit in terms of importing and acquiring more inputs and spare parts, among others. However, the construction of canals further resulted in the destruction of the natural resources in the area.

93 Cited in Oculi, "The Political Economy of Planning the Bakolori Irrigation Project," 102-103.

94 Abba *et al.*, *The Nigerian Economic Crisis*, 32.

95 Oculi, "The Political Economy of Planning the Bakolori Irrigation Project," 100.

96 Nwaubani, "For Bread Alone," 51-52.

97 Ibid., 52.
98 Watts, "Agriculture and Oil-Based Accumulation," 77.
99 For accounts of this protest and massacre, see Oculi, "The Political Economy of Planning the Bakolori Irrigation Project," 81-96; W. M. Adams, "Rural Protest, Land Policy, and the Planning Process on the Bakolori Project, Nigeria," *Africa*, Vol. 58, No. 3, 1988, 323-327; and Beckman, "Public Investment and Agrarian Transformation in Northern Nigeria," 128.
100 Adams, "Approaches to Water Resource Development," 314-322.
101 Oculi, "The Political Economy of Planning the Bakolori Irrigation Project," 106.
102 See Federal Republic of Nigeria, *Report of the Ministerial Committee on the Causes of Excessively High Cost of Government Contracts in Nigeria*, Lagos: Federal Government Printer, 1981, 13.
103 Adams, "Approaches to Water Resource Development," 313.
104 Abba *et al.*, *The Nigerian Economic Crisis*, 31.
105 Andrae and Beckman, *The Wheat Trap*.
106 World Bank, *Nigeria: Agricultural Sector Review*, Vol. 1, revised draft, Washington, D.C.: World Bank, 1987, cited in Forrest, *Politics and Economic Development in Nigeria*, 194.
107 See P. Lawrence, "The Political Economy of the 'Green Revolution' in Africa," *Review of African Political Economy*, No. 42, 1988, 72.
108 Elson, "Male Bias in the Development Process," 10.
109 B. N. Okigbo, "Sustainable Agricultural Systems in Tropical Africa," in C. A. Edwards *et. al.* eds., *Sustainable Agricultural Systems*, Ankeny, Iowa: Soil and Water Conservation Society, 1990, 323.
110 Cromwell, *Governments, Farmers and Seeds in a Changing Africa*, 23.
111 See A. I. Okpoko and P. U. Okpoko, "Traditional Farming Practices in Nigeria," *West African Journal of Archaeology*, Vol. 29, Nos. 1 and 2, 1999, 61-62.
112 See for instance, Richards, *Indigenous Agricultural Revolution*; Scott, *Seeing Like a State*; and Steiner, "Overcoming Soil Fertility Constraints to Crop Production in West Africa."
113 Okpoko and Okpoko, "Traditional Farming Practices in Nigeria," 63-65.

Chapter 7

Oil and Economic Development Strategies, 1970-1986

The influence of modernization on Nigeria's development trajectory was more clearly manifested in the economic development strategies that were pursued. As already noted, development economists, who greatly influenced the kind of developmentalist policies that were pursued in Nigeria before the introduction of the SAP in 1986, were consumed with the "stages of growth" linear conception of development. Their perception of a developmentalist state as crucial for economic transformation through the replication of the characteristics of Western capitalist societies, led to the recommendation of policies that promoted authoritarian and accumulationist state. Economic development strategies were therefore preoccupied with the Nigerian state mobilizing resources for the attainment of the Rostownian take-off stage, which was regarded as critical for attaining self-sustaining growth and development.

As was seen in the previous chapter, agriculture was the backbone of the Nigerian economy before 1970 and through the exploitative activities of the various commodity-marketing boards the agricultural sector constituted the primary source of surplus accumulation for the Nigerian state. However, with the poor performance of agricultural products in the world market in the 1960s, there was a sharp decline in the revenue derived from agriculture. From the late 1960s, oil started becoming an important source of revenue for the Nigerian state, a situation that was accentuated from the 1970s to the extent that from the mid 1970s, there was a near total dependence on oil for foreign exchange. Policy makers and their development economist advisors, among others, saw the very good performance of oil in the world market and the phenomenal increase in the revenue that Nigeria derived from oil as an opportunity for the rapid modernization of the Nigerian economy.

This chapter analyzes the influence of oil on the economic development strategies in Nigeria from the 1970s to 1986 when the SAP was introduced. It examines the extent to which the use of the revenue from oil contributed to the attainment of the modernization project of Nigeria's policy makers. The chapter analyzes why in spite of the enormous revenue from oil and the various projects aimed at transforming the economy that were executed, the country was plunged into a serious economic crisis by the early 1980s. Was the economic crisis primarily a product of corruption and poor implementation of otherwise sound economic development policies, as the apostles of the modernization paradigm would want us to believe? Alternatively, can the crisis be traced to some fundamental shortcomings of the modernization paradigm itself? This chapter addresses these and other issues. In addition, the chapter will highlight the kind of accumulation process that occurred because of the increased revenue from oil.

The Performance of Oil

The German-owned Nigerian Bitumen Company was the first company to start prospecting for oil in 1908 in the territories that eventually became Nigeria.[1] However, with the amalgamation of the Northern and Southern Protectorates in 1914 and the promulgation of the Mineral Act in that year, non-British companies were barred from prospecting for oil in the Nigerian colony. As a result, Shell-British Petroleum (Shell-BP) was the only company that was granted a license to prospect for oil in Nigeria in 1937. The company started exploring for oil in 1938 but suspended its activities with the outbreak of World War II the following year. It resumed its oil exploration activities in 1947, discovered oil in commercial quantity in 1956 and began commercial production of oil at Oloibiri in 1958. However, it was not until the 1970s that oil started occupying a dominant position in Nigeria's economy, rising from an average daily production of 5,140 barrels per day (bpd) to 1.08 million bpd in 1970 and 2.3 million bpd, in 1974. In the 1970s, over 90 percent of the annual oil production was exported while from 1980 to 2001, over 80 percent of the oil produced annually was exported.

The increase in oil production was accompanied by a phenomenal increase in the prices of crude oil thereby greatly increasing the amount of revenue that Nigeria derived from oil exports. These increases were due mainly to the activities of the OPEC, the powerful cartel of the non-Western oil-producing countries, which Nigeria joined in 1971 and the reaction of the Arab oil-producing nations to the Egyptian-Israeli war of October 1973. Because of the war, the Arab oil-producing nations, which dominated OPEC, decided to impose an oil embargo on the West by drastically reducing oil production with a view to forcing the United States to mediate in the Middle Eastern crisis while OPEC equally hiked the prices of oil. The average prices of Nigerian crude oil, which was $2.4 per barrel in 1970 and rose to $4.6 in 1973, more than tripled to $14.6 in 1975. The percentage share of oil in Nigeria's GDP rose from an average of 1.6 percent in 1960-69 to 17.4 percent in 1970-74, and 24.3 percent in 1975-79. The phenomenal increase in Nigeria's GDP clearly reflected the new prosperity from oil: for instance, the GDP at current factor cost rose from 5,205.1 million naira in 1970/71 to 18,298.3 million naira in 1974/75 and 49,632.3 million naira in 1980. At the same, Nigeria's external reserve rose from 104.6 million naira in 1970, to 3,380.1 million naira in 1975 and 5,445.6 million naira in 1980.

Table 7.1 Annual crude oil production and export, 1970-2002 ('000 barrels)

Year	Production	Export	Percentage	Domestic Consumption	Percentage
1970	395,689	383,455	96.9	12,234	3.1
1971	558,689	542,545	97.1	16,144	2.9
1972	665,295	650,640	97.8	14,655	2.2
1973	719,379	695,627	96.7	23,752	3.3
1974	823,320	795,710	96.6	27,610	3.4
1975	660,148	627,638	95.1	32,510	4.9
1976	758,058	736,822	97.2	21,236	2.8
1977	766,055	715,240	93.4	50,815	6.6
1978	696,324	674,125	96.8	22,199	3.2
1979	845,463	807,685	95.5	37,778	4.5
1980	760,117	656,260	86.3	103,857	13.7
1981	525,291	469,095	89.3	56,196	10.7
1982	470,638	401,658	85.3	68,980	14.7
1983	450,961	392,031	86.9	58,930	13.1
1984	507,487	450,580	88.8	56,907	11.2
1985	547,088	486,580	88.9	60,508	11.1
1986	535,929	486,584	90.8	49,345	9.2
1987	483,269	390,514	80.8	92,755	19.2
1988	529,602	435,797	82.3	93,805	17.7
1989	625,908	522,481	83.5	103,427	16.5
1990	660,559	548,249	83.0	112,310	17.0
1991	689,850	585,838	84.9	104,012	15.1
1992	711,340	604,300	85.0	107,040	15.0
1993	691,400	563,614	81.5	127,786	18.5
1994	696,190	578,044	83.0	118,146	17.0
1995	715,400	616,900	86.2	98,500	13.8
1996	740,190	648,690	87.6	91,500	12.4
1997	759,710	673,340	88.6	86,370	11.4
1998	776,190	687,390	88.6	88,620	11.4
1999	778,900	666,490	85.6	112,410	14.4
2000	797,880	688,080	86.2	109,800	13.8
2001	817,150	674,930	82.3	142,220	17.7
2002	685,773	521,973	76.1	163,800	23.9

Source: Computed from Central Bank of Nigeria, *Statistical Bulletin*, Vol. 13, 2003, 132.

Table 7.2 Percentage distribution of Nigeria's GDP at 1984 constant factor cost

Period Year	GDP (Billion Naira)	Crude Petroleum	Manufac-turing	Agricul-ture	Retail & Wholesale Trade	Other
1960-69	26.8	1.6	6.1	58.8	N.A	33.6
1970-74	58.2	17.4	2.5	33.2	11.0	35.9
1975-79	73.7	24.3	5.0	30.2	12.1	28.4
1980	73.2	22.0	8.1	30.8	12.4	26.7
1981	70.4	14.0	9.9	34.7	13.0	28.4
1982	70.2	12.5	11.2	35.8	13.6	26.9
1983	66.4	12.8	8.4	37.7	14.0	27.1
1984	63.0	15.2	7.8	37.8	13.6	25.6
1985	68.9	15.1	8.6	40.3	13.0	23.0
1986	71.1	13.8	8.0	42.7	13.0	22.5
1987	70.7	12.5	8.4	41.5	13.9	23.7
1988	79.8	12.3	8.7	41.5	13.8	23.7
1989	83.5	13.2	8.2	40.6	13.4	24.6
1990	90.4	12.8	8.2	39.0	12.7	27.3
1991	94.5	12.4	8.3	39.0	12.5	27.8
1992	97.4	13.4	7.9	38.3	12.5	27.9
1993	100.0	13.1	7.3	37.8	12.6	29.2
1994	101.0	12.6	7.2	37.3	12.5	30.4
1995	103.3	12.6	6.7	34.0	12.2	34.5
1996	107.0	13.1	6.5	39.0	11.8	29.6
1997	110.0	12.8	6.3	39.4	11.7	29.8
1998	112.0	11.9	5.9	40.4	11.8	30.0
1999	116.0	11.7	5.9	40.6	11.7	30.0

Source: B. E. Aigbokhan, "Resuscitating Agricultural Production (Cocoa, Cotton, Groundnuts, Palm Oil, Rubber, etc) for Exports," Central Bank of Nigeria, *Occasional Paper*, No. 6, 2001.

Table 7.3 Nigeria's GDP and external reserves, 1970-2002 (million naira)

(a) Gross Domestic Product			(b) Nigeria's External Reserves	
Year	GDP at 1984 Factor Cost	GDP at Current Factor Cost	Year	External Reserve
1970/71	54,148.9	5,205.1	1970	104.6
1971/72	65,707.0	6,570.7	1971	132.3
1972/73	69,310.6	7,208.3	1972	191.6
1973/74	73,763.1	10,990.7	1973	241.0
1974/75	82,424.8	18,298.3	1974	3,112.5
1975/76	79,988.5	20,957.0	1975	3,380.1
1976/77	88,854.3	26,656.3	1976	3,057.6
1977/78	96,098.5	31,520.3	1977	2,521.0
1978/79	89,020.9	34,540.1	1978	1,249.1
1979/80	91,190.7	41,947.7	1979	3,043.2
1980	96,186.6	49,632.3	1980	5,445.6
1981	70,395.9	50,456.1	1981	2,424.8
1982	70,157.0	51,570.4	1982	1,026.5
1983	66,389.5	56,709.1	1983	781.7
1984	63,006.4	63,006.4	1984	1,143.8
1985	68,916.3	71,368.1	1985	1,641.1
1986	71,075.9	72,128.3	1986	3,587.4
1987	70,741.4	106,883.2	1987	4,643.3
1988	77,752.5	142,678.4	1988	3,272.7
1989	83,495.2	222,457.7	1989	13,457.1
1990	90,342.1	257,873.0	1990	34,953.1
1991	94,614.1	320,247.4	1991	44,249.6
1992	97,431.1	544,330.6	1992	13,992.5
1993	100,015.2	691,606.8	1993	67,245.6
1994	101,040.0	911,091.3	1994	30,455.9
1995	103,503.0	1,960,689.0	1995	40,333.2
1996	107,020.0	2,740,459.0	1996	174,309.9
1997	110,400.0	2,834,998.9	1997	262,198.5
1998	112,950.0	2,765,670.0	1998	226,702.4
1999	116,140.0	3,193,660.0	1999	546,873.1
2000	120,640.0	4,842,190.0	2000	1,090,148.0
2001	125,720.0	5,545,410.0	2001	1,181,652.0
2002	129,820.0	5,726,190.0	2002	1,013,514.0

Source: Central Bank of Nigeria, *Statistical Bulletin*, Vol. 13, 2003, 112 and 190.

With the increasing revenue from oil, the sector replaced agriculture as the main foreign exchange earner. In fact, from 1974, Nigeria came to rely primarily on oil for its foreign exchange earnings as oil consistently accounted for over 90 percent (with the exception of 1978 when it accounted for 89 percent) of the country's foreign earnings. Indeed, between 1990 and 2002, there was a near total dependence on oil as it accounted for over 97 percent of the country's foreign earnings for most of the years. The resultant neglect of agriculture and the poor performance of the manufacturing sector virtually turned Nigeria into a monoculture economy. The increasing revenue from oil and the desire to have more control and access to the oil-based revenue resulted in increased participation of the Nigerian state in the oil sector. The Nigerian National Oil Company (NNOC), which was established in 1971, was merged with the inspectorate division of the federal ministry of petroleum resources to form the Nigerian National Petroleum Corporation (NNPC) in 1977. The NNPC was responsible for supervising and regulating the oil production process while also getting directly involved in oil production. By 1979, the Nigerian government through the NNPC acquired majority interest (60 percent share equity ownership) in all the major oil companies operating in the country. The only exception was Shell in which Nigeria's share equity ownership increased to 80 percent following the nationalization of the 20 percent shares of the British Petroleum component of the company in August 1979.[2]

The phenomenal increase in the prices of oil from 1973/74 and the near total dependence on oil for government revenue had a number of implications for the wellbeing of the Nigerian economy. The Nigerian state, which before the oil boom depended on peasant based agricultural production for the bulk of its foreign exchange, now came to rely solely on oil rents and royalties for its revenue. Thus, "the major part of state revenues was now derived largely independently of production activities in the domestic economy and independently of indigenous social classes."[3] The outcome was the neglect and decline of the peasant and rural-based production system, a situation that was accentuated by the unabashedly full-scale, modernization-inspired development strategies that were pursued from the 1970s. Furthermore, the dependence on oil, as was the case with raw materials, made the country's economy to be highly susceptible to the vagaries of the oil prices in the world market. Thus, when the "oil shocks" of 1977-78 and the large-scale oil crisis of the 1980s (due largely to the manipulative activities of the advanced capitalist countries that were intent on drastically reducing the prices of oil)[4] occurred, the Nigerian economy was plunged into crisis. The magnitude of the oil crisis was such that Nigeria's annual oil production drastically declined from 766 million barrels in 1977 to 450 million barrels in 1983.

In any case, with the enormous revenue from oil the Nigerian state greatly increased its expenditure. The country embarked on massive and reckless recurrent and capital expenditure while various international financial institutions, creditors and suppliers courted the Nigerian government. In addition, the oil revenue was

Table 7.4 Nigeria's oil and non-oil exports, 1970-2002 (million naira)

Year	Total Exports	Oil Exports	Percentage	Non-Oil Exports	Percentage
1970	885.4	510.0	57.6	375.4	42.4
1971	1,293.4	953.0	73.7	340.4	26.3
1972	1,434.2	1,176.2	82.0	258.0	18.0
1973	2,278.4	1,893.5	83.1	384.9	16.9
1974	5,794.8	5,365.7	92.6	429.1	7.4
1975	4,925.5	4,563.1	92.6	362.4	7.4
1976	6,751.1	6,321.6	93.6	429.5	6.4
1977	7,630.7	7,072.8	92.7	557.9	7.3
1978	6,064.4	5,401.6	89.1	662.8	10.9
1979	10,836.8	10,166.8	93.8	670.0	6.2
1980	14,186.7	13,632.3	96.1	554.4	3.9
1981	11,023.3	10,680.5	96.9	342.8	3.1
1982	8,206.4	8,003.2	97.5	203.2	2.5
1983	7,502.5	7,201.2	96.0	301.3	4.0
1984	9,088.0	8,840.6	97.3	247.4	2.7
1985	11,720.8	11,223.7	95.8	497.1	4.2
1986	8,920.6	8,368.5	93.8	552.1	6.2
1987	30,360.6	28,208.6	92.9	2,152.0	7.1
1988	31,192.8	28,435.4	91.2	2,757.4	8.8
1989	57,971.2	55,016.8	94.9	2,954.4	5.1
1990	109,886.1	106,626.5	97.0	3,259.6	3.0
1991	121, 535.4	116,858.1	96.2	4,677.3	3.8
1992	207, 266.0	203,292.7	98.1	3,973.3	1.9
1993	218,770.1	213,778.8	97.7	4,991.3	2.3
1994	206,059.2	200,710.2	97.4	5,349.0	2.6
1995	950,661.4	927,565.3	97.8	23,096.1	2.2
1996	1,309,543.4	1,286,215.9	98.2	23,327.5	1.8
1997	1,241,662.7	1,212,499.4	97.7	29,163.3	2.3
1998	751,856.7	717,786.5	95.5	34,070.2	4.5
1999	1,188,969.8	1,169,476.9	98.4	19,492.9	1.6
2000	1,945,723.3	1,920,900.4	98.7	24,822.9	1.3
2001	2,001,230.8	1,973,222.2	98.6	28,008.6	1.4
2002	1,874,874.3	1,780,221.6	95.0	94,651.6	5.0

Source: Computed from Central Bank of Nigeria, *Statistical Bulletin*, Vol. 13, 2003, 172.

seen as providing an opportunity for the rapid modernization of the Nigerian economy and society.

Oil and Public Expenditure

The period from 1973, which has been described as marking the beginning of "the rise of the oil state," witnessed a massive increase in the Nigerian government's recurrent and capital expenditure. Indeed, oil had its most significant impact via state expenditure since its direct contribution in terms of employment and related economic activity was limited.[5] The increases in state expenditure were reflected in areas such as wage increases, employment, social services such as education and housing, industrial investment and infrastructures. These were accompanied by a generous trade liberalization policy. Forrest has characterized the period from 1974 to 1977 as that of "loss of control" that witnessed "massive state expenditures, which maintained their momentum well after state revenues had declined." He noted that unlike the low-population oil producers of the Middle East, Nigeria did not invest its oil wealth in Western economies thereby securing a flow of investment income for the future, nor, was revenue set aside in a stabilization, or development, fund. He further noted that the phenomenal increase in government expenditure resulted in "an explosion of purchasing power that ignited an enormous consumption boom." The 1974 and 1975 federal budgets were described as "the great consumption budgets" in that both budgets greatly liberalized foreign trade by substantially reducing import duties and excises and further relaxing foreign exchange controls. This trade liberalization resulted in a substantial increase in the volume of imports.[6]

The oil boom certainly resulted in massive expenditure on the part of the Nigerian state. Among other things, the country embarked on enormous building and construction projects such as luxury hotels, stadia, international airports, low-cost housing and express roads while hosting various expensive international sports and cultural jamborees. Indeed, the degree of indiscipline and "loss of control" that characterized government expenditure was reflected in the naive declaration by a federal permanent secretary that Nigeria's problem was not lack of money, but rather, how to spend the "petro-naira."[7] The huge expansion in government expenditure as partly reflected in the massive construction and building projects created avenues for corrupt practices on the part of Nigerian government officials, business elites and their foreign collaborators while many of the projects were poorly executed. As a result of these factors, many studies (ranging from liberal to Marxist and neo-Marxist studies) on Nigeria's economic policies and development crisis have overwhelmingly blamed internal factors as primarily responsible for the country's economic debacle. They emphasized issues such as financial indiscipline, recklessness, "contractocracy," mismanagement and corruption, as well as poor implementation of government projects.[8]

There is no doubt that these factors characterized the Nigerian economy but most of the factors can only be properly understood when situated within the context of the transplanted capitalist system. The factors are symptomatic of the global capitalist system but were aggravated by the existence of a peripheral capitalist system in Nigeria. In other words, they do not constitute ends in themselves and it is wrong to analyze them from the perspective of the specificity of the so-called irrational internal policies. It is therefore not correct to attribute the causes of Nigeria's economic crisis that assumed acute proportions from the early 1980s, solely to the specificity of these internal factors as have been the case in most of the existing analyses. The fundamental causes of the crisis can be more properly located within the acute shortcomings of transnational capitalism and Nigeria's peripheral location within the global capitalist system. Thus, what has been overlooked in the analysis of the kind of public expenditure promoted by the oil money and the subsequent economic crisis is the critical influence of the modernization paradigm, as epitomized by the transplanted peripheral capitalist system, on the pattern of expenditure and economic development strategies. Bangura succinctly captured the situation, when he stated:

> Let us dispose of one myth about mismanagement, and that is, that there can never be a perfectly managed capitalist economy that will be permanently crisis-free; for capitalism is a system of competitive centrally planned autonomous corporate units in an anarchical environment. . . . The 'best managed' capitalist economies, US, Britain, France, etc, have experienced profound economic crises. Those who talk of mismanagement outside the context of capitalism as the cause of the crisis, are therefore chasing the shadows and are not being serious in their analysis. Surely, the Nigerian economy must rank among the most mismanaged in the world which has certainly made matters worse for the economy, but I don't see how the economy could have been managed in such a way as to permanently avoid crises, if that management (is done within the context of a peripheral capitalist system). Related to the above is what some authors have seen as the corrupt nature of public officials and private entrepreneurs who openly loot public funds or make illegal transactions in the foreign exchange market. Again, much as these have aggravated the problem, they cannot on their own constitute the cause of the (economic) crisis. In any case . . . corruption is an integral part of the accumulation process (in the capitalist system), especially at its most primitive stage. The special problem of the Nigerian context is the externalisation of the looted funds most of which find their way not in the circuit of reproduction of the local economy, but in the metropolitan economies either through investing in such economies or in squandering the looted wealth in the commodities of those economies. Such a problem has to do with the contradiction between national and international systems of accumulation and the structure of production and exchange relations that tie the Nigerian economy to the world capitalist economy.[9]

It is from the above perspective that the nature of the public expenditure of the fund derived from oil and the associated economic development strategies will be analyzed.

The great increase in the size of federal and state bureaucracies as a result of the creation of more states (twelve states in 1967 and then nineteen in 1976), and the subsequent dramatic increases in the salaries of public sector workers, greatly contributed to the expansion of public expenditure. Of much significance was the Udoji salary award of 1974. The Udoji Commission was set up in 1972 to recommend ways of reforming the civil service. The Commission's report, which was submitted in 1974, recommended the rationalization of the civil service in order to make it more development-oriented and recommended a two-phased increase in the salary of public sector workers.[10] However, in practice more attention was focussed on the wage increase aspect of the report. In January 1975, the minimum wage was raised by 130 percent, rising from 312 naira per annum to 720 naira per annum and similar increases were made for all levels of the public sector workers with the top echelon awarded a 90 percent salary increase. The backdating of the wage increases to April 1974 led to the payment of nine months salary arrears to workers. Private sector workers resorted to various industrial actions to demand for their own wage increases and were eventually granted increases of 30 percent or more.

Education, which was seen as crucial for the modernization project of the capitalist transformation of the Nigerian economy and society, was accorded very high priority in the 1970s. This period witnessed the launching of various national education policies. The Joint Admission and Matriculation Board (JAMB), a central admission board, which was charged with maintaining equity and fairness in university admissions by carefully balancing the issues of merit and national interest in the admission process was created. The role of the National Universities Commission (NUC) in regulating the activities of the universities and advising on the establishment of new universities was strengthened while the Universal Primary Education (UPE) program was launched in 1976. Indeed, the 1970-74 National Development Plan had "the development and expansion of education at various levels in order to achieve higher enrolment ratios as well as improved quality at these levels while at the same time, reducing the educational gap in the country by 'levelling upwards'" as a major objective.[11]

The federal and state governments therefore embarked on massive expansion and diffusion of educational institutions at all levels throughout the country. The federal government took over the funding of the existing state universities and established new federal universities thereby resulting in the rise of the number of university students from 14,000 in 1970 to 53,000 in 1978. Federal and state governments established more polytechnics, colleges of education, and secondary schools (state governments took over private schools from voluntary agencies) while the UPE program resulted in a phenomenal increase in primary school enrolment. The various costs associated with the establishment and running of the respective educational institutions resulted in a great expansion in educational expenditure, which at its peak in 1975 absorbed 1,051 million naira (19 percent) of federal current and capital expenditure (including all transfers).[12] The expansion of education especially at the tertiary level was perceived as crucial for the capitalist transformation of the Nigerian economy. According to Beckman:

> The growth of a trained professional class in the business sector (state and private) is an important aspect of (the) present capitalist transformation. Unlike the original, largely uneducated Nigerian business class . . . the new generation is more easily integrated with, and adopts the class outlook of, international capital. It is also important to stress the growing sophistication in the training of this new class. Many go to business schools in the United States. The teaching of (capitalist) management sciences spreads fast not only through the formal higher school system, but also through a variety of public and private bodies run by firms of business consultants, often with foreign partners.[13]

Massive building and construction projects greatly contributed to the expansion in government expenditure. The building of low-cost housing estates mainly directed at low-income earners, was first initiated by the Gowon military regime in 1972 and was a cornerstone of the policies of the civilian regime of Shagari under its "housing for all" program. A primary objective of the program was to redistribute income towards the low-income earners by reducing the proportion of their gross income spent on rent to no more than 20 percent.[14] A significant feature of the low-cost housing program was the use of contractors. The Nigerian Building Society was converted to the Federal Mortgage Bank in 1977 to provide soft loans to the middle- and high-income groups (with repayment periods of between seven to twenty years) to build their own houses. In all instances, the aim of the housing program was to create the conditions that would facilitate "affordable owner/occupier" houses.

A number of fraudulent practices were associated with the low-cost housing program, which became an avenue for accumulation of state resources by sections of the Nigerian elite and their foreign collaborators. The cost of building the low-cost housing estates was highly inflated while many of the planned housing projects were not completed. For instance, the civilian regime of Shagari planned to construct 120,000 housing units between 1980 and 1983, but by the end of 1983, only 32,227 units had been constructed at a total cost of 1.26 billion naira, that is, 40,000 Naira per unit. It has been estimated that about 50 percent of the amount spent on the housing projects were fraudulently misappropriated.[15] The high cost of the so-called low-cost houses made them unaffordable to the low-income earners. Even then, many of the completed housing units were poorly erected and lacked basic amenities such as electricity, roads and water. Furthermore, the low-income houses, which were mainly constructed in the urban centers "were constructed with little regard for the (culture) and values of those expected to occupy them."[16] In the name of modernization, attempts were made to transplant the kind of low-cost housing structures that existed in Western capitalist countries into Nigeria. Thus, a combination of the high cost of the housing projects and their lack of relevance to the culture and values of Nigerian low-income earners made them shun the housing estates.

Apart from the low-cost housing projects, there was a general construction boom in the 1970s and early 1980s. The end of the Nigerian civil war necessitated the reconstruction of many roads, bridges and other facilities that were destroyed during the war. Moreover, the creation of new states resulted in the construction of new state government houses, secretariats and official residential accommodation among others. There was also the construction of military barracks in different parts of the country and the building of dams for the various river basins. Beyond these was the belief among policy makers and their advisers that the sudden wealth derived from oil created the unique opportunity for the rapid transformation of Nigerian urban centers into replicas of Western urban centers. There was therefore the massive construction of luxury hotels, stadia, international airports, super-expressways and Lagos fly-overs, among others. All these building and construction projects created an overwhelming demand for construction materials, in particular cement, which made the federal government to embark on an uncontrolled importation of cement that resulted in the congestion of Nigerian ports in the mid-1970s.

The Nigerian government paid huge amounts of demurrage fees to foreign ship owners because of this port congestion. An estimated amount of 109 million naira was paid as demurrage charges for 1975 alone. Other costs arising from the ports congestion included 60 million naira surcharges on freights, 35 million naira penalty charges imposed by the haulage firms, extra interest charges of 32 million naira, in addition to losses due to deterioration of cargo estimated at 273 million naira.[17] Usman has pointed out that Western cement manufacturing and shipping companies used the opportunity of the cement importation to greatly exploit Nigerian resources. For instance, between 1974 and 1976, Nigeria paid an average of about $115 for each metric tonne of cement imported into the country, including shipping and demurrage charges. This was $75 higher than what should have been paid at the then prevailing world price of $25 for a single metric tonne of cement and $15 per tonne for the freight. In fact, the direct and indirect losses to the Nigerian economy from the cement "armada" amounted to about 1 billion naira for a single year.[18] The tribunal that was set up in 1980, under the chairmanship of a Nigerian Supreme Court Justice, to probe the cement crisis unearthed a number of fraudulent practices on the part of Nigerian elites and their foreign collaborators in connection with the contracts for cement importation.[19]

The enormous expansion in building and construction projects made the sector to become one of the most rapidly growing sectors of the Nigerian economy. For instance, in 1974-75, building and construction accounted for 70.8 percent of Nigeria's gross capital formation. The sector's contribution to the GDP at current factor cost rose from 884.1 million naira in 1973/74 to 3,491.8 million naira in 1979/80. Yet most of the contracts for the projects were awarded to foreign firms thereby resulting in massive capital flight from Nigeria while reinforcing the country's neocolonial dependency. To worsen the situation, these contracts were highly inflated. A ministerial committee headed by S. Essang, the then finance minister in the Shagari civilian administration, that was set up to investigate the reasons for the excessive costs of government contracts in Nigeria reported in July 1980 that the contracts were highly inflated. Among other things, the committee reported that the cost of government projects awarded to contractors was 200 percent higher in Nigeria than in Kenya, and 130 percent higher than in Algeria.[20] In addition, in February 1985, the Odama Committee reported that most contracts for construction works in Nigeria were deliberately inflated with the result that their costs were three times higher than those in East and North Africa, and four times higher than those in Asia.[21] The magnitude of the extent of inflation of construction contracts in Nigeria can be gleaned from the case of the 125 kilometers Lagos-Ibadan expressway, which was constructed at the cost of 178 million naira, that is, over one million naira per kilometer.[22] It has been pointed out that these contracts were deliberately inflated by the Western capitalist countries that were infuriated by OPEC's raising of oil prices, which they blamed for being mainly responsible for the recession in their economies that started at about the same period. This blaming of OPEC's pricing policy, failed to take into account the fact the economic crisis had its roots at the much deeper level of the structure and cycles of capitalist economies.[23] Indeed, the degree of inflation of government contracts was so blatant that in 1977, Joseph Garba, the then Nigerian commissioner for external affairs, publicly complained that Western capitalist nations were charging four to five times more for one kilometer of road in Nigeria, than they charged, for example, in Ghana.[24]

In spite of the role played by Western capitalist countries in sharply inflating Nigerian government contracts, there has been the tendency among scholars to analyze the abuse associated with the contract system, primarily from the perspective of the specificity of internal irrationalities of Nigerian government's policies. This has been characterized as "contractocracy" or "contractor syndrome" under which as a rule, government projects are usually contracted out to indigenous or foreign contracting or consulting firms.[25] This kind of analysis fails to take into account the fact that the contract system is an integral part of the transplanted Western capitalist system and that the Western capitalist economies rely greatly on contractors and consultants. It is true that the contract system was greatly abused in Nigeria (with the collaboration of Western capitalist firms) but there are also abuses associated with the contract system in the advanced capitalist economies. A good case in point is the various abuses associated with the no bid contract awarded by the United States government to the Halliburton firm for the reconstruction of Iraq. Yet analyses of economic recessions in Western capitalist countries have not isolated the widespread use of contractors and consultants in explaining their economic predicaments. In fact, the role of contractors can be more properly analyzed if situated within the context of the general dynamics of the world capitalist economy.[26]

In any case, the preoccupation with transplanting the institutions of the advanced capitalist economies into Nigeria led to the concentration of the building and construction projects in the urban centers. Since the indigenous structures such as buildings were seen as primitive and backward attempts were not made to adapt the projects to the indigenous social and cultural realities. To worsen the situation, the enormous government expenditure on building and construction did not make meaningful contribution to the stimulation of domestic production activities. Even though cement was the major item needed for these projects and there was an overwhelming demand for cement, the indigenous cement industries could not respond by increasing production to meet a significant part of this demand. Yet cement production was one of the earliest consumer goods industries established in Nigeria in the post World War II period and was considered to have the greatest comparative advantage and potential for success among the various import-substituting consumer goods industries established during this period.[27] However, as demonstrated by Adubifa's study of the Nigerian cement industry, the firms could not respond to the increased demand by significantly increasing their production capacity because of the limitations of the modernist-inspired import substitution strategy and the associated policy of technology transfer.[28]

The failure of the supposedly traditional, primitive and backward rural areas to benefit from the massive construction works because of the urban bias nature of the modernist transformation policies promoted the mass migration of rural youths to the urban centers. In addition, the massive expenditure associated with wage increases, the attempts at rapidly modernizing the Nigerian economy and society through the unbridled transplantation of Western institutions into the country and the various abuses and exploitative practices associated with the process promoted an enormous amount of deficit financing. Paradoxically the rate of deficit financing grew from 1975 when Nigeria's revenue from oil experienced a great amount of increase. This deficit financing resulted in a rapid buildup of the country's external debts.

The increases in wages among public and private sector workers created increased demands for various manufactured goods and services mainly among the urban dwellers. These demands were not met through increased domestic production. Rather, under the liberal modernist policy of trade liberalization, the government promoted the massive importation of these items to satisfy the foreign tastes that had been cultivated by the so-called modernizing elites residing in the urban centers, which had percolated to the other segments of urban dwellers. Under the auspices of modernization, there was a drive by the Western capitalist countries to promote global trade liberalization which would ultimately result in the "the globalisation of consumption" and the creation of a "global supermarket" that would not tolerate regional peculiarities and characteristics. It has been alleged that the United States championed the drive to liberalize trade with the aim of ultimately generalizing the US way of life, increasing the profits of US producers, as well as increasing US control over important sectors of other countries'

Table 7.5 Federal Government Finances, 1970-2002 (million naira)

Year	Total Revenue	Retained Revenue	Current Expenditure	Capital Expenditure	Surplus/ Deficit (-)	% of GDP
1970	634	448.8	716.1	187.8	-455.1	-8.7
1971	1168.8	1168.8	823.6	173.6	171.6	2.6
1972	1405.1	1404.4	1012.3	451.3	-58.8	-0.8
1973	1695.3	1695.3	963.5	565.7	166.1	1.5
1974	4537.4	4537	1517.1	1223.5	1796.4	9.8
1975	5514.7	5514.7	2734.9	3207.7	-427.9	-2.0
1976	6765.9	6765.9	3815.4	4041.3	-1090.8	-4.0
1977	8042.4	8042.4	3819.2	5004.6	-781.4	-2.4
1978	7371	5178.1	2800	5200	-2821.9	-7.8
1979	10912.4	8868.4	3187.2	4219.5	1461.7	3.4
1980	15233.5	12993.3	4805.2	10163.3	-1975.2	3.9
1981	13290.5	7511.6	4846.7	6567	-3902.1	-7.7
1982	11433.7	5819.1	5506	6417.2	-6104.1	-11.8
1983	10508.7	6272	4750.8	4885.7	-3364.5	-5.9
1984	11253.3	7267.2	5827.5	4100.1	-2660.4	-4.2
1985	15050.4	10001.4	7576.4	5464.7	-3039.7	-4.2
1986	12595.8	7969.4	7696.9	8526.8	-8254.3	-11.3
1987	25380.6	16129	15646.2	6372.5	-5889.7	-5.4
1988	27596.7	15588.6	19409.4	8340.1	-12161	-8.4
1989	53870.4	25893.6	25994.2	15034.1	-15135	-6.7
1990	98102.4	38152.1	36219.6	24048.6	-22116.1	-8.5
1991	100992	30829.2	38243.5	28340.9	-35755	-11.0
1992	190453.2	53264.9	53034.1	39763.3	-39532.5	-7.2
1993	192769.4	83493.6	136727.1	54501.8	-107735	-15.5
1994	201910.8	90622.6	89974.9	70918.3	-70270.6	-7.7
1995	459987.3	249768.1	127629.8	121138.3	1000	0.1
1996	520190	369267	124491.3	212926.3	32049.4	1.6
1997	582811.1	423215.2	158563.5	269651.7	-5000	-0.2
1998	463608.8	353724.1	178097.8	309015.6	-133389.3	-4.7
1999	949187.9	662585.3	449662.4	498027.6	-285104.7	-8.4
2000	1906159.7	597282.1	461608.5	239450.9	-103777.3	-2.9
2001	2231533	796977	579329	438697	-221048.9	-4.0
2002	1731837.5	716754.2	696777.7	321378.1	-301401.6	-5.1

Source: Central Bank of Nigeria, *Statistical Bulletin*, Vol. 13, 2003, 92-94.

economies.[29] The US and other Western capitalist countries sought to achieve this globalization of consumption through the promotion of agricultural modernization as largely embodied in the green revolution, bilateral and multilateral assistance, and international agricultural and development agencies.[30] Furthermore, the enormous government expenditure on various projects resulted in increased demand for imported materials, which further promoted massive importation of foreign goods into the country.

The rapid government expenditure generally promoted great increases in incomes, mainly among the urban dwellers, a situation that fuelled increased demand for food, goods and services. This increased demand and the resultant high increases in prices of these items contributed to the creation of an inflationary situation. Rather than put in place measures that would promote domestic production especially in the rural areas to meet the increased demand, the government decided to adopt the modernist policy of liberalizing imports through reduction in import duties as a means of curbing inflation. Thus, the government was more concerned with using import liberalization to control inflation rather than promoting domestic production that would contribute to reduction in imports thereby improving the balance of payments position. As a result, it was stated in the third national development plan that the government would remove all non-tariff barriers to trade as well as considerably reducing import and excise duties.[31] In the same vein, the guidelines to the fourth national development plan stated that import would be deliberately encouraged as an anti-inflationary measure.[32] This import syndrome can be better appreciated if situated within the capitalist diffusionist path promoted by the modernist development strategy.

Nevertheless, trade liberalization made imports to be cheaper than domestically produced food and goods thereby further fuelling imports while negatively affecting domestic production. Rural production of food and other agricultural products were more adversely affected. Women who dominated the food processing sector in the rural areas, and the manufacturing of various beverages and alcoholic drinks, were particularly more negatively affected as the imported products coupled with the new taste of the urban dwellers resulted in a further decrease in the demand for their products. Furthermore, the modernization paradigm which characterized rural production system and their products as primitive, backward, not subjected to acceptable hygienic practices and therefore unhealthy, greatly contributed to the depressed demands for the locally produced foods, beverages and alcoholic drinks. This was a continuation of the colonial attack and repression of the domestic production of food and drinks that were seen as offering stiff competition to the imported ones, a development that greatly contributed to the economic marginalization, and therefore, the status of rural women.

The rapid rise in the rate of imports was clearly reflected in the fact that between 1974 and 1978, imports increased almost fivefold, rising from 1,737.3 million naira to 8,211.7 million naira. Exports only experienced a marginal

Table 7.6 Nigeria's balance of payments, 1970-2002 (million naira)

Year	Oil Exports	Oil Imports	Balance of Trade	Non-oil Exports	Non-oil Imports	Balance of Trade	Total Balance of Trade
1970	510.0	52.2	457.8	375.4	704.2	-328.8	129.0
1971	953.0	50.4	902.6	340.4	1,028.5	-688.1	214.5
1972	1,176.2	45.2	1,131.0	258.0	944.9	-686.9	444.1
1973	1,893.5	41.0	1,852.5	384.9	1,183.8	-798.9	1,053.6
1974	5,365.7	52.4	5,313.3	429.1	1,684.9	-1,255.8	4,057.5
1975	4,563.1	118.0	4,445.1	362.4	3,603.5	-3,241.1	1,204.0
1976	6,321.6	95.0	6,226.6	429.5	5,053.5	-4,624.0	1,602.6
1977	7,072.8	102.2	6,970.6	557.9	6,991.5	-6,433.6	537.0
1978	5,401.6	110.0	5,291.6	662.8	8,101.7	-7,438.9	-2,147.3
1979	10,166.8	230.0	9,936.8	670.0	7,242.5	-6572.5	3,364.3
1980	13,632.3	227.4	13,404.9	554.4	8,868.2	-8313.8	5,091.1
1981	10,680.5	119.8	10,560.7	342.8	12,719.8	-12,377.0	-1,816.3
1982	8,003.2	225.5	7,777.7	203.2	10,545.0	-10,341.8	-2,564.1
1983	7,201.2	171.6	7,029.6	301.3	8,732.1	-8,430.8	-1,401.2
1984	8,840.6	282.4	8,558.2	247.4	6,895.9	-6,648.5	1,909.7
1985	11,223.7	51.8	11,171.9	497.1	7,010.8	-6,513.7	4,658.2
1986	8,368.5	913.9	7,454.6	552.1	5,069.7	-4,517.6	2,937.0
1987	28,208.6	3,170.1	25,038.5	2,152.0	14,691.6	-12,539.6	12,498.9
1988	28,435.4	3,803.1	24,632.3	2,757.4	17,642.6	-14,885.2	9,747.1
1989	55,016.8	4,671.6	50,345.2	2,954.4	26,188.6	-23,234.2	27,111.0
1990	106,626.5	6,073.1	100,553.4	3,259.6	39,644.8	-36,385.2	64,168.2
1991	116,858.1	7,595.3	109,262.8	4,677.3	79,424.9	-74,747.6	34,515.2
1992	203,292.7	19,937.2	183,355.5	3,973.3	125,974.2	-122,000.9	61,354.6
1993	213,778.8	41,329.3	172,449.5	4,991.3	124,771.1	-119,779.8	52,669.7
1994	200,710.2	42,349.6	158,360.6	5,349.0	120,439.2	-115,090.2	43,270.4
1995	927,565.3	155,825.9	771,739.4	23,096.1	599,301.8	-576,205.7	195,533.7
1996	1,286,215.9	162,178.7	1,124,037.2	23,327.5	400,447.9	-377,120.4	746,916.8
1997	1,212,499.4	166,902.5	1,045,596.9	29,163.3	678,814.1	-649,650.8	395,946.1
1998	717,786.5	175,854.2	541,932.3	34,070.2	661,564.5	-627,494.3	-85,562.0
1999	1,169,476.9	211,661.8	957,837.2	19,492.9	650,853.9	-631,338.0	326,499.2
2000	1,920,900.4	198,735.9	1,722,164.5	24,822.9	764,228.0	-739,405.1	982,759.4
2001	1,973,222.2	215,474.6	1,757,747.6	28,008.6	1,131,991.6	-1,103,983.0	653,764.6
2002	1,780,221.6	239,071.0	1,541,150.6	94,651.6	722,509.3	-627,857.7	913,292.9

Source: Central Bank of Nigeria, *Statistical Bulletin*, Vol. 13, 2003, 172-173.

increase during the same period, rising from 5,794.8 million naira in 1974 to 6,064.4 million naira in 1978. This figure does not even fully reflect the bleak situation in connection with exports because oil accounted for the bulk of the exports while non-oil exports performed miserably. The poor performance of non-oil exports in addition to the fact that non-oil imports accounted for the bulk of the country's imports had adverse negative effects on the balance of payment position. Moreover, the reliance on oil to finance the huge import bills meant that any shock in the oil market would adversely affect the balance of payment position. This was exactly what happened with the oil shocks of 1978/79 and 1981 to 1983 when Nigeria experienced huge balance of trade deficits.

The enormous wealth derived from oil promoted a pattern of expenditure that was supposedly aimed at modernizing the Nigerian economy, but in practice helped to further entrench the neocolonial dependence of the economy. Indeed, the modernization inspired development policies and the associated massive expenditure promoted a pattern of accumulation that sought to make the Nigerian state an agent of capitalist accumulation and development in general, thereby serving the interests of both the indigenous and foreign bourgeoisie.[33] In the process, the massive expenditure was mainly concentrated in the urban centers while the rural areas and the associated culturally adapted rural production process were neglected. As already noted, the neglect of the rural areas was based on the notion of the supposed primitivity and backwardness of the rural areas whose so-called irrational economy of affection had nothing meaningful to contribute to the development process.

Oil and Development Planning

Development planning which started in Nigeria in 1945 was squarely based on the modernization paradigm. Planning aimed at replicating the Western development trajectory by reproducing the Rostownian stages of growth in Nigeria. Indeed, the four plans that were drawn up between 1962 and 1985 followed the trajectory of the modernization paradigm as the various reformulations of the paradigm were reproduced and used to define the philosophy, objectives and targets of the respective plans. The first and second development plans, which were prepared during the period when the emphasis on Rostow's growth theory was at its peak, were primarily concerned with attaining a minimum level of growth as the means for establishing the conditions for the "take-off" of development. According to Stolper, the main architect of the first development plan, "the whole purpose of the planning exercise (was) to aid Nigeria in mobilising as many resources as possible and allocating them for growth."[34] Operating more clearly within the context of the "stages of growth" theory, the second development plan stated that Nigeria had "all the essential ingredients for a quick 'take off.'" The plan therefore placed emphasis "on growth as a pre-condition for a meaningful distribution of the fruits of development" stating that "the 'national cake' must first be baked before it is shared."[35]

However, by the mid-1970s, the primary focus of the modernization paradigm on growth came under widespread criticism because of the apparent failure of good growth performance to translate into meaningful economic development. This resulted in the reformulation of the paradigm, which now emphasized "redistribution with growth" and "basic needs" perspectives. These new perspectives were reflected in the third and fourth national development plans. Thus, the primary objective of the third plan was "to achieve a rapid increase in the standard of living of the average Nigerian." Noting that development is "not just a matter of growth in per capita income," the plan sought to "translate economic growth into meaningful development through income redistribution."[36] Continuing in the same tradition, the guidelines for the fourth development plan criticized the practice of measuring economic development in terms of the degree of growth in the GDP and capital formation. The guidelines stated, "true development must mean the development of man – the realisation of his creative potential, enabling him to improve his material conditions of living through the use of resources available to him."[37] As noted by Ajayi, this new sentiment did not remove the basic flaws in development planning because the redistribution and basic needs approaches with their vision of an egalitarian and individualistic society, conceived from above, constituted mere reformulations of the objectives of modernization.[38] Thus, in spite of the new sentiment regarding the need for development to be man-centered, the paradigm of modernity remained the essential paradigm that underlined all the plans.

Nigerian policy makers and their economic advisers saw the increased revenue from oil in the 1970s, as providing the perfect opportunity for the rapid modernization of the Nigerian economy and society through the replication of Western capitalist institutions. Development planning was regarded as the ideal agency through which oil money would be used to effect this rapid transformation. The third national development plan, which was prepared in the midst of the oil boom of the mid-1970s, stated that the increased revenue from oil would be used to develop the productive capacity of the economy in order to achieve self-sustaining growth within the shortest possible time. It was stated that the size of the plan, which was described as the biggest and most ambitious plan ever prepared for Nigeria, was deliberately made large to reflect the development problems of the country. Thus, while the 1962-68 and 1970-74 plans involved total capital expenditures of 2.4 billion naira and 3.3 billion naira respectively, the third plan initially envisaged a total capital expenditure of 30 billion naira, which was later revised upwards to 43.3 billion naira. This large allocation was justified on the ground that it would enable the government effect a radical transformation of the economy during the plan period.[39] As stated in the plan:

> Due to developments in the oil sector substantial resources are becoming available to Nigeria. Since oil is a wasting asset, it is the development strategy of the government to utilise the resources from oil to develop the productive capacity of the economy. In the relatively short time that the economy will enjoy a surplus of investible resources it is intended that maximum effort will be made to create the economic and social infrastructure necessary for self-sustaining growth in the longer run when resources scarcity may recur.[40]

In stating its intention to use the oil money to transform the Nigerian economy, the third national development plan launched a serious attack on the economic practices of peasant farmers and other rural dwellers, which were considered as backward and primitive. This was a continuation of the tradition of discountenancing indigenous economic practices in favor of the Western capitalist practices. The ways in which these unfair and ill-advised attitudes were applied to technological and agricultural development have been discussed in chapters 5 and 6. The next two sections will examine how the oil money was expected to contribute to the promotion of industrial development and for increasing the level of indigenous ownership over the industrial enterprises in the country.

Industrial Development

As already noted, the industrial development strategy was that of import substitution. However, from the 1970s, the main objective of the industrial development program was to use the revenue from oil to diversify the productive base of the economy in order to reduce the reliance on oil as the primary source of foreign exchange. To achieve this objective, the available local resources would be more effectively utilized, strategic industries such as iron and steel and petrochemical industries would be established while more efforts would be made to increase the level of ownership and management of industries by Nigerians, among others. A major strategy for achieving industrial development was the signing of partnership agreements between the federal government and foreign private investors in the establishment of industries considered strategic for the country's industrialization process. This period witnessed the establishment of many turnkey industries. Nigerians did not acquire any form of technical skills in the process of establishing these industries while the projects were highly exploitative.

The objectives of the industrial development policy, which were laid down in the second national development plan, provided the blueprint that generally guided the industrialization strategies up to the introduction of the SAP in 1986. The objectives included promoting even regional development and industrial diversification, continuing the program of import substitution and extending the ISI policy to intermediate and capital goods production, and raising the proportion of indigenous ownership of industrial investments. To achieve these objectives, priority would be placed on agro-allied, petrochemicals, textile, iron and steel, and automotive industries, among others. While emphasizing the desirability of partnership with foreign investors, the need for indigenous ownership and control of industries that were of strategic importance to the country's development was stressed. The government would own at least 55 percent of the equities in strategic industries such as iron and steel, petrochemicals, fertilizer and petroleum while in other large- and medium-scale industries where technical partnerships with overseas industries was desirable, government and private equity would not be less than 35 percent.[41] The third national development plan regarded the enormous revenue from oil as providing the opportunity for the actualization of the industrial development policies. The federal and state governments therefore became directly involved in the development of various categories of industries such as iron and steel, petrochemicals, fertilizer, petroleum refining, automobile assembly, pulp and paper and textiles.

The guiding philosophy for the industrialization program was the import substitution strategy, which was perceived as the ideal vehicle for the transplantation of foreign industrial technologies into the country. As has already been pointed out, import substitution promoted extreme technological and economic independence while greatly aiding the country's economic exploitation by the advanced capitalist industries. Import substitution largely promoted the establishment of consumer goods industries, which were mainly branches of TNCs. These industries were strategically dependent on the parent companies and home countries for raw materials, capital equipment and technical managerial staff, among others. For instance, the import of raw materials by the industries increased by 110 percent between 1975 and 1979, and 100 percent between 1979 and 1981, while that of capital equipment increased by 156 percent between 1975 and 1979, and 78 percent between 1979 and 1981. Indeed, in view of the high import content of these industries, about 70 percent of the value added accrued to foreigners.[42] The strategy of import substitution did not promote linkages between the import substituting industries and the rest of the Nigerian economy. Furthermore, the fact that the industries were mainly capital-intensive contributed to the massive importation of capital goods.

In view of the massive importation of capital goods and the perceived significance of capital goods industries for the country's industrialization, successive Nigerian governments stated their commitment to the development of an iron and steel industry. A successful iron and steel industry was regarded as the backbone of any meaningful industrialization in Nigeria. It was perceived as critical for laying the foundation for long-term steady and self-reliant industrialization and economic growth in the country. As noted by Shagari in June 1981, the industry constituted "a decisive step in determining the future status of the country and the pattern of her economic development."[43] The development of an iron and steel industry was therefore included in the various development plans.

However, this policy was perceived from the perspective of an import substitution strategy that relied exclusively on foreign technology while discountenancing the existing indigenous capacity in this sector. Nevertheless, although the development of an iron and steel industry appeared in successive development plans, the attempts at developing the industry became entangled in Cold War politics. In addition, the Western capitalist countries displayed lukewarm attitude toward the project because they saw it as capable of threatening the lucrative profits they were making from exporting capital goods to Nigeria. Western European companies were first approached by the pro-West Balewa administration of Nigeria's First Republic to assist in the establishment of an iron and steel industry but the companies advised that the project was not viable. Given the uncooperative attitude of the Western companies, the Nigerian government reluctantly approached the Soviet Union in 1967 to assist with the establishment of the industry. Although the Soviet Union advised that the project was viable, it was not until 1979, toward end of the 1975-80 national development plan, that the actual process of developing the industry was set in motion with the signing of a contract between the Nigerian government and the Soviet Union.

When the decision to commence the development of the iron and steel industry was taken, the Western capitalist industries that had initially advised against the viability of the industry used the influence of their governments over the Nigerian government to inject themselves into the process. Thus, the contract for the development of the Ajaokuta iron and steel industry was divided between the Soviet firm, Tiajpromexport (TPE) and Western-owned construction companies: Dumez and Fourgerolle of France, and Bilfinger and Berger of Germany. The Soviet firm was to supply the blast furnace-basic oxygen technology of iron and steel making while the Western firms were contracted to carry out the civil engineering works. More significant is the fact that some Western governments and industries succeeded in pressurizing the Nigerian government to award another contract for the construction of a second iron and steel industry at Aladja, to Western firms. In addition, contracts were awarded to German and Japanese firms to set up three steel rolling mills at Oshogbo, Jos and Katsina.

The award of these contracts to Soviet and Western industries had some negative effects on the development of the iron and steel industry. Ehiedu Iweriebor has clearly demonstrated the adverse effects with respect to the Ajaokuta industry. According to him:

> The award of (the civil engineering) contracts to Western companies was short-sighted and counterproductive for various reasons. First, in view of the well known fact that Western sources which had been contacted from the late 1950s to help Nigeria develop her steel industry had failed to do so for overt political (and self-serving economic) reasons; such an award meant putting the project's fate in the hands of historical opponents of Nigeria's steel development plans. Second, in the light of the East-West Cold War and especially the fact that Soviet Union's assistance had demonstrated the

> feasibility of Nigerian steel development, the project moved from wish to possibility. It was short-sighted, however, to award part of the contract to a company from the Soviet Union and the other contracts to companies based in Western countries. This merely placed the project in the destructive cauldron of Cold War politics.

Furthermore, the situation adversely affected the progress of the Ajaokuta project in the sense that whenever the Nigerian government experienced financial problems and failed to make regular payments, the Western companies stopped work on the project. Conversely, "the Soviet firm whose contract was on a government to government basis and partly due to diplomatic and friendship considerations, generally continued work, even when the Nigerian government was unable to pay regularly."[44]

The award of the contract to a German/Austrian consortium to establish another iron and steel plant at Aladja further adversely affected the development of the iron and steel industry. There was no coordination between the Ajaokuta and Aladja projects. As a result, the two industries were based on different technologies: the blast and furnace system for Ajaokuta and the direct reduction process for Aladja. This did not facilitate linkage between the two iron and steel plants as the Ajaokuta plant could not make use of the billets from the Aladja plant, for instance, because the size of the billets was different from what it needed. The Ajaokuta industry therefore had to import its own billets. In addition, the feasibility study on the Aladja industry stated that the locally available iron ore deposits needed to be refined and upgraded before they could be used by the industry. Yet provisions were not made for the upgrading of the iron ore before the construction of the Aladja industry, which therefore resorted to importing its iron ore requirements. The high cost of importing the raw materials and other inputs greatly contributed to the escalation of the prices of the products of the local iron and steel firms thereby making them costlier than the imported ones.

As noted in chapter 5, a major shortcoming of the Ajaokuta and Aladja plants is the fact that the materials they produced were not of strategic importance to the development of the manufacturing industry sector of the country's economy. They mainly produced items that were needed by the construction industries instead of the flat sheets needed by the manufacturing industries, a situation that, by 1984, made flat sheets to account for 58 percent of Nigeria's annual import of steel products. Furthermore, because of the modernist approach that underlined the development of the iron and steel industry, the immense indigenous knowledge and technology that already exist within the country were discountenanced as backward and irrational. As a result, attempts were not made to link the industry with the existing indigenous technological base. Indeed, because of various problems that plagued the iron and steel industry, such as poor conceptualization, poor planning, poor execution and mismanagement,[45] the iron and steel plants did not effectively take off and had virtually collapsed by the end of the 1980s. Both the Nigerian federal government and the foreign partners share culpability for these problems.

The problems experienced by the iron and steel industry provided a good opportunity for the apostles of the modernization paradigm championed by the World Bank and the *Economist*'s Economic Intelligence Unit, to analyze the problems from the modernist perspective. They then went ahead to proffer solutions that were aimed at serving the exploitative economic interests of the advanced capitalist countries. These views have been endorsed and reproduced by Paul Lubeck and Michael Watts:

> More alarmingly, (the Ajaokuta steel complex) is designed with antiquated Soviet blast furnace technology to produce 1 million tons per year for a market estimated at 300,000 tons per year and at a price six times the world market price. The World Bank has refused to commit funds, arguing that Ajaokuta will become a permanent foreign exchange guzzler requiring at least $200,000 a year just to import high-quality coal. It will be a net loser of foreign exchange even after capital costs are written off. *Instead, they recommend that the direct gas reduction steel plant at Aladja be expanded from 400,000 to 1 million tons per year.* (My emphasis)

The authors provided a Weberian and modernist justification for the World Bank's position on Ajaokuta, stating that by refusing to fund the project, "the World Bank injects a rationality and discipline that the country's indigenous and bureaucratic bourgeoisie have so far proven incapable of exercising on their own."[46] The least that can be said is that the disastrous consequences of the World Bank's SAP, which provided the context for their claim, clearly help to demonstrate the untenability of their assertion. It is significant to note that the World Bank recommended the discontinuation of the Soviet built Ajaokuta steel project while recommending the expansion of the Aladja plant constructed by Western-based firms. This is in spite of the fact that the performance of the Aladja firm was extremely poor, in a sense, even poorer than that of the Ajaokuta plant. This recommendation is a clear manifestation of how the World Bank champions the interests of Western capitalist countries.

The position of the World Bank and the other critics of the Nigerian iron and steel projects are seriously flawed, negate the quest for economic self-reliance while helping to serve the advanced capitalist economies interests of perpetuating Nigeria's dependence on their economies. It has been pointed out that "while all the present steel projects at full production capacity will produce about 2.5 million tonnes of round products, this will satisfy only 50% of the country's steel requirements." The other 50% of national demand, which is made up of flat, alloy, special and tube steel products that "are required by the engineering and machine building industries and are not currently produced in the country," are still being imported. In addition, it is misleading for the World Bank to use "the SAP-induced depressed demand for steel products to assert that there would be 'over production' of steel products from Ajaokuta and the other plants." Indeed, the real reason for the World Bank and other foreign opposition to the steel industry "is the fear that a viable and productive Nigerian steel industry will free the country from its current captivity to Western and Japanese steel and metal producers, suppliers and vendors."[47] There is no doubt that a successful iron and steel industry is critical for Nigeria's industrialization and self-reliant economic development. However, for the industry to be relevant, successful and contribute to economic and technological development, it should be closely linked to, and integrated into, the indigenous knowledge and technological base.

Economic Nationalism and the Indigenization Policy

The background to the indigenization policy of 1972 (revised in 1977) can be traced to the 1950s when Nigerian politicians and businessmen desired access to the country's economic resources and to the immense surplus accumulated by the colonial marketing boards. They therefore mounted great pressure on the colonial administration for more economic concessions. Thus, the indigenization decree can, in a sense, be seen as the culmination of previous attempts by the Nigerian bourgeoisie since the colonial times to create elbowroom for them within the foreign dominated capitalist economy. Nonetheless, the immediate events that provided the enabling environment for the promulgation of the decree can be traced to the 1960-70 decade, particularly the period of the Nigerian civil war, 1967-70. Among such events, were the discriminatory practices of the dominant foreign-owned commercial banks, the substantial shortfall in the anticipated foreign capital for the 1962-68 plan, and the increasing cost of Nigeria's continued dependence on foreign capital.[48]

The Nigerian civil war provided the immediate impetus for the promulgation of the indigenization decree. During the war, the Nigerian ruling class was shocked to discover that the country's "traditional Western friends," notably Britain and the United States were not committed to the unity of the country but were rather prepared to sacrifice the country's unity on the alter of their own economic interests. Since the seceding Biafran territory was rich in oil, these countries decided to stay on the fence, adopt an ambivalent attitude and watch the progress of the war and the possible outcome before fully committing themselves one way or the other. The United States secretary of state, Dean Rusk, stated that the solution to the Nigerian crisis was a British affair while the British government resorted to legalistic arguments in justifying the oil mongul, Shell-B.P's advance payment of oil royalties to Biafra. More significantly, the British government made it very difficult for Nigeria to procure arms from Britain.[49] The Nigerian government therefore had to resort to the Soviet Union, with which she had not been friendly because of her pro-Western position and the cold war politics, for the supply of arms and other forms of military assistance. The virtual recognition of Biafra by France further incensed many Nigerians.

The role of these Western countries, which many Nigerians regarded as "Western duplicity" led to a wave of anti-imperialist sentiments and the demand for the nationalization of all foreign-owned businesses. This demand for nationalization of foreign-owned enterprises was capitalized upon by the Nigerian bourgeoisie who had all along been advocating for a space within the private sector that would be under their own control. They therefore pressurized the Nigerian government under the guise of economic nationalism to come up with a policy that would transfer full or part ownership of different categories of enterprises to the Nigerian bourgeoisie.

The indigenization policy was first articulated in the 1970-74 national development plan, the immediate post civil war plan, which capitalizing on the nationalist fervor generated by the war, was full of nationalist and egalitarian rhetoric. The plan stated the government's commitment to "the progressive elimination of foreign dominance in the national economy, not merely in terms of nominal financial-ownership but really in terms of the level of managerial and technological control."[50] Indigenization as articulated in this plan had two dimensions: the Nigerianization of management positions in the private sector through the appointment of Nigerians to these positions, and the indigenization of the ownership and control of private enterprises.[51] The main objectives of the indigenization policy were the creation of opportunities for Nigerian indigenous businessmen to exercise more control over the economy, the maximization of local retention of profits, the transfer of technology and managerial expertise to the indigenous entrepreneurial and managerial classes, and the raising of the level of intermediate capital goods production.[52]

The Nigerian Enterprises Promotion Decree (indigenization decree) of 1972 and revised decree of 1977 were partially aimed at reducing the level of foreign dominance over Nigeria's economy.[53] The indigenization decree of 1972 contained two graduations of the percentage of indigenous ownership of foreign-owned enterprises while the revised decree of 1977 had three graduations. The graduations were divided into schedules (Schedule 1, 1972 and 1977: 100 percent, Schedule 2, 1972: 40 percent and 1977: 60 percent, and Schedule 3, 1977: 40 percent). The breakdown of indigenous ownership of the enterprises were: 100 percent for small-scale merchandizing, light manufacturing and low technology service enterprises, 40 percent (1972) and 60 percent (1977) for more technology-intensive manufacturing industries and financial firms such as insurance companies, and 40 percent for high technology manufacturing industries. It is significant to note that the small-scale enterprises that were to be completely taken over by Nigerians were those mainly owned by Asians especially the Lebanese while Western-based transnational corporations mainly owned those in which indigenous ownership ranged from 60 to 40 percent.

The revenue derived from oil, provided part of the financial resources for the implementation of the provisions of the decrees. To facilitate the takeover of these foreign-owned enterprises by Nigerians, a Nigerian Enterprises Promotion Board (NEPB) and a fully publicly funded National Bank for Commerce and Industry (NBCI) were created while commercial banks were directed to allocate at least 40 percent of all loans and advances to Nigerian businesses. The main beneficiaries of these loans were the business elite who had the necessary collateral to guarantee the loans, military and civilian office holders, as well as high-ranking members of the bureaucracy who used their influential position in government to secure these loans. Most of the political office holders and top bureaucrats secured these loans without the required collateral and without been subjected to the requirements of the normal lending process: they were able to use their influential positions in government to subvert the due process.[54]

Foreign-owned companies adopted various measures to subvert the provisions of the decrees. Partnership agreements were abused to ensure that effective control of the companies remained with the foreign partners. Some companies such as the UAC resorted to merging all their subsidiary companies into a single conglomerate so that they would be large enough to belong to either schedule 2 or 3. Yet some other companies that straddled Schedules 2 and 3, resorted to division rather than merging their operations by pursuing a "two-company strategy," under which transnational corporations incorporated two companies, one located in Schedule 2 and the other in Schedule 3. This made it possible for them to retain uninhibited control over many product lines while at the same time minimizing their tax liability to the Nigerian government. Other measures included, "lending" some of their top employees loans to buy shares in the companies at favorable terms so that the foreigners could retain significant influence over the board of directors, and outright fronting where well placed Nigerians claimed ownership of companies that in actuality were still foreign-owned. In addition, some foreign investors, mainly the Levantines resorted to the fraudulent acquisition of Nigerian citizenship in order to retain control over their companies.[55]

The indigenization policy was located within the framework of the modernization paradigm, partly in the sense that the state saw it as its responsibility to provide a favorable atmosphere for the operation of foreign-dominated high technology industries, such as the oil industry. Furthermore, indigenization was regarded as capable of facilitating the process of technology transfer hence technical partnership agreements was favored in the so-called high technology industries. As demonstrated by Biersteker and Ankie Hoogvelt, the state support, subsidization, encouragement of technical partnership agreements and protection of the foreign-dominated high-technology industries, in many respects, resulted in subversion of the indigenization decree. Some of the ways in which this subversion were done included the granting of the right to choose, maintain and adapt technology to the foreign partners and the negotiations of special arrangements and exemptions for foreign companies.[56]

Indeed, the technical partnership agreements further helped to entrench Nigeria's technological and economic dependence. The preoccupation with equity ownership rather than organizational and technical control, resulted in a situation where Nigerians were appointed to inconsequential managerial positions (that in reality amounted to being more of "glorified clerks"), such as personnel managers, legal officers, and public relation officers. Foreigners were the production and technical managers as well as the research management experts.[57] Given this situation, it is difficult to agree with Forrest's optimistic prediction that "in the long run, the increase in Nigerian senior management and directors will no doubt shift more (decision making) to Nigerian staff, continued technological dependence and the multinational nature of many enterprises notwithstanding."[58] In reality, while indigenization can be said to have largely promoted the ownership and control of the non-strategic merchandizing and small-scale industrial enterprises by the Nigerian bourgeoisie, it consolidated the ownership and control of the strategic, highly state protected and subsidized high-technology industries by the foreign bourgeoisie.[59] Indeed, the indigenization policy merely transformed "the distributive rather than productive sectors of the economy to a different or 'higher' level of dependency."[60] Thus, indigenization further entrenched the compradoral character of the Nigerian bourgeoisie while consolidating the dependence of Nigeria's economy on international monopoly capital.

It is thus evident that the indigenization decree resulted in the further consolidation of expatriate, international capital in Nigeria, in the further subordination of the indigenous capitalist class and indeed the entire Nigerian economy to the interests of foreign capital, thereby perpetuating neo-colonial dependence. The modernization paradigm that underlined the policy especially in terms of technology transfer acutely helps to illustrate the dependency-perpetuating phenomenon fostered by the paradigm. Indigenization did not help in attaining the federal government's objectives of promoting indigenous control of "the commanding heights of the economy," promoting a just and egalitarian society and fostering the redistribution of income, that were articulated in various national development plans.

Conclusion

Nigeria's policy makers and their economic advisers regarded the huge amount of revenue, which the country derived from oil in the 1970s as providing the opportunity for the rapid modernization of the Nigerian economy and society through the transplantation of Western economic and social institutions into the country. Development economists who were the main propagators of the modernization paradigm had a field day as the Rostownian linear conception of development became the yardstick for promoting economic development in the country. Successive Nigerian development plans were therefore preoccupied with achieving specific percentage of growth, attaining the "take-off" stage, redistributing the benefits of growth and meeting the basic needs of Nigerians – essentially corresponding with the various reformulations of the modernization paradigm. The preoccupation with replicating various Western institutions and "artifacts" of development underlined the various building and construction projects, socio-economic programs, industrialization, agricultural projects and even the supposedly nationalistic indigenization program.

In spite of the huge sum of money spent on replicating these institutions, the country remained in the throes of worsening underdevelopment. The economy remained undiversified as Nigeria continued to rely on oil as her primary source of foreign exchange earnings. In the circumstance, any fluctuation in the world market demand for, or prices of, crude oil was bound to have repercussion on the Nigerian economy especially given the peripheral location of the economy in the global capitalist system. This was precisely what happened in the early 1980s when the global capitalist crisis resulted in a depressed demand for crude oil, decreased oil prices and oil glut in the international market. The poor economic development strategies and the oil crisis triggered the debilitating debt and economic crises in the 1980s. However, it should be noted that these factors only helped to manifest an economic crisis that had been latent given the peripheral, neo-colonial and dependent economy that the modernization inspired development paradigm helped to promote. The economic crisis was all along, only masked by the windfall from oil and so, the oil crisis expectedly resulted in the manifestation of the crisis.

In analyzing the failure of the development programs, many scholars have adopted the modernist paradigm of blaming internal irrational and backward policies as the primary culprit. Emphasis has been placed on the specificity of irrational internal policies such as poor implementation, financial recklessness and indiscipline, mismanagement, corruption and contractocracy, among others.[61] These factors were certainly present but they were symptomatic of the peripheral capitalist diffusionist path of development promoted by the modernization paradigm and the resultant peripheral location of Nigeria in the global capitalist system. In essence, even if these factors were absent, there would still have been economic crisis because of the fundamental shortcomings of the modernization paradigm. The chief culprit therefore is the modernization paradigm, which promoted a development process that was out of tune with the prevailing social, economic and cultural realities. The paradigm and its emphasis on the transplantation of Western economic and social institutions into Nigeria merely helped to serve the exploitative economic interests of the advanced capitalist countries while simultaneously entrenching Nigeria's economic dependence and her peripheral location in the international capitalist system. Thus, the various building and construction projects which emphasized the use of imported materials, trade liberalization, import substitution strategy of industrialization, technical partnership agreements with the emphasis on the so-called technology transfer, among others, ended up promoting economic and technological dependence. Undoubtedly, the worsening level of corruption and mismanagement on the part of Nigerian elites and their foreign collaborators helped to worsen the development crisis. However, to regard these factors, as ends in themselves is to ignore the more fundamental structural factor manifested in the peripheral and neocolonial capitalist system existing in the country.

Perhaps the greatest shortcoming of the modernization-inspired economic development policies was the devaluation and marginalization of the indigenous culture, economic base, production systems and technologies. By characterizing them as primitive, backward and irrational, they were deprived of the opportunity of playing a fundamental role in the country's economic development process. Yet development is a cultural process that has meaning and relevance when based on a people's culture, social and material realities and the associated indigenously developed production systems and technology. By devaluing and marginalizing the indigenous culture, the economic development process was deprived of the cultural base necessary for a successful development process. Furthermore, the urban centered development strategies and the underlining modernization paradigm helped to undermine and truncate the indigenous production base. Significantly, the indigenous production base, which was largely located in the rural areas, was neglected, undermined and even repressed. In addition, rural women who occupied strategic position in food processing and brewing of beverages and alcoholic drinks in the rural areas were marginalized. In the circumstance, the economic development policies, which were in first place based on faulty development strategies, were deprived of the necessary indigenous cultural, social and material base upon which to strive.

Notes

1 F. Vivekananda and J. O. Ihonvbere, "Debts and Falling Oil Prices: A Case Study of Nigeria," *Scandinavian Journal of Development Alternatives*, Vol. VI, No. 4, 1987, 168.

2 The nationalization of British Petroleum was partly in retaliation for the company's role in an oil-swap agreement, which allowed Nigeria's oil to be subterraneously shipped to Apartheid South Africa and the racist regime of Ian Smith in Zimbabwe. The move was also to pressurize Britain (the colonial master of Zimbabwe before Ian Smith's Universal Declaration of Independence (UDI) from Britain in 1965) to support the holding of multiracial elections that would lead to the independence of Zimbabwe. It is alleged that this move forced the British government to accede to the demands for an all-party conference, which ultimately led to the independence of Zimbabwe in 1980. See Osaghae, *Crippled Giant*, 103 and 107.

3 Ohiorhenuan, *Capital and the State in Nigeria*, 71.

4 Vivekananda and Ihonvbere have pointed out that from the late 1970s, the Western capitalist countries and their TNCs had taken a firm decision to drastically bring down the price of oil by destabilizing OPEC. The actions they took to destabilize OPEC included, direct penetration and manipulation; stockpiling; political blackmail;

overproduction by non-OPEC states; and development of energy-saving devices. The outcome was an oil glut in the world market, which began from about 1978 and became worse in the early 1980s. See Vivekananda and Ihonvbere, "Debts and Falling Oil Prices," 172.

5 B. Beckman, "Neo-Colonialism, Capitalism, and the State in Nigeria," in H. Bernstein and B. K. Campbell eds., *Contradictions of Accumulation in Africa: Studies in Economy and State*, Beverly Hills and London: Sage Publications, 1985, 80.

6 Forrest, *Politics and Economic Development in Nigeria*, 142.

7 Onimode, *Imperialism and Underdevelopment in Nigeria*, 213.

8 See for instance *ibid.*; Forrest, *Politics and Economic Development in Nigeria*; Olaloku *et. al.*, *Structure of the Nigerian Economy*; A. Kirk-Greene and D. Rimmer eds., *Nigeria Since 1970: A Political and Economic Outline*, London: Hodder and Stoughton, 1981; and Y. B. Usman, "Middlemen, Consultants, Contractors and the Solutions to the Current Economic Crisis," *Studies in Politics and Society*, No. 2, 1984, 4-34.

9 Y. Bangura, "Overcoming Some Basic Misconceptions of the Nigerian Economic Crisis," *Studies in Politics and Society*, No. 2, 1984, 48.

10 Federal Government of Nigeria, *Public Service Review Commission, Main Report* (the Udoji Report), Lagos: Federal Government Printer, 1974.

11 Federal Republic of Nigeria, *Second National Development Plan, 1970-74*, 237.

12 Forrest, *Politics and Economic Development in Nigeria*, 148.

13 Beckman, "Neo-Colonialism, Capitalism, and the State in Nigeria," 83.

14 Forrest, *Politics and Economic Development in Nigeria*, 148-149.

15 Ibeanu, "Class Interest and Public Policy in Nigeria," 35.

16 Ibid., 36-37.

17 Forrest, *Politics and Economic Development in Nigeria*, 144.

18 Usman, "Middlemen, Consultants, Contractors," 28-29. Usman stated that the absurd high prices for cement and the resultant cement crisis, was a product of deliberate machinations on the part of Western cement monopolies and their collaborators in the Nigerian government and in the Nigerian chambers of commerce. According to him, they did everything to thwart attempts by the Nigerian government to import cement at much cheaper prices from the Soviet Union and other countries of the then Eastern bloc. He claimed that a "consignment of cement ordered by the (Nigerian) government from the USSR was hijacked in an open act of piracy near Lagos, in July 1974." Also see idem, *The Central Role of Corruption in a Dependent Capitalist Economy: The Nigerian Experience*, NISER Distinguished Lecture Series, Ibadan: NISER, 1983, 11.

19 For a summary of the findings of this tribunal, see Onimode, *Imperialism and Underdevelopment in Nigeria*, 214.

20 Federal Republic of Nigeria, *Report of the Ministerial Committee on the Causes of Excessively High Cost of Government Contracts in Nigeria*.

21 Cited in Usman, "Middlemen, Consultants, Contractors," 24.

22 Onimode, *Imperialism and Underdevelopment in Nigeria*, 214.

23 Usman, "Middlemen, Consultants, Contractors," 28.

24 Cited in Onimode, *Imperialism and Underdevelopment in Nigeria*, 214.

25 I. Eteng, "Indigenization for Lumpen-Bourgeois Development in Nigeria," in O. Nnoli ed., *Path to Nigerian Development*, Dakar: CODESRIA, 1981, 234.

26 Bangura, "Overcoming Some Basic Misconceptions of the Nigerian Economic Crisis," 49.

27 Kilby, *Industrialization in an Open Economy*, 100.

28 Adubifa, *Technology Policy in Nigeria*, 134-139.

29 Vivekananda and Ihonvbere, "Debts and Falling Oil Prices," 170.

30 In the Nigerian context, this drive for the globalization of consumption and the subsequent import dependency it created is clearly illustrated by the case of bread. For an interesting analysis of this phenomenon, see Andrae and Beckman, *The Wheat Trap*.

31 Federal Republic of Nigeria, *Third National Development Plan*, 34.

32 Federal Republic of Nigeria, *Guidelines to the Fourth National Development Plan*, 10.

33 B. U. Ekuerhare, "Recent Pattern of Accumulation in the Nigerian Economy," *Africa Development*, Vol. IX, No. 1, 1984; and Beckman, "Neo-Colonialism, Capitalism, and the State in Nigeria," 101-104.

34 Stolper, "The Main Features of the 1962-1968 National Plan," 85.

35 Federal Republic of Nigeria, *Second National Development Plan*, 31 and 33.

36 Federal Republic of Nigeria, *Third National Development Plan*, 29 and 33.

37 Federal Republic of Nigeria, *Guidelines to the Fourth National Development Plan*, 20-23.

38 Ajayi, *The Past in the Present*, 12.

39 Federal Republic of Nigeria, *Third National Development Plan*, 10.

40 Ibid., 31.

41 Federal Republic of Nigeria, *Second National Development Plan*, 143-146.

42 W. Arthur Lewis, "Reflections on the Structure of Nigerian Manufacturing Industry," in O. Teriba and M. O. Kayode eds., *Industrial Development in Nigeria*, Ibadan: Ibadan University Press, 1977, 35.

43 Quoted in *Newswatch* (Lagos, Nigeria), 8 July 1985, 11.

44 Iweriebor, *Nigerian Technology Development Since Independence*, 134-135.

45 Adubifa, *Technology Policy in Nigeria*, 146-154; and *Newswatch*, 5 October 1992, 39-41.

46 P. M. Lubeck and M. J. Watts, "An Alliance of Oil and Maize? The Response of Indigenous and State Capital to Structural Adjustment in Nigeria," in Berman and Leys eds., *African Capitalists in African Development*, 216-217.

47 Iweriebor, *Nigerian Technology Development Since Independence*, 137.

48 For details on the colonial and immediate postcolonial background to the promulgation of the decree, see Eteng, "Indigenization for Lumpen-Bourgeois Development," 219-220; and T. J. Biersteker, *Multinationals, the State, and Control of the Nigerian Economy*, Princeton: Princeton University Press, 1987, 52-69.

49 O. F. Onoge, "The Indigenisation Decree and Economic Independence: Another Case of Bourgeois Utopianism," in Nigerian Economic Society, *Nigeria's Indigenisation Policy: Proceedings of the November 1974 Symposium Organized by the Nigerian Economic Society on the Subject "Indigenisation: What Have We Achieved?"* Ibadan: The Nigerian Economic Society, 1974, 58.

50 Federal Republic of Nigeria, *Second National Development Plan*, 33.

51 Ibid., 288-289.

52 Eteng, "Indigenization for Lumpen-Bourgeois Development," 220-221; and V. I. Bello, "The Intentions, Implementation Processes and Problems of the Nigerian Enterprises Promotion Decree (No. 4) 1972," in Nigerian Economic Society, *Nigeria's Indigenisation Policy: Proceedings of the 1974 Symposium*, 8.

53 See Federal Republic of Nigeria, *Nigerian Enterprises Promotion Decree*, Decree No. 4, Lagos: Federal Government Printer, 1972; idem., *Nigerian Enterprises Promotion Decree*, Decree No. 3, Lagos: Federal Government Printer, 1977; and idem., *Second National Development Plan*, 288-289. In 1963, foreign interests accounted for 68.1 percent of the paid-up capital invested in the Nigerian economy while in 1965, foreign

ownership accounted for 61.9 percent of such capital. See P. C. Packard, "A Note on the Concentration and Profit Rates within the Manufacturing Sector, 1963 and 1965," in Teriba and Kayode eds., *Industrial Development in Nigeria*, 126.

54 The examples of two top government officials, Dr. Adetoro, a federal commissioner and Philip Asiodu, a federal permanent secretary, clearly help to illustrate the extent of abuse associated with the process. Dr. Adetoro obtained loans worth 118,932 naira from banks to purchase about 60,201 shares in 13 different companies even though at the time he was acquiring these loans and making the purchases, he was indebted to various banks to the tune of 121,959 naira. Philip Asiodu had a total credit account of 15,107 naira in various banks between 1974 and 1975 and yet was able to raise a loan of 345,000 naira in his personal capacity. A further loan of 1,105,000 naira was raised "by companies of which members of his immediate family alone or with himself as partner were sole owners." See Dudley, *An Introduction to Nigerian Government and Politics*, 118-119.

55 Ibid., 116-120; T. J. Biersteker, "Indigenization in Nigeria: Renationalization or Denationalization?" in I. W. Zartman ed., *The Political Economy of Nigeria*, New York: Praeger, 1983, 193-202; idem., *Multinationals, the State, and Control of the Nigerian Economy*, 112-154, 220-221; Ohiorhenuan, *Capital and the State in Nigeria*, 95-96; G. Williams, "Nigeria: The Neo-Colonial Political Economy," in D. L. Cohen and J. Daniel eds., *Political Economy of Africa*, Harlow, Essex: Longman, 1981, 48 and 58; and P. Collins, "Public Policy and the Development of Indigenous Capitalism: The Nigerian Experience," *Journal of Commonwealth and Comparative Politics*, Vol. XV, No. 2, 1977, 134-137.

56 Biersteker, "Indigenization in Nigeria,"; idem., *Multinationals, the State, and Control of the Nigerian Economy*, 225-242; A. Hoogvelt, "Indigenisation and Foreign Capital: Industrialization in Nigeria," *Review of African Political Economy*, No. 14, 1979, 58-68; and idem., "Indigenization and Technological Dependency," *Development and Change*, vol. 11, No. 2, 1980, 257-272.

57 Ohiorhenuan, *Capital and the State in Nigeria*, 93-94.

58 Forrest, *Politics and Economic Development in Nigeria*, 156.

59 Ekuerhare, "Recent Pattern of Accumulation in the Nigerian Economy," 63-64.

60 Graf, *The Nigerian State*, 56.

61 See for instance, Lubeck and Watts, "An Alliance of Oil and Maize," 205-207.

Chapter 8

Economic Crisis and Structural Adjustment Program

As noted in the preceding chapter, Nigeria's economy was plunged into a very severe crisis in the 1980s. Among other things, the crisis was manifested in balance of payment deficits, huge external and internal debts, heavy budget deficits, a high rate of inflation, smuggling, a low level of capacity utilization in the manufacturing industries and the worsening material condition of the majority of the populace. The severity of the economic crisis became manifest in 1982 with the rapidly diminishing foreign reserves and mounting external debts, but the crisis had been latent since the attainment of political independence in 1960 when a neocolonial political economy was foisted on the country. However, the collapse of the world oil market and the subsequent drastic reduction in government revenue from the late 1970s, which made the Nigerian government embark on heavy external borrowing and the associated high debt service ratio, aggravated the crisis. This resulted in a phenomenal growth of the country's external debt. For instance, Nigeria's external debt jumped from $1.2 billion in 1978 to $12.8 billion in 1983 and to $30 billion dollars in 1989. The external debt stabilized at between $30 and $33 billion dollars in the 1990s. In naira terms, Nigeria's external debt rose from 1.3 billion naira in 1978 to 10.6 billion naira in 1983 and then rose to 240.4 billion naira in 1989 and 3,780.2 billion naira in 2002. At the same time, the federal government's domestic debt rose from 6 billion naira in 1978 to 22.2 billion naira in 1983 and then 47.1 billion naira in 1989 and 1,166 billion naira in 2002. The huge amount needed to service the debts has siphoned a great deal of money out of the country.

Many scholars in explaining the causes of the economic crisis have advanced various Weberian and modernist explanations, which center on the irrationality of public policy and the poor implementation of development policies. Specifically, successive Nigerian governments from the late 1970s, the IFIs and various neoliberal scholars, have emphasized issues like the overvaluation of the naira, the overregulation of the economy, the uncontrolled public expenditure, the overdependence on oil as the main source of foreign exchange and government revenue, the high level of corruption, poor agricultural production and unemployment, among others.[1] It is argued that by introducing many distortions

Table 8.1 Nigeria's domestic and external debts outstanding and external reserves, 1970-2002 (million naira)

Year	Domestic Debt	External Debt	Debt Service Ratio	External Reserve
1970	1,111.9	175.0	4.3	104.6
1971	1,245.7	178.5	n.a.	132.3
1972	1,000.7	265.6	n.a.	191.6
1973	1,061.2	276.9	n.a.	241.0
1974	1,266.6	322.4	n.a.	3,112.5
1975	1,678.9	349.9	2.7	3,380.1
1976	2,630.0	374.6	n.a.	3,057.6
1977	4,636.0	365.1	n.a.	2,521.0
1978	5,983.1	1,252.1	n.a.	1,249.1
1979	7,231.2	1,611.5	n.a.	3,043.2
1980	8,231.5	1,866.8	4.2	5,445.6
1981	11,195.5	2,331.2	4.6	2,424.8
1982	15,010.5	8,819.4	16.2	1,026.5
1983	22,224.3	10,577.7	23.8	781.7
1984	25,675.0	14,808.7	33.8	1,143.8
1985	27,952.0	17,300.6	33.3	1,641.1
1986	28,440.2	41,452.4	32.6	3,587.4
1987	36,790.6	100,789.1	13.3	4,643.3
1988	47,031.1	133,956.3	29.0	3,272.7
1989	47,051.1	240,393.7	21.3	13,457.1
1990	84,124.6	298,614.4	n.a.	34,953.1
1991	116,200.2	328,054.3	n.a.	44,249.6
1992	161,200.2	544,264.1	n.a.	13,992.5
1993	261,093.6	633,144.4	n.a.	67,245.6
1994	259,360.9	648,813.0	n.a.	30,455.9
1995	248,774.6	716,865.6	n.a.	40,333.2
1996	343,674.1	617,320.0	n.a.	174,309.9
1997	359,029.1	595,931.9	n.a.	262,198.5
1998	537,490.9	633,017.0	n.a.	226,702.4
1999	794,806.3	2,577,383.4	n.a.	546,873.1
2000	898,253.9	3,097,383.8	n.a.	1,090,148.0
2001	1,016,974.0	3,176,291.0	n.a.	1,181,652.0
2002	1,166,000.7	3,780,208.9	n.a.	1,013,514.0

Sources: Central Bank of Nigeria, *Statiscal Bulletin*, Vol. 13, 2003, 100, 103 and 190; and Forrest, *Politics and Economic Development in Nigeria*, 147.

into Nigeria's economy, these factors made massive external borrowing and therefore the debt crisis (which is central to the economic crisis) inevitable.

Based on the above explanations of the causes of the economic crisis, a number of policies aimed at resolving it were implemented between 1978 and June 1985. The policies include the introduction of various forms of austerity measures; a ban on the importation of certain items in order to conserve scarce foreign exchange; an increase in import duties on a wide range of finished and intermediate goods; the encouragement and protection of local industries; and the restriction of government expenditure to essential projects. In spite of these measures, the country's economic crisis continued to worsen. On 1 October 1985, the Babangida administration promulgated a decree that imposed a National Economic Emergency on the country to last for fifteen months. The decree empowered Babangida "to introduce measures as deemed necessary to reorganise, stimulate, reactivate and improve the productive sectors of the economy." Based on this decree, the Babangida administration ordered compulsory deductions of between 2 and 15 percent from the wages, salaries and other incomes of all workers at source, to be paid into the National Economic Recovery Fund, which was established in the Central Bank. In addition, a ban was placed on the importation of rice, maize and wheat.[2]

In order to resolve the crisis the Shagari and Buhari administrations had respectively approached the IMF for a loan. However, the negotiations between the regimes and the IMF failed due to disagreements on the IFIs' insistence on the implementation of a SAP, which among other things required the massive devaluation of the Nigerian currency, the privatization of public enterprises, and the removal of government subsidies from social services. It was in the midst of the impasse between the Buhari regime and the IMF that Babangida carried out his coup. Babangida promised in his inaugural address to break the impasse with the IMF over the request for a loan – a development that tended to create the impression that his coup was a pro-IMF coup. Indeed, the *Financial Times* stated, "it was probably the first time in Africa that a government overthrow has been caused at least in part by failure to reach agreement with the IMF."[3] The appointment of Kalu Idika, a former World Bank official and a pro-IMF loan and pro-SAP advocate, as the finance minister tended to further lend credence to the perception of the coup as a pro- IMF coup.

However, given the widespread anti-IMF sentiments among most members of the public and sections of the armed forces, Babangida was weary of unilaterally committing the regime to the acceptance of the IMF loan. This would have involved the implementation of the conditions demanded by the financial institution. Hoping to win the support of the populace for the loan, he subjected the issue to a nationwide public debate. To Babangida's disappointment, the outcome of the debate was a massive rejection of the loan. Critical segments of the populace such as the Nigeria Labor Congress (NLC – which threatened a general strike if the loan was accepted), student bodies, university lecturers, market women, manufacturers, transporters, the lumpen proletariat, the urban unemployed and religious leaders, were against the taking of the loan.

In spite of the overwhelming rejection of the IMF loan by the Nigerian public, the Babangida administration was bent on implementing the measures recommended by the IFIs. Furthermore, by 1986, it was becoming increasingly difficult to service Nigeria's huge foreign debts while the IFIs and other external creditors refused to extend more credit facilities to the country unless the government implemented a structural adjustment program. The 1986 budget, dubbed a reform budget, marked the first step toward the implementation of the SAP policy. The budget, which was a balanced budget, included an 80 percent cut in petroleum subsidies, a package of export incentives aimed at liberalizing trade, the scrapping of commodity marketing boards, an adjustment of the exchange rate of the naira and a commitment to the privatization/commercialization of public enterprises. Further bans were placed on the importation of agricultural products like rice, maize, wheat and vegetable oil, various forms of taxes and levies were introduced while the servicing of foreign debts was restricted to no more than 30 percent of foreign exchange earnings. Although these measures were well received by the IFIs and Western creditors, they refused to reschedule Nigeria's debts because the reform policies did not include a commitment to a substantial devaluation of the naira. The Babangida administration introduced the Structural Adjustment Program in July 1986 within this context.

The Structural Adjustment Program

As already noted, Nigerians massively rejected the taking of the IMF loan and the associated economic reform package during the nationwide public debate. In line with Babangida's initial claim that the populace would be actively involved in the initiation of public policies, one would have expected the regime to defer to the will of the people by rejecting the implementation of the SAP. However, given the fact that the so-called commitment to public consultation was a ruse to win initial acceptability and legitimacy for his regime, Babangida went ahead to subvert the popular will by introducing SAP.[4] Indeed, this authoritarian manner of introducing and implementing SAP was in line with the position of the IFIs that only strong regimes with the political will to force the SAP measures on their populace were in the position to effectively implement the reform package. Thus, in the case of Nigeria, Rashid Faruqee observed that one factor that made the introduction of SAP an impressive beginning, was the fact that "the military government could initiate the reforms without worrying about how they might hurt some groups."[5] Nevertheless, given the widespread resentment against the meddling role of the IFIs in Nigeria's affairs, the Nigerian government decided to win general acceptability for SAP by claiming that it was an entirely internally devised and "home-grown" policy. As stated by Oyovbaire and Olagunju:

> Essentially, SAP is a nationally articulated and self-imposed economic recovery programme. It was decided upon by the (Babangida) leadership in preference to an IMF standby loan facility which on political grounds, was turned down by the Nigerian people because of what appeared to be burdensome economic conditions and implications of political subservience attached to such loan facility. But in essence, the policy measures of SAP are as rigorous as, and indeed much more rigorous than those of the IMF conditionalities, at least going by the experience of countries where programmes of economic recovery have been adopted largely to satisfy the conditions of IMF standby loans.[6]

However, it is deceptive to claim that SAP was a "home-grown" program. Realizing the resentment of Nigerians toward the imperialistic role of the IFIs, in particular, the IMF, the World Bank decided to assume the leading role in the preparation of the SAP package. Its officials covertly worked with Nigerian officials in an inter-ministerial committee set up by the Babangida regime to formulate a SAP program.[7] Forrest has clearly documented the World Bank's role in the preparation of the SAP program.

> With the political unacceptability of the IMF, the World Bank took the lead in writing and working towards the introduction of a Structural Adjustment Programme that would prove acceptable to the IMF and the Nigerian government and open the way to rescheduling. Key actors in this critical period were Vice-President Ernest Stern from Washington and the Bank's resident representative in Lagos, Ishrat Husain, a former Pakistani civil servant. Since his arrival in Nigeria in December 1983, Husain had adopted a high profile, participating vigorously in various policy debates, feeding up-to-date information to the Nigerian authorities, visiting Dodan Barracks (the then seat of power for successive military administrations), and establishing links with Nigerians favourable to World Bank policy. . . . The World Bank office in Lagos was strengthened to increase liaison with Nigerian ministries and improve data collection and analysis.[8]

In spite of its role in formulating the SAP package, the World Bank and some of its officials continued to claim that "a generally competent technical group" of Nigerian officials formulated the program after far-reaching consultations and an "intensive public debate." Furthermore, it was claimed that, the fact that the program was "not dictated by outside agencies" but, rather, was "made in Nigeria by Nigerians" made it to become a source of national pride thereby winning popular support from the populace.[9]

The centerpiece of SAP is the deregulation of the Nigerian economy through the peripheralization of the state and the ascendancy of market forces. A cardinal aspect of this deregulation is the massive devaluation of the naira through the agency of market forces. Other important aspects of the program include monetary contraction and interest rate reform, budgetary restraint and tax adjustment. Indeed, at the center of the SAP are demand-management policies through a credit squeeze and economic liberalization that will grant ascendancy to market forces.[10] In a nationwide address introducing the SAP, Babangida stated that the program "puts emphasis on price mechanism as a means of strengthening the existing demand management policies; it encourages . . . a more realistic rate of the naira; promotes replacement of direct administrative controls with greater reliance on market forces and the rationalisation of public enterprises."[11] The main objectives of the SAP are to dismantle exchange controls and adopt a market-determined exchange rate policy; to restructure and diversify the productive base of the economy in order to reduce dependence on the oil sector and on imports; to achieve fiscal and balance of payment viability; to liberalize the trade regime, rationalize customs tariffs and excise duties, and abolish price controls; to privatize and commercialize public enterprises and abolish marketing boards; to lay the basis for a sustainable noninflationary or minimally inflationary growth; and to lessen the dominance of unproductive investments in the public sector, improve the sector's efficiency, and intensify the growth potential of the private sector.[12]

Because of the overwhelming sentiment against SAP among Nigerians, Babangida sought to make the SAP pill more palatable and therefore, acceptable, by announcing that the program would only last until June 1988. The adjustment program however remained in operation after 1988. Although the Abacha regime claimed in 1994 that it had "suspended" SAP, what the regime actually did was to introduce a "guided deregulation" which lasted from 1994 to 1998. This policy did not tamper with the fundamental tenets of SAP. Thus, the adjustment program remained in operation into the 2000s. In fact, the Obasanjo civilian regime further strengthened the influence of the program on Nigeria's economic policy by appointing, in 2004, Okonjo-Iweala, a former Vice President of the World Bank as Nigeria's Finance Minister. At the same time, Soludo, who had strong connections with the World Bank, was appointed the Governor of the Central Bank.

Operating squarely from the Weberian and modernist perspectives, Lubeck and Watts justified the introduction of SAP in Nigeria based on the irrationality, indiscipline, mismanagement, and corruption that characterized the indigenous rentier capitalist class who control the Nigerian state. To them, SAP was needed to introduce discipline, rationality and calculability into the accumulation and development process in the country. According to them:

> Only greater competition, market forces, real prices, and learning from the more productive practices of foreign capital can create the social structure of accumulation to sustain indigenous capital and thus wean them from rentier distributive politics. . . . Accordingly, Babangida's decision to go for the World Bank's SAP implicitly recognized that the weakness of the state and indigenous capital required the resources of international finance capital (World Bank and IMF) in order to supply the discipline, calculability, and rationality necessary to rekindle the embers of accumulation. Thus, however painful for the weak, Babangida's SAP is best conceived as an alliance among unequal capitalist partners (international and local, state and private)-an alliance whose members are simultaneously engaged in both cooperation and competition, in order to institutionalize conditions that will enable them to "grow" their way out of the present

> crisis. Foreign capitalist involvement is, in other words, a necessary means to rationalize and discipline the restructuring of comparatively backward indigenous private and state capitalist accumulation, which is simultaneously strengthened and undermined by its dependence on petroleum rents.[13]

This analysis, which placed the reasons for Nigeria's economic crisis solely on irrational internal policies, ignores the fact that the fundamental factor responsible for the economic crisis lies in Nigeria's peripheral location in the global capitalist system. Contrary to the benevolent picture of the IFIs, painted by Lubeck and Watts in accordance with the typical Weberian fashion, the structural adjustment program of the IFIs, in fact, became the new agency through which the exploitation and peripheralization of Nigeria by international finance capital was perpetuated.

Devaluation and the Economic Crisis

Massive devaluation of the naira, which would lead to the attainment of what was described, as a market-determined realistic exchange rate for the currency constitutes the focal point of SAP.[14] This is based on the IFIs argument that the fundamental cause of Nigeria's economic crisis centers around the overvaluation of the naira, which introduced severe distortions into the country's economy. It is claimed that the nature of foreign exchange management in Nigeria in the period between 1960 and 1986 promoted a progressive overvaluation of the naira. For instance, when Nigeria joined the IMF in March 1961, its pound was pegged at par with the British pound sterling while the exchange rate between the American dollar and the British pound sterling was used to determine the exchange rate between the Nigerian pound and the dollar. However, when the dollar-gold convertibility was suspended in August 1971 and the dollar became the principal reserve currency, many countries responded by floating their exchange rates. Rather than float her exchange rate, Nigeria resorted to mainly using the floating rates of the pound sterling and the dollar to determine the value of the Nigerian pound vis-à-vis the various currencies. However, in April 1974 Nigeria stopped using the exchange rates of foreign currencies to determine the value of its own currency (the name of the currency had been changed from the pound to the naira in January 1973). An inflexible nominal exchange rate policy, which resulted in the progressive appreciation of the naira, was adopted. Thus, apart from a 10 percent devaluation of the naira in 1973 and a gradual devaluation of the naira between January 1984 and June 1986, no substantial devaluation of the Nigerian currency occurred before the introduction of SAP in 1986.[15]

In any case, it was claimed that the very high degree of the overvaluation of the naira introduced fundamental structural defects into the economy. It made imports cheaper while locally produced goods were overpriced, therefore more expensive, thereby creating import dependency and a disincentive for local industries to produce export-oriented goods. Furthermore, it was not profitable to produce primary commodities for export purposes, thus, resulting in agricultural stagnation. The result was a lack of diversification of the Nigerian economy, which continued to depend on oil as its sole source of foreign exchange. Furthermore, import dependency resulted in an extremely high demand for foreign exchange, a situation that led to a great deal of corruption in the state controlled import licensing system since demand far out weighed the available foreign exchange. In short, overvaluation was said to have introduced the following distortions into the Nigerian economy: corruption, lack of diversification of the economy, and a non-export orientation of the economy.

Given the claim that the grossly overvalued naira introduced severe distortions into Nigeria's economy, it is not surprising that a substantial devaluation of the currency constitutes a core element of SAP. The adjustment of the exchange rate was seen as crucial for the economic recovery program. It was seen as necessary in order "to curtail demand for imports, encourage capital inflows and nonoil exports, and eliminate the distortions imposed by the import licensing system-but above all to provide a realistic exchange rate for the (naira)."[16] However, this exchange rate adjustment was to be achieved through the agency of the "free" market system.

This fact accounts for the central position, which the Second-Tier Foreign Exchange Market (SFEM)-later replaced by the Foreign Exchange Market (FEM)-occupies in the adjustment program. In fact, it was specifically stated in the SAP document that the SFEM was set up to correct the serious overvaluation of the naira through the interplay of "free" market forces.[17] It was believed that massive devaluation of the naira would improve Nigeria's balance of payments position while at the same time diversifying the economy and improving the efficiency of resource allocation. This was to be achieved through the perceived positive effects of devaluation. The supposed positive effects included the discouragement of imports, which would become very expensive; the stimulation of non-oil exports, which would become more profitable; the achievement of a realistic exchange rate of the naira through the forces of supply and demand; a more efficient allocation of foreign exchange; eventual elimination of the black market involving the currency; an increase in industrial capacity utilization, an expansion of domestic production, and, therefore, a reduction in unemployment; and the restoration of creditors' confidence in the economy, thereby encouraging an inflow of capital and foreign investment.

In spite of the innovations that were introduced into the exchange rate market-the change from SFEM to FEM, the change from weekly bidding to fortnightly bidding, and subsequently the introduction of daily inter-bank bidding-the underlying philosophy remained the same. That is, reliance on the "free" market system of demand and supply to determine the appropriate value of the naira. However, it should be pointed out that reliance on the so-called free market forces of demand and supply to determine the realistic value of the naira is patently defective. For one thing, a "free" market system does not exist anywhere in the world. Even in the advanced capitalist economies, which are usually touted as "free" market economies, this is in practice not really the case. In fact since the post-World War II period, the governments of these countries have actively intervened in their economies in order to achieve their economic objectives, a phenomenon described by Callaghy as "embedded liberalism."[18]

Moreover, in developing countries, the conditions required for the effective functioning of the so-called "free" market system are completely lacking. For instance, in Nigeria, the efficient functioning of the FEM presupposes adequate funding, which in practice is not available. Furthermore, the Central Bank of Nigeria (CBN) is virtually the monopoly supplier of foreign exchange to the FEM in a system in which an oligopolistic group of banks bid for foreign exchange. From time to time, the CBN has been compelled to intervene in the market to change the "market"-determined exchange rate of the naira.[19] Thus, in such a grossly imperfect market situation it is unrealistic to rely on market forces to determine the actual value of the naira.

One of the reasons why the (S)FEM was introduced was to eliminate the bureaucratic corruption and bottlenecks associated with the import license system. Though the foreign exchange market succeeded in eliminating these problems, the locus of corruption shifted to the banks. This development is partly responsible for the unacceptable level of devaluation of the naira since the introduction of the SAP. Until January 1989, the FEM and the autonomous market existed side by side. Although the rate at which foreign currencies could be sold at the FEM was regulated, the same was not the case with the autonomous market. The cost of foreign currencies in the autonomous market was therefore very high (for instance, in December 1988, the exchange rate of the naira to the dollar at the autonomous market was N10 to $1 while the official exchange rate for the same period was N5.4 to $1). Thus, in order to make huge profits banks diverted most of the foreign exchange they earned from the bidding sessions into the autonomous market. This situation resulted in the proliferation of banks (over 100 merchant and commercial banks were established between 1986 and the early 1990s). Many of these banks did not have any branch, as their primary function was to buy foreign exchange at the official rate and sell them at huge profits, in the autonomous market. Thus, the preoccupation with foreign exchange speculation diverted the attention of most banks from those regular banking functions that are vital to the overall economic development of the country.

Table 8.2 Exchange rate of the naira to the U.S. dollar and rate of inflation, 1970-2002

Year	Official Exchange Rate	AFEM Exchange Rate	Nominal Effective Exchange Rate*	Inflation Rate (Percent)
1970	0.71	-	99.9	13.8
1971	0.70	-	100.9	16.0
1972	0.66	-	101.0	3.2
1973	0.66	-	94.3	5.4
1974	0.63	-	100.8	13.4
1975	0.62	-	100.4	33.9
1976	0.63	-	107.8	21.2
1977	0.65	-	102.6	15.4
1978	0.61	-	101.0	16.6
1979	0.60	-	98.2	11.8
1980	0.55	-	106.3	9.9
1981	0.61	-	110.4	20.9
1982	0.67	-	109.9	7.7
1983	0.72	-	109.8	23.2
1984	0.76	-	113.2	39.6
1985	0.89	-	100.0	5.5
1986	2.02	-	51.9	5.4
1987	4.02	-	14.7	10.2
1988	4.54	-	13.0	38.3
1989	7.39	-	8.9	40.9
1990	8.04	-	7.7	7.5
1991	9.91	-	6.3	13.0
1992	17.30	-	3.7	44.5
1993	22.05	-	3.0	57.2
1994	21.89	-	2.9	57.0
1995	21.89	81.02	0.7	72.8
1996	21.89	81.25	0.8	29.3
1997	21.89	81.65	0.8	8.5
1998	21.89	85.57	0.8	10.0
1999	96.02	96.02	0.2	6.6
2000	103.79	103.79	0.2	6.9
2001	111.49	111.49	n.a.	16.5
2002	120.56	120.56	n.a.	16.1

*Nominal Effective Naira Exchange Rate Indices is Trade-Weighted (Base Year: 1985=100)

Source: Central Bank of Nigeria, *Statistical Bulletin*, Vol. 13, 2003, 151, 184 & 186.

In an attempt to curb the corrupt practices of banks and shore up the value of the naira, the federal government in the 1989 budget merged the autonomous market with the FEM while introducing daily inter-bank foreign exchange bidding. However, this did not yield any positive results. The cancellation of the autonomous market did not go down well with the bankers and even with some exporters, who started clamoring for the reintroduction of the autonomous market.

Even though the government introduced Bureaux de Change where individuals could sell and buy foreign currencies using licensed private dealers, the ceiling on the volume of transactions did not make the Bureaux sufficiently attractive to exporters, many of whom preferred leaving their money in foreign banks. Consequently, the inflow of foreign exchange into the Bureaux was very low and this did not positively affect the fortunes of the naira.[20] In another attempt to deal with the situation, the CBN, in May 1989, ordered all government agencies and parastatals to withdraw their accounts from commercial and merchant banks and lodge them with the CBN. It was felt that the resultant liquidity squeeze would help to raise the value of the naira.

Due to the high degree of fluctuation in the official exchange rate of the naira, an attempt was made in 1994, with the introduction of a guided deregulation, to stabilize the exchange rate of the currency. The official exchange rate of the naira was fixed at N21.89 to $1.00. This official exchange rate remained in operation until the end of 1998. In addition, in February 1995, the Autonomous Foreign Exchange Market (AFEM) was introduced. All these measures yielded no positive result as the value of the naira continued its downward spiral. Between 1988 and 2002, the exchange rate of the naira against the dollar declined from N10 to $1 to over N120 to $1.

Thus, from a position of purported overvaluation of the naira, the currency became so extremely undervalued that the outcome was spiraling inflation. This high level of inflation in turn had adverse effects on the economy. For instance, official figures showed that the rate of inflation more than tripled between 1987 and 1988, rising from 10.2 percent to 38.3 percent and then to 72.8 percent in 1995. In spite of the very high level of inflation caused by the reckless devaluation of the naira and the severe adverse consequences of devaluation on other sectors of the Nigerian economy, neoliberal scholars have praised the massive devaluation as one of the most significant achievements of SAP. For instance, Faruqee noted that:

> Exchange rate reform has been one of the most important achievements of Nigeria's (adjustment) program. What has been most remarkable is the sustained devaluation of the naira's external value between 1985 and 1992...From 1988 to 1992, the quarterly average of the naira exchange rate per U.S. dollar depreciated by 27 percent, 58 percent, 61 percent, 67 percent, and 83 percent over the 1987 base period. . . . The dramatic decline in the exchange rate almost made (the naira) competitive, but the intermittent efforts to regulate the exchange rate have caused it to deviate significantly at times from an equilibrium rate as reflected in the observed divergence between the official and the parallel market rates.[21]

It is important to point out that in a dependent and peripheral capitalist system, such as Nigeria's, where there is shortage of foreign exchange, it is meaningless to talk of a market determined equilibrium rate for the domestic currency.

Other scholars have emphasized the supposed benefits of the "rational" devaluation of the naira on different sectors of the Nigerian economy. Such benefits include increase in government revenue, increase in the income of primary producers generally, and particularly those engaged in agricultural export production, increased efficiency in resource allocation, the ability of manufacturers to get imported raw materials relatively more easily, and improvement in capacity utilization of manufacturing industries.[22] Forrest stated that "the devaluation of the naira was a positive measure and long overdue." He noted that devaluation "strengthened the weight of the domestic market by bringing consumption more into line with domestically produced goods and services." Furthermore, by increasing the price of imports and agricultural exports, devaluation "acted to shift real incomes to rural areas where the majority of the population live."[23] The examination of the impact of devaluation and other SAP measures on Nigeria's economy will help to shed some light on the extent to which the above assertions are correct.

SAP and the Manufacturing Sector

One of the aims of SAP was to end import dependency and diversify the productive base of the economy through the resuscitation of the manufacturing sector. The program therefore "sought to correct the distorted incentive structure that encouraged excessive dependence on imports." However, the short-term strategy was to provide a sharp injection of imports that would enable production to recover while the medium-term strategy aimed at developing local technology, raw materials, and intermediate inputs.[24] These goals were to be achieved through the provision of the enabling conditions like devaluation, trade liberalization, abolition of import licensing, reduction in the number of banned import items, lifting of ex-factory price controls and the revision of tariffs.

The available evidence shows that the adjustment policies had adverse effects on the manufacturing sector, which experienced serious decline under SAP. Manufacturing output growth fell drastically from an annual average of 18.5 percent in the period 1976-85 to 2.6 percent during the 1986-98 period which was much less than the expected 8 percent growth rate needed to put the sector on the path to recovery. In fact, the period from 1993 to 1998 recorded an average negative growth in manufacturing output. Furthermore, the rate of capacity utilization in the sector experienced a downward trend, declining from an annual average of 53.6 percent in the immediate pre-SAP 1981-85 period to 41.1 percent in 1986-90. It further declined to an annual average of 35.4 and 31.8 percent in the 1991-95 and 1996-98 periods respectively.[25] The reasons given for the low level of output and capacity utilization include the massive devaluation of the naira, the high interest rates, and the inadequate credit supply to enterprises, all of which led to the escalation of the cost of production and the prices of finished goods.[26] In addition, the reports of the Manufacturers Association of Nigeria (MAN) indicate that local sourcing of raw materials declined from an average of 51 percent in 1988 to 46 percent in the first six months of 1989, and further declined to an average of 40 percent in 1999. The reasons adduced for this decline include the increases in both the cost of local raw materials, due to pressure from exports, and the cost of imported machines and spare parts due to the massive devaluation of the naira. Furthermore, between 1988 and 1989, the cost of both imported and local raw materials rose by an average of 111 percent and 98 percent respectively. This contributed to the rising cost of production and ex-factory prices of goods, and therefore a considerable decline in the demand for locally manufactured goods.[27]

Table 8.3 Average/annual growth rate of industrial production in Nigeria, 1966-1998

Year	All Industries	Manufacturing
1966-75	19.2	12.9
1976-85	5.3	18.5
1986-98	6.5	2.6
1991	6.3	9.3
1992	7.0	11.8
1993	12.3	(26.9)
1994	(1.9)	(0.9)
1995	(0.4)	(5.5)
1996	2.8	1.3
1997	6.2	0.4
1998	(4.7)	(3.9)

Source: C. M. Anyanwu, "Productivity in the Nigerian Manufacturing *Industry*," Central Bank of Nigeria, *Occasional Paper*, No. 7, December 2000, 134.

The World Bank and neoliberal scholars have asserted that devaluation, which made the prices of imported raw materials very expensive, forced Nigerian industries to be inward looking and therefore encouraged local sourcing of raw materials. Thus, there was a direct relationship between capacity and the use of domestic inputs as "capacity utilization among firms that responded to the new incentive structure by using domestic inputs tended to be higher."[28] In this regard, it is claimed that industries like textiles, leather, food, and beverages, which sourced their raw materials locally, performed well

Table 8.4 Nigeria's average manufacturing capacity utilization rates (selected industries), 1975-2002

Year	Bakery	Beer and Stout	Textiles	Leather	Radio/TV	Motor Vehicle Assembly	All Industries
1975	66.4	76.0	79.7	77.2	100.0	84.0	76.6
1976	68.2	78.7	79.8	77.2	100.0	90.5	77.4
1977	70.2	77.4	75.3	73.6	100.0	93.2	78.7
1978	71.3	83.5	80.1	72.0	58.3	85.0	72.9
1979	73.3	83.7	84.0	74.2	56.4	87.0	71.5
1980	74.4	91.9	84.4	78.4	43.3	88.5	70.1
1981	55.3	100.0	76.9	85.0	-	79.1	73.3
1982	73.9	86.0	73.6	71.8	50.1	61.4	63.6
1983	60.4	68.0	57.4	54.0	27.4	38.1	49.7
1984	60.9	62.2	46.7	36.2	27.4	24.9	43.0
1985	42.7	59.0	44.6	25.5	33.9	26.1	38.3
1986	41.5	49.8	41.3	33.1	31.1	24.9	38.8
1987	38.9	49.8	48.0	32.9	36.7	30.6	40.4
1988	35.1	59.2	54.8	45.7	34.6	22.2	42.4
1989	31.7	53.4	59.7	60.3	28.9	18.9	43.8
1990	42.3	59.2	52.2	53.0	42.3	27.9	40.3
1991	57.2	62.4	54.9	52.2	34.6	19.6	42.0
1992	32.2	-	44.3	51.2	18.2	12.7	38.1
1993	55.1	54.6	60.0	55.3	57.4	41.5	37.2
1994	25.9	28.4	38.2	25.6	30.4	31.6	30.4
1995	19.1	31.9	44.3	27.6	29.8	35.1	29.3
1996	25.9	30.5	46.5	29.1	38.7	51.0	32.5
1997	-	57.4	50.0	44.0	35.2	73.9	30.4
1998	14.5	54.2	33.4	38.7	35.9	30.5	32.4
1999	15.3	47.1	20.2	39.2	33.4	42.4	34.6
2000	30.1	49.4	21.4	37.9	36.7	41.9	36.1
2001	54.3	54.6	31.8	36.7	35.6	41.4	42.7
2002	60.6	56.3	35.5	31.8	39.6	32.8	44.3

Source: Central Bank of Nigeria, *Statistical Bulletin*, Vol. 13, 2003, 127-129.

under SAP and had a generally high percentage of capacity utilization. On the other hand, industries like motor vehicle assembly plants and electronics (radio and T.V.) which depended greatly on imported raw materials performed poorly. Furthermore, the beer and stout brewing industries and bakeries were forced to develop alternative sources of raw materials. This therefore promoted a great amount of increase in agro-industrial linkages. This optimistic assessment of the impact of SAP on some categories of industries is not quite accurate. It is true that relatively speaking, industries like textiles and leather performed better than motor vehicle assembly plants and electronic industries, but overall all industries performed uniformly poorly under SAP. In fact, the extremely high prices of locally produced raw materials made them unaffordable to industries that sourced their raw materials locally. Even then, the trend of sourcing raw materials locally started before SAP as the increasing economic crisis of the early 1980s, had forced some category of industries to start sourcing more of their inputs locally.

It has also been observed that the figure for the output of some manufacturing industries, such as textiles, were understated because "enormous amounts of Nigerian textiles are smuggled to neighboring states, due in part to overpriced currencies in the neighboring francophone states whose currency is backed by the French franc."[29] It is true that there were smuggling of some manufactured products to neighboring countries but it is debatable whether the amount of smuggled goods was "enormous." Even if allowance is made for the smuggled goods, the fact remains that the impact of SAP on industrial output and capacity utilization was quite adverse. It is important to point out that a study of the impact of SAP on the Nigerian textile industry by Adebayo Olukoshi and Hussainatu Olukoshi contradicts the optimistic picture usually painted by the proponents of SAP. Their study shows that "the Nigerian textile industry, which by 1980 was the third largest in Africa, surpassed only by Egypt and South Africa and boasting some 100 factories and 100,000 workers," was particularly hard hit by SAP. They noted that various policy measures of SAP placed the textile industry under great "strain, characterized by further closures and shortening of the working day and week." In addition, there was massive retrenchment of workers in the textile industry. Furthermore, "the collapse in purchasing power following the drastic devaluation of the Naira created a serious problem of realization for the textile industry as the market for textiles shrank and manufacturers were stuck with their products in warehouses all over the country."[30]

In the face of the astronomically high prices of goods, the income of workers remained virtually static while because of inflation, the real income of the working people declined considerably. The very high level of unemployment did not help the situation. It is therefore not surprising that various surveys by the MAN recorded a very marked decline in demand. The outcome was the closure of many medium and small-scale industries. Yet it is a well-known fact that small-scale industries in particular play a very crucial role in the economic development of developing countries. Indeed, in its half-year report for the period July to December 1999, MAN stated "a situation where over 130 member-companies of the Manufacturers Association of Nigeria shut down operations during the year under review . . . left much to be desired." Furthermore, the report observed that "unemployment in Nigeria, which at present, is at an unacceptable level, poses a great threat to the political, economic and social stability of the nation as crime, destitution, social exclusion and similar vices become prevalent."[31]

A related issue is the impact of liberalization of the trade regime on the industrial sector. The deregulation policy of the SAP failed to take into account the immense advantages that foreign and well-established industries have over Nigerian industries. Exposing Nigerian industries to the chilly winds of international competition under the pretext that the magic of the marketplace will force them to be more efficient is misguided, if not dishonest. In addition, the fact that the adjustment program ignored supportive policies specific to the industrial sector and the recessions caused by the harsh economic policies has led to "contraction without restructuring" in manufacturing. In the face of this stifling environment, Nigerian industries were not able to compete with cheap imported goods. The unfavorable policies resulted in a deindustrialization process in Nigeria. Ojo adequately captured the adverse impact of devaluation and trade liberalization on the industrial sector in Africa generally when he wrote:

> In Africa, the massive devaluation of most national currencies and the liberalization of trade regime inherent in current (SAP) policies are not geared toward an alteration of the existing comparative advantage. Indeed, they are favoring the indiscriminate importation of cheap foreign goods, while at the same time national industries are operating below capacity because of the devaluation-induced high domestic currency costs of imported raw materials and other restrictive policies. As a consequence, local industries cannot compete with these imports, and the stage is being set . . . for a gradual process of "Deindustrialization" in most-African countries.[32]

Moreover, the liberalization of imports adversely affected Nigeria's industries while overall entrenching the import dependency of the economy. Making foreign exchange considerations the centerpiece of the SAP is antithetical to the program's avowed intention of ending import dependency through the diversification of the economy. In fact, many local manufacturers abandoned their industries in favor of the importation and distribution of finished consumer goods. The demand for imported consumer goods did not contribute to the elimination of the parallel "black" market; on the contrary, it greatly helped to promote smuggling. At the same time, the industrial policy and the Debt Equity Swaps promoted by the SAP had the effect of significantly reversing some of the few gains of the indigenization program. Indeed, in order to attract foreign investment, the 40 to 60 percent limits that were placed on foreign equity participation in some sectors of the Nigerian economy under the indigenization program, were swept away. Furthermore, the procedures for foreign investment were streamlined. These policies had the potential of promoting the re-colonization of Nigeria's industries by foreign capitalists.[33]

A cardinal policy of SAP was the privatization, rationalization and commercialization of public enterprises, which were seen as inefficient, deficit-ridden and a drain on public finance. A rationale for privatization was that the public money that had been used to subsidize the enterprises could be diverted to other programs. At the same time, privatization will help to attract sorely needed foreign investors while creating more opportunities for indigenous private capital. Decree No. 25 of 1988 created the Technical Committee on Privatization and Commercialization (TCPC: renamed as the Bureau for Public Enterprises, BPE in 1995), which had the responsibility for privatizing and commercializing public enterprises. Public enterprises were classified into four categories. The first category involved the full privatization of enterprises (mainly hotels and agro-allied companies) that can be fully operational on a commercial basis. Enterprises such as oil companies, fertilizer companies, paper companies, cement companies, banks and steel rolling mills that can be partially privatized and would no longer receive subsidies from the government belonged to the second category. The third category comprised enterprises such as the Nigerian Railway Corporation (NRC), the National Electric Power Authority (NEPA), and federal television and radio stations that can be partially or fully commercialized with partial removal of subsidies. Finally, enterprises like the NNPC, the Nigerian Coal Corporation, the Nigerian Ports Authority (NPA) and the Nigerian Telecommunications Limited (NITEL), were to be fully commercialized while continuing to receive public subsidies.

By March 1992, about sixty-eight enterprises had been privatized with the government realizing about N3.3 billion from the sale of the enterprises. This was a very low amount given the number and quality of the enterprises involved. It has been asserted that by recommending the privatization of public enterprises, "the World Bank, performs a progressive role by rationalizing productive capital investment and by restraining the appetite of rentier capitalists in the interest of the majority of Nigerians."[34] The experience with privatization in Nigeria and other African countries does not quite support this assertion. Generally, privatization has led to the concentration of the resources of these countries in the hands of very few wealthy individuals while also increasing foreign control of African enterprises, yet the enterprises are sold to these individuals at very low rates. This has therefore resulted in discrimination against the poor in the disposition of collectively owned wealth, in the case of Nigeria, in the reversal of the few gains that had been made under previous indigenization policies.

Nevertheless, the poor performance of public enterprises is not necessarily due to state ownership *per se* but to a combination of factors, some of which have much to do with the inherently unfavorable neocolonial situation existing in Nigeria and other African countries. This unfavorable situation equally affects the performance of private enterprises. As noted by Riddell, the public sector in Africa is not necessarily less efficient than the private sector; it all depends on the prevailing domestic environment.[35] Furthermore, Barbara Grosh's study of Kenya's industrial sector has demonstrated that "efficiency levels in public manufacturing are comparable to those in private sector manufacturing, and that quasi-public firms combining both private and public control substantially surpass efficiency levels in the private sector considered separately."[36] Thus, privatization is not the appropriate solution to the poor performance of Nigeria's public enterprises. They should rather be reorganized and commercialized.

Moreover, the deregulation and privatization policy did not result in any substantial and sustained increase in the level of foreign private investment in Nigeria. For instance, private investment from Britain traditionally the largest foreign investors in Nigeria declined from 52.8 percent of the total foreign investment in the country in 1985 to 13.2 percent in 1995. In addition, after the 1989 to 1992 period which marked the peak of the debt equity swaps and during which the bulk of the public enterprises were sold, foreign private investment in the manufacturing and processing sector was consistently lower than in the mining and quarrying sector dominated by oil.

While the inflationary situation occasioned by the SAP created very difficult times for local manufacturing industries, the banking sector experienced an unprecedented boom, as demonstrated by the proliferation of banks, especially merchant banks. One factor that influenced this proliferation of banks was the monetarist as opposed to productionist policies promoted by the SAP. Perhaps more important is the huge amount of profit that the banks made, primarily from foreign exchange speculation. The fact that these banks concentrated on foreign exchange speculation to the neglect of the normal banking functions of helping to promote the development of the economy demonstrates the detrimental impact on the country's economy of the proliferation of banks. It is probable that it is the lucrativeness of the banking business that made the MAN (the umbrella organization of all manufacturers in the country) to apply for a license to establish a merchant bank in September 1989.[37]

The huge profit margin of the banks, among other things, introduced great distortions into the country's labor market. For instance, by offering emoluments that were far beyond what the manufacturing industries could pay, the banks attracted some strategically highly skilled personnel to the banking industry instead of the manufacturing industry. Yet as Phillips has argued, since Nigeria's economic crisis was caused mainly by the country's production structure, meaningful attempts at overcoming the crisis should comprise primarily structuralist rather than monetarist strategies.[38]

In addition, the debilitating effects of the devaluation and liberalization policies of SAP discouraged virtually all forms of manufacturing activities, and promoted capital flight, disinvestment, and worst of all, the flooding of Nigerian markets with used goods from various Western capitalist countries, a situation which Abutudu has appropriately described as the "*tokunboh*" culture.[39] Apart from the

Table 8.5 Cumulative foreign private investment in Nigeria by origin, 1970-2002 (million naira)

Year	United Kingdom	% of Total	U.S.A.	% of Total	Western Europe	% of Total
1970	444.4	44.3	230.0	22.9	224.8	22.4
1971	592.0	44.8	337.4	25.5	261.0	19.7
1972	769.7	49.0	286.6	18.2	367.0	23.4
1973	860.9	48.8	308.0	17.5	415.2	23.5
1974	832.8	46.0	300.0	16.6	459.8	25.4
1975	857.5	37.5	535.2	23.4	590.1	25.8
1976	947.2	40.5	376.2	16.1	653.1	27.9
1977	1072.8	42.4	287.2	11.3	739.0	29.2
1978	1195.3	41.7	342.4	12.0	847.6	29.6
1979	1103.6	35.0	565.8	17.9	976.0	31.0
1980	1421.8	39.3	566.2	15.6	1107.2	30.6
1981	1429.2	38.0	438.6	11.7	1350.0	35.9
1982	1993.8	37.0	1171.6	21.8	1557.6	28.9
1983	2606.8	43.8	973.0	16.4	1684.2	28.3
1984	3043.4	47.4	964.9	15.0	1659.1	25.8
1985	3594.2	52.8	860.2	12.6	1601.1	23.5
1986	5073.9	54.5	1381.5	14.8	1828.9	19.6
1987	5508.1	55.1	1198.5	12.0	2053.4	20.5
1988	4724.9	41.7	2734.8	24.1	2512.8	22.2
1989	6254.3	57.4	642.8	5.9	2440.6	22.4
1990	6828.6	65.4	209.3	2.0	1509.7	14.5
1991	7247.6	59.2	-826.7	-6.8	2840.1	23.2
1992	7808.0	38.1	6010.1	29.3	3587.1	17.5
1993*	11441.3	17.1	12051.8	18.0	39445.8	59.0
1994	12578.0	17.8	13439.4	19.0	39178.4	54.0
1995	15794.1	13.2	18482.9	15.5	77463.4	64.9
1996	16988.9	13.9	18673.2	15.2	78712.7	64.5
1997	17221.5	13.4	22442.0	17.5	80150.3	62.4
1998	31367.9	20.6	21573.6	14.2	82279.2	54.0
1999	32603.5	21.1	20084.1	13.0	83558.3	54.2
2000	32779.3	20.8	21939.6	13.9	84466.1	53.6
2001	35452.3	22.0	22626.6	14.1	86175.1	52.9
2002	36841.4	22.1	22446.9	13.5	86324.4	51.8

* The increase in the naira amount of foreign private investment between 1993 and 2002 is a product of the substantial devaluation of the naira. In real terms, the monetary value of the investment during this period was substantially lower than the pre-SAP value.

Source: Central Bank of Nigeria, *Statistical Bulletin*, Vol. 13, 2003, 195.

Table 8.6 Cumulative foreign private investment in Nigeria by type of activity, 1970- 2002 (million naira)

Year	Mining and Quarrying	% of Total	Manufacturing and Processing	% of Total
1970	515.4	51.4	224.8	22.4
1971	694.0	52.5	378.8	28.6
1972	859.7	54.7	356.6	22.7
1973	925.3	52.5	409.0	23.2
1974	818.1	45.1	520.4	28.7
1975	959.6	41.9	506.2	22.1
1976	918.9	39.3	550.7	23.5
1977	1090.8	43.1	703.8	27.8
1978	421.3	14.7	1263.4	44.1
1979	466.8	14.8	1402.5	44.5
1980	677.4	18.7	1503.9	41.5
1981	526.0	14.0	1705.7	45.4
1982	974.0	18.1	1922.5	35.7
1983	511.2	8.6	2128.1	35.8
1984	702.8	10.9	2109.3	32.9
1985	744.0	10.9	2278.1	33.5
1986	2510.4	27.0	2810.2	30.2
1987	2260.2	22.6	3122.3	31.2
1988	3403.0	30.0	3637.0	32.1
1989	636.7	5.8	5406.4	49.6
1990	1091.6	10.5	6339.0	60.7
1991	-810.0	-6.6	8692.4	71.0
1992	6417.2	31.3	9746.3	47.5
1993	27686.9	41.5	12885.1	19.3
1994	26680.0	37.7	14059.9	19.9
1995	56747.3	47.5	27668.8	23.2
1996	56792.3	46.3	29814.3	24.3
1997	59221.4	46.2	31297.2	24.4
1998	59970.5	39.3	34503.9	22.6
1999	58855.4	38.2	36282.1	23.5
2000	60710.9	38.5	37333.6	23.7
2001	61611.9	38.3	37779.6	23.5
2002	61611.9	37.0	39953.6	24.0

Source: Central Bank of Nigeria, *Statistical Bulletin*, Vol. 13, 2003, 197.

fact that these policies discouraged production, they not only reinforced and sustained the existing emphasis on distribution, but also in fact did this in the worst possible way. While previous distribution efforts concentrated primarily on the importation of new goods, the emphasis under the SAP regime has been on the importation of used goods. Moreover, the primary concern with foreign exchange speculation by Nigerian banks helped to promote the worst form of "buccaneer" or, at best, compradorial capitalism in Nigeria.

SAP, Agriculture and Rural Development

One of the main reasons used to justify the introduction of SAP was that it would help to end the reliance on crude oil as the principal source of foreign exchange through the diversification of the export base of the country. As a result, SAP "sought largely to change the incentive and price structure to enhance agricultural production, raise rural incomes, and make the regional mix of crop production more efficient."[40] These objectives were to be achieved through devaluation, trade liberalization and the abolition of commodity marketing boards. It was argued that making imports more expensive while at the same time significantly increasing the value of exports through devaluation would encourage Nigerian farmers to produce more cash crops for export. As a result, the ratio of non-oil exports would increase considerably. Furthermore, in line with the discredited policy of comparative advantage, it was argued that it was in Nigeria's interest to concentrate on agricultural production, in which the country has the advantage, as opposed to industrial production. It was equally stated that this would help to stimulate the rural economy and therefore improve the economic wellbeing of rural dwellers who had been neglected by the "urban bias" policies of successive Nigerian administrations.[41]

The abolition of the commodity marketing boards was generally hailed as a progressive measure that freed peasant farmers from the exploitative policies of the state controlled boards thereby allowing them to reap the benefits of the price increases promoted by devaluation. There are certainly some benefits associated with the abolition of the marketing boards but it is debatable whether leaving peasant farmers at the mercy of private traders and the market forces would help to protect them from exploitation, increased prices for inputs and fluctuating prices for their products. Although the abolition of the exploitative marketing boards was justified, it seems to me that there was the need to put in place some form of institutional measures that would help to protect peasant farmers from the vagaries of the free market system. The banning of the importation of selected agricultural products in order to boost domestic production and demand was not far reaching enough.

At the initial stage, it appeared as if devaluation and liberalization had helped to boost non-oil exports. This was because of the phenomenal increase in the prices of cash crops. For instance, a ton of cocoa, which sold for 1,500 naira in September 1986, sold for 27,000 naira in January 1989. However, by May 1989 (within a period of five months), the price of a ton of cocoa crashed to 7,000 naira per ton, representing an enormous 286 percent decrease. The initial great increase in the price of cocoa had made a number of farmers mobilize their resources and borrow a lot of money in order to increase the amount of cocoa they could cultivate. As would be expected, the sudden crash created a great deal of misery for cocoa farmers and even resulted in the dislocation of some families. It has been observed that the World Bank's strategy of development which is so strongly "agriculture-based and export-oriented," only exacerbates "dependence on hostile foreign markets – and indeed will lead to further impoverishment of those countries which can only export crops for which there is a limited, perhaps shrinking, demand." [42] A significant question is how do we account for this serious crash in prices? The conventional explanation usually given for this kind of occurrence includes the inelastic nature of the demand for primary commodities in the world market and the availability of synthetic substitutes. Nevertheless, Fadahunsi has pointed out that the phenomenal increases in the price of cocoa and other agricultural commodities were in the first place artificial. As he puts it:

> Between 1987 and 1989, bogus cocoa merchants invaded the cocoa trade once government yielded to IMF/World Bank pressure to disband the cocoa and other commodity marketing boards. The newbreed cocoa merchants turned out to be mostly foreigners and their Nigerian fronts who were desperately trying to repatriate some of their genuine and ill-gotten profits that had accumulated in Nigeria during the regime of controlled exchange rates. Because these foreign entrepreneurs no longer had confidence in the viability of the Nigerian monetary system and the economy, they were seeking for means to take their money out of Nigeria at all cost.

He further decried the fact that

> What makes the cocoa experience particularly unfortunate, and with it the blind ideological pursuit of the policy of deregulation by the political authorities, is the damage that has been done to the country's leading potential non-oil export and to the welfare of the cocoa farmer. There was no moment during the period when the "newbreed" cocoa farmers were offering over N20,000 per tonne to farmers that the export value of the commodity was more than . . . N15,000 . . . A more caring government should have become suspicious of the intentions of the merchants and therefore interfered in the interest of the nation and the farmers. The hands of the Nigerian state are apparently still tied by its avowed commitment to "deregulation" and the interplay of market forces in the commodity and foreign exchange markets.[43]

One significant effect of the collapse in the prices of primary commodities was the drastic decline in the volume of the exports of these commodities. Hence, cocoa exports declined from 19,526 metric tons in January 1989 to just 905 tons in

August of the same year, representing a 95 percent drop. Consequently, the contribution of non-oil exports to the country's foreign exchange earnings was very low. Of the expected revenue of $1.14 billion from non-oil exports between January and August 1989, only $405 million was realized.[44] In addition, the crash in prices of primary commodities negatively affected the income of the rural peasant producers. The very high degree of inflation considerably reduced their real incomes. The situation was not helped by the sharp rises in the prices of inputs for food crops production, which in turn promoted escalating increase in the prices of foodstuffs, thereby putting them virtually out of the reach of the overwhelming majority of farmers. Given this development, it is difficult to agree with the contention that "by increasing the price of imports and agricultural exports, the adjustment acted to shift real incomes to rural areas where the majority of the population live;"[45] thus, "the position of the poor actually improved during the (SAP)."[46] Indeed, in noting the worsening standard of living of the rural dwellers, the 1989 MAN mid-year report stated, "cases of hunger and malnutrition, the worst in the last decade were recorded in the rural areas of the country."[47] By the mid-1990s, the situation had become desperate and cases of kwashiokor, a disease caused by malnutrition in children, had become commonplace in the country.

These monumental economic hardships forced many farmers and youths to resort to what Hirschmann has described as the exit option by abandoning farming and migrating to the urban centers, thereby worsening the already acute employment situation in these areas.[48] From this perspective, the abolition of the commodity marketing boards occasioned by deregulation and liberalization can be said to have had a double-edged impact on the peasant farmers. As Bryceson and Bank noted:

> SAPs largely dismantled parastatal marketing boards that had serviced peasants' input requirements, enforced commodity standards, and provided single-channel marketing facilities and controlled prices. Their replacement by private traders was patchy, and left farmers with a more uncertain market environment, widely fluctuating producer prices, escalating input prices, and tenuous input supply.[49]

It is therefore ironic that devaluation and deregulation, which were supposedly aimed at increasing the income of farmers, ended up further impoverishing them. Indeed, the harvest of the SAP-induced agricultural reform turned out to be "a blighted one."[50] Given the empirical evidence that has been presented, the argument that devaluation, deregulation and liberalization would greatly stimulate the production and export of non-oil products, thereby enhancing the standard of living of the rural dwellers, has been proved incorrect.

SAP and the Social Sector

The SAP policies of devaluation deregulation and removal of subsidies promoted an astronomical increase in the cost of social services like health and education, thereby putting these crucial services out of the reach of the majority of the populace. In the midst of this increase in the cost of social services, government allocation of revenue to the services experienced a drastic decrease. For instance, total federal government's expenditures on health in 1990 were about 40 percent of their value in 1981 while the recurrent expenditure fell from 4.8 percent in 1978 to 2.2 percent in 1989, and capital expenditure fell from 5.4 percent in 1981 to 1.5 percent in 1989.[51] In 1987-88, education received half of what it received in 1980. Furthermore, primary school enrollment ratio, which was 98 percent in 1978-80, fell to 70 percent in 1989 while secondary school enrollment ratio declined from 29 percent in 1985 to 19 percent in 1989.[52]

Thus, while on the one hand SAP made social services unaffordable for the vast majority of the populace, the high costs of equipment occasioned by devaluation and the huge decline in government allocations led to a virtual collapse of the health and educational sectors in Nigeria. This collapse is manifested in the poor conditions of service for staff and the consequent extremely low morale, the lack of facilities, libraries that are devoid of current books and journals, and hospitals that have become consulting clinics and virtual mortuaries. Commenting on the sorry state of the health sector, Folasade Iyun, stated *inter alia*, "we are now in a position in which patients are not only required to purchase all their drugs but to shop for dressings and other medications required for even minor operations. We have thus reached the anomalous situation in which blood transfusions are not possible due to lack of blood-bags for willing donors."[53] It is from this perspective that the incessant strikes and other crises that have characterized the health and education sectors can be explained, as can the massive brain drain that these sectors experienced from the mid-1980s onward. Yet adequate performance of the health and educational sectors is crucial for the development of any country.

With regard to the effect of devaluation and the other adjustment programs on the social sector in Africa generally, Sahn has argued that the above scenario is not an adequate characterization of their impact on social services. He pointed out that there were many instances, where funding of education and health experienced considerable increases. To him, the major issue is not "whether adjustment affected the level of spending; but whether adjustment affected the way available resources were being allocated within the social sector." In a rehash of some of the familiar arguments of the proponents of devaluation and adjustment policies, he stated that too much money was being spent on secondary and university education as opposed to primary education, on subsidizing the urban elite as opposed to the rural dwellers, and on curative, hospital-based services for the urban population as opposed to preventive services, most of which would have benefited the rural dwellers.[54] Of course, this is not a correct assertion. The massive brain drain from both the health and education sectors, the frequent strikes by academics and health workers, and the numerous student demonstrations in Nigeria are clear manifestations of the adverse effects of the adjustment policies on these services.[55] Indeed, the ravages of the policies have worsened rather than helped to resolve Nigeria's economic crisis.

Nigerian Women and SAP

As is clearly illustrated by the title of the book on the impact of SAP on African women, edited by Gloria Thomas-Emeagwali, *Women Pay the Price*,[56] Nigerian women, particularly lower income women, were more adversely affected by the SAP. Indeed, official explanations of the economic crisis appeared to have taken the view that women played a special role in promoting national indiscipline. The Babangida administration therefore implemented policies on the price of food and other essential commodities, which identified women traders in the informal sector as being the "cause" of the problem and involved high levels of harassment of such women.[57] In fact, as is the case with modernist macro-economic paradigms, the macro-economic thinking in the structural adjustment program was presented in a language, which appeared to be gender neutral. However, this apparent gender neutrality is deceptive because it masked a deeper gender bias. Indeed, the macro economic thinking that underlined the SAP was based on a hidden set of assumptions that were deeply imbued with male bias.[58] The result of this gendered nature of the SAP is that "women as a social category and members of the lower class bear a disproportionate burden of adjustment."[59]

Given the modernist paradigm that underlined the adjustment program, its policies were essentially patriarchal. In view of the central role women occupied in the overall production process, the policies promoted by SAP greatly discriminated against them. For instance, in the agrarian sector, SAP's emphasis on the modernist principle of comparative advantage, which sought to promote the production and export of cash crops, favored men who dominated this sector. At the same time, the policy discriminated against women since the food crops production sector they dominated was not emphasized as investible funds were reallocated from the sector to the cash crops sector. In addition, since women play a leading role in the sale of local fast foods and small-scale food processing, they were "directly affected by the decline in purchasing power of their clientele."[60]

Furthermore, the central position women occupy in the home made them more negatively affected by SAP because they were placed in the difficult position of devising various survival strategies for the household. The women from poor households bore even greater burden. In fact:

> As home managers and mothers (women) are affected by expenditure cuts and the removal of subsidies on food and items such as fuel, etc., and are affected by cuts in

> health, education, and other social services. This is more so where women head households but is also applicable in other contexts since they are often expected to continue with household management on the lines of the pre-structural adjustment budget. In many cases the old allowances for running the household remain. In others they have shrunk or no longer exist, given the high incidence of retrenchment and unemployed husbands. For women, life after the adoption of a structural adjustment program is even worse than before, because they have to spend more time and energy in search of fewer commodities and less time is left for social activities in the community.[61]

Moreover, because of the transplanted masculinist conception of the modern sector, the adverse economic effects of SAP led to the retrenchment of more women than men in the manufacturing industries. Thus, the adjustment policies resulted in the slowing down of "the rate of proletarianization of women," in the manufacturing sector.[62] The great amount of difficulties experienced by women under SAP at both the household and non-household levels, contributed to a phenomenal increase in the degree of their participation in the so-called informal sector of the economy. The difficulties equally placed women in the forefront of the attempts at devising "multiple modes," or strategies, of survival.[63]

Conclusion

It is apparent from the preceding discussion that the role of state regulation and overvaluation in bringing about Nigeria's economic crisis has been exaggerated. As noted in chapter 7, the fundamental causes of the crisis can be located in the political economy of the dependent, neocolonial capitalist system existing in the country. In other words, the fundamental causes of the crisis go very much beyond the so-called state regulation and the inadequacies of the monetary policies pursued in Nigeria prior to 1986. It thus follows that solutions that emphasize deregulation and devaluation will not have much success; on the contrary, they are bound to aggravate the crisis.

Extreme devaluation of the naira set in motion a serious inflationary situation that resulted in the worsening of the distortions in the country's economy. Many manufacturing industries ceased to exist while the extreme decline in the real income of working people and the extremely high level of unemployment combined to pauperize the overwhelming majority of Nigerians. Phillips adequately captured the debilitating effects of devaluation and deregulation on Nigeria when he noted that the policies have made the cost of development so high that development might elude the country for a long time.[64] Similarly, in a statement released by the Nigerian Economic Society (NES) after its millennium conference on Economic Development held at Abuja in September 2000, it was noted that devaluation might make "good politics on the short run (but) dangerous economics in short to long run." The statement added that the effects of devaluation scare away foreign investment while promoting macroeconomic instability, unemployment, poverty, and low investment in the real productive sectors.[65] At the same time, extreme devaluation and deregulation helped to further entrench the peripheralization and subordination of Nigeria's economy to the interests and dictates of international monopoly capital. This is hardly surprising, for the IFIs that insisted on the implementation of these policies are agents of international monopoly capital.

A related issue is the fact that the implementation of the SAP marked a significant loss of autonomy on the part of the Nigerian government over the implementation of economic policies. Right from the Shagari period there has been widespread opposition in Nigeria to the IFIs dictated adjustment program. The public debate that the Babangida regime conducted over the IMF loan equally reflected widespread opposition to the taking of the loan and implementation of the SAP. However, acting contrary to popular opinion, the 1986 Babangida budget incorporated most of the main elements of the SAP. Among other things, the budget contained a package of export incentives incorporating trade liberalization, reduced the petroleum subsidy by 80 percent, and made a commitment to privatization. Nevertheless, although the budget mentioned an exchange rate adjustment, the naira was not devalued. The absence of devaluation from the budget made the Western creditors and the IFIs reject the reform package in the budget. In the face of this opposition, the Nigerian government decided to go against the popular will by introducing an adjustment program whose central features were the devaluation of the naira and the ascendancy of market forces, in August 1986. It is thus clear that the SAP was implemented under the *diktat* of the agents of international monopoly capital.

Given the ravaging effects of SAP it is clear that any solution aimed at overcoming Nigeria's worsening economic crisis should involve the termination of the adjustment program. Examples from all over Africa demonstrate that the structural adjustment policies have been highly detrimental to the development of African countries. In fact, in view of the contributions of neocolonial dependency to Nigeria's economic crisis, merely adjusting the neocolonial structures as prescribed by the SAP is not a credible solution. What the country needs is structural transformation programs that will help to terminate the prevailing neocolonial dependency.

Notes

1 See, for instance, D. Rimmer, "The Overvalued Currency and Over-Administered Economy of Nigeria," *African Affairs*, Vol. 84, No. 336, 1985, 435-446; N. B. Tallroth, "Structural Adjustment in Nigeria," *Finance and Development*, September 1987; R. Faruqee, "Nigeria: Ownership Abandoned," in I. Husain and R. Faruqee eds., *Adjustment in Africa: Lessons from Country Case Studies*, Washington, D.C.: World

Bank, 1994; Lubeck and Watts, "An Alliance of Oil and Maize?"; and Oyovbaire and Olagunju, *Foundations of a New Nigeria*, 33-34.

2 Oyovbaire and Olagunju, *Foundations of a New Nigeria*, 34-35.

3 *Financial Times*, 28 August 1985, cited in Forrest, *Politics and Economic Development in Nigeria*, 209. Forrest stated that Babangida appeared to have been convinced of the need for an agreement with the IMF, in the months preceding the coup.

4 Dibua, "Structural Adjustment Programme and the Subversion of Popular Will in Africa."

5 Faruqee, "Nigeria: Ownership Abandoned," 238.

6 Oyovbaire and Olagunju, *Foundations of a New Nigeria*, 35.

7 See Callaghy, "Lost Between State and Market," 306-309.

8 Forrest, *Politics and Economic Development in Nigeria*, 212.

9 Faruqee, "Nigeria: Ownership Abandoned," 238 and 245; and World Bank, *Sub-Saharan Africa: From Crisis to Sustainable Growth*, 48.

10 Federal Republic of Nigeria, *Structural Adjustment for Nigeria, July 1986-June 1988*, Lagos: Federal Government Printer, 1986. For a stimulating theoretical analysis of SAP, see M. I. Obadan and B. U. Ekuerhare, "The Theoretical Basis of Structural Adjustment Programs in Nigeria," *International Social Science Journal*, May 1989.

11 Cited by A. Fadahunsi, "Devaluation: Implications for Employment, Inflation, Growth and Development," in A. O. Olukoshi, ed., *The Politics of Structural Adjustment in Nigeria*, London, Ibadan and Portsmouth, NH: James Currey and Heinemann, 1993, 38.

12 Oyovbaire and Olagunju, eds., *Foundations of a New Nigeria*, 35-36; A. O. Phillips, "A General Overview of SAP," in A. O. Phillips and E. C. Ndekwu, eds., *Structural Adjustment in a Developing Economy: The Case of Nigeria*, Ibadan: NISER, 1987, 2; and Faruqee, "Nigeria: Ownership Abandoned," 247.

13 Lubeck and Watts, "An Alliance of Oil and Maize?," 209 and 213-214.

14 For elaborate discussion of the devaluation policy and its impact on the economic crisis, see J. I. Dibua, "Devaluation and Economic Crisis: A Political Economy Analysis," in A. Oyebade ed., *The Transformation of Nigeria: Essays in Honor of Toyin Falola*, Trenton, NJ: Africa World Press, 2002, 261-288; and Fadahunsi, "Devaluation: Implications for Employment, Inflation, Growth and Development."

15 For details on Nigeria's exchange rate policy before 1986, see I. Aluko-Olokun, "An Appraisal of the Second-Tier Foreign Exchange Market (SFEM)," in Phillips and Ndekwu, eds., *Structural Adjustment in a Developing Economy*, 56-57; and C. O. Obute, "Floating Exchange Rates and Structural Adjustment in Nigeria," in *Structural Adjustment in Nigeria: Proceedings of the Nigerian Economic Society Annual Conference, Ile-Ife, May 3-7, 1988*, Ibadan: Nigerian Economic Society, 1988.

16 Faruqee, "Nigeria: Ownership Abandoned," 255.

17 Federal Republic of Nigeria, *Structural Adjustment for Nigeria*, 9.

18 Callaghy, "Political Passions and Economic Interests," 507.

19 M. I. Obadan, "The Theory and Practice of the Second-Tier Foreign Exchange Market in Nigeria: Nine Months After," in Phillips and Ndekwu, eds., *Structural Adjustment in a Developing Economy*, 36-39.

20 The adverse effects of the limit placed on the amount of foreign exchange transactions the Bureaux de Change could carry out, made their umbrella body, the Association of Bureaux de Change Operators of Nigeria (ABCON), petition the Central Bank of Nigeria in September 2000, requesting a revision of the maximum amount allowed per transaction. Even though the maximum amount allowed per transaction had earlier in

the year been raised from $2,500 to $5,000, they argued that this amount was not enough. They further argued that the limit placed on the amount of transactions they could carry out was a contributory factor to the continuous depreciation of the value of the naira. See *The Guardian* (Lagos, Nigeria), 4 September 2000.

21 Faruqee, "Nigeria: Ownership Abandoned," 256.

22 Oyovbaire and Olagunju, *Foundations of a New Nigeria*, 36-37.

23 Forrest, *Politics and Economic Development in Nigeria*, 217.

24 Faruqee, Nigeria: Ownership Abandoned," 275.

25 C. M. Anyanwu, "Productivity in the Nigerian Manufacturing Industry," Central Bank of Nigeria, *Occasional Paper*, No. 7, December 2000, 128.

26 United Bank of Africa (UBA), *Monthly Business and Economic Digest*, August 1989, 1-2; and September/October 1995, 5.

27 See UBA, *Monthly Business and Economic Digest*, August 1989, 1-2; and *The Guardian*, 29 May 2000.

28 Faruqee, "Nigeria: Ownership Abandoned," 276.

29 Lubeck and Watts, "An Alliance of Oil and Maize?," 224.

30 Adebayo Olukoshi and Hussainatu Olukoshi, "Structural Adjustment and Female Wage Labor in the Nigerian Textile Industry," in G. Thomas-Emeagwali ed., *Women Pay the Price: Structural Adjustment in Africa and the Caribbean*, Trenton, NJ: Africa World Press, 1995, 41-42.

31 Cited in *The Guardian*, 30 May 2000.

32 O. Ojo, "Beyond Structural Adjustment: Policies for Sustainable Growth and Development in Africa," in G. A. Cornia and G. K. Helleiner eds., *From Adjustment to Development in Africa: Conflict, Controversy, Convergence, Consensus*, New York: St. Martins Press, 1994, 131.

33 J. F. E. Ohiorhenuan, "Re-Colonising Nigerian Industry: The First Year of the Structural Adjustment Programme," in Phillips and Ndekwu eds., *Structural Adjustment Programme in a Developing Economy*.

34 Lubeck and Watts, "An Alliance of Oil and Maize?," 217.

35 R. Riddell, "The Future of the Manufacturing Sector in Sub-Saharan Africa," in T. M. Callaghy and J. Ravenhill eds., *Hemmed In: Responses to Africa's Economic Decline*, New York: Columbia University Press, 1993.

36 B. Grosh, "Public, Quasi-Public and Private Manufacturing Firms in Kenya: The Surprising Case of a Cliché Gone Astray," *Development Policy Review*, Vol. 8, No. 1, 1990, cited in Riddell, "The Future of the Manufacturing Sector in Sub-Saharan Africa," 238. Also see B. Grosh, *Public Enterprise in Kenya: What Works, What Doesn't, and Why*, Boulder, CO: Lynne Rienner, 1991.

37 *The Guardian*, 28 September 1989.

38 Phillips, "A General Overview of SAP," 7.

39 *Tokunboh*, which is derived from the Yoruba language and usually given as a name to someone born overseas, was popularized in the SAP era in Nigeria by a company named *Tokunboh*, which specialized in the importation of used motor vehicles. Generally, the term is used to describe the massive importation of used consumer goods like motor vehicles, electrical and electronic equipment, clothing and shoes, and other items from Europe. See M. I. M. Abutudu, "Globalization and 'Tokunboh': Tentative Notes on Structural Adjustment, Culture and Politics in Nigeria," Paper Presented at the 22nd Annual Conference of the New York African Studies Association, Held at Binghamton University, Binghamton, 24-25 April 1998.

40 Faruqee, "Nigeria: Ownership Abandoned," 272.

41 It has been pointed out that the "urban bias" thesis which was relevant in the 1970s was no longer relevant in the 1980s. This is so because as the thesis was being deployed in the early 1980s to justify the implementation of SAP; urban populations were experiencing a drastic plunge in their real wages and salaries. When this reality eventually registered, "the urban bogey was replaced with the image of 'corrupt government officials' whose elimination propelled IFIs' stated policy objectives." See Bryceson and Bank, "End of an Era," 17.

42 M. J. Schultheis, "The World Bank and Accelerated Development: The Internationalization of Supply-Side Economics," *African Studies Review*, Vol. 27, No. 4, 1984, 13; and J. C. N. Paul, "The World Bank's Agenda for the Crises in Agriculture and Rural Development in Africa: An Introduction to a Debate," *African Studies Review*, Vol. 27, No. 4, 1984, 3-4.

43 Fadahunsi, "Devaluation: Implications for Employment, Inflation, Growth and Development," 48-49.

44 UBA, *Monthly Business and Economic Digest*, August 1989, 2 and 7.

45 Forrest, *Politics and Economic Development in Nigeria*, 217.

46 Faruqee, "Nigeria: Ownership Abandoned," 278.

47 UBA, *Monthly Business and Economic Digest*, August 1989.

48 A. O. Hirschmann, *Exit, Voice and Loyalty*, Cambridge, Mass: Harvard University Press, 1970.

49 Bryceson and Bank, "End of an Era," 13.

50 Gibbon, Havnevik and Hermele, *A Blighted Harvest*, 147.

51 F. Iyun, "The Impact of Structural Adjustment on Maternal and Child Health in Nigeria," in Thomas-Emeagwali ed., *Women Pay the Price*, 32.

52 See Faruqee, "Nigeria: Ownership Abandoned," 279-280.

53 Iyun, "The Impact of Structural Adjustment," 33.

54 D. E. Sahn, "Economic Crisis and Policy Reform in Africa: Lessons Learned and Implications for Policy," in idem ed., *Adjusting to Policy Failure in African Economies*, Ithaca, NY: Cornell University Press, 1994, 382.

55 See for instance, B. Beckman and A. Jega, "Scholars and Democratic Politics in Nigeria," *Review of African Political Economy (ROAPE)*, No. 64, 1995, 167-181; and K. A. Shettima, "Structural Adjustment and the Student Movement in Nigeria," *ROAPE*, No. 56, 1993, 83-91.

56 Thomas-Emeagwali, *Women Pay the Price*.

57 C. Dennis, "The Limits to Women's Independent Careers: Gender in the Formal and Informal Sectors in Nigeria," in D. Elson ed., *Male Bias in the Development Process*, Manchester and New York: Manchester University Press, 1995, 100.

58 D. Elson, "Male Bias in Macro-Economics: The Case of Structural Adjustment," in idem ed., *Male Bias in the Development Process*, 165-166.

59 Shettima, "Engendering Nigeria's Third Republic," 80.

60 G. Thomas-Emeagwali, "Introductory Perspectives: Monetarists, Liberals and Radicals: Contrasting Perspectives on Gender and Structural Adjustment in Africa," in Thomas-Emeagwali ed., *Women Pay the Price*, 4.

61 Ibid. Also see D. Elson, "Household Responses to Stabilisation and Structural Adjustment: Male Bias at the Micro Level," in idem ed., *Male Bias in the Development Process*, 211-252.

62 Adebayo and Hussainatu Olukoshi, "Structural Adjustment and Female Wage Labor," 45-47.

63 A. R. Mustapha, "Structural Adjustment and Multiple Modes of Social Livelihood in Nigeria," in P. Gibbon, Y. Bangura and A. Ofstad eds., *Authoritarianism, Democracy, and Adjustment: The Politics of Economic Reform in Africa*, Uppsala: Nordiska Afrikainstitutet, 1992, 188-216.

64 Phillips, "A General Overview of SAP," 7.

65 Cited in *The Guardian*, 20 September 2000.

Chapter 9

State, Youth and Women's Movements, 1986-1998

Youths and women constitute the largest constituencies that have been marginalized by the various modernization-inspired development policies in Nigeria. As has already been pointed out, the transplanted Western patriarchal model of development did not view women as important actors in the development process, rather, they were perceived as homemakers who were to play largely domestic roles. Furthermore, in spite of the enormous wealth derived from the oil boom in the 1970s, the various iniquities associated with neocolonial dependency, authoritarianism and corruption, resulted in a harvest of suffering and misery for the bulk of Nigerian youths and women in "the midst of plenty." The prevailing developmental state model of socio-economic transformation articulated by development economists promoted a bureaucratic, elitist and authoritarian state-led development process that relied on the advice of "experts" supplied by the IFIs and Western capitalist nations. This model did not only fail to involve women and youths in the development process; it equally failed to address issues pertinent to these segments of the population.

The fact that for most of its postcolonial history, authoritarian military regimes had ruled Nigeria resulted in the suppression of most institutions and avenues of dissent in the civil society. This posed some challenges that were taken up by youths whose idealism places them in a better position to oppose such regimes. Nevertheless, the struggle against authoritarian and corrupt regimes were usually championed by students because they constitute the most enlightened segment of the youths and are better organized to carry out well articulated opposition. Various women organizations were also formed in response to their marginalization and neglect as well as to various societal ills. Some women organizations, which operated mainly at the grassroots level, emphasized issues of self-help, mutual support and socio-economic empowerment.[1] There were also various market women associations that not only championed the trading interests of women but usually aligned with other deprived groups such as students and human rights organizations to protest the dictatorial and harsh economic policies of successive Nigerian administrations. These categories of women organizations largely drew their memberships from among non-elite women. Women in Nigeria (WIN), a radical feminist group, which comprised mainly radical female and male intellectuals, played in significant role in aligning with other oppositional groups to protest against various forms of authoritarianism in Nigeria. WIN was particularly active in the opposition against SAP, the endless transition programs of the Babangida and Abacha regimes, and human rights violations, among others. Indeed, it has been argued that without the leading roles played by WIN and market women, who boycotted the markets, the pro-democracy movement of the 1980s and 1990s, would not have achieved the amount of success it achieved.[2]

On the other hand, various elite women organizations, which were largely conformist organizations, and therefore did not protest against oppressive and harsh government policies in threatening ways, were formed. A significant example is the National Council of Women Societies (NCWS). Between 1986 and 1998, a new dimension was introduced into the elite-led women movement, that is, the creation of state-sponsored feminist movements – BLP for Rural Women and Family Support Program (FSP).

However, this chapter will focus on the student movement and state-sponsored feminism in the period between 1986 and 1999. Both movements exhibited contrasting tendencies in their attitude toward the World Bank sponsored SAP. The students were vigorously opposed to the structural adjustment program and the associated transition to civil rule program, which was equally aimed at perpetuating personal rule. On the other hand, the state-sponsored feminist organizations were pro-SAP, and also aimed at eliciting women's (in the case of the BLP, mainly rural women's) support for the respective self-succession bids of Babangida and Abacha.

The Students' Movement

Pre-SAP Students' Movement

Since the colonial period, Nigerian students have consistently championed the struggle against authoritarianism and corruption. They played an active role in the anticolonial nationalist activities. In 1944 the Nigerian Union of Students (NUS), which was formed in 1940, organized a series of meetings in Lagos, Nigeria: several trade union, professional, political, ethnic and literary associations were invited to these meetings. The meetings resulted in the formation of the first national political party in Nigeria, the NCNC, in August 1944. In the same year, students of Kings College, Lagos protested against the attempt to relocate them from their campus to another location so that the colonial military troops could be stationed on their campus.[3] This tradition of student activism continued into the postcolonial period. Between 1960 and 1962, students protested against the Anglo-Nigerian defence pact, which was eventually abrogated in 1962. In 1964, they protested against the outcome of the Nigerian general elections, which they perceived as massively rigged, and students of the University of Ibadan protested against the flawed Western Region of Nigeria election of 1965. However, students' activism in Nigeria assumed a greater dimension from the 1970s.

The advent of military rule in Nigeria witnessed a high amount of centralization of the administration of the country. This was accompanied by a great degree of authoritarianism and corruption. The federal system of government was subverted as the country was virtually administered as a unitary state in line with the command structure of the military. This centralization of administration at the political level was equally extended to university governance thereby subverting internal structures of democratic governance at the university level. Federal officials like the federal minister of education and the executive secretary of the NUC, on many occasions usurped the powers of university councils and made pronouncements affecting the running of universities without consulting the governing councils. The governing councils and senates of the respective universities lost their powers of setting up guidelines for the functioning of their universities, more importantly, lost the power to appoint, discipline, and sack vice-chancellors. The power to appoint vice-chancellors for the federal universities was vested in the head of state and in the case of state universities, on the governors of the state that owned the university: this resulted in the arbitrary appointment of vice-chancellors. Since the appointment of vice-chancellors became a source of patronage, many of the vice-chancellors no longer felt accountable to their university constituencies rather their primary loyalty were to those in government who made their appointment possible. The outcome was the exhibition of dictatorial tendencies as well as corruption on the part of many vice-chancellors. Similarly appointment of members of the university councils were not always based on competence and qualifications but became an arbitrary source of rewarding cronies. The undemocratic nature of university governance became a source of constant clashes between students and university authorities on the one hand, and the federal government on the other hand.

At the same time, as successive military regimes became more dictatorial and corrupt, draconian measures were taken to stifle voices of opposition in the civil society. The situation was not helped by the increasing amount of unemployment, poverty and misery in the Nigerian society. All these fuelled widespread discontent in the society but trade unions and other opposition organizations were for the most part either banned or rendered ineffective while individuals who opposed the regimes were incarcerated. With most institutions of dissent in the civil society rendered ineffective, students assumed the vanguard of dissent. Students' protests were therefore directed against authoritarianism and corruption at both the level of university governance and in the society.[4] They equally protested against the increasing rate of unemployment, poverty and misery in the face of the oil boom, as well as other manifestations of the crisis of development in the Nigerian neocolony. This linkage between issues specific to universities and societal issues became a significant mobilizational tool for the students, hence their protests became progressively more mass-based, more sustained and more radicalized.

Thus, protests over issues internal to a particular university were seen as opportunities to protest over national issues. Such crisis therefore usually spread to other Nigerian university campuses and to the cities where the disgruntled youths and other oppositional groups see students as championing their hopes and aspirations. This situation was facilitated by the increasing radicalization and the efficient organizational level of the national students' organization, which ensured that issues internal to specific universities were aggregated "into national ones, while simultaneously ensuring that issues of higher education are part of wider ideological and political concerns."[5]

However, students' crises were normally violently suppressed and extremely harsh punishment meted on those who were regarded as the principal actors in the protests. It is therefore not surprising that the first death resulting from students' protests was recorded in 1971, a situation that was to become the trend in subsequent protests. However, what can be regarded as a turning point in students' crisis occurred in 1978: this crisis set the pattern for future students' crises.

The 1978 crisis was caused by the announcement of a three-fold increase in fees by Jibril Aminu, the executive secretary of the NUC, in April 1978. Although this announcement was made in the third quarter of the 1977/78 academic year, it was backdated to the beginning of the session. The announcement was made without consultation with stakeholders in the university system and, in fact, constituted a usurpation of the powers of the respective university authorities. Students were irked by the announcement, which they saw as an unnecessary financial burden on their parents, and argued that the increase would make education an elitist commodity. Sensing that such a policy was in the offing, students had carried out widespread consultation and lobbying to ensure that it was not promulgated.

With the failure of various attempts to make the government cancel the increase in school fees, students resorted to hunger strikes, boycott of lectures and peaceful demonstrations. They argued that their parents should not be made to pay for the corruption and squandermania on the part of the government and that their action would continue until education was "made a popular commodity and not an exclusive elitist luxury."[6] The government reacted by sending a team of policemen and the military to brutally suppress the demonstrations and by April 20, ten people mostly students were killed in Zaria, Ile-Ife and Lagos. Ahmadu Bello University (ABU), Zaria was the worse hit: a combined team of policemen and soldiers were sent to the campus and by the time they left six students were dead. The brutal nature in which the demonstrations were suppressed generated massive resentment among members of the public, a situation which was not helped by the callous and arrogant statements of some federal government officials, particularly Aminu and Ahmadu Ali, the federal commissioner of education. The insensitivity of these two officials made students and the public demand their removal. The rallying demand of demonstrations, which spread to major Nigerian cities, became "Ali Must Go."

The mass-based nature of this crisis was unprecedented in Nigeria's history and indeed threatened the survival of the Obasanjo military regime. The effective mobilizational activities of the national students' body, the National Union of Nigerian Students (NUNS) ensured massive participation by students and members of the public at large. By effectively linking educational issues with national issues the public especially the youths saw students as effectively articulating their interests, frustrations, hopes and aspirations. This crisis marked a turning point in the history of student unionism in Nigeria as broader national issues rather than local welfare issues became the most significant issues on which students agitated. The crisis set the pattern for future demonstrations.

The commission that was set up to inquire into the crisis noted that "the crisis was an offshoot of the general indiscipline in the Nigerian society." It accused the federal government of operating a muddled up system of university governance and that there was an "absence of clear functional authority and role relationships among the various authorities concerned with university policy-making and execution." However, the most severe punishments were reserved for students and radical lecturers: the national leader of NUNS and leaders of the students union of ABU, the Universities of Ibadan and Benin were expelled from their respective universities. Eight professors from the Universities of Ibadan and Calabar, and Ibadan Polytechnic, as well as a student affairs officer at the University of Lagos and a journalist with the Calabar-based *The Chronicle* newspaper were dismissed from their respective positions. The sacked professors were accused of "not teaching what they were hired to teach but indulged in indoctrination of students with their preferred ideologies." Membership of student unions on individual campuses was made optional while the commission saw nothing wrong "in having a central students union body provided such a body knows its limits," but the federal government reiterated its ban on NUNS (students subsequently formed the National Association of Nigerian Students - NANS).[7] In addition, the vice-chancellors of the University of Lagos and ABU were sacked over the "ineffective" manner they handled the crisis on their respective campuses. On the other hand the police who were responsible for the massacre of students were found to have generally performed their functions adequately with the exception of Lagos where their conduct was found wanting. The commission's recommendation against the use of the army to suppress students' demonstrations was rejected by the federal government.[8]

Although student protests continued to take place on university campuses, the next one of national significance occurred in 1986. The 1986 students' crisis, which originated at ABU, Zaria, was caused by the authoritarian nature of the administration of Ango Abdullahi, the vice-chancellor, of the university. Abdullahi's administration was highly undemocratic and high-handed. He subverted the committee system of governance and was constantly at loggerheads with lecturers and students. His tenure as vice-chancellor was thus characterized by a number of disagreements with students, which usually resulted in the imposition of severe punishments on students.[9]

The factor that triggered the 1986 crisis was the commemoration of the "Ali Must Go Massacre Day" of 1978. In April 1986, the caretaker committee of ABU students' union obtained permission from the university authorities to observe the day with a peaceful procession round the campus. The procession, which from all accounts was peaceful, went through all the halls of residence in the campus including Amina hall, the female hall of residence. However, on 25 April, Mathias Yohanna, the chairperson of the students' caretaker committee, received a letter dated 23 April from the acting student affairs officer of the institution. The letter asked him to demonstrate within 24 hours why disciplinary action should not be taken against him for violating university rules and regulations banning male students from entering the female hostel. Yohanna replied that he only received the letter on 25 April, by which time the 24-hour deadline had expired. He stated that the 21 April procession was peaceful and that it was a common practice for processions to pass through all the halls of residence including the female hall. On 2 May, he received another letter from the student affairs officer asking him to show cause why he and his colleagues should not be held "fully responsible for the violation of university regulations concerning the female hostel." On 12 May, the vice-chancellor requested the chairman of the advisory committee on student discipline to convene an urgent meeting of the committee to consider a case of violation of university regulations by the students caretaker committee.

On 14 May, the six members of the students' caretaker committee wrote a letter of apology to the vice-chancellor stating among other things, that minor issues like a peaceful procession through the female hostel should not be allowed to degenerate into a crisis.[10] The students' disciplinary committee that looked into the case of the six student leaders acknowledged that it had seen the letter of apology the students wrote to the vice-chancellor, that all the students were in their final year of study, and that they showed "obvious remorse throughout their trial." In spite of these observations, the committee recommended their expulsion from the university merely adding that it "would not be averse to any lenient disciplinary action the vice-chancellor might consider appropriate in the circumstance."[11] The vice-chancellor expelled the chairman of the caretaker committee, suspended the public relations officer for the rest of the academic session and sent letters of warning to the other four members of the committee. In order to prevent the situation from deteriorating to this point the student leaders had approached various organizations and individuals to help plead their case but the vice-chancellor reportedly refused to meet with these individuals and representatives of the organizations. NANS even wrote a letter of apology on behalf of the students to the vice-chancellor.[12] The stage was therefore set for a crisis.

ABU students decided to embark on boycott of lectures and peaceful demonstration round the campus to drive home their demand for the reinstatement of the expelled and suspended student leaders. On 22 May after a peaceful procession round the campus, the students staged a sit-in action in the front of the building housing the vice chancellor's office. The vice-chancellor invited the police, which brutally dispersed the students. On the following day, mobile policemen (anti-riot police squad) invaded the campus although there was no violent demonstration: the outcome was the killing of four persons with several people injured. This police brutality generated negative reactions from all over the country, a situation that was not helped by the indifferent public statements made by the vice-chancellor and the Kaduna state police commissioner whose men were responsible for the carnage. On primetime national television news program, the vice-chancellor proclaimed that "only four" people were killed while the police commissioner justified the killings as been in conformity with the law of the land, adding, "we don't operate outside the laws of the land."[13]

The callous statements on the part of the central figures in the crisis further incensed students in other institutions of higher learning and members of the public resulting in widespread violent demonstrations in different parts of the country. The popular demands were for the sacking of the vice-chancellor of ABU, the Kaduna state police commissioner and Jibril Aminu, the minister of education (who was equally at the center of the 1978 crisis). Even usually conservative bodies like the NCWS and the Senate of the University of Ibadan described the killings as barbaric and should not be condoned in any society. The NLC - the central labor organization - condemned the killings, demanded the sacking of those individuals connected to the killings and declared 4 June 1986 a day of national mourning during which it will organize a nationwide peaceful protest. The NLC instructed its secretary general who was appointed a member of the commission set up to probe the crisis not to participate in the activities of the commission until the federal government acceded to popular demands to sack the three individuals regarded as culpable for the killings. The federal government reacted to the proposed nationwide protest by banning all public processions and declaring a state of emergency in the country. The offices of the NLC secretariat all over the country were sealed off while its key leaders were arrested. The government accused the NLC and other "extremist individuals" of using the ABU incident as a pretext to undermine the stability of the administration through subversive activities.[14]

At the sitting of the commission that was set up to probe the crisis the Academic Staff Union of Universities (ASUU), ABU branch, produced a number of compelling evidence to demonstrate that the crisis was caused by the callousness of the vice-chancellor. It further stated that the crisis could have been avoided and that the 23 May killings, "was a cold mindless multiple murder."[15] The commission exonerated the vice-chancellor stating that he was "blameless" but recommended that he should be reassigned to another position in the interest of peace. The Kaduna state police commissioner was equally found to have been "blameless" but should be posted out of the state. It recommended the retirement of the assistant police commissioner in charge of Zaria for his "gross incompetence, insensitivity and ineptitude" while the police officer that led the mobile police force into the campus should be tried for murder. The recommendation that the mobile police force should no longer be invited into the campus to suppress student demonstrations was rejected by the government with the argument that it would amount to "creating an immune territory within the nation." Similarly, the recommendation against the police use of live ammunition on demonstrating students was rejected.

Students received very severe punishments: the punishments imposed on members of the caretaker committee were upheld but the expulsion of the chairman of the committee was converted to suspension for one academic session. The ban on NANS was reiterated while student unionism in all university campuses and other institutions of higher learning was suspended. It was recommended that whenever the individual university authorities decide to lift the ban on student unionism on their respective campuses, membership should be made optional and the institutions should not assist in collecting union dues. This was aimed at causing division among the student body and paralyzing them thereby weakening their organization. The commemoration of "Ali Must Go" and similar activities were banned on all campuses. As was the case with the panel that investigated the 1978 students' crisis, some professors at ABU were accused of not teaching what they were paid to teach instead they were indoctrinating students with radical ideologies. The commission recommended that the government should look into the activities of these professors and that "if their role is inimical to the stability of government" they "should be flushed out of the universities." Furthermore, the NLC was warned not to interfere in student union activities.[16] In addition, the federal government announced that with the exception of the Obafemi Awolowo University, Ile-Ife and the Kaduna Polytechnic where acts of "intolerable lawlessness" accompanied the protests, other institutions of higher learning could reopen on 14 July 1986.

Although after 1986, Nigerian universities continued to experience students' crises, many of the crises, which originated from essentially local issues, remained localized with NANS lending its support. One important lesson that students learned from the 1986 crisis, was that the Babangida regime was determined to weaken student unionism in order to be able to successfully implement its modernist-inspired authoritarian programs, most importantly SAP. Student activists in most Nigerian universities therefore went underground to map out strategies for combating the authoritarian military rule.[17] Thus in the post 1986 period, NANS became much more political and concerned itself more with national issues. This was because the military regimes had not only become more authoritarian and corrupt but had imposed an unpopular structural adjustment program on the country, whose implementation further increased their degree of authoritarianism. The debilitating effects of SAP as well as the manipulation of the transition to civil rule program by first, Babangida, and later, Abacha, in such a way that they would perpetuate themselves in office, engaged most of the attention of NANS.

The Anti-SAP Demonstrations

As was pointed out in chapter 8, the severity of Nigeria's economic crisis, which became apparent in 1982, resulted in the introduction of various neoliberal policies supposedly aimed at resolving the crisis. Since one of the most significant ways in which the crisis manifested itself was the debt crisis, successive governments had sought the assistance of IFIs, notably the World Bank and the IMF, in rescheduling the debt and in providing further loans. However, the Shagari and Buhari regimes saw the implementation of some of the conditions of the IFIs like massive devaluation of the national currency and removal of subsidy from petroleum products and the social sector as politically risky. While they were prepared to implement some of the conditions, issues like massive devaluation of the currency and the removal of petroleum subsidy were seen as too sensitive: this resulted in an impasse in the negotiations between the World Bank, and the Shagari and Buhari regimes respectively. In spite of these disagreements, the two regimes took some incremental steps to meet some of the demands of the World Bank. In the educational sector, the measures included the closing down of many institutions of learning especially at the primary and secondary school levels, the reduction in the level of subvention to institutions of learning and the removal of centralized catering services. In addition, various forms of fees and levies as well as user charges were introduced.[18] In line with its modernist perspective, the World Bank argued that these measures would help to bring the educational system in line with the practice in the Western countries. However, the measures had significant negative impacts on the educational sector. The drastic reduction in the level of subventions to the universities had adverse impact on teaching, research and infrastructural development. For instance, in 1987, the recurrent grant to the universities was reduced to just 30 percent of the amount normally received and by 1989, the grants available to the universities were only sufficient to pay staff salaries. Furthermore, drastic devaluation adversely affected the local book industry while imported books became so expensive that many students could not afford them.[19]

Although contrary to popular opposition the Babangida regime introduced SAP in 1986, some of the economic policies of the regime were seen as not far reaching enough by the IFIs. They insisted that there should be substantial removal of subsidy from petroleum products and social services, as well as more drastic devaluation of the national currency. Nevertheless, the manner in which the adjustment program was introduced, its debilitating effects on students and other Nigerians, and the attempts to satisfy the further demands of the World Bank became sources of conflicts between students and the government leading to anti-SAP demonstrations, notably in 1988, 1989 and 1990. Students were strongly opposed to the neomodernization policies of SAP, which they saw as having serious adverse effects on the overwhelming majority of the populace.

By April 1988, the main outstanding issue between the IFIs and Nigeria over the country's request for the IFIs' endorsement of its structural adjustment program was the removal of petroleum subsidy.[20] The World Bank and the IMF were scheduled to meet in April/May 1988 during which Nigeria's request for an endorsement of its SAP would be considered.[21] This meeting was therefore critical for Nigeria's debt rescheduling efforts but there had been widespread opposition from students, the NLC, market women associations, WIN, ASUU, and other organizations in the country to the removal of petroleum subsidy. The Babangida administration realized that such a move was politically risky and decided to shift the responsibility to the NNPC. In preparation for this move, the government had instructed the NNPC to operate along commercial lines in March 1988. It was within this context that the NNPC announced increases in the prices of petroleum products on 10 April 1988.

This increase attracted massive opposition from students and some other organized interest groups. Students argued that the increase would make prices of various essential commodities to skyrocket and so worsen the economic predicament of Nigerians: they and other Nigerians called on the federal government to rescind the decision. Since the government refused to accede to this request, students decided to embark on boycott of lectures and peaceful demonstrations until the government rescinded the decision. Students of the University of Jos marched to the government house to present their letter of protest to the state governor who promised to forward the letter to the head of state. The peaceful demonstration at Jos turned violent when the law enforcement agents resorted to the use of force to suppress the student protesters whose ranks had been swelled by other members of the public who joined the protests. By the end of the day, the police killed at least six people. This repressive reaction and the skyrocketing prices of essential items like food and transportation made the protests to spread to other Nigerian cities. The massive nature of the participation in the protests and the fear of a mutiny within the ranks and file of the armed forces led to further brutal repression of the protests.

The government accused the students of been manipulated by enemies of the administration that were bent on bringing about the collapse of the regime. David Mark, the minister of communications clearly stated this point when he argued that students were acting under the spell of external influence because they do not own cars and were therefore not affected by the increase in the prices of petroleum products.[22] The government ordered the closure of higher educational institutions in the country and the head of state assumed the power of reopening the institutions. NANS was banned while its leadership and leaders of some student unions in some institutions were detained.

After this demonstration, the government embarked on measures aimed at dividing the student body and weakening NANS. The police and university vice-chancellors started taking measures to prevent the holding of NANS national leadership and delegates meetings on university campuses. Rival pro-government student organizations were sponsored on campuses while members of secret cults were enlisted to intimidate and harass NANS leadership and leaders of campus student unions affiliated to NANS (the beginning of the destructive role of secret cults on Nigerian university campuses can be largely traced to this period). Attempts were equally made to use religious and ethnic differences to cause disagreement among NANS members. These measures largely failed as NANS continued to operate and command the loyalty of the majority of the student body in spite of all the intimidation. As noted by Ade Ajayi, government's reliance on the destruction of student unionism as the only effective answer to student protests did not succeed in stopping these protests. On the contrary, "it encouraged outside financing of students and perhaps also contributed to the spread of (destructive) cultism," on the campuses of institutions of higher learning.[23]

Given the worsening harsh economic effects of SAP, students were determined to prevail on the government to abandon the SAP-based policies. The 20th Senate meeting of NANS in November 1988 came up with a ten-point demand, which the government was expected to fulfill within six weeks. The demands were essentially opposed to the SAP-induced free market enterprise. They included the abolition of SAP, the stoppage of SAP-induced rationalization of courses in higher institutions, increase in university funding and the guarantee of free education for all Nigerians up to the secondary school level.[24] The failure to meet these demands sparked the nationwide anti-SAP protests in May 1989. Various members of the society like unemployed youths, workers, and market women participated in the protests, which turned out to be violent. The government again blamed the protests on the hands of enemies of the government who were making use of students as proxies and the head of state specifically appealed to the military not to allow such elements to force the government out of office. Government ordered the closure of universities and other institutions of higher learning while leaders of NANS and other Nigerian citizens were arrested and detained. The government eventually ordered that the closed institutions be reopened in early July 1989, but six universities would remain closed until March 31, 1990, because of "the intolerable lawlessness displayed by their students with widespread riots, arson and rampage spreading into the surrounding city areas."[25] The closure of these institutions attracted widespread condemnation and the government eventually reversed the decision after series of appeals from Nigerians.

In spite of the draconian response to the anti-SAP protests, the government realized that the public who were suffering from the serious negative effects of SAP supported the students' actions. The government therefore announced SAP relief measures, which included the allocation of money to the education sector, employment of more teachers and the creation of more jobs. Nevertheless, the government was still determined to curb the influence of students. It promulgated the Student Union Activities (Control and Regulation) Decree 47 of 1989 under which student unionism was confined to individual campuses and membership was made voluntary. Student unions could be proscribed if their activities were determined to be inimical to the interest of the nation. In a direct usurpation of the powers of individual university authorities, the decree stated that the minister of education could expel any student from any higher institution of learning.[26]

The decision to take a World Bank loan to be used to restructure the educational sector sparked the students' protest of April 1990. Students' grudge centered on the conditions associated with the loan, which were seen as highly detrimental to the educational sector and would truncate the desire by many Nigerian youths to acquire higher education. In complete disregard to the realities of the Nigerian situation, the conditions sought to transplant the prevailing situation in the education sector in the advanced Western capitalist economies, into Nigeria. The conditions included increase in school fees, rationalization of undergraduate and graduate programs, retrenchment of university staff, an increase in internally generated revenue, and reduction of government's expenditure on the university sector. Student protest against this loan started at ABU, Zaria and subsequently spread to other Nigerian universities. Students' pointed out that these conditions amounted to the deregulation of the education sector and the introduction of the unfair so-called free market system into the sector. They noted that the commercialization of university education and the rationalization of academic programs would make higher education elitist and beyond the reach of majority of Nigerians. They equally protested the role of the IFIs in Nigeria's affairs and saw this as amounting to the recolonization of the country. The government resorted to its usual reaction of closing down universities and reaffirming its ban on NANS. Events have proved that student protest against this loan was justified as it is now generally accepted that the loan largely created an opportunity for the sale of obsolete books, other instructional materials, and irrelevant and obsolete technologies to Nigerian universities.[27] This is a clear example of the use of the IFIs and the modernization paradigm to serve the economic interests of the advanced capitalist countries.

Students' protest against the harsh effects of SAP continued well into the 1990s. In April 1991, NANS issued a thirty-day ultimatum to the federal government, which clearly called for the termination of the neoliberal economic and social policies. Its demands included the scrapping of SAP, the institution of a social security scheme for all Nigerians, provision of employment for Nigerians, nationalization of all transnational corporations in Nigeria and stoppage of the practice of closing institutions of higher learning during students' crisis. The government took this ultimatum seriously because the period of its expiration coincided with the OAU ministerial and heads of state meetings to be held at Abuja in May/June. It therefore prevailed on different interest groups and prominent Nigerians to put pressure on NANS not to embark on protest at the expiration of the ultimatum. NANS eventually decided to withdraw the ultimatum.

In May 1992, NANS decided to protest against the deteriorating material conditions of Nigerians occasioned by the continued implementation of SAP. May 13 was billed as a day of non-violent mass protest against the Babangida administration and the prevailing harsh effects of SAP. NANS planned to launch an economic manifesto during that day, which was to serve as "an alternative agenda to the IMF-induced structural adjustment programme." The manifesto demanded the dissolution of the presidential advisory committee, which was accused of having failed to live up to its expectation of properly articulating the country's economic problems and providing the proper focus for development. The manifesto also demanded considerable increase of the value of the currency, the discontinuation of the interests paid on Nigeria's external loans and the imposition of a 10 percent education tax on the profits of transnational companies operating in Nigeria.[28]

The protests, which started in Lagos spread to other parts of the country. The attempts by the law enforcement agencies to suppress the demonstrations increased their level of violence. Various government properties were destroyed while a number of people were killed. In order to curb the protests various institutions of higher learning were closed down. The minister of information accused some misguided persons of taking advantage of an otherwise peaceful demonstration by students to create social chaos. It is important to point out that students had consistently criticized the nature of the inherited authoritarian neocolonial state apparatus and, they in fact, advocated the reform of the state apparatus. However, they were extremely critical of the power of the market in effecting the necessary changes. Indeed, their alternative programs to the SAP insisted "on an extension of the state sector, under popular control, and the introduction of a planning system." Such alternative programs would help in protecting some of the few postcolonial gains in public welfare and living standards threatened by the structural adjustment program.[29] Nevertheless, another significant issue that attracted the attention of students was the authoritarian manner of the implementation of the transition to civil rule program.

Students and the Transition to Civil Rule Programs

Nigerian students' consistently opposed military intervention in the country's politics. They saw such interventions as detrimental to Nigeria's development as well as the democratization process as they constantly bred authoritarianism and corruption in the Nigerian society. Students constituted a constant thorn on the flesh of the Gowon regime because of its failure to come up with a credible transition to civil rule program. Thus, when Mohammed seized power from Gowon in July 1975 and immediately committed to a transition program, as well as introducing measures to curb corruption in the Nigerian polity, students massively supported his administration. His assassination in a failed coup in February 1976 was widely condemned by students who defied the threats and warnings of the coup plotters and took to the streets to protest against the coup. The commitment of Obasanjo to the transition program initially won him the support of students but this support ended with the 1978 crisis.

Students opposed the Buhari regime, which overthrew the civilian regime of Shagari, because of its failure to commit to a definite democratization process and the draconian policies that it pursued. Babangida capitalized on these shortcomings of the Buhari regime when he seized power in July 1985. He immediately promised a transition to civil rule process and that the policies of his regime would be anchored on the respect for human rights. This won his regime initial massive support from students and other Nigerians.

However, as the Babangida transition to civil rule program unfolded and it soon became clear that he was not really intent on handing over power to a civilian regime unless the process led to his succeeding himself in office, students championed the opposition to the program. Students also opposed Abacha's self-serving transition to civil rule program on similar grounds. As discussed in chapter 4, both Babangida and Abacha embarked on repressive and authoritarian transition to civil rule programs that were aimed at perpetuating themselves in office. Individuals and groups who opposed their self-serving transition programs were intimidated and repressed. In the case of Babangida, the consolidation of SAP was made an integral part of his regime's transition program. Thus, the objectives of SAP were to be consolidated at every stage of the program. Democratization therefore appeared to be more of a strategy of checkmating popular opposition to SAP and fostering self-perpetuation in office. This making of the structural adjustment program an integral part of the democratization process and the seriously flawed nature of the transition program, made students to join forces with other relevant groups in opposing the transition program. In essence, students' criticism was directed at the authoritarian and repressive manner of the implementation of the structural adjustment and transition programs, and not to a genuine and credible democratization process. They were also critical of the neoliberal linkage of free market economy to liberal democracy as well as the neoliberal endorsement of authoritarian state sponsored democratization process that would help in consolidating the objectives of SAP.

Based on the senseless manipulation of the transition program and the realization that the program constituted a journey to nowhere, students joined other democratic forces in demanding an end to the transition program and the scrapping of various so-called transition institutions, like the Mass Mobilization for Social Justice and Economic Recovery (MAMSER) and the BLP that the regime had established. They equally demanded the convening of a sovereign national conference, which will fashion out a democratization program for the country as well as the establishment of an interim national government to implement the democratization program. For instance, the 1991 NANS ultimatum called for the scrapping of the political transition program and the BLP, which was seen as an avenue for the private accumulation of Nigeria's resources and for mobilizing support for Babangida's self-succession bid. In order to make their campaign for the termination of military rule more effective, students and other civil society groups decided to coordinate their campaign by coming together to form an umbrella organization, the Campaign for Democracy (CD) on 11 November 1991. The CD campaigned vigorously for the termination of military rule no later than October 1992 and persistently called for the convening of a sovereign national conference. When therefore in June 1993, the Babangida administration annulled the result of the generally acclaimed free and fair presidential election, the resentment of students could not be contained. They aligned with other democratic forces to champion the protests that accompanied that annulment and helped to put in place a sustained massive resistance that led to Babangida quickly handing over power to a hastily contrived interim national government under the leadership of Shonekan.

In addition, when Abacha overthrew the interim regime and went on to institute a naked dictatorship and a transition program designed to lead to his self-perpetuation in office, students played a leading role in opposing his designs. NANS embarked on sustained criticism and protest against the policies of this regime in spite of its extremely repressive character and the fact that it resorted to political assassinations against its enemies. It is not an exaggeration to say that the eventual inauguration of the Fourth Republic in Nigeria in 1999 can be largely attributed to the fearless and sustained struggle for democracy waged by students and other pro-democracy groups. Indeed, the 1990s, which can be characterized as the pinnacle of opposition against authoritarianism and in favor of democratization in Nigeria, owe this distinction to the sustained protests of students working in alliance with other pro-democracy groups.[30] They became the main voice of dissent when many other civil institutions in the country were emasculated.

State-sponsored Feminism

Better Life Program

The Better Life Program, launched in September 1987, was one of state-sponsored programs supposedly aimed at empowering the grassroots that the Babangida regime launched between 1985 and 1993. The other programs included the DFRRI, National Directorate of Employment (NDE), MAMSER, and local government reforms. The significance of these programs can be better understood if they are situated within the context of the massive resentment generated among the populace over the debilitating effects of SAP. Indeed, as previously pointed out, in Nigeria and other African countries, the harsh effects of the adjustment policies had resulted in various popular protests against the programs and demands for their termination. The World Bank and other proponents of SAPs, argued that these protests only emanated from disgruntled urban-based individuals and organizations, as well as students. They recommended the implementation of policies that would empower rural dwellers in order to counter the influence of urban dwellers and create alternative basis of support for the structural adjustment policies. Perhaps the most profound statement in this regard, was contained in the 1989 World Bank publication entitled *Sub-Saharan Africa, From Crisis to Sustainable Growth: A Long-Term Perspective Study*. The report, which was couched in populist language, recommended issues like democratization, grassroots empowerment, women empowerment and rural development.[31]

Beckman's incisive critique of the World Bank's report has clearly demonstrated that by emphasizing the need to empower the civil society, particularly the grassroots, the World Bank sought to delegitimize the nationalist and popular resistance to SAP through the appropriation of some of the ideological armor of the opposition.[32] It is from this perspective that the various contradictions in the report can be understood. For instance while the document advocated grassroots empowerment, it at the same time supported authoritarian tendencies so long as this would lead to the consolidation of the objectives of SAP.[33] In fact, the World Bank's version of empowerment, which is for those who support SAP rather than its opponents, is a managerial populist approach that fits well with the populist political practices of the regimes implementing SAP and even helps to justify repression against the "vested interests" that resist SAP.[34]

Thus, in order to correctly appreciate the *raison d' être* for the populist policies of the Babangida administration, the policies should be situated within the context of the desire to undermine the opposition to its unpopular policies, especially SAP. This resulted in the attempt to create alternative basis of support, for the regime and its adjustment policies from among the rural dwellers who were supposedly the beneficiaries of the adjustment policies. According to Bangura, given the belief that price reforms and devaluation would benefit the rural dwellers, some African governments "tried to mobilise the rural groups to counter the political weight of the organised urban sector." But this did not succeed as peasants remained "sceptical of crucial aspects of the reforms such as fluctuations in prices, the withdrawal of subsidies from farm inputs, escalating costs of production, and general levels of inflation that affect their consumption of traded goods."[35] Nevertheless, as was the case with the state-sponsored 31st December women's movement in Ghana,[36] the Babangida administration in Nigeria decided to single out rural women as an important group among the rural dwellers on which to create an alternative basis of popular support for his regime's policies. In fact, the BLP was portrayed as part of the structural adjustment program with both programs committed to "tackling the social, cultural, political and economic disabilities afflicting the (rural) women folk in Nigerian society."[37] Although the name of the BLP was changed to Better Life Program for Rural Dwellers in 1990, women remained the primary focus of the program.

The main aim of the BLP was the creation of a new rural woman who would be economically strong, politically active, socially aware, psychologically fulfilled and, therefore, adequately equipped to play her role in the society more maximally.[38] Toward this end, the following objectives were to be pursued:

1. The creation of awareness in women so that they could realize, utilize and develop their potentials in order to lead a more fulfilling life.
2. Encouragement of the education of women in all its ramifications - functional, formal and informal.
3. Raising the social consciousness of women about their rights as well as their social, political and economic responsibilities.
4. Encouragement of self-sufficiency and income generating activities in order for women to be able to reap adequate benefit from their labor and therefore enjoy some economic independence.
5. Bringing women together and closer for a better understanding and resolution of their problems through collective action.
6. Mobilizing women for concrete activities towards achieving specific objectives, including seeking leadership roles in all spheres of national life.
7. Highlighting the plight of women in all aspects of life in Nigeria.
8. Educating rural women on simple hygiene, family planning, the importance of childcare and increased literacy rates.
9. Drawing attention to the problems and needs of rural communities.[39]

These objectives were to be achieved through enlightenment campaigns, workshops, seminars, and trade fairs. In addition, social and economic projects would be executed in the rural areas while efforts would be made to facilitate the access of rural women to funds and credit facilities. Issues like adult literacy, home economics, crafts, improved agricultural practices, improved water supply, primary health care programs such as immunization, oral rehydration therapy and family planning would be emphasized.

The organizational structure of the BLP clearly reflected the elitist nature of the movement. Better Life Committees (BLC) were set up at the national, state and local government levels, with the wife of the head of state, wives of state governors and wives of local government chairmen, as the chairpersons at the various levels. The other members of these committees were drawn from the elite class. In addition, each state had an advisory board for the BLP comprising elite women like commissioners, director generals, heads of parastatals, high court judges and general managers. In any case, while the better life committees at the local government level were charged with initiating and executing projects in the rural areas, those at the state and national levels were responsible for monitoring the implementation of the projects. According to Mariam Babangida, this integrated and coordinated feedback strategy would provide a systematic networking and help to facilitate the constant review of projects so that fresh ideas could be introduced as soon as they became necessary.[40]

In line with the recommendation of the United Nations Decade for women, Decree 30 of 1989 established the National Commission for Women (NCW) with the primary responsibility of promoting the welfare of Nigerian women in all its ramifications.[41] Among other things, the NCW was supposed to supervise and streamline the activities of the BLP. In the words of Mariam Babangida, the NCW was the "ideological and administrative wagon of the Better Life Programme."[42] In spite of this claim, the first lady was not happy with the idea of subordinating the BLP to the NCW and, so, refused to allow the BLP to become a department under the NCW. However, Decree 42 of August 1992 restructured the NCW to include the appointment of an advisory council with the first lady as the chairperson, as well as a Director General for the Commission. The advisory council was responsible for "advising, guiding and monitoring the National Commission and better life programme for rural women."[43] It was only after this restructuring that the BLP was made a department of the NCW. Each state had its own commission on women located in the state governor's office.

With the elitist orientation and organization of the BLP, rural women whose plight was supposedly the main reason for the creation of the program were not involved in the initiation and execution of projects that were purportedly aimed at improving their material and social conditions. Rather, in a patronizing way, the urban-based elite women saw it as their responsibility to determine the projects that would serve the interests of rural women. Mariam Babangida justified this attitude by stating:

> The blind cannot lead the blind. The people at the top are educated, more educated and more comfortable than the people in the rural areas. They need educated urban women who must map out strategies to assist in solving the problems of the rural poor. We have the privilege, we are very influential and so we are certain and well assured that whatever plans we have would be for the benefit of the rural people . . . . The rural people are voteless and powerless. How then can they lead themselves? It is the urban educated women that would have to lead them.[44]

It is ironic that elite women who "are almost by definition unproductive, even at the household level"[45] and whose interests coincided with those of the patriarchal state which exploited and undermined the rural women, could claim that they were better placed to decide what would benefit the rural women.

There is no doubt that rural women were in the best position to understand their own plight and therefore recommend programs that would help to emancipate and empower them. Jadesola Akande has criticized the belief by policy makers and elite women that they are better placed to know what would benefit rural women as patronizing and condescending. She noted that given the different situation and experience of the urban-based elite women on the one hand, and the rural women on the other hand, there are always serious divergences of opinion between them on most issues.[46] Indeed, one of the greatest factors that have militated against the success of rural development programs in Nigeria is the patronizing attitude of urban-based government officials.[47]

In practice, the various activities of the BLP like the organization of seminars, trade fairs and the commissioning of projects were reduced to occasions for fanfare, flamboyant and ostentatious display of wealth by the first ladies at the various levels of government and other elite women. Apart from the display of some products of rural women during the trade fairs, they were hardly visible on these occasions that were supposedly for their empowerment. It is because of this that the better life program was derisively dubbed by members of the public as "Better Life for Rulers Women."[48]

As already pointed out, the significance of the BLP can be better understood if the program is situated within the context of the Babangida regime's attempt at undermining popular and democratic opposition to SAP while creating a new basis of popular support for the regime's SAP influenced policies. In essence, a primary aim of the regime was to use the BLP to construct a new basis of popular support for its SAP-inspired undemocratic, carefully teleguided and "test-tube" programs of political and socio-economic transformations. Hussaina Abdullah has observed that the BLP and similar elitist and conservative women organizations "have taken their role to be the mobilisation of women in support of the transition programme and the SAP."[49] Given the regime's belief that the opponents of its policies were mainly urban-based elites, it felt that one way to undermine the opposition was by wooing the rural dwellers, particularly rural women. According to Mariam Babangida "there is need for us to create the necessary awareness among our rural womenfolk of government's efforts in ensuring a smooth transition to civil rule."[50] Beckman clearly put the issue in perspective when he stated:

> In the face of nationalist and popular resistance, the theoreticians of SAP - along side the attempt to delegitimise resistance - seek to establish an alternative basis of popular legitimacy. The notion of grassroots empowerment seems central to this exercise.[51]

Bujra has noted that state-sponsored feminist organizations such as the BLP "play a role of social control on behalf of (the ruling) class as a whole; they do almost nothing to transform the position of the majority of women."[52]

An important question that arises is, to what extent was the BLP able to promote the empowerment of rural women in particular and Nigerian women in general. Some scholars have identified two types of gender interests, which feminist movements serve: they are practical gender interests and strategic gender interests.[53] Practical gender interests are related to women's immediate concerns such as health care, provision of water, and material goods, all of which are important for family survival and community welfare. These conform to the patriarchal notion of socially accepted role for women and so do not challenge gender inequality and women's subordination.[54] According to Maxine Molyneux, practical gender interests "do not generally entail a strategic goal such as women's emancipation or gender equality . . . nor do they challenge the prevailing forms of subordination even though they arise directly out of them."[55]

On the other hand, strategic gender interests pursue transformative goals in the sense that they are committed to women's emancipation and equality through the eradication of policies, such as, gender division of labor and unfair relations of power. Caroline Moser states that: "strategic gender needs are those needs which are formulated from the *analysis of women's subordination to men,* and deriving out of this the strategic gender interest identified for an alternative, more equal and satisfactory organization of society than that which exists at present, in terms of both the structure and nature of relationships between men and women. (emphsis in the original)"[56] Strategic gender interests therefore involves the pursuit of women's interests in a way that is perceived to be threatening and subversive of the patriarchal order. Thus by their nature, practical gender interests aim at meeting immediate and short term gender needs while strategic gender interests aim at meeting long term gender needs. It follows that any meaningful attempt at promoting women empowerment should not only meet practical gender needs, but should also meet strategic gender needs. The assessment of the BLP would therefore involve the extent to which the program was able to bring about positive transformation in the social, cultural, economic and political status of women - particularly the rural women, as well as promote women's emancipation, autonomy and gender equality.

An analysis of the activities of the BLP would show that attempts were made only at addressing the practical needs of women to the neglect of their strategic needs. For instance, the BLP did not seriously address issues like social, political, legal and cultural discrimination against women. The BLP clearly accepted the inherited western patriarchal viewpoint of women as homemakers who are primarily concerned with the survival of the family and welfare issues. As observed by Amina Mama:

> The BLP was not only high profile and expensive. It was also extremely conservative. On no occasion did Mrs Babangida give a public address without distancing herself from any kind of 'women's lib' or feminism, by stressing that the first duties of women are the traditional ones of wifehood and motherhood.[57]

At best, the activities of the BLP were based on the Women in Development (WID) paradigm, which itself was squarely situated within the modernization paradigm.[58] Indeed, the better life program's WID approach to the gender question rested "on the principle of 'integrating women into the development process', and on the assumption that women's 'backwardness' will end once women are absorbed into the mainstream of industry, commerce, education and politics."[59] This WID approach has been criticized for its preoccupation with the integration of women into development programs without seriously addressing the important issues of empowering women, particularly rural women, through freeing them from various forms of cultural, societal, patriarchal, gender, and class oppression and exploitation.[60] Furthermore, the approach tended to view "development" as something done by development agencies and women are "in" it as far as they are recipients of projects and programs. Thus, third world women were assigned a passive role in a development process guided by mainly Western modernist "experts."[61]

Moreover, the failure of the BLP to address the issue of rural women empowerment from the wholistic and strategic perspective further helped to perpetuate the subordinate position of women in the Nigerian society. In addition, since rural women were not involved in the initiation and implementation of rural development projects, such projects tended to be conceived from the point of view of satisfying the needs of rural men. Women continued to carry out the cumbersome, low esteemed and low paying activities such as domestic activities, farming, food processing and retail trading. For programs like the BLP to be effective, rural women have to be involved in initiating and implementing projects that would substantially improve their economic, social, educational and psychological status. An analysis of the better life projects commissioned in the former Bendel State, Nigeria, in the period between November 1987 and December 1990, will help to substantiate the fact that the BLP was mainly concerned with the traditional areas of food production and processing, handicrafts and gin distillery. For instance of the 59 projects, which were commissioned, 46, that is, 77.97 percent were food related while 13, that is, 22.03 percent were non-food related. The emphasis on these traditional domestic activities helped to reinforce the unequal sexual division of labor and the subordination of women. However, it was hoped that by encouraging rural women to produce more food, which could be sold at cheaper prices especially in urban markets, some of the harsh effects of SAP could be minimized and urban riots prevented.[62] In fact, the emphasis on food production was meant to serve dual purposes. As the most marginalized segment of the Nigerian society and given the domestic functions of rural women as producers, home managers and mothers, they were at the forefront of the receiving end of the adverse effects of SAP.[63] Increased food production was therefore expected to meet the food requirements of rural families while the money derived from the sale of surplus could be used to meet some other family requirements. Furthermore, the emphasis on food production was meant to continue to promote the domestic orientation of women.[64]

Unfortunately, Mariam Babangida and other urban-based women elite extravagantly spent the enormous resources that accrued to the BLP from the federal and state governments, and their agencies. For instance, at the national level, the better life fairs became avenues for ostentatious and extravagant display of wealth as well as wastage of the nation's resources. Particularly notorious in this

Table 9.1 Number and type of BLP projects in Bendel State, Nigeria, November 1987-December 1990

Type of Project	Number of Projects	Food Related	Non-Food Related
Garri Processing	32	Yes	No
Home Economics	1	Yes	No
Nursery/Primary Schools	1	No	Yes
Corn Milling	1	Yes	No
Food Canteen	1	Yes	No
Cloth Weaving	4	No	Yes
Shopping Complex	4	No	Yes
Gin Distillery	2	No	Yes
Rubber Processing	1	No	Yes
Fishing Boat	1	Yes	No
Yam and Plantain Flour	3	Yes	No
Transportation Boats	1	No	Yes
Goatery	3	Yes	No
Citrus Farm	1	Yes	No
Sugar Cane Farm	1	Yes	No
Piggery	1	Yes	No
Starch and Cassava Processing	1	Yes	No
Total	59	46	13
Percentage	77.97	22.03	

Source: Bendel State Government, *Handbook on Better Life Programme in Bendel State*, 34.

regard was the second better life fair, which was held at Abuja in September 1990. All the delegates from the then 21 states of the federation were flown to Abuja and accommodated in five star hotels at government's expense. Indeed, apart from the high amount of publicity which the BLP attracted for the first ladies at the respective levels of government (particularly Mariam Babangida at both the national and international levels), the program did not, and could not, contribute meaningfully to the empowerment of rural women. Nor did it succeed in the enterprise of creating an alternative basis of popular support among the rural women for the Babangida regime and its unpopular structural adjustment policies.

Rather than seriously address the issue of women empowerment, the BLP was busy using the country's resources to attract international attention to Mariam Babangida and to win international support for the policies of the Babangida regime. For instance, the BLP co-sponsored and hosted the United Nations Economic Commission for Africa women's meeting in November 1989, which attracted women delegates including some first ladies from different parts of

Africa. The BLP sent delegates to various international trade fairs with the ostensible purpose of displaying the products of rural women. These activities succeeded in attracting some international recognition to Mariam Babangida: the most significant being the award of the 1991 African leadership prize for the sustainable end of hunger, which was awarded to her and Wagari Maathai (the 2004 Nobel Peace Prize Winner). It is significant that while Mariam Babangida accommodated and supported the patriarchal policies of the Nigerian state, Wangari Maathai, transformed her Green Belt Movement (GBM) from an environmental movement into an activist movement that genuinely advocated environmental sustainability, rural development and women empowerment. Furthermore, she joined forces with other popular activist groups to advocate for genuine democratization and the empowerment of the vast majority of the Kenyan populace. Wangari Maathai's activist and confrontational posture earned her the anger of the Kenyan government and as a result, she was subjected to various forms of official intimidation and even death threats.[65] Wangari Maathai and Mariam Babangida were therefore not on the same pedestal in terms of fighting for women's rights, empowerment, and democratization.

The most generous thing that can probably be said about the state-sponsored BLP is that its so-called feminism merely amounted to tokenism. In any case, since the BLP was a creation of the patriarchal neocolonial state, the program rapidly became a reflection of the undemocratic and decadent structures of the Nigerian state as epitomized by the authoritarian and corrupt practices. Indeed, the case of the BLP is a clear example of how an undemocratic state cannot promote popular and democratic movements and structures. This point becomes more apparent when it is realized that in spite of the fact that all women suffer from societal oppression, they do not experience oppression and exploitation equally. The social classes to which they belong determine the experiences of Nigerian women. Thus, the interests and aspirations of women are dictated by their class positions.[66] It should be realized that most Nigerian elite women attained their social status by virtue of their affiliations and linkages to the male ruling class. As a result, the interests they pursue coincide with those of the neocolonial patriarchal state. As observed by Staudt "elite women, increasingly dependent on husbands and privileges of their household and class, may work politically to advance the interests of their class."[67] According to Fatton:

> While (all) women suffer similar patriarchal impediments, they do not have the same aspirations, desires, and needs. Urban women and peasant women, bourgeois women and proletarian women, old women and young women have more contradictory interests and lifestyles than could ever be surmounted by their common experience of sexual submission.[68]

Family Support Program

With the demise of the Babangida regime and that of the Shonekan-led interim national government, Mariam Abacha, the wife of the new head of state decided to launch a new state-sponsored feminist movement, the family support program, instead of continuing with the implementation of the BLP. The introduction of the FSP was justified on the ground that unlike the BLP, which was "elitist, theoretical and flamboyant (in) nature and outlook", the new program was geared toward promoting "not only the cause of women but the entire family system for wholistic development of the society."[69] However, in spite of this explanation, the FSP was nothing more than a mere modification of the BLP. The structure, nature of operation and focus of the FSP were essentially similar to that of the BLP. In fact, as was the case with the better life program, the family support program was largely a personality and first lady issue. As noted by O. Alubo, the launching of the FSP could be seen as just another first lady program whose life span would depend on that of the regime.[70] Furthermore, the FSP was equally aimed at creating a new basis of popular support for the Abacha regime, which was perhaps, far more draconian and authoritarian than previous military regimes. Like the BLP, the significance of the FSP can be situated within the context of trying to divert attention from the untold hardship caused by the continued implementation of SAP, and the effects of the unprecedented draconian, authoritarian and repressive policies of the Abacha regime, on the average Nigerian family. It follows that the observations that were made with regard to the BLP are equally applicable to the FSP.

The FSP was inaugurated in 1994 and was purportedly primarily aimed at supporting and protecting the family as an entity and its living conditions. The focus of the FSP was the family, but the main targets were women and children, particularly rural women and children who are usually most affected by poverty. The program was expected to concentrate its activities on poverty alleviation, community mobilization, child welfare and youth development, disability and destitution, health, education, women in development, agriculture and income generation.[71] To accomplish these tasks, the program would focus on microenterprise, microfinance and microcredit schemes in addition to promoting infrastructural development particularly in the rural areas. A Family Support Trust Fund (FSTF) was created by Decree No. 10 of 1995, to provide the funds for the implementation of the activities of the FSP. A management board set up to administer the trust fund was responsible, among other things, for:

1. Receiving monies accruing to the Fund.
2. Disbursing monies from the Fund to such programs as may be determined, from time to time, by the head of state.

3. Promoting decent health care delivery with the general purport of reducing maternal and child mortality and morbidity through improved health care delivery system for the family.
4. Assisting families identify economically viable enterprises for income generation and provide technical and financial support for their implementation.
5. Assisting rural families increase their agricultural productivity and other skills for the improvement of their wellbeing.
6. Enhancing the capacity of parents to act as role models to their children through guidance and counseling and public enlightenment programs.
7. Creating, arousing and sustaining the interests of the federal, state and local governments, the Nigerian people, and the international community on the activities of the family support program.
8. Sensitizing government on the need to provide adequate shelter for all Nigerians.
9. Promoting and improving the welfare of the most vulnerable and disadvantaged groups in the society, notably women.
10. Carrying out public enlightenment campaigns for the general public on matters of human decency, civic responsibility and concern for the welfare of the disadvantaged.[72]

The organizational structure of the FSP was similar to that of the BLP: it was elitist and emphasized first ladyism. The first lady headed the national committee at the federal level, the wives of state administrators headed the state committees, and the wives of local government chairmen headed the local government committees. The common people were not involved in the decision making process. Like the BLP, the FSP cashed on the newfound populism on the part of the World Bank and other development agencies, which as already pointed out, were actually aimed at delegitimizing popular opposition to the harsh effects of the neoliberal economic policies. This attempt at portraying the FSP as a populist and grassroots development oriented program led to the launching of the Family Economic Advancement Program (FEAP).

Family Economic Advancement Program

The family economic advancement program was launched in 1996 to help in actualizing the FSP's commitment to the empowerment of Nigerian families through poverty alleviation. FEAP, which was an offshoot of the FSP, was organizationally under the control of the first lady who was the chairperson of the board. At the state level, the chairperson of the FSP chaired the state coordinating committee of FEAP while local government chairmen chaired the local government coordinating committees with the local government chairpersons of the FSP as members of the committees. Coordinating committees were also created at the ward level. FEAP was therefore largely a first lady affair. Nevertheless, FEAP mainly aimed at economically empowering the low-income Nigerian families "by providing them with opportunities for harnessing indigenous technologies and also to encourage local initiatives through increase in local productivity and income."[73] Thus, as an economic empowerment program, FEAP was expected to "mobilise and support the rural economy and the urban informal sector of Nigerian economy so as to improve the standard of living of the low income group."[74] Furthermore, it was expected that indigenous skills, plant, machinery and equipment fabricated in Nigeria would largely constitute the cornerstone of the program thereby helping to lay the foundation for the country's technological take-off.[75] Some of the objectives of FEAP include:

1. To provide loans directly to people at ward level thereby providing them with the capital needed to set up and run cottage enterprises.
2. To encourage the design and manufacture of appropriate plants, machinery and equipment.
3. To create employment opportunities at the ward levels.
4. To improve the standard of living of the people.
5. To encourage producers at the ward level to form cooperative societies.
6. To utilize all available local resources for the benefit of Nigerians, through improved production, storage, preservation, processing, recycling, packaging and marketing.
7. To involve the private sector, states and local governments in the funding of the production activities.[76]

The initial funding for the program was to be provided by the federal government and the funds were to be disbursed to qualified groups through selected financial institutions: subsequent funding would be provided by states, local governments, the private sector, international agencies and organizations. FEAP would only fund the microenterprises of cooperative societies that have been formed by individuals with common interests and objectives. The primary target was cooperative societies formed by low-income groups in the rural areas and the urban informal sector who usually lack the required collateral to obtain loans from commercial banks. It was believed that given the "apparent feminization of poverty" in the sense that women constitute the bulk of the poor and low-income groups, this microfinancing strategy would considerably contribute to the empowerment of women.[77] Thus, any cooperative society applying for a FEAP loan must comprise both men and women. The group applying for the loan must provide 10 percent of the amount requested as a sign of commitment to the proposed project. Since no collateral was required, this amount and the machinery and equipment purchased with the loan would serve as the security for the loan. The interest rate for the loans was fixed at 10 percent and the loan would be redeemed within a period ranging from three months after the commencement of production to three years from the lending date of the loan.[78] It has been claimed that from its inception in 1997 to May 1999, the sum of 6.8 billion naira was disbursed as loans to 20,719 cooperative societies.[79]

At the superficial level, it can be said that FEAP targeted the group of people that had been neglected by successive government policies. However, as previously pointed out the significance of programs such as FEAP can be properly understood if they are situated within the context of the attempts by the IFIs and the Abacha regime to undermine the popular opposition against the harsh effects of SAP. The concepts of microenterprises, microfinance and microcredit that underlined FEAP were based on the modernist populist policies propounded by the World Bank, the United Nations Development Program (UNDP), other international financial and aid agencies, and Western capitalist governments in the wake of the devastating effects of SAPs on third world countries.[80] In addition, the extremely dictatorial Abacha regime saw FEAP as a means of winning some form of legitimacy for the regime. Furthermore, even the little amount of benefits that would have been derived from FEAP was vitiated by the fact that as a first lady program, FEAP was essentially used to promote massive corruption and the personal aggrandizement of the first lady. The fact that the FSP and FEAP were merely first lady programs was clearly demonstrated by the decision of the Obasanjo civilian regime to strip the first ladies at various levels of government of their roles as chairpersons of the programs in October 2000. This was because their activities constituted a usurpation of the functions of the women affairs ministries.[81] The FSP and FEAP were eventually scrapped and their functions transferred to the ministries of women affairs at the federal and state levels.

It is clear from the discussion of the BLP, FSP and FEAP, that the programs were mainly elitist and self-serving. Indeed, under the guise of women empowerment, the first ladies sought to use the programs to mobilize the support of rural women for the oppressive and self-serving policies of their husbands' regimes. Ifi Amadiume has argued that the BLP and FSP were used by the first ladies as instruments for undermining the autonomy of women's organizations and to take-over the control of the women's movement with a view to gaining wealth, status and prestige. She noted that the first lady cult became an instrument for class reproduction and personal aggrandizement in the name of empowering women.[82] These state-sponsored feminist movements promoted what has been characterized as "femocracy" rather than women empowerment.[83] Furthermore, femocracy exploits "the commitments of the international movement for greater gender equality while actually only advancing the interests of a small female elite, and in the long-term undermining women's interests by upholding the patriarchal status quo." It is therefore apparent that the BLP, FSP and FEAP only paid lip service to the interests of the poor rural women while serving as avenues for the consolidation of gender inequality, and the oppressive, exploitative and patriarchal social order.

Conclusion

The majority of youths and women constitute part of the most marginalized segments of the Nigerian society in spite of the immense contributions they have made to different aspects of the society. The Political Bureau traced the origin of this marginalization to the colonial period. Since students (the most active segment of youths) were in the forefront of the anticolonial movement and, in fact, constituted the militant wing of the movement, the colonial regime harbored a large dose of anti-student sentiments. This anti-student sentiment was carried over into the postcolonial period as students' protests against various forms of injustice, oppression and exploitation, were often ruthlessly suppressed. The introduction of capitalist relations under colonialism greatly contributed to the decline of the role of women in the Nigerian society. The influence of the transplanted western modernist and patriarchal policies on development and social policies fostered the marginalization of the majority of Nigerian women who were mainly rural peasant producers and members of the informal urban sector.[84] The consistent students' protests against authoritarian and dictatorial regimes in postcolonial Nigeria resulted in the constant attempts at ruthlessly suppressing the student movement. In the case of women, various tokenist policies that sought to incorporate a few elite conformist women into the male dominated power structure were put in place but the majority rural and urban poor women remained neglected.

The severe adverse effects of the SAP, the high level of authoritarianism the implementation of the program fostered, and the authoritarian and self-serving construction of democratization process by the Babangida and Abacha regimes, promoted an unprecedented high level of popular opposition against both regimes. This popular opposition got to its peak in the 1990s. Since students were uncompromisingly opposed to the neomodernist structural adjustment policies, which the IFIs and Western creditor nations insisted that the Nigerian administrations continue to implement in spite of the debilitating effects of the program, students crises were ruthlessly suppressed. Furthermore, some women organizations notably market women and the radical WIN joined forces with students and other popular opposition groups to mount a sustained campaign against SAP and the authoritarian construction of the transition to civil rule program. The desire to undermine the popular opposition to SAPs in various African countries and create an alternative basis of support for its neoliberal policies, made the World Bank to come up with its own version of populist policies that were supposedly aimed at empowering rural women, and other rural dwellers. It is from this perspective that the launching of the BLP, FSP and FEAP can be partly understood.

As already pointed out, the BLP, FSP and FEAP constituted attempts at delegitimizing and undermining the democratic and popular opposition to the SAP-inspired harsh and unpopular policies of the Babangida and Abacha regimes. Since the regimes felt that the opposition was mainly from urban-based associational groups and individuals, they sought to create a new basis of popular support from among the rural dwellers. Hence, the emphasis on programs purportedly aimed at empowering the grassroots. Nevertheless, given the fact that the state-sponsored feminist programs emphasized short-term practical gender interests, as opposed to long-term strategic gender interests that are crucial for ending gender inequality and for transforming the status of women, the programs were not in the position to promote women empowerment. Thus, the state-feminist programs did not succeed in empowering rural women or in creating a new basis of popular support for the Babangida and Abacha regimes. Among other things, their antecedents, class alignment, authoritarian and undemocratic nature, were inimical to the fostering of women empowerment. The examples of the BLP and FSP clearly show that state-sponsored feminist movements merely amount to tokenism: they cannot promote women empowerment.

Notes

1 See E. T. Lucas, "Social Development Strategies of a Non-Governmental Grassroots Women's Organisation in Nigeria," *International Journal of Social Welfare*, Vol. 10, No. 3, 2001, 185-193; and idem., "We Decide, They Decide For Us: Popular Participation as an Issue in Two Nigerian Women's Development Programmes," *Africa Development*, Vol. XXV, Nos. 1 and 2, 2000, 75-98.

2 Shettima, "Engendering Nigeria's Third Republic," 86.

3 Olusanya, *The Second World War and Politics in Nigeria*, 66-74.

4 For a detailed discussion of this form of protest, see J. I. Dibua, "Students and the Struggle Against Authoritarianism in University Governance in Nigeria," in P. T. Zeleza and A. Olukoshi eds., *African Universities in the Twenty-First Century: Vol. II: Knowledge and Society*, Dakar: CODESRIA, 2004, 459-479.

5 Beckman and Jega, "Scholars and Democratic Politics in Nigeria," 177.

6 U. Sani, *The Dynamics of Students' Unionism in Nigeria*, Kano: Bagauda Press, 1979, 83.

7 Although successive Nigerian governments refused to recognize NANS, except for a brief period in 1985-1986, when the new Babangida administration in search of legitimacy and acceptance from students removed the ban, the organization continued to operate effectively and continued to command the respect of students all over the country. Indeed, unlike NUNS, whose membership was restricted to university students, NANS represented universities, polytechnics and colleges of education students. It therefore had a very large constituency, which helped to make its activities more widespread thereby making it difficult for the government to ignore it. In the early 1990s, NANS represented a student population of 220,000 at the university level and 320,000 at the polytechnic and colleges of education level. See Beckman and Jega, "Scholars and Democratic Politics in Nigeria," 175.

8 For the commission's full report and the federal government's reaction to it, see Federal Republic of Nigeria, *Government Views on the Report of the Commission of Inquiry into the Nigerian Universities Crisis, 1978*, Lagos: Federal Ministry of Information, 1978.

9 See *Newswatch* (Lagos, Nigeria), 23 June 1986, 16.

10 All the letters cited were reproduced in Academic Staff Union of Universities (ASUU), *The Killings at A.B.U.: Friday 23 May, 1986*, Zaria: Academic Staff Union of Universities, 1986, 67-77.

11 Ibid., 77-82.

12 See Ibid., 87-96; and *Newswatch*, 23 June 1986, 18.

13 *Newswatch*, 9 June 1986, 15-16; and 16 June 1986, 4.

14 *The African Guardian* (Lagos, Nigeria), 19 June 1986, 20.

15 *Newswatch*, 23 June 1986, 14. Also see J. D. Ojo, *Students' Unrest in Nigerian Universities: A Legal and Historical Approach*, Ibadan: Spectrum Books and IFRA, 1995, 53-54.

16 For details on the recommendation of the commission and the federal government's views on the report, see Federal Republic of Nigeria, *The Federal Military Government's Views on the Commission of Inquiry into Student Crisis at the Ahmadu Bello University, Zaria, May 1986*, Lagos: The Federal Government Printer, 1986.

17 I. O. Albert, "University Students in the Politics of Structural Adjustment in Nigeria," in T. Mkandawire and A. Olukoshi eds., *Between Liberalism and Oppression: The Politics of Structural Adjustment in Africa*, Dakar: CODESRIA, 1995, 380.

18 Shettima, "Structural Adjustment and the Student Movement in Nigeria," 83.

19 Albert, "University Students in the Politics of Structural Adjustment in Nigeria," 377.

20 The IFIs' endorsement of Nigeria's structural adjustment program was crucial because both the IFIs and Western creditor nations made such an endorsement a condition for further loans and for debt rescheduling. This therefore placed the IFIs in a position to dictate economic rescheduling policies to Nigeria and other African countries. See Dibua, "Journey to Nowhere," 119.

21 Shettima, "Structural Adjustment and the Student Movement," 84.

22 *The African Guardian*, 2 May 1988.

23 J. F. Ade Ajayi, "Foreword," in Ojo, *Students' Unrest in Nigerian Universities*, xiii.

24 Shettima, "Structural Adjustment and the Student Movement," 86.

25 *Newswatch*, 10 July 1989, 9.

26 Shettima, "Structural Adjustment and the Student Movement," 86.

27 See B. Bollag, "Nigerian Universities Start to Recover from Years of Violence, Corruption and Neglect," *The Chronicle of Higher Education*, 1 February 2002.

28 *Newswatch*, 25 May 1992, 11-17.

29 Y. Bangura, "Authoritarian Rule and Democracy in Africa: A Theoretical Discourse," in Gibbon, Bangura and Ofstad eds., *Authoritarianism, Democracy and Adjustment*, 67 and 75.

30 See Dibua, "Nigeria: Opposition, 1990s, to the Fourth Republic," 1123-1125.

31 World Bank, *Sub-Saharan Africa: From Crisis to Sustainable Growth*. These issues were reiterated in subsequent reports. See for instance, idem., *World Development Report: The Challenge of Development*, Washington, D.C.: The World Bank, 1991; and idem., *Adjustment in Africa*.

32 Beckman, "Empowerment or Repression?," Africa Development, 45-72.

33 World Bank, *Sub-Saharan Africa: From Crisis to Sustainable Growth*, 54-62.

34 Beckman, "Empowerment or Repression," 58.

35 Bangura, "Authoritarian Rule and Democracy in Africa," 66.

36 For a general discussion on the attempt by the Jerry Rawlings administration to create an alternative basis of popular support for his regime and the structural adjustment policies of his regime, see D. Rothchild, "Rawlings and the Engineering of Legitimacy in Ghana," in I. W. Zartman ed., *Collapsed States: The Disintegration and Restoration of Legitimate Authority*, Boulder, CO: Lynne Rienner, 1995, 49-65.

37 National Commission for Women, *SAP and the Nigerian Women: The Better Life Programme Experience*, Abuja: National Commission for Women, n.d., 6-7.

38 Mariam Babangida, "Women: The Nutritional Bedrock of African Society," Text of an Acceptance Speech at the Award Ceremony of the 1991 African Leadership Prize for the Sustainable End of Hunger, Church House Conference Center, London, 30 September 1991; and Oyovbaire and Olagunju eds., *Foundations of a New Nigeria*, 45-46.

39 Better Life Programme, *Better Life Programme for Rural Women*, Lagos: 1990, 9; Better Life Programme, *Better Life Fair for Rural Dwellers*, Lagos: Alimbar Tribune, 9; and Bendel State Government, *Handbook on Better Life Programme in Bendel State*, Benin City: n.d., 7.

40 Babangida, "Women: The Nutritional Bedrock of African Society."

41 Federal Republic of Nigeria, *The National Commission for Women*, Decree No. 30 of 1989, Lagos: The Federal Government Printer, 1989.

42 Babangida, "Women: The Nutritional Bedrock of African Society."

43 *The African Guardian*, 16 November 1992, 25.

44 Cited in *The Guardian* (Lagos, Nigeria), 28 September 1991. Also see *West Africa* (London), 30 September - 6 October 1991, 52.

45 A. Mama, "Feminism or Femocracy?: State Feminism and Democratisation in Nigeria," *Africa Development*, Vol. XX, No. 1, 1995, 52.

46 J. Akande, "Women and the Law," in A. O. Obilade ed., *Women in Law*, Louisiana and Lagos: Southern University Law Center and Faculty of Law, University of Lagos, 1993, 23-24.

47 See for example, Dibua, "Government's Agricultural Policy and Rural Development in Nigeria," 40-53; idem, "Local Government and Rural Development in Nigeria Within the Context of Development Planning," *Journal of Rural Development and Administration*, Vol. XXII, No. 1, 1990, 1-16; S. K. T. Williams, *Rural Development in Nigeria*, Ile-Ife: University of Ife Press, 1978; and Idode, *Rural Development and Bureaucracy in Nigeria*.

48 A. Ogundeji, "Better Life for the Current Mariam?," *The African Guardian*, 25 July 1994.

49 Abdullah, " 'Transition Politics' and the Challenge of Gender in Nigeria," 33.

50 Cited in *Newbreed Magazine* (Lagos, Nigeria), March 1989, 14.

51 Beckman, "Empowerment or Repression?," 57.

52 J. M. Bujra, " 'Urging Women to Redouble Their Efforts...': Class, Gender and Capitalist Transformation in Africa," in C. Robertson and I. Berger eds., *Women and Class in Africa*, New York and London: Africana Publishing Company, 1986, 136.

53 See for instance, M. Molyneux, "Mobilising Without Emancipation?: Women's Interests, State and Revolution in Nicaragua," *Feminist Studies*, Vol. 11, No. 2, 1985, 227-254; C. O. N. Moser, "Gender Planning in the Third World: Meeting Practical and Strategic Gender Needs," *World Development*, Vol. 17, No. 11, 1989,1799-1825; idem, *Gender Planning and Development: Theory, Practice and Training*, New York: Routeledge, 1993.

54 See C. Baylies and J. Bujra, "Challenging Gender Inequalities," *Review of African Political Economy*, No. 56, 1993, 3-10.

55 Molyneux, "Mobilising Without Emancipation?," 233.

56 Moser, "Gender Planning in the Third World," 1803.

57 Mama, "Feminism or Femocracy?," 52.

58 See J. L. Parpart, "Who is the 'Other'?: A Postmodern Feminist Critique of Women and Development Theory and Practice," *Development and Change*, Vol. 24, 1993, 448-449.

59 Abdullah, "'Transition Politics' and the Challenge of Gender," 32-33.

60 See for instance, H. Afshar ed., *Women, Development and Survival in the Third World*, London: Longman, 1991; and A. Goebel and M. Epprecht, "Women and Employment in Sub-Saharan Africa: Testing the World Bank and WID Models with a Lesotho Case Study," *African Studies Review*, Vol. 38, No. 1, 1995, 1-22.

61 D. Elson, "Rethinking Strategies for Development: From Male-biased to Human-centered Development," in idem ed., *Male Bias in the Development Process*, 265.

62 J. I. Dibua, "Better Life Programme and the Empowerment of Rural Women in Nigeria: An Appraisal," Paper Presented at the 37th Congress of the Historical Society of Nigeria, Held at the University of Calabar, Calabar, Nigeria, 18-20 May 1992.

63 P. Elabor-Idemudia, "Rural Women's Quality of Life under Structural Adjustment Policy and Programmes: A Nigerian Case Study," Ph. D. Dissertation, University of Toronto, 1993. Also see D. Elson, "The Impact of Structural Adjustment on Women: Concepts and Issues," in B. Onimode (ed.), *The IMF, the World Bank and the African Debt Vol. 2: The Social and Political Impact*, London: IFAA and Zed Books, 1989, 56-74; and H. Afshar and C. Dennis (eds.), *Women and Adjustment Policies in the Third World*, Macmillan, 1992.

64 See R. Pittin, "Women, Work and Ideology in Nigeria," *Review of African Political Economy*, No. 52, 1991, 39.

65 For details on Wangari Maathai's activities, see M. Michaelson, "Wangari Maathai and Kenyan's Green Belt Movement: Exploring the Evolution and Potentialities of Consensus Movement and Mobilisation," *Social Problems*, Vol. 41, No. 4, 1994, 540-561. Also see S. N. Ndegwa, *The Two Faces of Civil Society: NGOs and Politics in Africa*, West Hartford, Connecticut: Kumarin Press, 1996, 84-97.

66 J. L. Parpart, "Women and the State in Africa," in D. Rothchild and N. Chazan eds., *The Precarious Balance: State and Society in Africa*, Boulder, CO: Westview, 1988; J. L. Parpart and K. A. Staudt, "Women and the State in Africa," in J. L. Parpart and K. A. Staudt eds., *Women and the State in Africa*, Boulder, CO: Lynne Rienner, 1990, 1-16; and Staudt, "Women's Politics," 193-208.

67 K. A. Staudt, "Stratification: Implications for Women's Politics," in Robertson and Berger eds., *Women and Class in Africa*, 87.

68 R. Fatton, "Gender, Class, and State in Africa," in Parpart and Staudt eds., *Women and the State in Africa*, 51.

69 Cited in Ogundeji, "Better Life for the Current Mariam?"

70 O. Alubo, "Supporting the Family," Newswatch, 20 February 1995.

71 International Labor Organization, "Government Programmes in Nigeria – Work and Family," *http://www.ilo.org/public/english/employment/gems/eeo/program/nigeria/fami.htm*; and H. Gbadamosi, "A Support for the Family," *Nigerian Tribune* (Ibadan, Nigeria), 28 April 1999, 10.

72 International Labor Organization, "Government Programmes in Nigeria – Work and Family."

73 Gbadamosi, "A Support for the Family," 10.

74 H. Imam, "Clearing the Hurdles to FEAP Funds Disbursement," *Business Times* (Lagos, Nigeria), 21 April 1997, 15.

75 Federal Republic of Nigeria, *Blueprint of Family Economic Advancement Programme*, Abuja: Federal Government Printer, 1997, 1.

76 Ibid., 3-4.

77 N. G. Iheduru, "Women Entrepreneurship and Development: The Gendering of Microfinance in Nigeria," Paper Presented at the 8th International Interdisciplinary Congress on Women, Held at Makerere University, Kampala, Uganda, 21-26 July 2002.

78 For details, see Federal Republic of Nigeria, *Blueprint of Family Economic Advancement Programme*, 21-25.

79 T. Obiechina, "FEAP Gulped N6b," *Nigerian Tribune*, 27 May 1999, 32.

80 For a detailed discussion of the modernist and neoliberal theoretical underpinnings of the microenterprise, microfinance and microcredit policies, see Iheduru, "Women Entrepreneurship and Development."

81 F. Owete, "Governors Wives Stripped of Roles in FSP," *The Punch*, 7 October 2000, 31.

82 I. Amadiume, *Daughters of the Goddess, Daughters of Imperialism: African Women Struggle for Culture, Power and Democracy*, London: Zed Books, 2000.

83 Femocracy has been described as "an anti-democratic female power structure which claims to exist for the advancement of ordinary women, but is unable to do so because it is dominated by a small clique of women whose authority derives from their being married to powerful men, rather than from any actions or ideas of their own." See Mama, "Feminism or Femocracy?," 41.

84 Federal Republic of Nigeria, *Report of the Political Bureau*, 152-153, and 159.

Chapter 10

Conclusion

Modernization has played a dominant role in Africa's development trajectory from the 1950s. From the 1950s to the 1970s, neo-Keynesianism, which occupied an ascendant position in the modernization paradigm, advocated state intervention in the economies of African countries. This gave rise to the developmental state philosophy during which state-centrist development policies were implemented in various African countries. Development economists who were the main apostles of the developmental state philosophy used the influential position they occupied in the IFIs, Western governments' development and aid agencies, and non-governmental Western-based international aid agencies to ensure the implementation of state-centrist development programs. This was a period of great optimism and belief in the statist development model and therefore witnessed the granting of ascendancy to the state over the markets. The failure of this statist model to promote the desired level of development by the 1970s was generally blamed on the public sector, which was accused of poorly implementing government programs. Remarkably, the solutions usually proffered by both development economists and their neoliberal colleagues, and other modernist social scientists, on how to improve economic performance generally centered on reforming the state sector in order for it to more effectively play its developmental role. In all these cases there was continued faith in state-centrist development model albeit subject to some reforms of the state sector.

As was pointed out in chapter 2, this belief in the statist development model lost a considerable degree of influence from 1981 with the publication of the World Bank's Berg Report. This publication, which marked the ascendancy of the neoclassical economists, criticized the state-centrist development policies as the primary culprit for the acute economic crisis because it was claimed that it did not allow the free operation of market forces. The resultant neoliberal revolution led to a situation in which monetary economists replaced development economists as the most influential group in shaping the development policies of the IFIs, donor agencies and Western governments, toward Africa. The new orthodoxy assigned the sole responsibility for promoting "rational" development in Africa to the market forces. The neoclassical economists, particularly the monetary economists, were the high priests of the neoliberal school and produced the grand theory on which the school's basic tenet rests. However, the social sciences "supplied the apostles who attempted to apply the explanatory model to their own disciplinary concerns, spinning a host of mini-models that sought to capture the character of the African state and society in line with the logic of neo-liberalism."[1] This enterprise which was dominated by North American based social scientists, particularly political scientists, led to the proliferation of various adjectival phrases that sought to locate the reasons for the failure of the statist model on the highly corrupt, patrimonial, clientelist and prebendal nature of the postcolonial African state.

A significant feature of the neoliberal orthodoxy is the extremely high degree of Afro-pessimism contained in their writings. They painted a picture of an inexorable descent into decay and that this state of affairs was entirely a product of internal irrational corrupt, patrimonial and prebendal proclivities on the part of state officials. In essence, Afro-pessimism maintain that Africa's development crisis is primarily, or some would even say, entirely of Africa's making (in spite of the benevolent attempts by the West to promote Africa's development), thereby absolving the West of any culpability in the crisis. Abubakar Momoh has pointed out that Afro-pessimism is an invented ideology aimed at blaming the victims of exploitation while masking Western culpability in the emergence and continuation of Africa's development crisis.[2] Thus, like the development economists, the main blame for the economic crisis was placed on internal factors although the degree of Afro-pessimism and the magnitude of the blame placed on internal factors appear higher among the neoliberals. However, this explanation amounts to blaming the victims. As was shown in the preceding chapters, the primary culprits for the economic crisis should be located in the shortcomings of the modernization paradigm on which both the statist neo-Keynesian and the neoliberal economic policies were based and the peripheral location of African countries in the international economic system. Indeed, there was an intricate connection between modernization and the peripheralization of African countries as the economic policies associated with the paradigm were largely aimed at subordinating African economies to the interests of the advanced capitalist economies. It is important to note that the decline or decay of the economies of African countries actually became worse after the introduction of the neoliberal adjustment policies, a factor that accounted for the high degree of hostility toward SAPs. In short, it can be argued that Africa's development crisis occurred in spite of, and not because of, the so-called internal "irrational" acts of patrimonialism and prebendalism, among others. These internal factors were largely the effects or consequences of the modernist development policies and Africa's peripheral location in the global capitalist system. Osaghae argued that these internal factors could at best be seen as dependent rather than independent variables.[3] In fact, the debilitating neocolonial structure and the modernist policies that sustained it were major contributory factors to Africa's development crisis.

The point here is not that internal factors such as corruption and poor implementation of government programs did not contribute to aggravating the crisis. Nor is it my intention to defend corruption and the poor implementation of public programs. Indeed, the monumental level of corruption, ineptitude and lack of vision among Nigerian and indeed, most African elites, politicians, operators of the state and their business allies, make them highly culpable for the crisis. Nevertheless, the point I am making is that internal factors (bad as they were), are not the fundamental causes of the economic crisis; even if these factors were absent, the crisis would still have occurred. The fundamental causes of the crisis are traceable to the acute limitations of the modernization paradigm and the peripheral location of African countries in the global capitalist system. A significant shortcoming of modernization is the contradictory relationship between it and the indigenous cultural, material and social realities. By denigrating the African culture as irrational, primitive, backward and barbaric, and therefore irrelevant to the development process, the indigenous basis and foundation for development was undermined. The attendant contention that development can only occur in African countries through the transplanting of Western institutions, technologies and the associated cultural norms into Africa, not only amounted to cultural imperialism but was also detrimental to the development process. This perspective made development to become a process of alienation with the attendant negative consequences. According to Ake, "instead of looking at traditional (African) culture as something that the development paradigm has to come to terms with and even build on positively, many disdained it." He added that this disdain for the African culture "has been a costly error. African culture has fiercely resisted and threatened every project that fails to come to terms with it, even as it is acted upon and changed."[4]

It is important to point out that contrary to the claim of modernization proponents, the European modernization experience is a specific cultural phenomenon that cannot be universalized; it is therefore Eurocentric and intimately bound to the social and historical realities of European societies. Furthermore, it should be noted that development is a cultural process and so, it cannot occur in any society if it is not rooted in the culture of that society. As aptly noted by Thierry Verhelst, "development is an all-inclusive process that is, in the final analysis, cultural." He added, "it is the idea of culture that gives both meaning and direction to economic activity, political decisions, community life, social conflict, technology, and so on. It is in fact culture that gives development its raison d'être and its goal."[5] In this regard, it is important to note for example, the significant role that culture played in the development of Japan, and the contributions of Confucianism to the development process in China and South Korea. In fact, the attempts at transplanting Western institutions and ideologies into Africa caused various disarticulations in African societies, which negatively affected the development process. Thus, the contradictory relationship between the transplanted institutions and technologies and the African social, economic and cultural realities, turned out to be counterproductive. As was demonstrated in chapters 5, 6 and 7, this was largely responsible for the crisis of technological development and industrialization, agricultural transformation, and indeed, the failure of the overall modernist development strategies in Nigeria.

In addition, the process of replicating the European experience resulted in the transplanting of the European patriarchal and sexist ideology into Africa – a situation that undermined the crucial roles that women played in the indigenous African economies while greatly marginalizing them. This deprived the development process of most of the crucial contributions of women. In response to the criticisms from African feminist and other interest groups to this marginalization of women by the modernist development model, some attempts were made to rectify the situation. Significant examples were the WID paradigm, which sought to integrate women into male-biased development programs and the World Bank's "populist" ideology of the 1990s that sought to empower women in relation to their governments while leaving them at the mercy of the exploitative interests of private enterprises and market forces. These half-hearted measures could not replicate the significant contributions women made to precolonial African economies. What is therefore called for is the rethinking of development strategies such that women would be accorded their proper roles and recognition in the development process.[6] In this regard, there is a lot to be learnt from the indigenous economic practices of many precolonial and traditional African societies.

Moreover, the primary preoccupation with surplus extraction by the colonial administrations helped to entrench the subordination of African economies to the interests of the international capitalist system while also entrenching the role of the state as primarily a surplus accumulator. The reproduction of this situation in the postcolonial period had adverse consequences for the development process. The reliance on the production of cash crops and minerals as the main source of foreign exchange made African economies susceptible to the vagaries in the prices of these products thereby entrenching their dependence on the international economic system. Furthermore, since the postcolonial African state is not directly involved in production, great reliance is placed on taxes and rents from cash crops production and mineral exploitation, giving rise to what has been described as a rentier state. According to Graf:

> The essential feature of the rentier state in the world market is that it severs the link between production and distribution. State revenues accrue from taxes or "rents" on production, rather than from productive activity. This production depends, however, on techniques, expertise, investments – and markets – generated outside the territory controlled by the state. For this reason, practically all aspects of exploration, production and marketing are dominated by international capital, typically in the form of the transnational corporation.[7]

Furthermore, the economies of the rentier states are susceptible to the fluctuations and shocks in the prices of commodities in the global market, and hence tendentially unstable. In addition, the economies are locked into, and dependent upon, North-South trade patterns.[8] These factors, which accentuated the peripheralization of African economies, greatly contributed to the development crisis.

Moreover, the externalist orientation of the modernist development policies enhanced Africa's dependence on the advanced capitalist countries and promoted the massive flight of capital out of African countries. As already, noted, the modernization paradigm discountenanced the use of indigenous technologies while promoting the massive importation of Western technologies and other inputs, under the guise of replicating the Western development experience. As the examination of technological and industrial development in chapters 5 and 7, and agricultural development in chapter 6 show, this reliance on the massive importation of foreign technology led to the stagnation of indigenous technologies, technological dependence and the massive flight of capital out of Africa. Although this reliance on foreign technologies and the other externalist features of the modernization paradigm contributed to, and aggravated, the development crisis, the tendency among modernist scholars is to portray them as benevolent acts aimed at fostering Africa's development. As a result, they tend to blame internal irrational acts that did not allow the transplanted technologies to operate effectively thereby depriving African countries of the benefits of the instrumental rationality associated with them.[9] Similar arguments have been used to explain the failure of the neoliberal policies in spite of the apparent acute shortcomings of the policies.

The modernist discourse has placed great emphasis on the failure of liberal democracy, as one of the greatest manifestations of the crisis of development in Africa – a discourse that assumed more prominence with the neoliberal political economy from the 1980s. Given the linkage that they make between liberal democracy and economic reforms, the failure of the democracy project has received a great deal of attention with emphasis placed on patrimonial and prebendal features for the failure of the democratization processes. Again, the issue of Western benevolence especially in the form of the political conditionality associated with SAPs is injected into the discussion. However, as was pointed out in chapter 4, the failure of liberal democracy is largely attributable to the modernization paradigm that underlined the project. Moreover, the high degrees of corruption associated with the democratic experiments are themselves factors inherent in the liberal democracy model. These factors more adversely affected Nigeria and other African countries because of the peripheral capitalist nature of their economies. Nevertheless, because of the structure of control over the production and dissemination of knowledge in the social sciences, these factors are portrayed as entirely products of the irrationality of African politicians and societies. While rather derogatory terms such as prebendalism, patrimonialism and corruption are used to describe these features in African politics, they are less derogatorily referred to as lobbying in the Western capitalist societies.

In any case, an important issue that needs to be addressed is the way out of the economic crisis. With the ascendant position of the neoclassical and neoliberal scholars, modernist discourse continue to insist that the neoliberal political economy of minimizing the role of the state through the ascendancy of market forces remains the way out of the crisis. Douglas Rimmer has argued that the operation of the principle of comparative advantage, and free international trade would contribute more to economic growth and the "trickling down" of the gains of growth rather than redistribution, and so, this represents the viable way to poverty alleviation and development in Africa.[10] It is important to note that even the advanced capitalist countries that are preaching the gospel of economic liberalism and free trade are themselves massively subsidizing their farmers and adopting various protectionist policies to advance the interests of their economies. As stated in an editorial article in the *New York Times*:

> The club of rich nations that wrote the rules of global trade has been aggressive in dismantling barriers when it comes to industrial goods and services, in which they hold a comparative advantage. But they refuse to do the same when it comes to agriculture. Politically powerful farm lobbies in Japan, Europe and the United States are not willing to face global competition on fair terms. So agriculture remains the hypocritical asterisk to our fervent free-trade and free-enterprise creed.

The article further stated that America's protectionist trade barriers and the billions in subsidies doled out to American farmers "contribute mightily to the hardships felt by poor farmers in the developing world."[11] Yet African countries, which are more disadvantageously placed, were advised to stop subsidizing farmers and to allow the unfettered operation of free international trade. This therefore amounts to continuing the peripheralization of Africa in the international economic system and the outcome is the worsening of the economic crisis.

The issue of the role of the state in Africa's development trajectory has occupied a central position in the discourse of the twin themes of success/failure of Africa's development. As already noted, development economists placed a great faith on the role of the state in promoting economic development while the neoliberal orthodoxy castigated the state for the development crisis and therefore advocated state-retrenching policies. Nevertheless, by placing the greatest emphasis on the so-called irrational policies of the African state, the neoliberal orthodoxy, perhaps inadvertently, accord the state a central position in the discourse of Africa's development. Furthermore, the neoliberals' call for state minimization is deceptive because their policies favor the existence of strong and authoritarian pro-SAPs states that would be able to push through the neoliberal reform agenda in the face of massive opposition from African peoples. In addition, the neoliberal position on state minimization is hypocritical because even in the advanced capitalist West, a free enterprise economy does not exist in any of the countries. Their governments actively intervene in the economies to protect the economic interests of the respective countries.

Given the interventionist role that the state plays even in the Western bastion of neoliberalism, does the solution to Africa's development crisis rest on the minimization of the African state in favor of market forces? My answer to this question is an unequivocal "no." In fact, since the end of the Great Depression in the 1930s and more so, after World War II, state intervention has been the norm in the economies of different countries in the world. Given the peripheral position of Africa in the international economic system and the urgent need for development, state intervention is even more compelling than before. As aptly stated by Olukoshi, it is "necessary to recognise that in Africa, there can be no question of a trade-off between the state and the market; the state does have a decisive role to play in the developmental process and its reinstatement, without the encumbrances which previously undermined its efficacy, must be a central concern of post-adjustment Africa."[12] Thus, the important issue "is not to 'roll back' the state but to re-design it" so that it can play a more effective role in Africa's development.[13]

The critical point, therefore, is not whether the state should intervene or play a developmentalist role in Africa; in fact, the need for developmental state in Africa is not in doubt. However, as is clear from the analysis in the preceding chapters, the postcolonial state has failed to promote development largely because of the encumbrances of modernization and the peripheral location of African states in the international economic system, which foster extraversion and dependence rather than development. The fundamental issue then, is the form, quality and scope of state intervention in order for it to promote development. Alan Carter has argued that because of the neo-colonial form of third world states, they, along with the advanced capitalist states are responsible for the exploitation and underdevelopment of third world countries.[14] As stated by Abdi and Ahmed Samatar:

> Critical thinkers have certainly *written off* the African state in its *post-colonial form*. . . . However, . . . their analytical animus is focused on the incapacity of the post-colonial state in history *rather than the state per se*. In other words, African development has stalled because the state is of the wrong kind and, therefore, a re-thinking of its form seems to be of utmost necessity. . . . the new agenda is not necessarily to side-step the state. (Emphasis in the original)[15]

A crucial consideration in the redefinition of the African state is that of autonomy: the state must attain a very high degree of autonomy both in internal and external affairs in order for it to be able to perform its developmental role. Thus, the autonomy would not only free the state from being captured by a domestic social class but would also result in the deperipheralization of the state in the international arena. The development of productive forces and therefore the transformation of the state from a rentier state into a productive and developmental state are crucial for the attainment and sustenance of its autonomy. The attainment of these objectives requires the development of a democratic system that is internally generated, emanating from the people and their institutions, and indeed, the product of a consensus between the different social forces. In this regard, the various non-governmental organizations, which represent the popular interests and aspirations of the people, must play an important role in the arrival at the consensus. It is important to distinguish here between the civil society groups that emanate from the people and genuinely represent their interests and the mainly self-serving and externalist oriented civil society groups that largely proliferated under the neoliberal regime. Many of the latter civil society groups are largely motivated by selfish considerations and perceive African realities from the perspective of their external mentors rather than from the perspective of the internal realities and interests of African peoples. They therefore cannot be counted upon to help to advance the democratic and economic interests and aspirations of the majority of the African peoples.

Under the new democratic dispensation, the state can count on the support and aspirations of the people and expect them to make the necessary sacrifices, if political and economic reforms are domestically formulated and based on a clear social consensus. Such a situation will help to assure the people of the domestic ownership of the political and economic reforms while also creating the basis for satisfying the social and welfare aspirations of the populace. The resultant social contract "will also provide a framework within which state and governmental legitimacy can be reconstructed for the formulation and implementation of policies."[16] The goal of the social contract between the state and the people should be to promote a self-reliant and sustainable development process. In this regard, in spite of the great amount of negative assessments particularly from some Western Africanists and some of its obvious shortcomings, Julius Nyerere's *Ujamaa* remains a good experiment that can provide relevant insights on how to work toward the attainment of self-reliance in Africa. As has been argued elsewhere, if stripped of its modernist developmentalism, which was a product of the developmentalist philosophy of the 1960s and 1970s, it can be clearly seen that the *Ujamaa* philosophy essentially reflected an inward orientation aimed at achieving a self-reliant development. In fact, if properly deconstructed, it would be apparent that beyond being a political ideology, *Ujamaa* was "conceived as a development strategy, a path to social equity and distributive justice based on a self-reliant development strategy."[17] African countries therefore have a lot to learn from this aspect of *Ujamaa* especially within the context of the prevailing neoliberal policies that have entrenched Africa's extraversion, dependence and, indeed, the crisis of development.

Nevertheless, culture must be accorded a crucial role in order for a meaningful, self-reliant and sustainable development to be attained by African countries. It should be realized that culture encompasses every aspect of life:

> know-how, technical knowledge, customs of food and dress, religion, mentality, values, language, symbols, socio-political and economic behavior, indigenous methods of taking decisions and exercising power, methods of production and economic relations, and so on.[18]

Culture should therefore form the basis and starting point for any meaningful development project for as already pointed out; development is itself a cultural process. As Verhelst aptly noted, "in order to be sustainable, development must be meaningful to the people concerned, consequently it must be embedded in their culture."[19] It follows that in place of the Eurocentrism or Westernization promoted by the modernist development paradigm, the culture and realities of African societies should form the basis for development. This would help to make development a process of de-alienation thereby eliminating the adverse effects of modernization on the development project.

However, ultimately, the development agenda in Africa can be better served within a pan-African context. The launching of both the African Union (AU) and the New Partnership for Africa's Development (NEPAD) in 2001 have been hailed by many scholars and policy makers as marking significant attempts at finding "homegrown" and pan-African solutions to Africa's developmental problems. For instance, Kempe Hope stated that:

> The NEPAD . . . represents a pledge by African leaders, based on a common vision and a firm and shared conviction that they have a pressing duty to eradicate poverty and place their countries, both individually and collectively, on a path of sustainable growth and development, and at the same time participate actively in the world economy and body politic. It is therefore anchored on the determination of Africans to extricate themselves and the continent from the malaise of underdevelopment and exclusion in a globalizing world. In other words, it is an attempt at a homegrown solution to overcoming Africa's marginalization in the world economy and international affairs, while improving the standard of living of the African people.[20]

But to what extent does NEPAD represent a Pan-African and homegrown solution to Africa's development crisis? Even though it emphasizes the need for self-reliance and various other developmental issues, NEPAD like similar programs drawn up by African heads of states in the past, such as the 1980 Lagos Plan of Action, is firmly based on the modernization program. However, although NEPAD emphasize self-reliance, its strategy for development is essentially externalist in orientation, with great emphasis placed on massive injection of foreign capital as the best route to Africa's development. Such reliance on foreign capital in the first place led Africa into the debt peonage that in turn provided the justification for the introduction of SAPs. Furthermore, NEPAD's approach to development is based on the neoclassical paradigm, which as already pointed out, has greatly contributed to the worsening of Africa's development crisis. In addition, African heads of states drew up NEPAD without involving the African peoples, contrary to the African Charter for Popular Participation in Development and Transformation (ACOOD), which was adopted in Arusha, Tanzania, in February 1990 and by the Organization of African Unity (OAU) Summit in July 1990.[21] As a top-bottom initiative that is situated within the modernization paradigm and prone to extraversion, NEPAD does not appear to be in the position to promote meaningful development in Africa.

Thus, although NEPAD's goal of a self-reliant development is praiseworthy, it is not in the position to lead African countries toward the attainment of this objective.

Given the pressing need for the attainment of a self-reliant and sustainable development in Africa, the people and their organizations, and not their governments should be in the forefront of the movement toward the achievement of these objectives. They should strive to attain the objectives within a pan-African context that would work toward achieving the kind of continental unity advocated by Kwame Nkrumah. Already there exist continental-wide non-governmental organizations such as those representing trade unions, formal and informal trans-territorial contacts between organizations such as those representing students, and between ordinary people such as traders, etc. These can form the building blocks toward the attainment of continental unity. Given the orientations and shortcomings of African governments, they cannot be expected to take the lead in this regard. A grassroots-led movement toward continental unity would eventually present African governments with a fait accompli and this would facilitate the entering into a social contract between a continental government and the African peoples. As stated by Carter, "it is to the peoples of this world . . . and to the (genuine) nongovernmental organisations which help them to help themselves that we must look for a future" that promotes enduring, self-reliant and sustainable development.[22] Such a people-led and people-oriented development process would be based on the culture and institutions of the people as well as grant them ownership and control over the process.

Notes

1 A. O. Olukoshi, "Extending the Frontiers of Structural Adjustment Research in Africa: Some Notes on the Objectives of Phase II of the NAI Research Programme," in P. Gibbon and A. O. Olukoshi, *Structural Adjustment and Socio-Economic Change in Sub-Saharan Africa: Some Conceptual, Methodological and Research Issues*, Uppsala: Nordiska Afrikainstitutet, 1996, 55.

2 A. Momoh, "Does Pan-Africanism Have a Future in Africa?: In Search of the Ideational Basis of Afro-Pessimism," *African Journal of Political Science*, Vol. 8, No. 1, 2003, 31-57.

3 Osaghae, *Crippled Giant*, 311.

4 Ake, *Democracy and Development in Africa*, 15.

5 T. G. Verhelst (Translated by B. Cumming), *No Life Without Roots: Culture and Development*, London: Zed Books, 1990, 159-160. Also see Ajayi, *The Past in the Present*; and O. Oladipo, "Imagination, Tradition and Development: A Review Essay," *CODESRIA Bulletin*, No. 4, 1994, 13-15.

6 For details, see Elson, "Rethinking Strategies for Development," 253-279.

7 Graf, *The Nigerian State*, 219.

8 Ibid., 220-221.

9 J. I. Dibua, "Benevolence, Received Wisdom and Africa's Development Trajectory," Paper Presented at the 46th Annual Meetings of the African Studies Association (USA) and the Canadian Association of African Studies, Held at New Orleans, Louisiana, USA, 11-14 November 2004.

10 D. Rimmer, "Learning About Economic Development from Africa," *African Affairs*, Vol. 102, 2003, 469-491.

11 "Harvesting Poverty: The Unkept Promise," *New York Times*, 30 December 2003. Also see T. Egan, "Big Farms Reap Two Harvests with Subsidies a Bumper Crop," *New York Times*, 26 December 2004.

12 Olukoshi, *The Elusive Prince of Denmark*, 50. Also see Mkandawire, "The Crisis in Economic Development Theory," 230.

13 Tsie, "State and Markets in the Southern African Development Community," 95.

14 See A. Carter, "The Nation-State and Underdevelopment," *Third World Quarterly*, Vol. 16, No. 4, 1995, 595-618.

15 Samatar and Samatar, "Introduction," 5.

16 Olukoshi, *The Elusive Prince of Denmark*, 52.

17 See B. Ibhawoh and J. I. Dibua, "Deconstructing Ujamaa: The Legacy of Julius Nyerere in the Quest for Social and Economic Development in Africa," *African Journal of Political Science*, Vol. 8, No. 1, 2003, 61 and 78. Also, see A. Mbelle, G. D. Mjema and A. A. L. Kilindo eds., *The Nyerere Legacy and Economic Policy Making in Tanzania*, Dar es Salaam: Dar es Salaam University Press, 2002.

18 Verhelst, *No Life Without Roots*, 17.

19 T. G. Verhelst, "What Do We Mean by Culture and Development?" *The Development Policy Management Network (DPMN) Bulletin*, Vol. 2, No. 2, 1994, 5.

20 K. R. Hope, "From Crisis to Renewal: Towards a Successful Implementation of the New Partnership for Africa's Development," *African Affairs*, Vol. 101, 2002, 389.

21 P. Egede, "African Labour Unions Meet, Pick Holes in NEPAD," *The Guardian*, 9 July 2002.

22 Carter, "The Nation-State and Underdevelopment," 615.

Bibliography

Abba, A., *et al.*, *The Nigerian Economic Crisis: Causes and Solutions* (Zaria, Nigeria: Academic Staff Union of Universities, 1985).

Abdullah, H., " 'Transition Politics' and the Challenge of Gender in Nigeria," *Review of African Political Economy*, 56 (1993).

Abernethy, D., "Bureaucratic Growth and Economic Stagnation in Sub-Saharan Africa," in S.K. Commins (ed.), *Africa's development Challenges and the World Bank* (Boulder, CO: Lynne Rienner, 1988).

Abrahamsen, R., "African Studies and the Postcolonial Challenge," *African Affairs*, 102(407) (2003).

Abubakar, A., "My Transition Agenda for Development," Text of a National Broadcast to the Nation by Head of State, General Abdulsalami Abubakar on 20 July 1998, *Vanguard* (Lagos, Nigeria), 21 July 1998.

---, "Time to Break Cycle of Instability and Mistrust," Text of General Abdulsalami Abubakar's Address to the Nation, on the Hand-over of Government and Inauguration of the President-elect, 29 May 1999.

Abutudu, M.I.M., *The State, Civil Society and the Democratization Process in Nigeria*, Monograph Series, No. 1 (Dakar: CODESRIA, 1995).

---, "Confronting Political Shock: Civil Society and the Annulment of the 1993 Presidential Election in Nigeria," Unpublished Research Report Submitted to the Social Science Research Council (SSRC), New York, 1996.

---,"Globalization and 'Tokunboh': Tentative Notes on Structural Adjustment, Culture and Politics in Nigeria," Paper Presented at the 22nd Annual Conference of the New York African Studies Association, Held at Binghamton University, Binghamton, 24-25 April 1998.

Academic Staff Union of Universities, *The Killings at A.B.U.: Friday 23 May, 1986* (Zaria: Academic Staff Union of Universities, 1986).

Adamolekun, L., *The Fall of the Second Republic* (Ibadan, Nigeria: Spectrum Books, 1985).

Adams, W.M., "Approaches to Water Resource Development, Sokoto Valley, Nigeria: The Problem of Sustainability," in D. Anderson and R. Grove (eds.), *Conservation in Africa: People, Policies and Practice* (Cambridge: Cambridge University Press, 1987).

---, "Rural Protest, Land Policy, and the Planning Process on the Bakolori Project, Nigeria," *Africa*, 58(3) (1988).

Adekson, J., "Dilemma of Military Disengagement," in O. Oyediran (ed.), *Nigerian Government and Politics under Military Rule, 1969-79* (New York: St. Martins, 1979).

Adelman, B.I., *Theories of Economic Growth and Development* (Stanford: Stanford University Press, 1962).

Adeoye, A.O., "Understanding the Crisis in Modern Nigerian Historiography," *History in Africa*, 19 (1992).

Aderibigbe, Y., "Women: Continued Search for Political Relevance," *The Guardian*, 8 April 2004.

---, "Rising Clamour for National Conference," *The Guardian*, 2 June 2004.

Adesina, O.C., "Politics and Nigerian Agriculture in the First Decade of 'Oil Boom,' 1970-1980: A Preliminary Assessment," *The Nigerian Journal of Economic History*, 1 (1998).

Adubifa, A., *Technology Policy in Nigeria* (Ibadan: Nigerian Institute of Social and Economic Research, 1990).

Afigbo, A.E., *The Warrant Chiefs: Indirect Rule in South-Eastern Nigeria, 1891-1929* (London: Longmans, 1972).

Afshar, H. (ed.), *Women, Development and Survival in the Third World* (London: Longman, 1991).

Afshar, H. and Dennis, C., *Women and Adjustment Policies in the Third World* (Macmillan, 1992).

Agbonifo, P.O., "State Farms and Rural Development: A Case Study of the Agbede and Warrake Farm Project in Bendel State of Nigeria," Unpublished PhD Dissertation, University of Wisconsin, Madison, 1980.

Agozino, B., *Counter-Colonial Criminology: A Critique of Imperialist Reason* (London: Pluto Press, 2003).

Ahluwalia, M.S. and Carter, N.G., "Growth and Poverty in Developing Countries," in H. Chinery (ed.), *Structural Change and Development Policy* (New York: Oxford University Press, 1979).

Aigbokhan, B.E., "Resuscitating Agricultural Production (Cocoa, Cotton, Groundnuts, Palm Oil, Rubber, etc) for Exports," Central Bank of Nigeria, *Occasional Paper*, 6 (2001).

Ajayi, J.F.A., *The Past in the Present: The Factor of Tradition in Development* (Lagos: Nigerian Institute of International Affairs, 1990).

---, "Foreword," in J.D. Ojo, *Students' Unrest in Nigerian Universities: A Legal and Historical Approach* (Ibadan: Spectrum Books and IFRA, 1995).

Akande, J., "Women and the Law," in A.O. Obilade (ed.), *Women in Law* (Louisiana and Lagos: Southern University Law Center and Faculty of Law, University of Lagos, 1993).

Akande, L., "Bush, Kerry Campaigns Cost $400m as Polls Draw Near," *The Guardian* (Lagos, Nigeria), 27 October 2004.

Ake, C., *Social Science as Imperialism: The Theory of Political Development* (Ibadan: Ibadan University Press, 1982).

---, "The State of the Nation: Intimations of Disaster," Presidential Address to the Nigerian Political Science Association, 1982.

---, "Introduction," *Africa Development*, IX(3) (1984).

---, "The State in Contemporary Africa," in C. Ake (ed.), *Political Economy of Nigeria* (London and Lagos: Longman, 1985).

---, "The State, Democracy and Development," in S. Rasheed and S. Tomori (eds), *The Political Economy of Development: An African Perspective*, Vol. 1 (Nairobi: ICIPE Science Press, 1996).

---, *Democracy and Development in Africa* (Washington, D.C.: The Brookings Institution, 1996).

Akeredolu-Ale, E.O., *The Underdevelopment of Indigenous Entrepreneurship in Nigeria* (Ibadan: Ibadan University Press, 1975).

Akindele, R.A., "The Constituent Assembly, 1988-1989," Paper Presented at the Conference on Democratic Transition and Structural Adjustment in Nigeria, Held at Hoover Institute, Stanford University, California, 27-29 August 1990.

Akintunde, J.O., "The Demise of Democracy in the First Republic of Nigeria: A Causal Analysis," *ODU*, 4 (1967).

Albert, I.O., "University Students in the Politics of Structural Adjustment in Nigeria," in T. Mkandawire and A. Olukoshi (eds), *Between Liberalisation and Oppression: The Politics of Structural Adjustment in Africa* (Dakar: CODESRIA, 1995).

Almond, G.A., *Political Development: Essays in Beuristic Theory* (Boston: Little, Brown, 1970).

Almond, G.A. and Coleman, J.S. (eds), *The Politics of Developing Areas* (Princeton: Princeton University Press, 1960).

Almond, G.A. and Powell, B., *Comparative Politics: Developmental Approach* (Boston: Little, Brown, 1966).

Alubo, O., "Supporting the Family," *Newswatch* (Lagos, Nigeria), 20 February 1995.

Aluko, O., "Politics of Decolonisation in British West Africa 1945-1960," in J. F. A. Ajayi and M. Crowder (eds), *History of West Africa*, Vol. 2 (London: Longman, 1975).

Aluko-Olokun, I., "An Appraisal of the Second-Tier Foreign Exchange Market (SFEM)," in A.O. Phillips and E.C. Ndekwu (eds), *Structural Adjustment in a Developing Economy: The Case of Nigeria* (Ibadan: NISER, 1987).

Amadiume, I., *Daughters of the Goddess, Daughters of Imperialism: African Women Struggle for Culture, Power and Democracy* (London: Zed Books, 2000).

Amin, S., *Eurocentrism* (London: Zed, 1988).

Amsden, A., *Asia's Next Giant: South Korea and Late Industrialization* (New York: Oxford University Press, 1985).

Amsden, A. (ed.), "The World Bank's East Asian Miracle: Economic Growth and Public Policy," Special Section, *World Development*, 22(4) (1994).

Amuwo, K., "Democracy by Fiat: Why it Will Not Work," *Africa Quarterly*, 35(3) (1995).

Andrae, G. and Beckman, B., *The Wheat Trap: Bread and Underdevelopment in Nigeria* (London and Uppsala: Zed Books and Scandinavian Institute of African Studies, 1985).

Anene, J. C., *Southern Nigeria in Transition, 1884-1906: Theory and Practice in a Colonial Dependency* (Cambridge: Cambridge University Press, 1965).

Animalu, A.O.E., "Models for Technology Transfer between Nigeria and the United States of America," in M. Amoda and C.D. Tyson (eds), *Technological Development in Nigeria* (Lagos and New York: Third Press International, 1979).

Anyang, S., "In Defence of the Small Farmer," *National Concord* (Lagos, Nigeria), 15 May 1985.

Anyanwu, C.M., "Productivity in the Nigerian Manufacturing Industry," Central Bank of Nigeria, *Occasional Paper*, 7 (2000).

Apter, D., *Ghana in Transition* (Princeton: Princeton University Press, 1957).

---, *The Politics of Modernization* (Chicago: Chicago University Press, 1965).

Arikpo, O., *The Development of Modern Nigeria* (Middlesex, England: Penguin Books, 1967).

Asiodu, P.C., "The Civil Service: An Insider's View," in O. Oyediran (ed.), *Nigerian Government and Politics under Military Rule, 1969-79* (New York: St. Martins, 1979).

Assie-Lumumba, N. and Lumumba-Kasongo, T., "The 'Silent Crisis' in the International Transfer of Knowledge in African Societies and Their Education Systems: A Theoretical Perspective," *CODESRIA Bulletin*, 4 (1994).

Atanda, J.A., "The Iseyin-Okeiho Rising of 1916: An Example of Socio-Political Conflict in Colonial Nigeria," *Journal of the Historical Society of Nigeria*, 4(4) 1969.

---, *The New Oyo Empire: Indirect Rule and Change in Western Nigeria, 1894-1934* (London: Longman, 1973).

Awolowo, O., *Thoughts on Nigerian Constitution* (Oxford: Oxford University Press, 1966).

---, *Adventures in Power, Book 1: My March Through Prison* (Ibadan: Macmillan, 1985).

Ayandele, E.A., *The Missionary Impact on Modern Nigeria, 1842-1914: A Political and Social Analysis* (London: Longman, 1966).

---, *The Educated Elite in Nigerian Society* (Ibadan: Ibadan University Press, 1974).

Ayiku, M.N.B., "Science and Technology in the Development Process," in S. Rasheed and S. Tomori (eds), *The Political Economy of Development: An African Perspective*, Vol. 1 (Nairobi: ICIPE Science Press, 1996).

Ayittey, G.B.N., *Africa in Chaos* (St. Martins, 1999).

Babangida, M., "Women: The Nutritional Bedrock of African Society," Text of an Acceptance Speech at the Award Ceremony of the 1991 African Leadership

Prize for the Sustainable End of Hunger, Church House Conference Center, London, 30 September 1991.

Bach, D.C., "Indigeneity, Ethnicity and Federalism," in L. Diamond *et. al.* (eds), *Transition Without End: Nigerian Politics and Civil Society Under Babangida* (Boulder: Lynne Rienner, 1997).

Bagchi, AK., "Technological Self-Reliance, Dependence and Underdevelopment," in A. Wad (ed.), *Science, Technology, and Development* (Boulder, Co and London: Westview and IT Publications, 1988).

Baker, K.M., *Case Studies in the Developing World: Agricultural Change in Nigeria* (London: John Murray, 1989).

Bangura, Y., "Overcoming Some Basic Misconceptions of the Nigerian Economic Crisis," *Studies in Politics and Society*, 2 (1984).

---, *Crisis, Adjustment and Politics in Nigeria* (Stockholm and Uppsala: AKUT Group, 1989).

---, "Authoritarian Rule and Democracy in Africa: A Theoretical Discourse," in P. Gibbon, Y. Bangura and A. Ofstad (eds), *Authoritarianism, Democracy, and Adjustment: The Politics of Economic Reform in Africa* (Uppsala: Nordiska Afrikainstitutet, 1992).

Bangura, Y. and Gibbon, P., "Adjustment, Authoritarianism and Democracy: An Introduction to Some Conceptual and Empirical Issues," in P. Gibbon, Y. Bangura and A. Ofstad (eds), *Authoritarianism, Democracy, and Adjustment: The Politics of Economic Reform in Africa* (Uppsala: Nordiska Afrikainstitutet, 1992).

Bates, R.H., *Markets and States in Tropical Africa: The Political Basis of Agricultural Policies* (Los Angeles: University of California Press, 1981).

---, "The Politics of Agricultural Pricing in Sub-Saharan Africa," in Z. Ergas (ed.), *The African State in Transition* (London: Macmillan, 1987).

---, *Towards a Political Economy of Development: A Rational Choice Perspective* (Berkeley, CA: University of California Press, 1988).

---, *Beyond the Miracles of the Market* (Cambridge: Cambridge University Press, 1989).

---, "The Impulse to Reform in Africa," in J. Widner (ed.), *Economic Changes and Political Liberalization in Sub-Saharan Africa* (Baltimore: Johns Hopkins University Press, 1994).

Bauer, P.T., *West African Trade: A Study of Competition, Oligopoly and Monopoly in a Changing Economy* (Cambridge: Cambridge University Press, 1954).

Bayart, J.F., "Civil Society in Africa," in P. Chabal (ed.), *Political Domination in Africa: Reflections on the Limits of Power* (Cambridge: Cambridge University Press, 1986).

Baylies, C. and Bujra, J., "Challenging Gender Inequalities," *Review of African Political economy*, 56 (1993).

Beckman, B., "Imperialism and Capitalist Transformation: Critique of the Kenya Debate," *Review of African Political Economy*, 19 (1980).

---, "Whose State? State and Capitalist Development in Nigeria," *Review of African Political Economy*, 23 (1982).

---, "Neo-Colonialism, Capitalism, and the State in Nigeria," in H. Bernstein and B.K. Campbell (eds), *Contradictions of Accumulation in Africa: Studies in Economy and State* (Beverly Hills and London: Sage Publications, 1985.

---, "Public Investment and Agrarian Transformation in Northern Nigeria," in M.J. Watts (ed.), *State, Oil and Agriculture in Nigeria* (Berkeley, CA: University of California Press, 1987).

---, "Empowerment or Repression? The World Bank and the Politics of African Adjustment," *Africa Development*, 16(1) (1991).

---, "The Liberation of Civil Society: Neo-Liberal Ideology and Political Theory," *Review of African Political Economy*, 58 (1993).

Beckman, B. and Jega, A., "Scholars and Democratic Politics in Nigeria," *Review of African Political Economy*, 64 (1995).

Bello, V.I., "The Intentions, Implementation Processes and Problems of the Nigerian Enterprises Promotion Decree (No. 4) 1972," in Nigerian Economic Society, *Nigeria's Indigenisation Policy: Proceedings of the November 1974 Symposium Organized by the Nigerian Economic Society on the Subject "Indigenisation: What Have We Achieved?"* (Ibadan: The Nigerian Economic Society, 1974).

Bendel State Government, "Press Release," Military Governor's Office, Benin City, Nigeria, 21 August 1984.

---, *Handbook on Better Life Programme in Bendel State* (Benin City, n.d.).

Berman, B.J., *Control and Crisis in Colonial Kenya: The Dialectic of Domination* (London and Athens, OH: James Currey and Ohio University Press, 1990).

---, "African Capitalism and the Paradigm of Modernity: Culture, Technology, and the State," in B.J. Berman and C. Leys (eds), *African Capitalists in African Development* (Boulder, CO: Lynne Rienner, 1994).

Better Life Programme, *Better Life Fair for Rural Dwellers* (Lagos: Alimbar Tribune, n.d.).

---, *Better Life Programme for Rural Women* (Lagos: 1990).

Bhalla, A.S., *Facing the Technological Challenge* (London and New York: Macmillan and St. Martins, 1996).

Biersteker, T.J., "Indigenization in Nigeria: Rationalization or Denationalization?" in I. W. Zartman (ed.), *The Political Economy of Nigeria* (New York: Praeger, 1983).

---, *Multinationals, the State, and Control of the Nigerian Economy* (Princeton: Princeton University Press, 1987).

---, "Reducing the Role of the State in the Economy: A Conceptual Exploration of IMF and World Bank Prescriptions," *International Studies Quarterly*, 34(4) (1990).

---, "The 'Triumph' of Neo-Classical Economics in the Developing World," in J. N. Rosenau and E.O. Cziempiel (eds), *Governance Without Government:*

Order and Change in World Politics (Cambridge: Cambridge University Press, 1992).

Bolaji, L., *Shagari: President by Mathematics* (Ibadan: Automatic Printing Press, 1980).

Bollag, B., "Nigerian Universities Start to Recover from Years of Violence, Corruption and Neglect," *The Chronicle of Higher Education*, 1 February 2002.

Boserup, E., *Woman's Role in Economic Development* (London: Allen and Unwin, 1970).

Bratton, M., "Beyond the State: Civil Society and Associational Life in Africa," *World Politics*, 51(3) (1989).

Brett, E.A., *Colonialism and Underdevelopment in East Africa* (New York: NOK Publishers, 1973).

Brown, M.B., *Africa's Choices: After Thirty Years of the World Bank* (Boulder, CO: Westview, 1995).

Bryceson, D.F. and L. Bank, "End of an Era: Africa's Development Policy Parallax," *Journal of Contemporary African Studies*, 19(1) (2001).

Bujra, J.M., " 'Urging Women to Redouble Their Efforts . . .': Class, Gender and Capitalist Transformation in Africa," in C. Robertson and I. Berger (eds.), *Women and Class in Africa* (New York and London: Africana Publishing Company, 1986).

Byfield, J.A., *The Bluest Hands: A Social and Economic History of Women Dyers in Abeokuta (Nigeria), 1890-1940* (Portsmouth, NH: Heinemann, 2002).

Callaghy, T.M., *The State-Society Struggle: Zaire in Comparative Perspective* (New York: Columbia University Press, 1984).

---, "The State as Lame Leviathan: The Patrimonial Administrative State in Africa," in Z. Ergas (eds.), *The African State in Transition* (London and New York: Macmillan and St. Martins, 1987).

---, "Absolutism, Bonapartism, and the Formation of Ruling Classes: Zaire in Comparative Perspective," in I.L. Markovitz (ed.), *Studies in Power and Class in Africa* (New York: Oxford University Press, 1987).

---, "The State and the Development of Capitalism in Africa: Theoretical, Historical, and Comparative Reflections," in D. Rothchild and N. Chazan (eds.), *The Precarious Balance: State and Society in Africa* (Boulder, CO: Westview, 1988).

---, "Political Passions and Economic Interests: Economic Reform and Political Structure in Africa," in T.M. Callaghy and J. Ravenhill (eds), *Hemmed In: Responses to Africa's Economic Decline* (New York: Columbia University Press, 1993).

---, "Lost Between State and Market: The Politics of Economic Adjustment in Ghana, Zambia, and Nigeria," in J.M. Nelson (ed.), *Economic Crisis and Policy Choice: The Politics of Adjustment in the Third World* (Princeton: Princeton University Press, 1994).

Carter, A., "The Nation-State and Underdevelopment," *Third World Quarterly*, 16(4) (1995).

Central Bank of Nigeria, *Statistical Bulletin*, 13 (2003).

Chazan, N., "Patterns of State-Society Incorporation and Disengagement in Africa," in D. Rothchild and N. Chazan (eds), *The Precarious Balance: State and Society in Africa* (Boulder, CO: Westview, 1988).

---, "State and Society in Africa: Images and Challenges," in Rothchild and Chazan (eds.), *The Precarious Balance*.

Chenery, H. *et al.*, *Redistribution with Growth* (New York: Oxford University Press, 1974).

Chinweizu, *The West and the Rest of Us* (New York: NOK, 1978).

Clapham, C., *Private Patronage and Public Power* (New York: St. Martins Press, 1982).

Coleman, J.S., *Nigeria: Background to Nationalism* (Berkeley, CA: University of California Press, 1958).

Collins, P., "Public Policy and the Development of Indigenous Capitalism: The Nigerian Experience," *Journal of Commonwealth and Comparative Politics*, XV(2) (1977).

Connolly, M. and Arokoyo, T., "Alleviating Fertilizer Technology Transfer Constraints," in A. U. Mokwunye (ed.), *Alleviating Soil Fertility Constraints to Increased Crop Production in West Africa* (Dordrecht, Boston, London: Kluwer Academic Publishers, 1991).

Coquery-Vidrovitch, C. (translated by B.G. Raps), *African Women: A Modern History* (Boulder, CO: Westview, 1997).

Cromwell, E., *Governments, Farmers and Seeds in a Changing Africa* (London: CAB International and Overseas Development Institute, 1996).

Crook, R.C., "Patrimonialism, Administrative Effectiveness and Economic Development in Cote d'Ivoire," *African Affairs*, 88(351) (1989).

Dasgupta, B., *Agrarian Change and the New Technology in India* (Geneva: United Nations Research Institute for Social Development, 1975).

Dei, G.J.S., "Sustainable Development in the African Context: Revisiting Some Theoretical and Methodological Issues," *Africa Development*, XVIII(2) (1993).

Dennis, C., "Capitalist Development and Women's Work: A Nigerian Case Study," *Review of African Political Economy*, 27/28 (1983).

---, "The Limits to Women's Independent Careers: Gender in the Formal and Informal Sectors in Nigeria," in D. Elson (ed), *Male Bias in the Development Process* (Manchester and New York: Manchester University Press, 1995).

Deutsch, K., "Nation-Building and National Development," in K. Deutsch and W. Foltz, *Nation-Building* (Chicago: Atherton Press, 1963).

Diamond, L., "Cleavage, Conflict and Anxiety in the Second Nigerian Republic," *Journal of Modern African Studies*, 20(4) (1982).

---, "Social Change and Political Conflict in Nigeria's Second Republic," in I.W. Zartman (ed.), *The Political Economy of Nigeria* (New York: Praeger, 1983).

---, "Class Formation in the Swollen African State," *Journal of Modern African Studies*, 25(4) (1987).

---, "Nigeria: Pluralism, Statism and the Struggle for Democracy," in L. Diamond *et. al.* (eds), *Democracy in Developing Countries* (Boulder, CO: Lynne Rienner, 1988).

---, *Class, Ethnicity and Democracy in Nigeria: The Failure of the First Republic* (Syracuse: Syracuse University Press, 1988).

---, "Postscript and Postmodern," in L. Diamond *et al.*, *Transition Without End: Nigerian Politics and Civil Society Under Babangida* (Boulder, CO: Lynne Rienner, 1997).

Diamond, L., Kirk-Greene, A. and Oyediran, O. (eds), *Transition Without End: Nigerian Politics and Civil Society Under Babangida* (Boulder, CO: Lynne Rienner, 1997).

Dibua, J.I., "Competition Among the Nigerian Bourgeoisie and the Demise of the First Republic," *The Herodotian*, 5(1) (1982).

---, "Conflict Among the Nigerian Bourgeoisie and the Demise of the Second Republic," *Africa Development*, XIII(4) (1988).

---, "Government's Agricultural Policy and Rural Development in Nigeria: The Case of Bendel State, 1964-1988," *The African Review*, 16(1/2) (1989).

---, "Local Government and Rural Transformation in Nigeria Within the Context of Development Planning," *Journal of Rural Development and Administration*, XXII(1) (1990).

---, "Better Life Programme and the Empowerment of Rural Women in Nigeria: An Appraisal," Paper Presented at the 37th Congress of the Historical Society of Nigeria, Held at the University of Calabar, Calabar, Nigeria, 18-20 May 1992.

---, "Structural Adjustment Programme and the Subversion of Popular Will in Africa: The Case of the Transition to Civil Rule in Nigeria," in S.G. Tyoden (ed.), *The Transition to Civil Rule: The Journey So Far – The Proceedings of the 19th Annual Conference of the Nigerian Political Science Association* (Lagos: The Nigerian Political Science Association, 1992).

---, "The Structural Adjustment Programme and the Transition to Civil Rule in Nigeria," in L.A. Thompson (ed.), *Democracy, Democratization and Africa* (Ibadan, Enugu and Abuja: Afrika-Link Books, 1994).

---, "The Post-Colonial State and Development Planning in Nigeria, 1962-1985," *Journal of Eastern African Research and Development*, 24 (1994).

---, "The Idol, Its Worshippers, and the Crisis of Relevance of Historical Scholarship in Nigeria," *History in Africa*, 24 (1997).

---, "Journey to Nowhere: Neo-Liberalism and Africa's Development Crisis," *Comparative Studies of South Asia, Africa and the Middle East*, XVIII(2) (1998).

---, "Pan-Africanism," in T. Falola (ed.), *Africa: Volume 4:The End of Colonial Rule: Nationalism and Decolonization* (Durham, NC: Carolina Academic Press, 2002).

---, "Devaluation and Economic Crisis: A Political Economy Analysis," in A. Oyebade (ed.), *The Transformation of Nigeria: Essays Honor of Toyin Falola* (Trenton, NJ: Africa World Press, 2002).

---, "Economic Crisis and Structural Adjustment Programs," in T. Falola (ed.), *Africa: Volume 5: Contemporary Africa* (Durham, NC: Carolina Academic Press, 2003).

---, "Benevolence, Received Wisdom and Africa's Development Trajectory," Paper Presented at the 46th Annual Meetings of the African Studies Association (USA) and the Canadian Association of African Studies, Held at New Orleans, Louisiana, USA, 11-14 November 2004.

---, "Collapse of Purpose: Ibrahim Babangida, 1985-1993," L.A. Nwachuku and G. N. Uzoigwe (eds), *Troubled Journey: Nigeria Since the Civil War* (Lanham: University Press of America, 2004).

---, "Students and the Struggle Against Authoritarianism in University Governance in Nigeria," in P.T. Zeleza and A. Olukoshi (eds.), *African Universities in the Twenty-First Century: Vol. II: Knowledge and Society* (Dakar: CODESRIA, 2004).

---, "Conflict over Control of Natural Resources in Nigeria: The Case of the Oil-Producing Niger Delta Communities of the South-South States, 1990-2004," *Lagos Historical Review*, 4 (2004).

---, "Citizenship and Resource Control in Nigeria: The Case of Minority Communities in the Niger Delta," *Africa Spectrum*, 39(1) (2005).

---, "Nigeria: Conferences, Commissions, Nigerian Constitution: 1956-1960," in K. Shillington (ed.), *Encyclopedia of African History*, Vol. 2 (New York and London: Fitzroy Dearborn, 2005).

---, "Nigeria: Murtala Muhammed, Obasanjo and Return to Civilian Rule, 1975-1979," in K. Shillington (ed.), *Encyclopedia of African History*, Vol. 2.

---, "Nigeria: Second Republic, 1979-1983," in K. Shillington (ed.), *Encyclopedia of African History*, Vol. 2.

---, "Nigeria: Opposition, 1990s, to the Fourth Republic," in K. Shillington (ed.), *Encyclopedia of African History*, Vol. 2.

---, "World Bank, International Monetary Fund, and Structural Adjustment," in K. Shillington (ed.), *Encyclopedia of African History*, Vol. 3.

Dike, K. O., *Trade and Politics in the Niger Delta, 1830-1885* (Oxford: Oxford University Press, 1956).

Dudley, B.J., "Western Nigeria and the Nigerian Crisis," in S.K. Panter-Brick (ed.), *Nigerian Politics and Military Rule* (London: Athlene Press, 1970).

---, *Instability and Political Order: Politics and Crisis in Nigeria* (Ibadan: Ibadan University Press, 1973).

---, *An Introduction to Nigerian Government and Politics* (Bloomington: Indiana University Press, 1982).

Dutt, A. *et al.*, *The State, Markets and Development: Beyond the Neoclassical Dichotomy* (Aldershot: Edward Elgar, 1994).

Economic Commission for Africa, *African Alternative Framework to Structural Adjustment Programme for Economic Recovery and Transformation (AAF-SAP)*, (Addis Ababa: United Nations Economic Commission for Africa, 1989).

Edsall, T.B., "Fundraising Doubles the Pace of 2000," *Washington Post*, 21 August 2004.

Effah-Attoe, S.A. and Jaja, S.O., *Margaret Ekpo: Lioness in Nigerian Politics* (Abeokuta: ALF Publications, 1993).

Egan, T., "Built With Steel, Perhaps, but Greased With Pork," *New York Times*, 10 April 2004.

---, "Big Farms Reap Two Harvests with Subsidies a Bumper Crop," *New York Times*, 26 December 2004.

Egede, P., "African Labour Unions Meet, Pick Holes in NEPAD," *The Guardian*, 9 July 2002.

Eisenstadt, S. N. and Lemarchand, R. (eds), *Political Clientelism, Patronage and Development* (Beverly Hills and London: Sage Publications, 1981).

Ekechi, F. K., "Perceiving Women as Catalysts," *Africa Today*, 43(3) (1996).

---, "Historical Women in the Fight for Liberation," in V.U. James and J.S.Etim (eds.), *The Feminization of Development Processes in Africa: Current and Future Perspectives* (Westport, Connecticut and London: PRAEGER, 1999).

Ekeh, P.P., "Citizenship and Political Conflict: A Sociological Interpretation of the Nigerian Crisis," in J. Okpaku (ed.), *Nigeria: Dilemma of Nationhood* (New York: The Third Press, 1972).

---, "Colonialism and the Two Publics in Africa: A Theoretical Statement," *Comparative Studies in Society and History*, 17(1) (1975).

---, "Colonialism and the Development of Citizenship in Africa: A Study inIdeologies of Legitimation," in O. Otite (ed.), *Themes in African Social and Political Thought* (Enugu: Fourth Dimension, 1978).

Ekeh, P.P. and Osaghae, E.E. (eds), *Federal Character and Federalism in Nigeria* (Ibadan: Heinemann, 1989).

Ekuerhare, B.U. "Recent Pattern of Accumulation in the Nigerian Economy," *Africa Development*, IX(1) (1984).

---, "The Theory and Concepts of Capital Goods and Technology Development in Nigeria," Paper Presented at the Annual Conference of the Nigerian Economic Society, Held at Minna, Nigeria, 22-25 May 1990.

Elabor-Idemudia, P., "Rural Women's Quality of Life under Structural Adjustment Policy and Programmes: A Nigerian Case Study," Ph. D Dissertation, University of Toronto, 1993.

Elaigwu, J.I., *Gowon: The Biography of a Soldier-Statesman* (Ibadan: West Books, 1986).

Eleazu, U.O., *Federalism and Nation-Building: The Nigerian Experience, 1954-1964* (Ilfracombe: Stockwell, 1977).

Elson, D., "The Impact of Structural Adjustment on Women: Concepts and Issues," in B. Onimode (ed.), *The IMF, the World Bank and the African Debt, Vol. 2: The Social and Political Impact* (London: IFAA and Zed Books, 1989).

---, "Male Bias in the Development Process: An Overview," in idem (ed.), *Male Bias in the Development Process* (Manchester and New York: Manchester University Press, 1995).

---, "Male Bias in Macro-Economics: The Case of Structural Adjustment," in idem (ed), *Male Bias in the Development Process.*

---, "Household Responses to Stabilisation and Structural Adjustment: Male Bias at the Micro Level," in idem (ed), *Male Bias in the Development Process.*

---, "Rethinking Strategies for Development: From Male-Biased to Human-Centered Development," in idem (ed.), *Male Bias in the Development Process.*

Enahoro, A., "The National Question: Towards a New Constitutional Order," *The Guardian*, 5 July 2002.

Enwerem, I.M., *A Dangerous Awakening: The Politicization of Religion in Nigeria* (Ibadan: IFRA, 1995).

Etakibuebu, G., "Future Uncertain Without a National Conference," *The Guardian*, 31 May 2004.

Eteng, I., "Indigenization for Lumpen-Bourgeois Development in Nigeria," in O. Nnoli (ed.), *Path to Nigerian Development* (Dakar: CODESRIA, 1981).

Evans, P. *et al.* (eds), *Bringing the State Back In* (Cambridge: Cambridge University Press, 1985).

Evans, P., "Class, State, and Dependence in East Asia: Lessons for Latin Americanists," in F.C. Deyo (eds), *The Political Economy of the New Asian Industrialization* (Ithaca: Cornell University Press, 1987).

---, *Embedded Autonomy: States and Industrial Transformation* (Princeton: Princeton University Press, 1995).

Eyoh, D., "From Economic Crisis to Political Liberalization: Pitfalls of the New Political Sociology of Africa," *African Studies Review*, 39(3) (1996).

Fadahunsi, A., "Devaluation: Implications for Employment, Inflation, Growth and Development," in A.O. Olukoshi (ed.), *The Politics of Structural Adjustment in Nigeria* (London, Ibadan and Portsmouth, NH: James Currey and Heinemann, 1993).

Falola, T., *Development Planning and Decolonization in Nigeria* (Gainesville: University Press of Florida, 1996).

---, *The History of Nigeria* (Westport, Connecticut and London: Greenwood, 1999).

---, *Economic Reforms and Modernization in Nigeria, 1945-1965* (Kent, Ohio: The Kent State University Press, 2004).

Falola, T. and Ihonvbere, J., *The Rise and Fall of Nigeria's Second Republic, 1979-1984* (London: Zed Books, 1985).

Famariyo, S., "Food Production Policies in Nigeria," *Food Policy*, February 1978.

Faruqee, R., "Nigeria: Ownership Abandoned," in I. Husain and R. Faruqee (eds.), *Adjustment in Africa: Lessons from Country Case Studies* (Washington, D.C.: World Bank, 1994).

Fatton, R., "Gender, Class, and State in Africa," in J.L. Parpart and K.A. Staudt (eds.), *Women and the State in Africa* (Boulder, CO: Lynne Rienner, 1990).

Federal Government of Nigeria, *Public Service Review Commission, Main Report* (the Udoji Report) (Lagos: Federal Government Printer, 1974).

---, *Report of the Constitution Drafting Committee*, Vol. 1 (Lagos: Federal Government Printer, 1976).

---, *The Constitution of the Federal Republic of Nigeria* (Lagos: Federal Government Printer, 1979).

---, *National Policy on Science and Technology* (Lagos: Federal Ministry of Science and Technology, 1986).

Federal Republic of Nigeria, *First National Development Plan, 1962-68* (Lagos: Federal Ministry of Information, 1962).

---, *Second National Development Plan, 1970-74* (Lagos: Federal Ministry of Information, 1970).

---, *Nigerian Enterprises Promotion Decree*, Decree No. 4 (Lagos: Federal Government Printer, 1972).

---, *Third National Development Plan, 1975-80* (Lagos: The Federal Ministry of National Planning, 1975).

---, *Nigerian Enterprises Promotion Decree*, Decree No. 3 (Lagos: Federal Government Printer, 1977).

---, *Government Views on the Report of the Commission of Inquiry into the Nigerian Universities Crisis, 1978* (Lagos: Federal Ministry of Information, 1978).

---, *Guidelines for the Fourth National Development Plan, 1981-85* (Lagos: The Federal Ministry of National Planning, 1980).

---, *Report of the Ministerial Committee on the Causes of Excessively High Cost of Government Contracts in Nigeria* (Lagos: Federal Government Printer, 1981).

---, *The Federal Military Government's Views on the Commission of Inquiry into Student Crisis at the Ahmadu Bello University, Zaria, May 1986* (Lagos: The Federal Government Printer, 1986).

---, *Structural Adjustment for Nigeria, July 1986-June 1988* (Lagos: Federal Government Printer, 1986).

---, *Report of the Political Bureau* (Lagos: Federal Government Printer, 1987).

---, *Government's Views and Comments on the Findings and Recommendations of the Political Bureau* (Lagos: Federal Government Printer, 1987).

---, *Transition to Civil Rule (Political Programme), Decree No. 9* (Lagos: Federal Government Printer, 1987).

---, *Constituent Assembly Decree: Decree No. 14* (Lagos: Federal Government Press, 1988).

---, *The National Commission for Women*, Decree No. 30 of 1989 (Lagos: The Federal Government Printer, 1989).

---, *Blueprint of Family Economic Advancement Programme* (Abuja: Federal Government Printer, 1997).

Ferguson, J., *The Anti-Politics Machine: "Development," Depoliticization, and Bureaucratic Power in Lesotho* (Cambridge: Cambridge University Press, 1990).

Fine, B. and Stoneman, C., "Introduction: State and Development," *Journal of Southern African Studies*, 22(1) (1996).

Flint, J.E., *Sir George Goldie and the Making of Nigeria* (Oxford: Oxford University Press, 1960).

Forrest, T., "Agricultural Policies in Nigeria 1900-78," in J. Heyer, P. Roberts and G. Williams (eds), *Rural Development in Tropical Africa* (London: Macmillan, 1981).

---, *Politics and Economic Development in Nigeria* (Boulder, CO: Westview, 1993).

Founou-Tchuigoua, B., "Africa Confronted with the Ravages of Neo-Liberalism," *Africa Development*, 21(2) (1996).

Francis, P., "For the Use and Common Benefit of All Nigeria: Consequences of the 1978 Land Nationalisation," *Africa*, 54(3) (1984).

Fukuyama, F., "The End of History?," *The National Interest*, 16 (1989).

---, *The End of History and the Last Man* (Penguin, 1992).

Gana, A.T., *The Limits of Political Engineering: A Critique of the Transition Programme* (Jos: Covenant Press, 1990).

Gbadamosi, H., "A Support for the Family," *Nigerian Tribune* (Ibadan, Nigeria), 28 April 1999.

Gerschenkron, A., *Economic Backwardness in Historical Perspectives* (Cambridge, Mass: Harvard University Press, 1962).

---, *Continuity in History and Other Essays* (Cambridge, Mass: Harvard University Press, 1968).

Gibbon, P., "Towards a Political Economy of the World Bank, 1970-90,"in T. Mkandawire and A. Olukoshi (eds), *Between Liberalisation and Oppression: The Politics of Structural Adjustment in Africa* (Dakar: CODESRIA, 1995).

Gibbon, P., Havnevik, K.J., and Hermele, K., *A Blighted Harvest: The World Bank and African Agriculture in the 1980s* (Trenton, NJ: Africa World Press, 1993).

Glaeser, B., *Ecodevelopment: Concepts, Projects, Strategies* (Oxford: Pergamon Press, 1984).

Glickman, H., "Reflections on State-Centrism as Ideology in Africa," in Z. Ergas (ed.), *The African State in Transition* (New York: St. Martins, 1987).

Goebel, A. and Epprecht, M., "Women and Employment in Sub-Saharan Africa: Testing the World Bank and WID Models with a Lesotho Case Study," *African Studies Review*, 38(1) (1995).

Goldsmith, A.A., "Africa's Overgrown State Reconsidered: Bureaucracy and Economic Growth," *World Politics*, 51(4) (1999).

Graf, W.D., *The Nigerian State: Political Economy, State Class and Political System in the Post-Colonial Era* (London and Portsmouth, NH: James Currey and Heinemann, 1988).

Green, R.H., "The IMF and the World Bank in Africa: How Much Learning?," in T.M. Callaghy and J. Ravenhill (eds), *Hemmed In: Responses to Africa's Economic Decline* (New York: Columbia University Press, 1993).

Grosh, B., *Public Enterprise in Kenya: What Works, What Doesn't, and Why* (Boulder, CO: Lynne Rienner, 1991).

Hammond, R. W., "Relevant Technology and the University," in M. Amoda and C. D. Tyson (eds), *Technological Development in Nigeria* (Lagos and New York: Third Press International, 1979).

Harbeson, J. *et. al.*, (eds), *Civil Society an the State in Africa* (Boulder, CO: Lynne Rienner, 1985).

Hayami, Y. and Ruttan, V., *Agricultural Development: An International Perspective* (Baltimore: The Johns Hopkins University Press, 1985).

Helleiner, G.K., *Peasant Agriculture, Government, and Economic Growth in Nigeria* (Homewood, Illinois: Richard D. Irwin, 1966).

Hettne, B., *Development Theory and the Three Worlds* (London: Longman, 1990).

Hirschmann, A.O., *Exit, Voice and Loyalty* (Cambridge, Mass: Harvard University Press, 1970).

Hirshman, A., "The Rise and Decline of Development Economics," in A. Hirshman, *Essays in Trespassing: Economics to Politics and Beyond* (Cambridge: Cambridge University Press, 1981).

Hoeven, R.V.D. and Kraaij, F.V.D. (eds), *Structural Adjustment and Beyond in Sub-Saharan Africa: Research and Policy Issues* (The Hague, London and Portsmouth, NH: Ministry of Foreign Affairs, James Currey and Heinemann, 1994).

Hoogvelt, A., "Indigenisation and Foreign Capital: Industrialization in Nigeria," *Review of African Political Economy*, 14 (1979).

---, "Indigenization and Technological Dependency," *Development and Change*, 11(2) (1980).

Hope, K.R., "From Crisis to Renewal: Towards a Successful Implementation of the New Partnership for Africa's Development," *African Affairs*, 101 (2002).

House-Midamba, B. and Ekechi, F.K. (eds), *African Market Women and Economic Power: The Role of Women in African Economic Development* (Westport, CT: Greenwood Press, 1995).

Huff, W., "The Developmental State, Government, and Singapore's Economic Development Since 1960," *World Development*, 23(8) (1995).

Husain, I., "Structural Adjustment and the Long-Term Development of Sub-Saharan Africa," in R.V.D. Hoeven and F.V.D. Kraaij (eds), *Structural Adjustment and Beyond in Sub-Saharan Africa: Research and Policy Issues*

(The Hague, London and Portsmouth, NH: Ministry of Foreign Affairs, James Currey and Heinemann, 1994).

Hyden, G., *Beyond Ujamaa in Tanzania: Underdevelopment and an Uncaptured Peasantry* (Berkeley: University of California Press, 1980).

---, *No Shortcuts to Progress: African Development Management in Perspective* (Berkeley, CA: University of California Press, 1983).

---, "The Anomaly of African Peasantry," *Development and Change*, 17(4) (1986).

---, "Rethinking Theories of the State: An Africanist Perspective," *Africa Insight*, 26(1) (1996).

Ibeanu, O.O., "Class Interest and Public Policy in Nigeria: An Analysis of Government Policies on Agriculture and Housing," *The African Review*, 16(1/2) (1989).

---, "The Deteriorating Condition of the Nigerian Peasantry," in O. Nnoli (ed.), *Deadend to Nigerian Development: An Analysis of the Political Economy of Nigeria, 1979-1989* (Dakar: CODESRIA, 1993).

Ibhawoh, B. and Dibua, J.I., "Deconstructing Ujamaa: The Legacy of Julius Nyerere in the Quest for Social and Economic Development in Africa," *African Journal of Political Science*, 8(1) (2003).

Idode, J.B., *Rural Development and Bureaucracy in Nigeria* (Lagos: Longman, 1987).

Igbafe, P.A., *Benin Under British Administration: The Impact of Colonial Rule on an African Kingdom, 1897-1938* (London: Longman, 1979).

Iheduru, N.G., "Women Entrepreneurship and Development: The Gendering of Microfinance in Nigeria," Paper Presented at the 8th International Interdisciplinary Congress on Women, Held at Makerere University, Kampala, Uganda, 21-26 July 2002.

Ihonvbere, J., "A Critical Evaluation of the Failed 1990 Coup in Nigeria," *Journal of Modern African Studies*, 29(4) (1991).

Ihuoma, A., "Economic Implications of Underdeveloped Capital Goods Industry in Nigeria," M. Sc Thesis, Ahmadu Bello University, Zaria, Nigeria, 1983.

Ikime, O., *The Fall of Nigeria: The British Conquest* (London: Heinemann, 1977).

---, (ed.), *Groundwork of Nigerian History* (Ibadan: Ibadan University Press, 1980).

---, *In Search of Nigerians: Changing Patterns of Inter-Group Relations in an Evolving Nation State* (Ibadan: Historical Society of Nigeria, 1985).

Imam, H., "Clearing the Hurdles to FEAP Funds Disbursement," *Business Times* (Lagos, Nigeria), 21 April 1997.

International Bank for Reconstruction and Development, *The Economic Development of Nigeria* (Lagos: Government Printer, 1954).

International Labor Organization, *First Things First: Meeting the Basic Needs of the People of Nigeria* (Addis Ababa: Jobs and Skills Program for Africa, 1981).

---, "Government Programmes in Nigeria–Work and Family," http://www.ilo.org/public/english/employment/gems/eeo/program/nigeria/fami.htm.

International Monetary Fund, *Recent Multilateral Debt Reschedulings with Official and Bank Creditors*, Occasional Paper No. 25, (Washington, D.C.: International Monetary Fund, 1983).

Iweriebor, E.E.G., *Radical Politics in Nigeria, 1945-1950: The Significance of the Zikist Movement* (Zaria: Ahmadu Bello University Press, 1996).

---, *Nigerian Technology Development Since Independence: The State of Development and the Strategy of Transformation* (Ibadan: BookBuilders, 2004).

Iyun, F., "The Impact of Structural Adjustment on Maternal and Child Health in Nigeria," in G. Thomas-Emeagwali (ed.), *Women Pay the Price: Structural Adjustment in Africa and the Caribbean* (Trenton, NJ: Africa World Press, 1995).

Jackson, R.H. and Rosberg, C.G., *Personal Rule in Black Africa: Prince, Autocrat, Prophet, Tyrant* (Berkeley, CA: University of California Press, 1981).

Jakande, L. K., *The Trial of Obafemi Awolowo* (Lagos: John West, 1980).

Johnson, C., *MITI and Japanese Miracle: The Growth of Industrial Policy, 1925-1975* (Stanford: Stanford University Press, 1982).

---, "Political Institutions and Economic Performance: The Government-Business Relationship in Japan, South Korea and Taiwan," in F. Deyo (ed.), *The Political Economy of the New Asian Industrialization* (Ithaca, NY: Cornell University Press, 1987).

Johnson, Cheryl, "Grass Roots Organizing: Women in Anticolonial Activity in Southern Nigeria," *African Studies Review*, XXV(2/3), 1982.

Johnson-Odim, C. and Mba, N.E., *For Women and the Nation: Funmilayo Ransome-Kuti of Nigeria* (Urbana: University of Illinois Press, 1997).

Johnston, B.F. and Kilby, P., *Agricultural and Structural Transformation: Economic Strategies in Late-Developing Countries* (London and New York: Oxford University Press, 1975).

Joseph, R.A., *Democracy and Prebendal Politics in Nigeria: The Rise and Fall of the Second Republic* (Cambridge: Cambridge University Press, 1987).

---, "Class, State, and Prebendal Politics in Nigeria," in P. Lewis (ed.), *Africa: Dilemmas of Development and Change* (Boulder, CO: Westview, 1998).

Justice, G., "Republicans Rush to Form New Finance Groups," *New York Times*, 29 May 2004.

---, "Despite New Financing Rules, Parties Collect Record $1 Billion," *New York Times*, 26 October 2004.

---, "Even with Campaign Finance Law, Money Talks Louder Than Ever," *New York Times*, 8 November 2004.

Kennedy, P., *African Capitalism: The Struggle for Ascendancy* (Cambridge: Cambridge University Press, 1988).

Kilby, P., *Industrialization in an Open Economy: Nigeria 1945-1966* (Cambridge: Cambridge University Press, 1969).

Kirk-Greene, A.H.M., *Crisis and Conflict in Nigeria: A Documentary Source Book, 1966-1967*, Vol. 1, (Oxford: Oxford University Press, 1971).

Kirk-Greene, A.H.M. and Rimmer, D. (eds), *Nigeria Since 1970: A Political and Economic Outline* (London: Hodder and Stoughton, 1981).

Kitching, G., "Politics, Method and Evidence in the 'Kenya Debate'" in H. Bernstein and B. Campbell (eds), *Contradictions of Accumulation in Africa* (London and Beverly Hills: Sage, 1985).

Kodjo, E. and Chanaiwa, D., "Pan-Africanism and Liberation," in A.A. Mazrui and C. Wondji (eds), *UNESCO General History of Africa: Vol. VIII: Africa Since 1935* (Paris: UNESCO, 1999).

Koinyan, L.D., *Integrated Rural Development* (Lagos: Federal Government Press, 1987).

---, *Food Self-Sufficiency and Much More* (Lagos: Federal Government Press, 1988).

Korieh, C.J., "Agricultural Transformation, State Policy, and Agricultural Decline in Eastern Nigeria, 1960-1970," in A. Oyebade (ed.), *The Transformation of Nigeria: Essays in Honor of Toyin Falola* (Trenton, NJ: Africa World Press, 2002).

Krugman, P., "Toward a Counter-Counterrevolution in Development Theory," in World Bank, *Proceedings of the World Bank Conference on Development Economics* (Washington, D.C.: The World Bank, 1992).

Kukah, M.H., *Religion, Politics and Power in Northern Nigeria* (Ibadan: Spectrum, 1993).

Kumer, N., "Intellectual Property Protection, Market Orientation and Location of Overseas R and D Activities by Multinational Enterprises," *World Development*, 24(4), (1996).

Lancaster, C., "Economic Reform in Africa: Is it Working?," O. Obasanjo and H. d'Orville (eds), *The Leadership Challenge in Economic Reforms in Africa* (New York: Crane Russak, 1991).

Lansing, J.S., *Priests and Programmers: Technologies of Power in the Engineered Landscape of Bali* (Princeton: Princeton University Press, 1991).

Lawrence, P., "The Political Economy of the 'Green Revolution' in Africa," *Review of African Political Economy*, 42 (1988).

Lee, J.M., *Colonial Development and Good Government: A Study of the Ideas Expressed by the British Official Classes in Planning Decolonization 1939-1964* (Oxford: Oxford University Press, 1967).

Leechor, C., "Ghana: Frontrunner in Adjustment," in I. Husain and R. Faruqee (eds), *Adjustment in Africa: Lessons from Country Case Studies* (Washington, D.C.: The World Bank, 1994).

Lewis, W.A., "Reflections on the Structure of Nigerian Manufacturing Industry," in O. Teriba and M.O. Kayode (eds), *Industrial Development in Nigeria* (Ibadan: Ibadan University Press, 1977).

Lewis, P.M., "From Prebendalism to Predation: The Political Economy of Decline in Nigeria," *Journal of Modern African Studies*, 34(1) 1996.

Leys, C., "African Capitalists and Development: Theoretical Questions," in B.J. Berman and C. Leys (eds), *African Capitalists in African Development* (Boulder, CO: Lynne Rienner, 1994).

Leys, C. and B.J. Berman, "Introduction," in Berman and Leys (eds), *African Capitalists in African Development.*

Lovett, M., "Gender Relations, Class Formation, and the Colonial State in Africa," in J.L. Parpart and K.A. Staudt (eds), *Women and the State in Africa* (Boulder, CO: Lynne Rienner, 1989).

Lubeck, P.M. and Watts, M.J., "An Alliance of Oil and Maize? The Response of Indigenous and State Capital to Structural Adjustment in Nigeria," in B.J. Berman and C. Leys (eds), *African Capitalists in African Development* (Boulder, CO: Lynne Rienner, 1994).

Lucas, E.T., "We Decide, They Decide For Us: Popular Participation as an Issue in Two Nigerian Women's Development Programmes," *Africa Development*, XXV(1/2) (2000).

---, "Social Development Strategies of a Non-Governmental Grassroots Women's Organisation in Nigeria," *International Journal of Social Welfare*, 10(3) (2001).

Macfie, A.L. (ed.), *Orientalism: A Reader* (New York: New York University Press, 2000).

Mackintosh, J.P. (ed.), *Nigerian Government and Politics* (London: George Allen and Unwin, 1966).

Mama, A., "Feminism or Femocracy?: State Feminism and Democratisation in Nigeria," *Africa Development*, XX(1) (1995).

Mamdani, M., "State and Civil Society in Contemporary Africa: Reconceptualizing the Birth of State Nationalism and the Defeat of Popular Movements," *Africa Development*, 15(4) (1990).

---, "A Critique of the State and Civil Society Paradigm in Africanist Studies," in M. Mamdani and E. Wamba-dia-Wamba (eds), *African Studies in Social Movements and Democracy* (Dakar: CODESRIA, 1995).

---, *Citizen and Subject: Contemporary Africa and the Legacy of Late Colonialism* (Princeton: Princeton University Press, 1996).

Mangwvat, M.Y., "The Early Phase of Colonial Rule in Nigeria and the Beginnings of New Political Entities, 1885-1913: Some Reflections," Paper Presented at the Seminar on Historical Roots of the Contemporary Nigerian Nation, held at Durbar Hotel, Kaduna, Nigeria, 4-8 June 1986.

Mba, N., *Nigerian Women Mobilized: Women's Political Activity in Southern Nigeria, 1900-1965* (Berkeley, CA: University of California Institute of International Studies, 1982).

Mbelle, A., Mjema, G.D. and Kilindo, A.A.L. (eds), *The Nyerere Legacy and Economic Policy Making in Tanzania* (Dar es Salaam: Dar es Salaam University Press, 2002).

Michaelson, M., "Wangari Maathai and Kenyan's Green Belt Movement: Exploring the Evolution and Potentialities of Consensus Movement and Mobilisation," *Social Problems*, 41(4) (1994).

Mid-Western State Government, *Agricultural Newsletter*, 2(1) (1973).

---, *The National Council for Agriculture and Natural Resources, Fifth Meeting, June 20-22, 1974, Benin City, Mid-Western Nigeria* (Benin City: Ministry of Home Affairs and Information, Information Division, 1974).

Mkandawire, T., "The Crisis in Economic Development Theory," *Africa Development*, XV(3/4) (1990).

---, "The Political Economy of Privatization in Africa," in G.A. Cornia and G.K. Helleiner (eds), *From Adjustment to Development in Africa: Conflict, Controversy, Convergence, Consensus* (New York: St. Martins Press, 1994).

---, "Adjustment, Political Conditionality and Democratization in Africa," in Cornia and Helleiner (eds), *From Adjustment to Development in Africa.*

Mohammed, S. and Edoh, T.A., *A Republic in Ruins* (Zaria: Ahmadu Bello University Press, 1986).

Molyneux, M., "Mobilising Without Emancipation?: Women's Interests, State and Revolution in Nicaragua," *Feminist Studies*, 11(2) (1985).

Momoh, A., "The Structural Adjustment Programme and the Transition to Civil Rule in Nigeria (1986-1993)," *Africa Development*, XXI(1) (1996).

---, *Even Birds Have a Home: Explaining the Pathologies of the Citizenship Question in Nigeria* (Lagos: EMPARC, 2001).

---, "Does Pan-Africanism Have a Future in Africa?: In Search of the Ideational Basis of Afro-Pessimism," *African Journal of Political Science*, 8(1) (2003).

Morgan, D., "$275 Billion Highway Bill Passes Easily in the House: Pork-Laden Measure Above Bush Spending Limit," *Washington Post*, 3 April 2004.

Moser, C.O.N., "Gender Planning in the Third World: Meeting Practical and Strategic Gender Needs," *World Development*, 17(11) (1989).

---, *Gender Planning and Development: Theory, Practice and Training* (New York: Routeledge, 1993).

Mosley, P., "Decomposing the Effects of Structural Adjustment: The Case of Sub-Saharan Africa," in R.V.D. Hoeven and F.V.D. Kraaij (eds), *Structural Adjustment and Beyond in Sub-Saharan Africa: Research and Policy Issues* (The Hague, London and Portsmouth, NH: Ministry of Foreign Affairs, James Currey and Heinemann, 1994).

Mureithi, L.P., "Development Planning in Kenya," in M. Urrutia and S. Yukawa (eds.), *Development Planning in Mixed Economies* (Tokyo: The United Nations University, 1988).

Mustapha, A.R., "Structural Adjustment and Multiple Modes of Social Livelihood in Nigeria," in P. Gibbon, Y. Bangura and A. Ofstad (eds), *Authoritarianism, Democracy, and Adjustment: The Politics of Economic Reform in Africa* (Uppsala: Nordiska Afrikainstitutet, 1992).

Mytelka, L.K., "The Unfulfilled Promise of African Industrialization," *African Studies Review*, 32(3) (1989).

Naanen, B., "Oil-Producing Minorities and the Restructuring of Nigerian Federalism: The Case of the Ogoni People," *Journal of Commonwealth and Comparative Politics*, 33(1) (1995).

National Commission for Women, *SAP and the Nigerian Women: The Better Life Programme Experience* (Abuja: National Commission for Women, n.d.).

National Orientation Agency, *Abacha's Transition Programme* (Abuja, Nigeria: National Orientation Agency, 1995).

Ndegwa, S.N., *The Two Faces of Civil Society: NGOs and Politics in Africa* (West Harford, Connecticut: Kumarin Press, 1996).

Ndujihe, C., "The Changing Story of Women in Politics," *The Guardian*, 5 August 2004.

Nelson, J.M. (ed.), *Economic Crisis and Policy Choice: The Politics of Adjustment in the Third World* (Princeton: Princeton University Press, 1994).

Newbreed Magazine (Lagos, Nigeria), March 1989.

New Nigerian (Kaduna, Nigeria), 9 May 1988.

New York Times, 30 December 2003.

New York Times, 16 April 2004.

New York Times, 8 July 2004.

Newswatch (Lagos, Nigeria), 8 June 1985.

Newswatch, 8 July 1985.

Newswatch, 9 June 1986.

Newswatch, 16 June 1986.

Newswatch, 23 June 1986.

Newswatch, 10 July 1989.

Newswatch, 25 May 1992.

Newswatch, 5 October 1992.

Newswatch, 23 January 1995.

Nicolson, I.F., *The Administration of Nigeria, 1900-1960: Men, Methods and Myths* (Oxford: Clarendon Press, 1975).

Nigeria, *Preliminary Statement on Development Planning in Nigeria*, Sessional Paper No. 6 (Lagos: Government Printer, 1945).

---, *A Ten-Year Plan of Development and Welfare for Nigeria*, Sessional Paper No. 24 (Lagos: Government Printer, 1946).

---, *Statement of the Policy Proposed for the Future Marketing of Nigerian Oil, Oil Seeds and Cotton*, Sessional Paper No. 18 (Lagos: Government Printer, 1948).

---, *Report of the Commission on Revenue Allocation* (Lagos: Government Printer, 1951).

---, *A Revised Plan of Development and Welfare for Nigeria 1951-56*, Sessional Paper No. 6 (Lagos: Government Printer, 1951).

---, *The Economic Programme of the Government of the Federation of Nigeria, 1955-60*, Sessional Paper No. 2 (Lagos: Government Printer, 1956).

---, *Federation of Nigeria: Opportunities for Overseas Investment: Joint Statement by the Federal and Regional Governments of Nigeria* (Lagos: Federal Government Printer, 1956).

---, *The Role of the Federal Government in Promoting Industrial Development in Nigeria*, Sessional Paper No. 3 (Lagos: Federal Government Printer, 1958).

---, *Report of the Commission Appointed to Enquire into the Fears of Minorities and the Means of Allaying Them* (Willink Commission), (London: HMSO, 1958).

Njoku, O.N., "Era of Misguided Good Feeling: Yakubu Gowon and the Birth of a New Nigeria, 1970-1975," in L.A. Nwachuku and G.N. Uzoigwe (eds), *Troubled Journey: Nigeria Since the Civil War* (Lanham, MD: University Press of America, 2004).

Nkemdirim, B., *Social Change and Political Violence in Colonial Nigeria* (Ilfracombe: Stockwell, 1975).

Nnoli, O., *Ethnic Politics in Nigeria* (Enugu: Fourth Dimension, 1980).

---, "Development/Underdevelopment: Is Nigeria Developing?," in O. Nnoli (ed.), *Path to Nigerian Development* (Dakar: CODESRIA, 1981).

Nwabueze, B.O., *Nigeria '93: The Political Crisis and Solutions* (Ibadan: Spectrum, 1994).

Nwaubani, E., "For Bread Alone: A Postscript on Nigeria's Wheat Entrapment," *Scandinavian Journal of Development Alternatives and Area Studies*, 18(2/3) (1999).

---, "Constitution-Making and the Nigerian Identity, 1914-1960," in A. Oyebade (ed.), *The Transformation of Nigeria: Essays in Honor of Toyin Falola* (Trenton, NJ: Africa World Press, 2002).

Nwosu, A.C., *Agricultural Mechanization in Nigeria (Assessing the Strategies and Technologies for Land Preparation)*, NISER Monograph Series, 2 (Ibadan: Nigerian Institute of Social and Economic Research, 1989).

Nzimiro, I., *The Green Revolution in Nigeria or Modernization of Hunger* (Oguta, Nigeria: Zim Pan-African Publishers, 1985).

Obadan, M.I. and Ekuerhare, B.U., "The Theoretical Bases of Structural Adjustment Programmes in Nigeria: An Appraisal," *International Social Science Journal*, 120 (1989).

Obadan, M.I., "The Theory and Practice of the Second-Tier Foreign Exchange Market in Nigeria: Nine Months After," in A.O. Phillips and E.C. Ndekwu (eds.), *Structural Adjustment in a Developing Economy: The Case of Nigeria* (Ibadan: NISER, 1987).

---, "A Critical Assessment of the SFEM as an Instrument of Policy," in J. Attah, M. Kwanashie and O. Ojowu (eds), *The Nigerian Economy under S(FEM)* (Zaria: Department of Economics, Ahmadu Bello University, 1987).

---, "Agricultural Development Strategies and Performance in Nigeria: From OFN to DFRRI," *IRORO*, 3(1/2) (1990).

Obasanjo, O., "The New Dawn," Inaugural Speech of His Excellency, President Olusegun Obasanjo, Following his Swearing-in as President of the Federal Republic of Nigeria, 29 May 1999, *Vanguard*, 30 May 1999.

Obiechina, T., "FEAP Gulped N6b," *Nigerian Tribune*, 27 May 1999.

Obute, C.O., "Floating Exchange Rates and Structural Adjustment in Nigeria," in *Structural Adjustment in Nigeria: Proceedings of the Nigerian Economic Society Annual Conference, Ile-Ife, May 3-7, 1988* (Ibadan: Nigerian Economic Society, 1988).

Oculi, O., "The Political Economy of Planning the Bakolori Irrigation Project: 1974-1980," Y.B. Usman (ed.), *Political Repression in Nigeria, Vol. 1: A Selection of Basic Documents 1979-1981* (Zaria, Nigeria: Gaskiya Corporation, 1982).

Odiaka, P., "Many Questions as the Nation Celebrates Democracy Day," *The Guardian*, 28 May 2004.

Offiong, D., *Imperialism and Dependency* (Washington, D.C.: Howard University Press, 1982).

Ogbodo, J.A. and Njoku, L., "Northern Govs, Ohanaeze, Others, Endorse National Conference," *The Guardian*, 6 June 2004.

Ogbomo, O.W., *When men and Women Mattered: A History of Gender Relations among the Owan of Nigeria* (Rochester, NY: University of Rochester Press, 1997).

Ogirri, D.A., "An Empirical Study of the Effects of State Land-reform Policies on Agricultural and Socioeconomic Developments in Nigeria from Colonial to Military Rule: A Macro Perspective," *The Journal of African Policy Studies*, 3(2) (1997).

Ogundeji, A., "Better Life for the Current Mariam?," *The African Guardian*, 25 July 1994.

Ohadike, D.C., *The Ekumeku Movement: Western Igbo Resistance to the British Conquest of Nigeria, 1883-1914* (Athens: Ohio University Press, 1991).

Ohiorhenuan, J.F.E., "Some Critical Issues in the Theory of Development Planning," Paper Presented at the National Seminar on Innovative Approaches to Development Theory, Held at the Conference Center, University of Ibadan, Ibadan, Nigeria, 23-27 January 1984.

---, "Re-Colonising Nigerian Industry: The First Year of the Structural Adjustment Programme," in A.O. Phillips and E.C. Ndekwu (eds), *Structural Adjustment in a Developing Economy: The Case of Nigeria* (Ibadan: NISER, 1987).

---, *Capital and State in Nigeria* (Westport, Connecticut: Greenwood Press, 1989).

Ojiako, J.O., *Nigeria: Yesterday, Today, and . . .?* (Onitsha, Nigeria: Africana Educational Publishers, 1981).

Ojo, M.O. *et al.*, "Sustaining Agricultural Development in a Deregulated Economy," *Central Bank of Nigeria: Economic and Financial Review*, 13(2) (1993).

Ojo, O., "Beyond Structural Adjustment: Policies for Sustainable Growth and Development in Africa," in G.A. Cornia and G.K. Helleiner (eds), *From Adjustment to Development in Africa: Conflict, Controversy, Convergence, Consensus* (New York: St. Martins Press, 1994).

Ojo, J.D., *Students' Unrest in Nigerian Universities: A Legal and Historical Approach* (Ibadan: Spectrum Books and IFRA, 1995).

Okeke, O., "Legacy of National Paralysis: Ernest Shonekan and Sani Abacha, 1993-1998," in L.A. Nwachuku and G.N. Uzoigwe (eds), *Troubled Journey: Nigeria Since the Civil War* (Lanham: University Press of America, 2004).

Okigbo, B.N., "Sustainable Agricultural Systems in Tropical Africa," in C.A. Edwards *et al.* (eds), *Sustainable Agricultural Systems* (Ankeny, Iowa: Soil and Water Conservation Society, 1990).

Okonjo, I.M., *British Administration in Nigeria, 1900-1950: A Nigerian View* (New York: NOK Publishers, 1974).

Okonjo, K., "The Dual-Sex Political System in Operation: Igbo Women and Community Politics in Midwestern Nigeria," in N.J. Hafkin and E.G. Bay (eds), *Women in Africa: Studies in Social and Economic Change* (Stanford: Stanford University Press, 1976).

Okoye, M., *A Letter to Dr. Nnamdi Azikiwe* (Enugu: Fourth Dimension, 1979).

Okpoko, A.I., "Indigenous Technology and Sustainable Development," *West African Journal of Archaeology*, 29(1/2) (1999).

Okpoko, A.I. and Ibeanu, A.M., "Early Metal-working in Nigeria," *West African Journal of Archaeology*, 29(1/2) (1999).

Okpoko, A.I. and Okpoko, P.U., "Traditional Farming Practices in Nigeria," *West African Journal of Archaeology*, 29(1/2) (1999).

Okpu, U., *Ethnic Minority Problems in Nigerian Politics, 1960-1965* (Uppsala: Acta Universitalis Uppsaliensis, 1977).

---, "Nigeria's Dilemma: Development or New States," *Africa, Revista trimestrale di studie documentazione dell' Intituto Italo-Africano*, 38 (1983).

---, "Inter-Party Political Relations in Nigeria 1979-1983," *Afrika Spectrum*, 19(2) (1985).

Oladipo, O., "Imagination, Tradition and Development: A Review Essay," *CODESRIA Bulletin*, 4 (1994).

Olagunju, T. and Oyovbaire, S. (eds), *Portrait of a New Nigeria: Selected Speeches of IBB*, Vol. 1 (London: Precision Press, 1989).

---, *For Their Tomorrow We Gave Our Today: Selected Speeches of IBB*, Vol. 2 (St. Helier, UK: Safari Books, 1991).

Olagunju, T. *et al.*, *Transition to Democracy in Nigeria, 1985-1993* (St. Helier, UK and Ibadan, Nigeria: Safari and Spectrum Books, 1993).

Olaoye, R.A., "Intrinsic Values of Traditional Arts and Crafts to the Development of Modern Science and Technology in Nigeria," in S. Bello and Y. Nasidi (eds), *Culture, Economy and National Development: Proceedings of the National Seminar Events of NAFEST '89* (Lagos: National Council for Arts and Culture, 1991).

Olarewaju, T., "Fury of the Amazons," *The Guardian*, 9 July 1999.

Olatunbosun, D., *Nigerian Farm Settlements and School Leavers' Farms: Profitability, Resource Use and Social Psychological Considerations*, Report 9, (East Lansing, Michigan: Consortium for the Study of Nigerian Rural Development, Michigan State University, n.d.).

Olukoshi, A.O., "Extending the Frontiers of Structural Adjustment Research in Africa: Some Notes on the Objectives of Phase II of the NAI Research Programme," in P. Gibbon and A.O. Olukoshi, *Structural Adjustment and Socio-Economic Change in Sub-Saharan Africa: Some Conceptual, Methodological and Research Issues* (Uppsala: Nordiska Afrikainstitutet, 1996).

Olukoshi, A., *The Elusive Prince of Denmark: Structural Adjustment and the Crisis of Governance in Africa* (Uppsala: Nordiska Afrikainstitutet, 1998).

Olukoshi, A. and Olukoshi, H., "Structural Adjustment and Female Wage Labor in the Nigerian Textile Industry," in G. Thomas-Emeagwali (ed.), *Women Pay the Price: Structural Adjustment in Africa and the Caribbean* (Trenton, NJ: Africa World Press, 1995).

Olurode, L., "The Limits of Democracy," *The Guardian*, 1 June 2004.

Olusanya, G.O., *The Second World War and Politics in Nigeria: 1939-1953* (Ibadan: Evans Brothers, 1973).

---, *The Evolution of the Nigerian Civil Service, 1861-1960: The Problems of Nigerianization* (Lagos: University of Lagos Press, 1975).

Oluwasanmi, H. A., *Agriculture and Nigerian Economic Development* (Ibadan: Oxford University Press, 1966).

Omoruyi, O., *The Tale of June 12: The Betrayal of the Democratic Rights of Nigerians (1993)* (Lagos and London: Press Alliance Network, 1999).

---, "Democratic Transitions in Africa: The Case of Nigeria," A Lecture Delivered under the auspices of the Dr. Sidney D. Redmond Lecture Series, Jackson State University, Jackson, Mississippi, USA, 24 February 2003.

Oniemola, D., *The World Bank and Capitalist Agricultural Development: The Ilorin Agricultural Development Project in Nigeria*, Nr. 22 (Berlin: Das Arabische Buch. KnesebeckstrBe 16, 1989).

Onimode, B., *Imperialism and Underdevelopment in Nigeria* (London: Zed Books, 1982).

---, *A Political Economy of the African Crisis* (London: Zed Books and IFAA, 1988).

---, (ed.), *The IMF, the World Bank and the African Debt*, 2 Vols. (London: IFAA and Zed Books, 1989).
Onoge, O.F., "The Indigenisation Decree and Economic Independence: Another Case of Bourgeois Utopianism," in Nigerian Economic Society, *Nigeria's Indigenisation Policy: Proceedings of the November 1974 Symposium Organized by the Nigerian Economic Society on the Subject "Indigenisation: What Have We Achieved?"* (Ibadan: The Nigerian Economic Society, 1974).
Onwudiwe, E. (ed.), *African Perspectives on Civil Society* (New York: Tri-Atlantic, 1998).
Onwuejeogwu, M.A., "The Place of Indigenous Technology in Present-day Africa," *West African Journal of Archaeology*, 29(1/2) (1999).
Osaghae, E. (ed.), *Between State and Civil Society in Africa* (Dakar: CODESRIA, 1994).
---, *Crippled Giant: Nigeria Since Independence* (Bloomington and Indianapolis: Indiana University Press, 1998).
Osoba, S. and Usman, Y.B., "A General Report on the Work of the Constitution Drafting Committee: A Minority Submission," (Lagos: August 1976, mimeo).
Osoba, S., "Decolonization in Nigeria as a Programmed Transition to Neo-Colonial Dependence," Department of History, Obafemi Awolowo University, Ile-Ife, Seminar Paper, March 1977.
Owete, F., "Governors Wives Stripped of Roles in FSP," *The Punch*, 7 October 2000.
Owomoyela, O., "With Friends Like These . . . . A Critique of Pervasive Anti-Africanisms in Current African Studies Epistemology and Methodology," *African Studies Review*, 37(3) (1994).
Owusu, M., "Democracy in Africa: A View from the Village," *Journal of Modern African Studies*, 30(2) (1992).
Oyovbaire, S. and Olagunju, T. (eds), *Foundations of a New Nigeria: The IBB Era* (London: Precision Press, 1989).
Packard, P.C., "A Note on the Concentration and Profit Rates within the Manufacturing Sector, 1963 and 1965," in O. Teriba and M.O. Kayode (eds), *Industrial Development in Nigeria* (Ibadan: Ibadan University Press, 1977).
Packingham, R.A., *Liberal America and the Third World: Political Development Ideas in Foreign Aid and Social Science* (Princeton: Princeton University Press, 1973).
Palmer-Jones, R., "Irrigation and Politics of Agricultural Development in Nigeria," in M. J. Watts (ed.), *State, Oil and Agriculture in Nigeria* (Berkeley, CA: University of California Press, 1987).
Parpart, J.L., "Women and the State in Africa," in D. Rothchild and N. Chazan (eds), *The Precarious Balance: State and Society in Africa* (Boulder, CO: Westview, 1988).
---, "Who is the 'Other'?: A Postmodern Feminist Critique of Women and Development Theory and Practice," *Development and Change*, 24 (1993).

Parpart, J.L. and Staudt, K.A., "Women and the State in Africa," in J.L. Parpart and K. A. Staudt (eds), *Women and the State in Africa* (Boulder, CO: Lynne Rienner, 1990).

Parsons, T., *The Social System* (London: Routledge and Kegan Paul, 1951).

Paul, J.C.N., "The World Bank's Agenda for the Crises in Agriculture and Rural Development in Africa: An Introduction to a Debate," *African Studies Review*, 27(4) (1984).

Phillips, A.O., "A General Overview of SAP," in A.O. Phillips and E.C. Ndekwu (eds.), *Structural Adjustment in a Developing Economy: The Case of Nigeria* (Ibadan: NISER, 1987).

Pittin, R., "Women, Work and Ideology in Nigeria," *Review of African Political Economy*, 52 (1991).

Post, K. and Vickers, M., *Structure and Conflict in Nigeria* (London: Heinemann, 1973).

Reubens, E.P., "Appropriate Technology for Nigerian Development," in M. Amoda and C.D. Tyson (eds), *Technological Development in Nigeria* (Lagos and New York: Third Press International, 1979).

Richards, P., *Indigenous Agricultural Revolution: Ecology and Food Production in West Africa* (London and Boulder, CO: Hutchinson and Westview, 1985).

Ricupero, R., "Trade and Technology: Issues at Stake for Developing Countries," in UNCTAD, *Technology, Trade Policy and the Uruguay Round* (New York: United Nations, 1990).

Riddell, R., "The Future of the Manufacturing Sector in Sub-Saharan Africa," in T. M. Callaghy and J. Ravenhill (eds), *Hemmed In: Responses to Africa's Economic Decline* (New York: Columbia University Press, 1993).

Rimmer, D., "The Overvalued Currency and Over-Administered Economy of Nigeria," *African Affairs*, 84(336) (1985).

---, "Learning About Economic Development from Africa," *African Affairs*, 102 (2003).

Rodney, W., *How Europe Underdeveloped Africa*, (Washington, D.C.: Howard University Press, 1982).

Rostow, W.W., "The Take-off into Self-sustained Growth," *Economic Journal*, 66 (1956).

---, *The Stages of Economic Growth: A Non-Communis Manifesto* (Cambridge: Cambridge University Press, 1960).

Rothchild, D., "Hegemony and State Softness: Some Variations in Elite Responses," in Z. Ergas (ed.), *The African State in Transition* (London and New York: Macmillan and St. Martins, 1987).

---, "Rawlings and the Engineering of Legitimacy in Ghana," in I.W. Zartman (ed.), *Collapsed States: The Disintegration and Restoration of Legitimate Authority* (Boulder, CO: Lynne Rienner, 1995).

Rothchild, D. and N. Chazan (eds), *The Precarious Balance: State and* Civil *Society in Africa* (Boulder, CO: Westview, 1988).

Roy, S., "Agrarian Crisis and Technology in Nigeria," *Africa Quarterly*, XXV(1/2) (1988).

---, *Agriculture and Technology in Developing Countries: India and Nigeria* (New Delhi and London: SAGE Publications, 1990).

Ruttan, V.W., "What Happened to Political Development?" *Economic Development and Cultural Change*, 39(2) (1991).

Sahn, D.E., "Economic Crisis and Policy Reform in Africa: Lessons Learned and Implications for Policy," idem (ed.), *Adjusting to Policy Failure in African Economies* (Ithaca, NY: Cornell University Press, 1994).

---, *Adjusting to Policy Failure in African Economies* (Ithaca, NY: Cornell University Press, 1994).

Said, E., *Orientalism* (New York: Random House, 1978).

---, *Culture and Imperialism* (London: Chatto and Windus, 1993).

Samatar, Abdi I. and Ahmed I. Samatar (eds), *The African State: Reconsiderations* (Portsmouth, NH: Heinemann, 2002).

Sandbrook, R., 'Patrons, Clients, and Factions: New Dimensions of Conflict Analysis in Africa," *Canadian Journal of Political Science*, 5(1) (1972).

---, *The Politics of Africa's Economic Stagnation* (Cambridge: Cambridge University Press, 1985).

Sani, U., *The Dynamics of Students' Unionism in Nigeria* (Kano: Bagauda Press, 1979).

Schultheis, M.J., "The World Bank and Accelerated Development: The Internationalization of Supply-Side Economics," *African Studies Review*, 27(4) (1984).

Schumacher, E.F., *Small is Beautiful* (London: Sphere, 1973).

Schweitzer, G.E., "Technology Transfer: The Nigerian Model," in M. Amoda and C.D. Tyson (eds), *Technological Development in Nigeria* (Lagos and New York: Third Press International, 1979).

Scott, J.C., *Seeing Like a State: How Schemes to Improve the Human Condition Have Failed* (New Haven: Yale University Press, 1998).

Seddon, D. and Betto-Jones, T., "The Political Determinants of Economic Flexibility, with Special Reference to the East Asian NICs," in T. Killick (ed.), *The Flexible Economy: Causes and Consequences of Adaptability on National Economies* (New York: Routledge, 1995).

Seers, D., "The Birth, Life and Death of Development Economics," *Development and Change*, 10 (1979).

Shettima, K.A., "Structural Adjustment and the Student Movement in Nigeria," *Review of African Political Economy*, 56 (1993).

---, "Engendering Nigeria's Third Republic," *African Studies Review*, 38(3) (1995).

Sklar, R.L., *Nigerian Political Parties: Power in an Emergent African Nation* (Princeton: Princeton University Press, 1963).

---, "The New Modernization," *ISSUE*, Vol. XXIII(1) (1995).

Soete, L., "Opportunities For and Limitations To Technology Leapfrogging," in United Nations Conference on Trade and Development, *Technology, Trade Policy and the Uruguay Round* (New York: United Nations, 1990).

Staudt, K.A., "Stratification: Implications for Women's Politics," in C. Robertson and I. Berger (eds), *Women and Class in Africa* (New York and London: Africana Publishing Company, 1986).

Staudt, K., "Women's Politics, the State, and Capitalist Transformation in Africa," in Markovitz, I. L. (ed.), *Studies in Power and Class in Africa* (New York and Oxford: Oxford University Press, 1987).

Stein, H. (ed.), *Asian Industrialization and Africa: Studies in Policy Alternatives to Structural Adjustment* (New York: St. Martins, 1994).

Steiner, K.G., "Overcoming Soil Fertility Constraints to Crop Production in West Africa: Impact of Traditional and Improved Cropping Systems on Soil Fertility," in A.U. Mokwunye (ed.), *Alleviating Soil Fertility Constraints to Increased Crop Production in West Africa* (Dordrecht, Boston, London: Kluwer Academic Publishers, 1991).

Stewart, F., "Capital Goods in Developing Countries," in I. Livingstone (ed.), *Development Economics and Policy: Readings* (London: Allen and Unwin, 1976).

---, *Planning to Meet Basic Needs* (London: Macmillan, 1985).

Stolper, W.F., "The Main Features of the 1962-1968 National Plan," *Nigerian Journal of Economic and Social Studies*, 4(2) (1962).

---, *Planning Without Facts: Lessons in Resource Allocation from Nigeria's Development*, (Cambridge, Massachusetts: Harvard University Press, 1966).

Suberu, R.T., "The Politics of Fiscal Federalism in Nigeria," in W. Reno (ed.), *Nigeria After Military Rule: Federalism, Resource Allocation, and Ethnic Politics*, PAS Working Papers No. 12, (Evanston, IL: Program of African Studies, Northwestern University, 2003).

Sunday Punch (Lagos, Nigeria), 5 June 2004.

Tachau, F. (ed.), *The Developing Nations: What Path to Modernization?* New York and Toronto: Dodd, Mead and Company, 1972).

Tallroth, N.B., "Structural Adjustment in Nigeria," *Finance and Development*, September 1987.

Tamuno, T., *The Evolution of the Nigerian State: The Southern Phase, 1898-1914* (London: Longman, 1972).

Tell (Lagos, Nigeria), 14 October 1996.

Temu, A. and Swai, B., *Historians and Africanist History: A Critique*, (London: Zed Books, 1981).

The African Guardian (Lagos, Nigeria), 19 June 1986.

The African Guardian, 2 May 1988.

The African Guardian, 16 November 1992.

The Guardian (Lagos, Nigeria), 8 July 1985.

The Guardian, 28 September 1989.

The Guardian, 28 September 1991.

The Guardian, 29 May 2000.

The Guardian, 4 September 2000.

The Guardian, 20 September 2000.

The News (Lagos, Nigeria), 14 October 1996.

The Nigerian Observer (Benin City, Nigeria), 10 January 1985.

The Punch (Lagos, Nigeria), 21 June 2004.

The Punch, 23 June 2004.

Thomas-Emeagwali, G., "Introductory Perspectives: Monetarists, Liberals and Radicals: Contrasting Perspectives on Gender and Structural Adjustment in Africa," in idem (ed.), *Women Pay the Price: Structural Adjustment in Africa and the Caribbean* (Trenton, NJ: Africa World Press, 1995).

Tiffin, S. and Osotimehin, F., *New Technologies and Enterprise Development in Africa* (Paris: Organisation for Economic Cooperation and development, 1992).

Tomori, S., "Agriculture, Forestry and Fishing," in F. A. Olaloku *et al.* (eds), *Structure of the Nigerian Economy* (New York: St. Martins, 1979).

Toye, J., "Interest Group Politics and the Implementation of Adjustment Policies in Sub-Saharan Africa," in P. Gibbon *et al.* (eds), *Authoritarianism, Democracy and Adjustment: The Politics of Economic Reform in Africa* (Uppsala: Scandinavian Institute of African Studies, 1992).

---, *Dilemmas of Development: Reflections on the Counter-Revolution in Development Economics*, Second Edition, (Oxford, UK and Cambridge, Massachusetts: Blackwell Publishers, 1993).

---, "Structural Adjustment: Context, Assumptions, Origin and Diversity," in R.V. D. Hoeven and F.V.D. Kraaij (eds), *Structural Adjustment and Beyond in Sub-Saharan Africa: Research and Policy Issues* (The Hague, London and Portsmouth, NH: Ministry of Foreign Affairs, James Currey and Heinemann, 1994).

Trevor-Roper, H., "The Rise of Christian Europe," *The Listener*, 28 November 1963.

Trickovic, V., "Science Policy and Development Strategy in Developing Countries," in B. R. Williams (ed.), *Science and Technology in Economic Growth* (London: Macmillan, 1973).

Tsie, B., "States and Markets in the Southern African Development Community (SADC): Beyond the Neo-liberal Paradigm," *Journal of Southern African Studies*, 22(1) (1996).

Turner, T. and Badru, P., "Oil and Instability: Class Contradictions and the 1983 Coup in Nigeria," *Journal of African Marxists*, 7 (1985).

Ukeje, E.U., "Productivity in the Agricultural Sector," *Central Bank of Nigeria*, Occasional Paper, 8 (2000).

Ukpevo, G., "Still-Born: Nigeria's Steel Industry, Dogged by Mismanagement and Corruption, is, According to Critics, a Steal Industry," *Newswatch*, 5 October 1992.

Uniamikogbo, S.O., "The State of the Capital Goods Industry in a Developing Economy: The Case of Nigeria," *The Indian Journal of Economics*, LXXII(286) (1992).

United Bank of Africa, *Monthly Business and Economic Digest*, August (1989).

---, *Monthly Business and Economic Digest*, September/October (1995).

United Kingdom, *Colonial Development Act, 1929* (London: HMSO, 1929).

United Nations Conference on Trade and Development (UNCTAD), *Transfer and Development of Technology in Developing Countries: A Compendium of Policy Issues* (New York: United Nations, 1990).

---, *The Implementation of Laws and Conventions on Transfer of Technology: The Experience of the Republic of Korea* (New York: United Nations, n.d.).

Usman, Y.B., *The Central Role of Corruption in a Dependent Capitalist Economy: The Nigerian Experience*, NISER Distinguished Lecture Series (Ibadan: NISER, 1983).

---, "Middlemen, Consultants, Contractors and the Solutions to the Current Economic Crisis," *Studies in Politics and Society*, 2 (1984).

---, *The Manipulation of Religion in Nigeria, 1977-1987* (Kaduna: Vanguard Publishers, 1987).

Uwadibie, N.O. and Luma, A., "Decentralization and Agricultural Policy: The Case of Nigeria, 1976-1993," *The Journal of African Policy Studies*, 3(1) (1997).

Uwujaren, G.P., "The Political Economy of Nigeria's Dependent Industrialization via Import Substitution," *Nigerian Journal of International Studies*, 5-7 (1981-1983).

van Lave, T., *The World Revolution in Westernization: The 20th Century in Global Perspective* (New York: Oxford University Press, 1987).

Verhelst, T.G. (Translated by B. Cumming), *No Life Without Roots: Culture and Development* (London: Zed Books, 1990).

---, "What Do We Mean by Culture and Development?," *The Development Policy Management Network (DPMN) Bulletin*, 2(2) (1994).

Vivekananda, F. and Ihonvbere, J.O., "Debts and Falling Oil Prices: A Case Study of Nigeria," *Scandinavian Journal of Development Alternatives*, VI(4) (1987).

Wad, A., "Introduction," in idem. (ed.), *Science, Technology, and Development* (Boulder, CO and London: Westview and IT Publications, 1988).

Wade, R., *Governing the Market: Economic Theory and the Role of Government in East Asian Industrialization* (Princeton: Princeton University Press, 1990).

Wallace, T., "The Challenge of Food: Nigeria's Approach to Agriculture 1975-80," *Canadian Journal of African Studies*, 15(2) (1981).

Watts, M.J., "Agriculture and Oil-Based Accumulation: Stagnation or Transformation?" in idem. (ed.), *State, Oil and Agriculture in Nigeria* (Berkeley, CA: University of California Press, 1987).

Weber, M., *General Economic History* (Glencoe: Free Press, 1950).

---, *The Protestant Ethic and the Spirit of Capitalism* (New York: Scribner, 1958).

Wells, J. C., *Agricultural Policy and Economic Growth in Nigeria* (Ibadan: Oxford University Press, 1974).

West Africa (London), 30 September – 6 October 1991.

Western Region of Nigeria, *Western Nigeria Development Plan, 1962-68* (Ibadan: Government Printer, 1962).

Whitaker, C.S., *The Politics of Tradition: Continuity and Change in Northern Nigeria, 1946-1966* (Princeton: Princeton University Press, 1970).

Williams, S.K.T., *Rural Development in Nigeria* (Ile-Ife: University of Ife Press, 1978).

Williams, G., *State and Society in Nigeria* (Idanre, Nigeria: Afrografika, 1980).

---, "Nigeria: The Neo-Colonial Political Economy," in D. L. Cohen and J. Daniel (eds), *Political Economy of Africa* (Harlow, Essex: Longman, 1981).

---, "The World Bank and the Peasant Problem," in J. Heyer *et al.* (eds), *Rural Development in Tropical Africa* (London: Macmillan, 1981).

---, "The World Bank in Rural Nigeria, Revisited: A Review of the World Bank's Nigeria: Agricultural Sector Review 1987," *Review of African Political Economy*, 43 (1988).

Williams, D.C., "Measuring the Impact of Land-reform Policy in Nigeria," *Journal of Modern African Studies*, 30(4) (1992).

Williams, A., "A Cross Nigeria Must Bear,"*The Guardian*, 6 June 2004.

Wisner, B., *Power and Need in Africa: Basic Human Needs and Development Policies* (London: Earthscan, 1988).

Wolf, E.R., *Europe and the People Without History* (Berkeley, CA: The University of California Press, 1982).

World Bank, *Sector Policy Paper on Rural Development* (Washington, D.C.: World Bank, 1975).

---, *Accelerated Development in Sub-Saharan Africa: An Agenda for Action* (Washington, D.C.: The World Bank, 1981).

---, *World Development Report, 1983* (New York: Oxford University Press, 1983).

---, *Toward Sustained Development in Sub-Saharan Africa: A Joint Program of Action* (Washington, D.C.: The World Bank, 1984).

---, *World Development Report, 1985* (New York: Oxford University Press, 1985).

---, *Africa's Adjustment and Growth in the 1980s* (Washington, D.C.: The World Bank, 1989).

---, *Sub-Saharan Africa: From Crisis to Sustainable Growth, A Long-Term Perspective Study* (Washington, D.C.: The World Bank, 1989).

---, *World Development Report: The Challenge of Development* (Washington, D.C.: The World Bank, 1991).

---, *The East Asian Miracle: Economic Growth and Public Policy, A World Bank Policy Research Report* (Oxford: Oxford University Press, 1993).

---, *Adjustment in Africa: Reforms, Results and the Road Ahead* (Oxford: Oxford University Press, 1994).

---, *Can Africa Claim the 21st Century* (Washington, D.C.: The World Bank, 2000).

---, *World Development Report 2000/1: A World Free of Poverty* (New York: Oxford University Press, 2000).

World Commission on Environment and Development, *Our Common Future* (New York: Oxford University Press, 1987).

Wunsch, J.S. and D. Olowu (eds), *The Failure of the Centralized State: Institutions and Self-governance in Africa* (Boulder, CO: Westview, 1990).

Yankah, K., "Displaced Academies and the Quest for a New World Academic Order," *Africa Today*, 42(3) (1995).

Young, C., "The End of the Post-Colonial State in Africa? Reflections on Changing African Political Dynamics," *African Affairs*, 103(410) (2004).

Young, C. and Turner, T., *The Rise and Decline of the Zairian State* (Madison: University of Wisconsin Press, 1985).

Zartman, I.W. (ed.), *Collapsed States: The Disintegration and Restoration of Legitimate Authority* (Boulder, CO: Lynne Rienner, 1995).

Zeleza, P.T., "NOMA Award Acceptance Speech," *ISSUE*, XXIII(1) (1995).

---, "The Perpetual Solitudes and Crises of African Studies in the United States," *Africa Today*, 44(2) (1997).

---, *Manufacturing African Studies and Crises* (Dakar: CODESRIA, 1997).

Index

www.ingramcontent.com/pod-product-compliance
Lightning Source LLC
LaVergne TN
LVHW011108300926
849160LV00008B/310
9781138356535